AMERICAN UNEMPLOYMENT

AMERICAN
UNEMPLOYMENT

PAST, PRESENT, AND FUTURE

FRANK STRICKER

UNIVERSITY OF
ILLINOIS PRESS
Urbana, Chicago, and Springfield

Library of Congress Cataloging-in-Publication Data
Names: Stricker, Frank, author.
Title: American unemployment : past, present, and future / Frank
    Stricker.
Description: Urbana : University of Illinois Press, 2020. | Includes
    bibliographical references and index.
Identifiers: LCCN 2019052185 (print) | LCCN 2019052186
    (ebook) | ISBN 9780252043154 (cloth) | ISBN 9780252085024
    (paperback) | ISBN 9780252052033 (ebook)
Subjects: LCSH: Unemployment—United States—History. |
    United States—Economic conditions. | United States—Social
    conditions.
Classification: LCC HD5724 .S7343 2020 (print) | LCC HD5724
    (ebook) | DDC 331.13/7973—dc23
LC record available at https://lccn.loc.gov/2019052185
LC ebook record available at https://lccn.loc.gov/2019052186

To my wife, Deborah Schopp,
to Vonn, Alexis, Nancy, and Ray,
and to everyone who supported the project

"The only difference between a derelict and a man is a job."

—William Powell at the Hooverville Dump,
in *My Man Godfrey* (1936)

Contents

Acknowledgments

Some of the learning that went into *American Unemployment* occurred over several decades. I was not trained as an economist, but I began paying attention to the U.S. economy in the 1970s and 1980s. The people in the Los Angeles chapter of the New American Movement (NAM) in the early 1970s taught me much, and I learned more in the Westcoast Association of Marxist Historians (WAMH) in the early 1980s. An offshoot of WAMH was a research group whose members shared drafts of articles and chapters for critical evaluation. These colleagues read every chapter of my book, and sometimes more than once. They include Craig Loftin, Steve Ross, Nancy Fitch, Leila Zenderland, Bob Slayton, Jan Reiff, Hal Baron, Becky Nicolaides, and Tobie Higbie.

In recent years, the organization that has most shaped my understanding of unemployment is the National Jobs for All Network (formerly the National Jobs for All Coalition). I was moving toward NJFAC's position on the importance of hidden unemployment when I published my first book, *Why America Lost the War on Poverty—and How to Win It*. As I contacted people about the poverty book, Sheila Collins suggested that I become a member of NJFAC. She was right. I joined and have worked in the coalition for a decade now. Many individuals in the organization have helped me think about the subjects of my book. I cannot name them all but they include June Zaccone, who creates NJFAN's monthly alternative unemployment rate; Trudy Goldberg, who read chapters and was always supportive; Logan Martinez, the lead organizer; Helen Ginsburg, who read chapters, gave me insights into organizations that preceded NJFAC, and supplied several sources; and, finally, a group that included William Darity Jr. and involved an online discussion of definitions of full employment.

Over the years, many people have been generous. Social work expert David Wagner read sections and gave me sources and a statement for chapter 1. Labor lawyer Tom Donahoe answered questions in his specialty, and economists Jim Devine and Tom Larson responded to many inquiries over many years. Sharla Solsma and Liz Tamoush offered psychological perspectives. Forty people responded to an informal survey about job-searching. Matthew Hart provided key facts and perspectives about grocery employees and the United Food and Commercial Workers, and Mike McGrorty educated me about welder training classes and other work issues.

Federal employees provided speedy answers to my questions. They include, at the Bureau of Labor Statistics, Ben Cover, John Mullins, Hyun Choi, Terence McMenamin, Fran Horvath, Michelle Mayfield, Catherine Wood, John Galvin, Eliot Davila, and Emy Sok; and at the Bureau of Economic Analysis, Lisa Mataloni, who tutored me on GDP measurements. The librarians at California State University, Dominguez Hills, especially Robert Downs, were very helpful. Many sections of this book could not have been written without the work of journalists and blog writers. They receive credit in the endnotes, and include Don Lee and Alana Semuels at the *Los Angeles Times* and Peter S. Goodman at the *New York Times*.

I am sure I am leaving out people who critiqued the manuscript, but readers include Lois Feuer and the late Tony Garavente. At a key point, Edward Kantowicz gave the whole manuscript a thorough, speedy, and sympathetic going-over. He helped me cut and paste. Marc Holcombe read the whole manuscript with care, and Joan Williams evaluated several chapters. Retired English teachers Bill and Jeri Roberts read several chapters at different times, and near the end, they proofed the whole manuscript. Derk Richardson, an author and editor, gave the entire manuscript a close read and recommended many needed corrections. My niece, Deborah Stricker Josephs, commented on several sections.

The two outside readers at the University of Illinois Press, Phil Harvey and Melvyn Dubofsky, and my editor, James Engelhardt, helped me turn the manuscript into a viable book. I started learning from James's recommendations almost as soon as we began corresponding. Mel offered many criticisms, and the revisions I produced in response made the book fairer and stronger. Phil's review provided a big boost. Once the book went into production, Tad Ringo managed the process with diligence and a gentle touch.

Finally, my wife Deborah Schopp read every chapter many times and without complaint. And whether she was reading the manuscript or not, she was making my life much better in so many ways.

Introduction

In retrospect, it is clear that my job history has not been typical of what many Americans go through. Many have to deal with extended periods of unemployment and low pay, even in their mature years, and most employees change jobs quite a few times. I had periods of unemployment and several years of worry about whether my job as a professor would last, but as it turned out, most of the time I had work, and at two jobs that paid me well and made me feel that I was doing something useful.

Up until the time I went away to graduate school, I had an excellent part-time job. I was well paid and never laid off. I was the only employee in a painting company and the painter-owner was my father.

After graduate school, it took me a while to find permanent employment. I did not like the job-search process. There weren't enough jobs and I did not have confidence that I would get a position. And I was struggling to finish my dissertation. I traveled for interviews and presentations to Gary, Indiana, upstate New York, and Ottawa, Canada, where there were two positions at Carleton University. One of the interviewers there told me he was sure I would get the job. I did not. Two friends of mine, one from my pre-college years and one from graduate school, got hired. That worked out okay.

I taught as a visiting professor at UCLA for one year and then was out of work for another. I did some job-searching but found nothing. No unemployment compensation either. I did not know enough to think about whether I could get it. My spouse had a job, but we weren't affluent. I returned to Chicago to paint houses with my dad for a couple of weeks. Later, my brother hooked me up with a friend who owned a shoe store in Los Angeles, and that man paid me for several days of work straightening out boxes in the back room. I doubt that the work I performed was very important, but I appreciate the kindness. It was a nice thing that the owner did for me.

Late in the summer of 1972, someone told me about a history job at California State University, Dominguez Hills. I had not even heard of the place. I did the interview, people were welcoming, and I secured a position teaching history and labor studies. I kept that job for thirty-five years. I was lucky because around the time I was hired, demand for historians was beginning to sag. After I and one other person were taken on, my department stopped hiring tenure-track faculty for twenty years. I had friends who left the field and others who became freeway flyers, teaching a course here and a course there, and juggling a stack of credit cards to pay their bills. Eventually I earned tenure, but it wasn't always easy. Budget cuts and layoff threats were regular occurrences, and the threat was dire in 1978 when California's Proposition 13 slashed property taxes and forced budget cuts. But faculty and administrators organized to save jobs. I was not laid off and for many years I was able to teach United States history, labor history, and courses about unemployment and poverty.

Did I suffer from being unemployed off and on for a couple of years? Not as much as many people suffer from unemployment, but I had experienced enough of it to know I did not want to be unemployed. And I had enough trouble finding a job to understand the role that luck played in people's employment success. The experience gave me a special interest in thinking about unemployment and poverty.

As I researched unemployment and its history, I came to believe that key assumptions guiding mainstream opinion and policy were misleading. In the late 1960s and 1970s, a handful of government officials, scholars, and activists showed how the government's official rate underestimated unemployment. But in 1978, Congress rejected legislation to guarantee a job to everyone who needed one. Inflation was one excuse for nixing full employment that year. Some economists in the 1960s believed that 4 percent unemployment was virtually full employment, but in the later 1970s, many economists, and not just conservatives, began to believe that unemployment had to be as high as 6 or 7 percent to keep prices and wages down. In 1979 President Jimmy Carter chose Paul Volcker to lead the Federal Reserve's war on wage and price inflation. He would use very high interest rates to generate very high unemployment and limit economic demand. Carter's successor, President Ronald Reagan, quietly supported Volcker's big squeeze, which brought the worst recession since the 1930s. But it did slash the rate of inflation.

Job growth resumed but real full employment had not been achieved when another recession began. And this has been the norm. In the long view, and regardless of the level of inflation or what is happening to other indexes, there has almost never been full employment during peacetime in America in the last century and a half. The private sector does not bring it, and while government officials have learned to manage spending and credit to encourage job creation, there is no enforceable obligation for the president, Congress, or the Federal Reserve to produce real full employment.

The fact that real full employment has been a rarity in American history is a major theme of the book. The rest of this introduction expands the point and sketches other themes. I provide definitions and discussions of key terms for the study of unemployment in the United States. It is crucial that we understand that official and conventional definitions can hide as much as they reveal. Part of the project of this book is to evaluate big-picture terms and meanings, in order to get closer to the actualities of unemployment and, where appropriate, to challenge intellectual constructs that stand in the way of full employment.

The effort to revise our concepts is one part of my project. Another is a history of unemployment in the United States. For any discussion of current problems and solutions, the history is important. For example, it shows that there is no going back to some full-employment utopia in the late 1800s or the 1920s or the 1950s. While some periods were better than others, there was rarely full employment. The central fact about employment history is not mostly full employment, occasionally punctuated by recessions and depressions, but rather periodic slumps—big and small slumps—and in between, unemployment often on the high side. High unemployment has been more common than full employment in United States history.

Excessive Unemployment, Not Full Employment, Is the Norm for U.S. Capitalism

In the nineteenth and early twentieth centuries, many economists in the United States and in Europe lived by the axiom that unregulated capitalist markets tended toward full employment. This idea was one form of the general argument for laissez faire, namely, that capitalist markets were most efficient when government interfered with them as little as possible. But in the later 1800s and early 1900s, when capitalists enjoyed free rein, big depressions were common and unemployment was quite high even between depressions. How high and how bad? Many scholars and policy experts in our time accept that a 4 percent unemployment rate is essentially full employment. Those 4 percent are the frictionally unemployed—people just about to get another job. For reasons that will be clear later, the position that 4 percent unemployment is virtually full employment is one I find profoundly misleading. But if we say that for non-farm private-sector workers, an unemployment rate of 4 percent or less is full employment, we find that of forty years (1890–1929) in a mostly laissez-faire period, only three averaged full employment, and two of those were war years (1906, 1918, 1919). If we want to be more lenient about this period when ideas, data, and tools relevant to unemployment were primitive, and allow that anything under 5 percent unemployment was full employment, we find just six full-employment years (1906, 1907, 1918, 1919, 1926, 1929).

Real full employment should mean that people who need a job can find one fairly quickly and at a wage that pays the bills. Today, many workers cannot pay their bills at the wage offered. And even at 4 percent unemployment, there are millions of people outside the labor force who want a job but are not actively searching for one, and so are not counted as unemployed. In the generally prosperous year of 2018, there were often five million part-timers who wanted full-time work and five million people outside the labor force who said they wanted a job but were not counted as searching for one and thus not counted as unemployed. In other words, there is unemployment that is not included in the official unemployment rate, and when the official rate is 4 percent, the real rate may be 8 or 9 percent or more. For this reason and others that will be discussed later, it seems clear that the official unemployment rate leaves out too many people. We need a more inclusive estimation of unemployment, but there is not much support for new methods. At the moment it may be more practical to assume that truly full employment requires that the current official unemployment rate be 2 percent or less. That's the level that was reached in the red-hot labor market of World War II. At the 2 percent level almost everyone who wants a job would have one. There would not be much uncounted unemployment at the 2 percent level.

There has not been a single year when unemployment averaged 2.0% percent since World War II, but on average there has been less unemployment than in the seventy years before that war. Much more federal spending on military and civilian programs has helped to bring fuller employment. In the postwar era, government economic policy was much more activist, and that meant less unemployment. Also, powerful trade unions assured that some groups of workers got a little more income.

Even then, real full employment was unusual. The "Keynesian revolution" of World War II showed that massive federal spending—based on huge sums of borrowed money—could help to bring truly full employment, but that lesson was not applied in a consistent and straightforward manner to civilian spending in the postwar period. Keynesian tax cuts were tried in the early 1960s and they stimulated job creation, but they were soon overshadowed by spending on the Vietnam War, which kept unemployment below 4 percent for four years. Even in that period there were still many people without work.

In the late 1960s and early 1970s, war spending and soaring oil prices ignited high inflation rates and high anxiety, too. Cutting inflation became the key rationale for raising unemployment levels. Many conservative economists and quite a few liberals agreed that there had to be sustained high unemployment to quash inflation. A new term was invented: the Non-Accelerating Inflation Rate of Unemployment (NAIRU); it meant the level of unemployment at which the rate of inflation was not increasing. There was still talk of full employment, but that phrase was, at times, a mangled concept. Many economists operated as though NAIRU were identical with full employment, so full employment could be claimed when unemployment was 6 or 7 percent. But NAIRU had nothing to do with how many people needed jobs.

As a result of NAIRU-style beliefs, unemployment was pushed up to 10.8 percent in the Volcker-Reagan recession of 1981–1982. But inflation rates were cut. The high-unemployment solution to inflation stayed popular, and Democratic economic policy became more conservative. In the mid-1980s, after Reagan's presidential victories, moderate to conservative Democrats organized to turn the party away from Rooseveltian liberalism, which they believed was a loser at the polls. They formed the Democratic Leadership Council. This move was part of something called neoliberalism. That was an odd term for Americans who had associated liberalism with activist government policies. Roosevelt's New Deal, with dozens of new laws and programs such as Social Security and protections for unionization, marked the birth of modern American liberalism. In the late 1970s and the 1980s, neoliberalism was a program to reduce government and allow private-sector decisions and freer competitive markets to work their magic. Proponents argued that owners and consumers made better judgments than government bureaucrats. Less government and more freedom for the private sector was supposed to mean more economic growth, better schools, and much more. In practice, neoliberalism meant removing people from welfare programs, privatizing public schools, cutting taxes to favor the rich, accepting and even causing higher unemployment to control inflation, obsessing about and sometimes cutting federal deficits and federal spending, limiting unionization, rejecting direct-government job creation, and cutting labor and environmental restrictions on the home front and in international trade pacts.

President Bill Clinton was a quasi-neoliberal. When he first came into office in 1993, the chair of the Federal Reserve, a pragmatic conservative named Alan Greenspan, convinced him that more government spending would mean more borrowing, and that would lead to higher interest rates and, ultimately, less job creation. Clinton had campaigned on a promise to invest $50 billion in people and in jobs, but he gave in to Greenspan. Greenspan mostly kept to his pledge to hold down interest rates, and the late '90s saw the best job markets since the 1960s. But the magic that boosted job creation was an uncontrolled expansion of private debt, especially in new technologies and commercial real estate. The economy crashed in 2001. But Greenspan tried again, supporting even larger increases in debt, especially in the housing market. But mortgage payments were too high for many working-class Americans, whose incomes had not increased much. Eventually, in 2008, the system crashed again. The result was the Great Recession—the worst depression since the 1930s.

The crisis pushed some Democrats a few steps back from neoliberalism. President Barack Obama, with fairly widespread support among economists but little support from Republicans in Congress, applied a high level of Keynesian deficit spending, and the government also funded several specific job programs. The Federal Reserve cut interest rates to zero to stop the economic slide. Eventually economic recovery took hold, but the principle of large-scale borrowing to finance job creation did not win support from Republicans or from most neoliberal Democrats.[1]

In general Democrats were more Rooseveltian-liberal than Republicans, and many supported such things as federal food stamps, expanded health-care access, and a new agency to defend consumers against the financial industry. But they rarely offered a vigorous defense of higher minimum wages, unionization, or government job-creation programs. The most ardent defender of an updated Rooseveltian liberalism for the 2010s was not a Democrat, but Bernie Sanders, a socialist who ran for the Democratic presidential nomination in 2016.

The economy improved slowly in the 2010s. Unemployment rates fell below 4 percent in 2018, and there was widespread agreement that something close to full employment had been reached. But there were a lot of people who should have been working and were not even searching for jobs; and real wages weren't increasing much.[2]

Economists and journalists knew these things, but few thought that federal direct job creation was the way to get enough good jobs to draw more people into the workforce, to assure that more new jobs were good ones, and to direct jobs to depressed areas. For some economists the goal of full employment has not seemed very important. Many people on the left side of the political spectrum, including some newly elected members of Congress in 2019, want full employment, but I could not find it in the index or in appropriate sections of the left-leaning *Economics: An Introduction to Traditional and Progressive Views* (2008), by Howard J. Sherman and others. In the conservative Harvard Economist N. Gregory Mankiw's popular *Macroeconomics* (2016), full employment barely makes an appearance. For Mankiw and quite a few other economists, full employment has been replaced by the Non-Accelerating Inflation Rate of Unemployment. That term is not about how many people need jobs, but about the level of unemployment necessary to keep inflation under control.

The record of the period 1970–2018 was not a good one on many fronts. Income inequalities widened, and average real wages for rank-and-file workers advanced slowly or not at all. There were many unemployed persons just outside the labor force who were not counted as unemployed. In recent years, unemployment has been quite low, but these years have been the exceptions. If we use 4.0 percent unemployment or less as an indicator of full employment, Americans have rarely experienced full employment since 1970: one month in 1999, ten in 2000, and thirteen from January 2018 through April 2019. That's it.

The Concepts of the Official Rate of Unemployment, Structural Unemployment, and Frictional Unemployment Capture Some Realities and Hide Others

The unemployment history of the last forty-five years is bad enough if we use official rates and embrace the common idea that 4 percent unemployment is really full employment. But to get a better idea of the number of people who need and want jobs, we should pay attention to the unemployed who are not counted as such. To be labeled unemployed, you must have looked for work in the previous four weeks. If, for example, you want to work but haven't searched for a job for a long time because you are very discouraged about finding one, you are not considered unemployed. This is one of the ways the government's unemployment rate omits people who would work if jobs were available. Government's monthly headline rate also does not include people who are working part-time and want full-time work. When we include the two groups, actual unemployment is twice the official unemployment rate.

The fact that more people than expected are out of the labor force has been discussed for years by journalists, scholars, and experts in the White House. But that discussion has not had the effect of moving economists and policymakers to consider a fundamental revision of the official unemployment rate. Nor has the failure of real wages to enter a period of substantial and sustained improvement. In 2017 and 2018 federal officials and reporters at major media outlets like the *Los Angeles Times* conversed as though the nation were at full employment. Full employment should mean general labor shortages, but most employers were not having a lot of trouble finding new workers, and they were not raising wages as much as we'd expect in really tight labor markets. From January 2016 through January 2019, real wages for rank-and-file workers increased a total of 2.1 percent. That's a plus, but it is less than 1 percent a year and less than expected in a red-hot, full-employment labor market.[3]

The official unemployment rate is just one concept with large policy implications that ought to be revised, or at least used with caution. Two other important ones are structural unemployment and frictional unemployment. Structural unemployment is said to be due not to a shortage of jobs but to things that get between job-seekers and jobs. For example, job-seekers may not have the skills demanded; employers may discriminate against ethnic minorities or women or older people; jobs may have shrunk in Detroit and West Virginia but be plentiful in Texas and South Dakota. Sometimes, conservatives and neoliberals assert that unions and wage laws make labor too costly. But the opposite may be true as well: low rates of unionization and low wages discourage people from looking for work.

Structural unemployment focuses on joblessness owing to factors that are occurring whatever the general state of the economy. It means that the jobs are there but people cannot connect with them. Clearly, this must be true to some extent; not everyone has the right training for jobs that are within reach, and specific occupations are always changing. But the structural concept can be a way to avoid the possibility that, even in good times, the economy is not producing enough jobs. If there were more good jobs available, and if people had faith that these jobs would not soon go away, more people would take jobs, more would get the training they needed, and more would be willing to move to job-rich towns and cities.

A third important concept that describes something real but also adds confusion to our understanding of unemployment is the idea of frictional unemployment. Many economists accept that when unemployment is around 4 percent, the majority of the unemployed are hardly unemployed at all. They are in transit. They are experiencing the normal frictions and time-lags that must be expected in the job search. They will find a job and often a better job. This is the cheery narrative of frictional unemployment. It is the reason some believe that 4 percent unemployment can be called full employment.

But while some of the unemployed fit the frictional story, the concept is misleading. Many of those included in the full-employment 4 percent unemployment rate do not find work, or at least not soon. About two million unemployed people every month don't find jobs; they stop looking for work and drop out of the labor force. Some may be experiencing life changes; others are discouraged about their prospects. Many people do find jobs every month, but many of them do not pass through the phase where they are counted as unemployed. There is a nearby labor force of people who want jobs and are on the alert for them but aren't in the official labor force. Obviously, the frictional idea describes something real; people without jobs search for jobs but do not get them right away because it takes time to search, find an opening, apply, fill out the paperwork, and so on. A number of these people will find jobs and sometimes even better jobs. But many will not. The frictional story describes too few of the people who are actually unemployed, and it makes life seem easy: be unemployed, search for work, and find it. But in fact, as many as two million people even in good times will exit the unemployed population every month not by finding a job but by dropping out of the labor force.

Unemployment Hurts

There are still politicians and economists who believe, as did their predecessors in the 1800s, that involuntary unemployment is rare and that jobless people are freeloaders or that they just want to be paid too much. At the University of Chicago, the economist and Nobel Laureate Robert Lucas believes that even in the Great Depression, unemployment was a matter of choice. During our Great Recession, Senator Orrin Hatch of Utah focused not on creating good jobs but on drug-testing for recipients of unemployment benefits: "we should not be giving cash to people who basically are just going to blow it on drugs and not take care of their own children." He fought against extending unemployment benefits: "A lot of these people don't want to work unless they get really high-paying jobs, and they're not going to get them ever. So, they just stay home and watch television." Of course, some people, especially in left-behind communities, are addicted to drugs, some have a frail work ethic, and more are dying every year from drug-related causes. But for many of them, the scarcity of good jobs has been a more important cause of their personal tragedies than the desire for very high pay or overly generous government benefits.[4]

The basic facts are clear. Recessions, unemployment, and lousy jobs add millions of people to the poverty population and spread misery. Long-term unemployment can be devastating for individuals, and catastrophic if it is a mass phenomenon that shatters the economic bones of a community or attacks specific social groups with extra cruelty. For many decades we have seen the results in Detroit and Flint, Michigan; Youngstown, Ohio; East St. Louis, Illinois; poor African American neighborhoods in Chicago; Paterson, New Jersey; West Virginia mining areas; and dozens of other hollowed-out communities. It is well known that there are hundreds of thousands of jobless workers in these left-behind communities. Millions of prime-age people who could use a job are not even looking for work. Recently, two Princeton scholars, Anne Case and Angus Deaton, found that mortality rates among whites, especially working-class whites, have been rising. Case and Deaton linked rising mortality and the opioid epidemic to limited economic opportunities.

Government Can Create Good Jobs

If high unemployment is common, if the business system creates too few jobs and too many that don't come with decent wages and benefits, and if that is a terrible thing for millions of individuals and for communities whose main businesses are shuttered, why isn't real full employment always on the front burner as a national policy goal? The reason is not that politicians and scholars cannot imagine something like new and improved versions of the New Deal's CCC, the WPA, the PWA, and the CWA or more recent direct job-creation programs. There are a variety of motives for opposition to federal job-creation programs, including the belief that such government programs must always be inefficient, or that they will drive up wages and force private companies out of business, or that they will require higher taxes on the rich. Some people will be in opposition for partisan reasons; they fear that the success of such a program could provide political recruits for the party that puts the program into action. These issues will be discussed in more detail in the text, but the advantages of a large-scale government program of direct job creation include the following: it can create millions of jobs that are not being created by the private sector; it can guarantee that those jobs come with a living wage and decent benefits, which many private-sector jobs do not provide; it can direct jobs to communities where they are most needed; and it is a more cost-effective way to use government expenditures than tax cuts that favor rich people and corporations, but come with no job-creation obligations.[5]

Learning from the Past; Using All the Tools We Have

The American intellectual infrastructure has advanced by leaps and bounds since the late 1800s. It now includes many sophisticated tools for analyzing and managing the economy, for example by adjusting federal spending and manipulating interest rates to restrain or fuel economic growth. The intellectual infrastructure includes a vast treasury of statistics and indexes that did not exist in 1900. There were no reliable national unemployment numbers back then; we have them now, and tons of other facts on many social and occupational groups. We have enough employment numbers that people outside the government and in the Bureau of Labor Statistics itself can construct a fuller unemployment count than the official monthly rate. We have information about wage rates in hundreds of occupations and a lot of data on annual incomes. From the latter poverty rates are derived every year. We can argue about whether the poverty line is too low or too high, but we have an abundance of numbers from which to construct alternative rates. We had none of these things in 1900. And we have something else: the history of the last century and a half of unemployment, of the ups and downs of the American economy, and of the way that people of different social and economic backgrounds dealt with chronic and recession-level unemployment.

Americans collectively have much, much more information than a hundred years ago and many more highly trained specialists in economics, politics, and history. Is America better for that? In some respects, the answer is a strong yes. For one thing, there has been less unemployment in the last forty years than there was in 1870–1910. In modern decades, the economy grows more often than it did in the decades before World War II. In modern times, most people seem to agree that the unemployed deserve unemployment benefits and other forms of support. Most but not all politicians and voters believe that it is the duty of government officials to fight recessions and depressions.

However, despite the huge advantages we moderns have in the level of skills and data that we can mobilize against unemployment, the results for average Americans aren't as positive as we might imagine. While there were four major depressions between 1873 and 1915 (1873–1879, the 1890s, 1907–1908, 1913–1914), there were almost as many—three—between 1973 and 2018 (1973–1975, 1981–1982, 2007–2009). And as in the past, between these modern depressions there have been milder recessions with high unemployment, including several that came with "jobless recoveries." Furthermore, in modern times, such things as racism, uneven economic growth, and drastic structural change have cast off millions of workers in coal-mining regions, industrial towns and cities, and, now, from retail businesses across the land. There is a large population of essentially unemployed people who are not counted as such. And there are millions of employed people who do not receive a living wage, nor enough hours of work to pay the bills.

The voices of jobless Americans are rarely heard in protests and demonstrations. They sometimes come to us through the efforts of journalists and scholars, and sometimes through their own writings. They may come to our attention in stories about spectacularly harsh outcomes that have been visited upon those being left behind by weak or changing economies and by racism: a very high number of shooting deaths in depressed black neighborhoods in Chicago, widespread opioid-related deaths in rural America, and unemployment and black lung disease in West Virginia coal mines. I have tried to pay attention to the economically oppressed, and especially those without jobs, starting in the 1870s and not just in depression years, but in commonly labeled prosperous periods such as the Progressive era before World War I, the roaring 1920s, the 1950s and the 1960s, and in recoveries from recessions such as the later 1980s and the mid-2010s. Donald Trump paid selective attention to a relative handful of such people, but not much has been done to make life better for them. Whether political changes visible on the national scene in 2019 will make a real difference remains to be seen.

This book is a contribution to the public discussion of unemployment and stagnant pay in the United States. It uses history, stories, and analysis to show that high unemployment has been the norm for most of modern American history. It argues that there are many more people who are truly unemployed than our headline numbers show, and that they are not unemployed because they haven't tried to work, but because influential political and economic groups ensure that there are not enough good jobs for all of those who need them. It does not have to be that way. The United States can have real full employment. There is too much unemployment and poverty, not mainly because the poor and the unemployed are defective, nor because the nation has insufficient information or too few trained economists. It is because of political and economic decisions that some influential Americans and their supporters have made and that others have not effectively countered.

PART I

History Lessons: 1873–2018

CHAPTER 1

Discipline for the Unemployed; Laissez-Faire for Business (1873–1920)

This chapter shows that during the foundational period of modern American capitalism, depressions were frequent, unemployment was common, and poverty rates probably fell. The federal government was, mostly, the accomplice of capital rather than of workers. Federal officials intervened to quash strikes but not to counteract depressions or to create a system of unemployment benefits. The chapter starts with a sketch of two big ideas that limited federal action for the working class and rationalized harsh measures used by charity organizations to control the unemployed and other poor people.

Unemployment and Its Deniers

Although economic growth over the whole period covered by this chapter was often strong, it was frequently interrupted by severe depressions. Average real incomes increased 48 percent between 1890 and 1915, but averages can be deceptive. Millions stayed poor and a relative handful became fabulously rich. Many immigrants did better than in the old country, and poverty rates for the whole population were inching down, but the average working-class family was often on the edge. When Louise More studied a sample of two hundred working-class families in New York City in 1903–1905, she found that the average family income was $851 (about $19,200 of purchasing power in our time).

She estimated that working-class families needed $800 for the basics, so half of her families were poor or nearly so. More believed that low wages and unemployment were significant causes of family poverty.

There was a lot of unemployment in this half century. Major depressions in the 1870s, 1890s, 1908, and 1913–1915, and small dips in between. In times of depression, suffering was widespread and cities swarmed with people who had no income, no home, and not much public or private aid. Governments did little to stimulate job creation; this was the dream world of modern libertarian free-marketers.[1]

The economic system often failed, but powerful business, political, and intellectual interests resisted fundamental reforms. Two big ideas helped them justify harsh policies. The first one was simple: most people, and especially the poor and the unemployed, were of weak character. Giving them economic aid encouraged laziness and other bad traits, so charity reformers strove to limit material aid. They believed that the unemployed and poor people needed instruction, regulation, and, sometimes, in the case of homeless people, imprisonment.[2]

Another set of ideas bolstered the power of captains of industry and finance and limited public and private assistance to people who were victimized by unemployment and poverty; this was the economic model that many mainstream economists believed in. Here the idea was that capitalism tended always to work smoothly. Free markets produced more income and plenty of jobs. For the most part, government should stay out. Of course, there were exceptions to this laissez-faire dogma. Railroad builders accepted huge grants of land from the federal government, and all capitalists wanted government assistance at times, including federal troops to suppress strikers. But the theory was that an economy free of government interference worked best. Government must not intrude upon the market system by encouraging unions or passing wage laws or giving unemployed persons living expenses while they searched for work. Workers had to save for a rainy day. When out of a job, they just had to try harder to find another one. There were always jobs out there waiting to be filled.

At the extreme, there was a social Darwinian version of the two big ideas. Government and charities must not interfere with the winnowing process that resulted in the survival of the fittest. Out of the competitive struggle, the fittest rose to positions of leadership and the least fit fell by the wayside. That was how it was meant to be. Yale sociology professor and social Darwinist William Graham Sumner said, "a drunkard in the gutter is just where he ought to be. Nature is working away at him to get him out of the way."[3]

Though Sumner's rhetoric was extreme, his biases were not unusual. There were major depressions in the late 1800s and plenty of evidence in most cities of high unemployment between depressions. One might have concluded that there was something outside the minds and wills of unemployed people causing unemployment. But many mainstream economists at home and abroad virtually denied the reality of unemployment. Some economists in America and in England believed as an act of faith that capitalism normally provided full employment. Many "denied or minimized the existence of involuntary unemployment, except perhaps as a transitory phenomenon that could be cured by lower wages." Unemployment, they argued, often owed to laziness, intemperance, ignorance, incompetence, and other bad traits and behaviors. The antidote to unemployment was not government spending or government job programs but Christian teachings, which would make the jobless person improve his character and make him a more valuable worker.

In the late 1800s and early 1900s, more economists began to challenge laissez-faire dogma and the comforting economic model that supported it. They would eventually come to understand that depressions occurred periodically because of the inner workings of the system and through no fault of the unemployed. Some economists and business leaders too came to understand that production could outpace consumer incomes and cause an economic decline that had nothing to do with how virtuous workers were. A corollary of new views that planted responsibility in the economy was that unemployed persons deserved government assistance—money, jobs, job search assistance, or something else. In this liberal minority were Richard Ely, John Commons, Charles Tuttle, and Wesley Mitchell. But most leaders of the profession and a majority of economists in America and in England were in denial about the fact that full employment was a rarity. They continued to assume that the economy tended toward full employment, barring unusual occurrences. The British economist H. Stanley Jevons, in "The Causes of Unemployment" (1909), claimed that what looked like unemployment resulted from three causes: a school system that turned out unemployable children; trade unions that made wages too high; and solar activity that affected agriculture and caused trade fluctuations.

One of the most admired economists in the Anglo-American world, Alfred Marshall, started from the view that the economy moved always toward full employment. The depression of the 1890s affected his view as it did other economists, but not so much. In 1903 he distinguished between cyclical depressions, like that of the 1890s, which were occasional and would become less frequent in the future as people learned to save money in good times, and something more important, which he called "systemic" unemployment. You might think the latter term meant something intrinsic to the economy, but Marshall was talking about people who could not or would not work. He labeled systemic unemployment a disease and thought it could be cured not by fixing job markets or the economy but by deurbanization and by kind but severe discipline of the culprits who refused to work. This is the kind of thing that came from the man who brought the neo to neoclassical economics by inventing something called marginal utility. Marginal utility did not make Marshall more realistic about unemployment.[4]

Outside the economics profession, there was plenty of opposition to capitalist economics and stingy charity practices in the late 1800s. A more realistic and generous view of the poor and the unemployed was promoted by labor-liberals and socialists like Eugene Debs, unemployed workers who demanded government work programs, unionists like Terrence Powderly, settlement house workers including Jane Addams, liberal Protestant leaders including George Herron, and progressive writers such as Henry George, Edward Bellamy, and Henry Demarest Lloyd. Many of these people were the left-wing and smaller fraction of the professional-intellectual class. They argued that the unemployed and the poor were not the cause of their own conditions. Low wages, technological change, depressions, and capitalism itself were the causes. It seemed to follow that if the main reasons for unemployment were large and impersonal, then solutions should not be about mending individuals but about fixing the economy and government, for example, with unions, public works, unemployment insurance, and even socialism.

Labor-liberals gained knowledge and numbers over fifty years of economic turbulence, but they had slight impact on government policy and legislation. Workers battled capitalists, and more intellectuals came to believe that poverty and unemployment was due to bad systems rather than bad people. But labor-liberals faced a mostly capitalist press, a reactionary Supreme Court, and a conservative majority in the professional-intellectual class. Unions increased their numbers, but even after an organizing surge, they covered just 7 percent of workers in 1915. Conservative intellectuals and professionals continued to wield influence through hundreds of papers, magazines, pulpits, universities, and charitable enterprises. They believed that capitalist institutions were sound and that the unemployed were defective. Many continued to believe that workers were poor because they were weak, ignorant, and even "depraved." Some considered that people who lacked income were predestined by God to fail. They lectured needy people on how to live on less while natural economic events took their course; they blamed working-class protest on communism and other foreign doctrines, not genuine grievances.[5]

The 1870s Depression, Unemployment Ideas, and the Middle Classes

From 1873 through 1877, Americans were shaken by their first modern depression. The depression was caused by international events that shrank the money supply and by business overinvestment, especially in railroads. We don't have precise unemployment numbers, but we know that the homeless population and the number of free riders on the railroads soared in many places. New York City police stations were filthy, but they were crammed every night with unemployed homeless people. Because the homeless were allowed to stay just one night in any single station, they moved from station to station and were called "revolvers."[6]

The unemployed demanded government assistance, and workers fought wage cuts. But many politicians, mainstream editors, and capitalists were unsympathetic. Sugar millionaire and New York City mayor William Havemeyer told protesters they had to save for a rainy day. Public works, one newspaper claimed, was "sheer unadulterated bosh." Beggars belonged in jail. The unemployed had to be patient while natural laws took effect and wages fell. Those who could not be patient, wrote one journalist, should be swept off the earth by "yellow fever, cholera, or any other blessing." In New York City's Tompkins Square, the unemployed who were protesting for government work projects were beaten by mounted police. It was a scene that the *New York Times* found amusing. But sometimes the unemployed succeeded in getting help from local governments.[7]

Middle- and upper-middle-class Americans had nightmares about disorderly poor people, whether beggars on the corner or thousands of people demanding jobs and money. The rowdy working class threatened their security and comfort. Some who were affluent became radical reformers and focused on changing the economy, but many charity officials stayed hard-hearted, even in depressions. They responded to threats from below with policies that denied material aid but ramped up home visitations as a way to persuade poor people to behave properly. Some charity leaders pushed for tougher laws against vagrants. Officials of the New York Society for the Condition of the Poor deplored expressions of sympathy that came in the form of free meals and shelters for needy people. Such things demoralized the poor by encouraging them not to look for work. Charity Organization Societies supervised an army of volunteer "friendly visitors" who entered people's homes and helped to determine whether people deserved assistance and what kind.

The charity reformers' ideas were not completely new. Since the Protestant Reformation of the 1500s in western Europe, public policy made provision for material relief to needy people, but it was usually assumed that many poor people, especially able-bodied males, did not deserve help. If people were to receive aid, they had to demonstrate that they were really needy, and they did so by performing hard labor. Hence the spread of workhouses in England, a country where huge numbers of people were often without work and income. The workhouses degraded and debased their inhabitants, in part to guarantee that only the very needy would enter.

There were workhouses and poorhouses in America in the 1800s, but not enough, especially as industrial capitalism took off after the Civil War. Much of the work of social control was organized by charity organizations, through home visitations and, in extreme cases, the police. There was nothing new in the links between relief policy and extreme methods of discipline, but the charity reformers were organized and militant, and they often thought of themselves as the vanguard of a newly realistic and scientific approach to the poor, the homeless, and the unemployed. Interestingly, their campaign against material assistance occurred in a period when capitalists had vastly increased the amount of wealth held by the rich, so there was more money for wages and cash aid for people who had been pushed into poverty by low pay and unemployment.

Needy people were more likely to receive help from city governments and local political machines than from charity organizations. One-tenth of Brooklyn's population was getting government aid in the depression of the 1870s, while a private New York charity organization hired fifty investigators to weed out unworthy applicants. It is not surprising that most applicants were judged to be undeserving, or that the few who received cash or vouchers had to perform hard labor.[8]

When the press, intellectuals, and charity reformers degraded the poor, they took some of the heat off millionaires like Andrew Carnegie and John D. Rockefeller. It is true that many middle- and upper-middle-class Americans worried about the immense power wielded by the robber barons, but it was easier to do something about poor people than about the barons. And some charity organizations depended on rich Americans for donations. So, conservative intellectuals and professionals frequently dehumanized the unemployed, and the depression of the 1870s seemed to unhinge them. The homeless, jobless person was "incorrigible," "incurable," and an "utterly depraved savage," according to Yale professor Francis Wayland. Harsh measures were necessary. A gun company produced the "Tramp Terror," a shotgun to use on tramps. The *Chicago Tribune* suggested that a little arsenic in food handouts at the back door would discourage begging hobos.[9]

The railroad strikes of 1877 really frightened the middle classes. The depression was in its fourth year. Some railroad companies had collapsed, and some kept paying dividends by cutting wages and increasing workloads. Worker discontent boiled over. A strike erupted against the Baltimore and Ohio Railroad. Federal troops arrived and suppressed it, but protest spread like wildfire. Workers forcibly stopped the trains. Local authorities had difficulty controlling the situation, for the uprising was massive and chaotic, unlike the mostly orderly strikes of modern times. A number of the unemployed became strikebreakers, but others joined strikers to seize control of neighborhoods and businesses. In St. Louis, a Marxist Workingman's Party led the uprising.

In Pittsburgh strikers initially enjoyed support from a community that hated the Pennsylvania Railroad; the local militia even fraternized with strikers. Then, 650 soldiers arrived from Philadelphia. In a pitched battle, they killed twenty-five people and seized the roundhouse and machine shops. In response, enraged strikers and their supporters burned company buildings, railcars, and locomotives. In the fourth year of the depression, it seemed obvious that capitalists and governments would not meet people's needs, so people began using direct action. They pillaged on a scale not seen again until the urban riots of the 1960s. Here were women using aprons to carry away eggs, dry goods, and other foodstuffs. There was a lady with an infant, "rolling a barrel of flour along the sidewalk, using her feet as the propelling power." The angry masses had their weekend. Then, the combined power of police, armed citizens, state militias, and the United States Army quelled the uprising.[10]

Opinion-makers were often vicious in their responses to the uprisings. The *New York Times* described the strikers as "hoodlums, rabble, bummers, looters, blacklegs, thieves, tramps, incendiaries, enemies of society, brigands, rapscallions, riff-raff, felons, and idiots." Workers had to learn to accept poverty-level wages and layoffs; otherwise they were scum. E. L. Godkin, editor of the *Nation* magazine, blamed immigrants and others whom he characterized as ignorant people for the uprisings of 1877. He asserted that governments that gave cash or jobs to the poor were communistic, European, and un-American. Military force was the best labor policy. The wealthy Reverend Henry Ward Beecher admitted to his congregation that the economy required an occasional depression and shrinkage of wages—necessities, he asserted, that workers could not understand. But why worry? "It was true that $1 a day was not enough to support a man and five children, if a man would insist on smoking and drinking beer. Was not a dollar a day enough to buy bread? Water costs nothing." And the congregation laughed. "Men cannot live on bread . . . but the man who cannot live on bread and water is not fit to live." More laughter.[11]

These authorities were about as far as could be from wanting to understand unemployment and low wages. On the other side, single-taxer Henry George and other progressives and socialists wrote about the impersonal causes of joblessness, but the idea that individuals caused their own misery was common among professors, editors, preachers, charity experts, and other leaders of the professional-intellectual class in the late 1800s. On six thousand occasions, Russell Conwell preached that a poor man is one "whom God has punished for his sins . . . let us remember that there is not a poor person in the United States who was not made poor by his own shortcomings or the shortcomings of someone else. It is all wrong to be poor anyhow." The Reverend Beecher said the same thing: "God intended the great to be great and the little to be little."[12]

The Great Depression of the 1890s

Depressions were milder in the 1880s, but unemployment remained high. In Massachusetts 29 percent of the workforce experienced unemployment in 1885. Worker discontent about pay and hours culminated in a strike wave in 1886. Meanwhile, economic rethinking continued. One example was Edward Bellamy's popular *Looking Backward* (1887), about a socialist utopia that provided jobs for all.[13]

In 1893 there began another depression, the biggest yet. Unemployment was very high and there was no help from Washington. Federal money could be spent to suppress the working class, but Senator James Berry of Arkansas, expressing a common view, opposed creating jobs "by appropriating money which belongs to other people and does not belong to the Senate."[14]

How bad was unemployment in the 1890s? There was no official government unemployment survey, but experts then and later made estimates. Here are some from 1894: half of the membership of the German Waiters Union in New York City was out of work; on the east side of New York, 40 percent of all the workers were unemployed and 40 percent on part-time; in Boston, 19 percent unemployed; in Chicago, 40 percent; in Paterson, New Jersey, 50 percent; and in Newark, 40 percent. In 1970 historian Charles Hoffman estimated that unemployment reached 19 percent in the winter of 1893–1894 and was still 15 percent in 1896–1897, the second trough in the depression. In the 1920s, economist Paul Douglas calculated that blue-collar unemployment was 17 percent in 1894. In 1990 economist David Weir found that nonfarm unemployment averaged 17 percent for 1894.[15]

These numbers were not as high as those for the 1930s (30 percent in some years). But unemployment in the '30s would be softened by federal cash grants and work-relief programs. The virtual absence of federal assistance in the 1890s meant that cities were flooded with people who had nothing. In Chicago, there may have been 100,000 unemployed workers. Some papers described widespread suffering among schoolchildren, servants, and homeless people seeking shelter in churches and public buildings. Police stations were jammed with unemployed people who had nowhere else to sleep. As many as fifteen hundred people slept in city hall.[16]

The depression was deep and long-lasting. The economy first slumped in 1893–1894 and then again in 1896–1897. Full recovery may not have been reached until 1901. What caused such a prolonged slump? The following factors were probably the most important. The U.S. economy had often grown strongly in the past, but by the 1890s there was significant overproduction and too many businesses in some areas. Building construction peaked in the spring of 1892; railroads, some of them burdened with very high interest payments, began to collapse in 1893. First went the Philadelphia and Reading Railroad in February 1893, and later the Northern Pacific, the Union Pacific, and the Atchison, Topeka & Santa Fe. The financial sector was unregulated; bankers speculated in the stock market with bank reserves, and when railroads and other businesses collapsed, so did the banks. Then there was a credit crunch as some banks failed and others tightened lending. Also, global competition had been depressing income in the farm sector since the late 1880s. Finally, once the depression was underway, the federal government did almost nothing to stimulate economic activity.[17]

A Convenient Failure of Imagination

The general cause of government neglect was not mainly that Americans did not know what to do. Nor was it that economists had to wait until the 1920s and 1930s for John Maynard Keynes to publish theories justifying government spending and budget deficits to spur job creation. It did not take a Ph.D. in economics or familiarity with Keynes's ideas to understand people's pain and to want to find painkillers and cures. The problem was a lack of desire to empathize and experiment. In 1893 Congressman Wilkinson Call of Florida urged members to stay in session to deal with distress among the unemployed, but he received no support. They could have stayed and come up with something. Governments had experience with public works in the normal course of events. Some reformers were urging public job programs as a response to mass unemployment. Congress could have created new projects to employ the unemployed. With good will, the thought process wasn't difficult: the private economy was not providing enough jobs; people needed jobs and income; government, therefore, should create jobs or pay people until the depression passed.[18]

But weren't Americans opposed to strong government? Such a bias is part of the American creed, but so is the opposite. There were examples of powerful government action. There were tariffs to bolster manufacturing prices and federal troops to beat down strikers. The nation had fairly recently undertaken a massive big-government effort to win the Civil War. Now, in the 1890s, workers needed help and often demanded it; there were reasonable solutions in the air. Ohio businessman Jacob Coxey wanted governments to employ people on public roads. A bill had been introduced in Congress to allow the Treasury to finance roadwork. Coxey supported that one and another law to authorize loans to cities, states, and territories to fund public improvements. Coxey's program aimed to employ the unemployed and to promote economic recovery by increasing purchasing power.

Coxey led a march on Washington; he hoped that 100,000 people would ride the rails to gather in Washington on Easter Sunday, 1894. But the unemployed and the working class mostly stayed home. Many of those who began to march from many parts of the country never made it to Washington. The logistics of this first national protest march must have been daunting. Also, union leaders were divided about solutions to unemployment, and, perhaps, not confident that Coxey's protest would lead to anything. When they reached the capital, Coxey's group numbered five hundred. The press was hostile, most middle-class Americans feared or hated tramps, and Coxey's weak showing encouraged ridicule. But many were hostile from the start. The dean of the Yale Law School called one group of Coxey marchers "soap-shunning and vermin-haunted rabble."[19]

President Grover Cleveland crushed the ragtag army. Coxey and his lieutenants were arrested and convicted of carrying banners on the Capitol grounds. Coxey and another person were also convicted of walking on the grass. That was federal power in action. Coxey's protest was over, but there would be others. Some marchers were warmly greeted, but there was never a mass movement large enough to compel federal officials to spend on job creation.

Even had unemployed demonstrations been substantially larger than Coxey's, they could have been squelched by local police, state troops, and the U.S. Army. We can understand this if we examine what happened to the Pullman strikers, a group that had the support of hundreds of thousands of railroad workers. The Pullman story illustrates the kind of conspiracy of ruthless federal officials and capitalists that large protests evoked. In 1893, the first year of the depression, employment in one Pullman car factory fell from five thousand to eleven hundred. Then George Pullman began selling railroad cars at a loss and reemployed some of his workers. But he cut wages five times, did not reduce rents on company housing, and refused to meet with worker representatives. And he asserted that workers contributed nothing to the success of the enterprise; only managers and stockholders did. Forget the value he extracted from his employees every day. Forget that employees' underpaid labor allowed the company to pay out $3 million in dividends in the depression year of 1894. Pullman employees rebelled and won the support of Eugene Debs's new American Railway Union for a general strike of railroad workers. Federal officials then plotted with railroad managers to use injunction law and the U.S. Army to quash the strike.[20]

If such power could be mobilized against a large union of several hundred thousand members, what hope had the unorganized unemployed millions? The working class and especially its leaders were not united about the shortcomings of narrow craft unions or the value of worker-oriented government programs. Some labor leaders urged shorter hours and public works as antidotes to unemployment; some thought less immigration would create more jobs. Most mainline union leaders, with Samuel Gompers in the lead, did not support militant protests to win government action on unemployment. Some radicals, including socialists, wanted government unemployment insurance, but others opposed it.[21]

Federal officials offered no relief to the unemployed and no effective recovery policy. In his second inaugural address in March 1893, President Cleveland stated that "The lessons of paternalism ought to be unlearned . . . while people should patriotically and cheerfully support their Government, its functions do not include support of the people." During this depression he worried more about the gold standard than helping the unemployed. From J. P. Morgan he borrowed $65 million worth of gold to bolster the gold supply that backed U.S. money. The gold standard based the quantity of money on the gold supply. Bankers liked the gold standard and low inflation, but there was little danger of inflation, and sticking with gold meant less spending money and longer depressions. Populist farmers and some workers and reformers wanted higher prices and more money in circulation, but the easy-money candidate of Democrats and Populists, William Jennings Bryan, was trounced by Republican William McKinley in 1896. Gold won, and economic recovery had to wait for new mines and new methods to increase the supply of gold and money. In later times, a monetary system based on gold could be seen as mysticism.[22]

Unemployment Relief in the 1890s

The federal government offered no aid, local governments offered not enough, and officers of the Charity Organization Societies obsessed about people's poor work ethic. There were organizations offering help, ranging from fragment societies that collected unwanted clothing for the needy and some job programs run by urban political machines. But the impact of all public and private assistance must have been very small.[23]

Apparent exceptions are revealing. New York City's East Side Relief Committee involved charity professionals and welfare organizations led by Josephine Shaw Lowell. She and her co-workers did not believe in work projects for the unemployed. But the extent of the unemployment crisis temporarily overwhelmed dogma. Members of the East Side Relief Committee raised money to employ several thousand people sewing, sweeping streets, and rehabilitating tenements. On average, individuals took home a total of $36, 1/15 of a subsistence budget for a year. In Lynn, Massachusetts, people were given $10 for a month's work on the streets. Ten dollars was not much even in the late 1800s, and hundreds of Lynn citizens did not even get that. Only 295 passed home investigations that were used to weed out supposed impostors.[24]

Some cities and states offered work projects that showed what could be done. But conservative opposition was strong. When Boston's unemployed demonstrated for public works, the state's governor did not give them jobs. He gave them mean-spirited individualism. Most people, he said, took care of themselves and they should not have to subsidize jobs for people who could not. Charity leaders opposed job-creation projects involving useful production because, they said, such programs would attract lazy people who would do bad work but have to be paid anyway. Charity officials found reasons to argue against every proposal to really help the unemployed, even plans to put them to work.[25]

Hardliners often dominated public debate in the 1890s, despite the fact that soaring unemployment could not have been caused by the collapse of people's work ethic. Yet even people who had other sophisticated ideas about the economy did not hold realistic and compassionate views of the unemployed. Charity bigwig Lowell had founded the New York Consumers League in 1890 to support better pay and conditions for women workers, and she organized the East Side Relief Project. But she seemed to believe that when working-class people fell into unemployment and poverty, their work ethic crumbled. Individuals on work-relief had to be given jobs that were "continuous, hard, and underpaid," and, preferably, under rigorous supervision in a workhouse. Lowell's dark view of human nature seemed, at times, so lacking in compassion and common sense as to suggest that she and professionals like her were not only worried about managing the working class, but grappling with personal anxieties about control and independence in an economy increasingly dominated by powerful capitalists and shaken by uncontrollable forces. In the mid-1880s she warned that charitable aid to a widow in poverty had to come with work requirements, or the lady would be tempted to spend "her days in idleness and her nights in debauchery." Honestly?[26]

Conservative members of the professional-intellectual class could have found more constructive channels for relieving their anxieties. In addition to Coxey's plan, demonstrators in New York City pressured the state legislature to authorize park commissioners to spend $1 million to employ the unemployed. The city of Denver, flooded with thousands of unemployed workers, including many miners, made a special appropriation of $15,000 for roadwork. Denver unions, with the cooperation of government officials and citizen committees, provided shelter and meals for up to fifteen hundred men for seven weeks at Camp Relief. Denver religious organizations organized the Maverick Restaurant, which provided good food at a minimal cost. Some people lacked even five cents for a meal, so officials opened a woodyard where the unemployed could earn enough to pay for food and a night's shelter. As always, there were naysayers; Denver's mayor claimed that many of the needy were impostors. But there was wide support in Denver for the view that jobless people were not to blame. Why the liberal slant? It was not that a few middle-class progressive leaders happened to live in Denver. It was that unions and a powerful working class, not the middle classes, set the agenda in the city.[27]

Across the nation many intellectuals, politicians, and professionals were like journalist William Allen White and, in White's words, "ten thousand other fools across the land" who still thought that laissez-faire economics was fine. Over time, the ranks of economic progressives were increasing, although slowly. Economist John Commons wrote a dozen articles urging public works as the antidote to depression. Governor Lorenzo D. Lewelling of Kansas declared a state vagrancy law unconstitutional and instructed the police not to molest tramps. "It is no crime to be without visible means of support," he said. Some historians think that the '90s saw a turn toward softer views, and there was movement along these lines, but it was only a half turn. Populism in the Democratic Party was routed in the presidential election of 1896, and liberal professors were harassed and even fired. The final report of the U.S. Industrial Commission in 1900, while noting that a regular job was the most important "privilege for which working men can ask," devoted only sixteen of 1,134 pages to unemployment. This occurred at the end of a period (1865–1900) in which half the years had depression levels of unemployment.

A revealing exchange occurred at the 1901 meeting of the American Economic Association. Economist Charles Tuttle criticized colleagues for accentuating the positive and saying little about unemployment. He proposed that since much unemployment was caused by technological change rather than lazy workers, the unemployed should be helped with free public employment bureaus and free railroad transportation paid out of government revenues. The participants, except for John Commons, laid into him. They declared, as historian Joseph Dorfman put it later, that his proposals were "a threat to the foundation of social order." They would "reduce initiative, the State would eventually have to enforce compulsory employment, the government would become the sole employer, and slavery would be necessary." Laissez-faire lived on among economists—but some of them seemed to be unhinged.[28]

Full Employment Was Rare, Even in Good Times; Job Tenure for Most Blue-Collar Workers Was Short

The years from 1900 through 1916, often called The Progressive era, were a period of a variety of reform movements. Successes included the creation of the Federal Reserve, limits on monopolistic business practices, and constitutional changes that expanded democracy via the popular election of senators and woman suffrage. But not much was done to lift wages or protect people against unemployment. And unemployment did not disappear. Although the period is often considered a prosperous one, there were lesser economic slumps in 1903–1904 and 1910–1911, and depressions in 1908 and 1913–1914. Unemployment was often quite high between cyclical downturns. Later estimates developed by economists Paul Douglas (for blue-collar workers), Stanley Lebergott (nonfarm workers), and David Weir (private-sector nonfarm workers) showed that high unemployment was typical, especially in the second half of the period. For the years 1900 through 1908, unemployment averaged 8.6 percent, 9.8 percent, and 6.9 percent in the three estimates; for 1908 through 1915, it averaged 11.1 percent, 12.35 percent, and 10.4 percent.

Exactly what constitutes full employment is a difficult issue and especially so for, say, 1890–1929, when the government did not carry out comprehensive monthly surveys. Nor do we have numbers akin to modern estimates of hidden unemployment. But if we say that only unemployment under 3 percent was really full employment, then there was just one year that averaged full employment out of forty years. If we say that anything at or below 4.0 percent—which is close to mainstream views in 2019—was full employment, then there were only three years in which unemployment on average was not excessive unemployment (1906, 1918, 1919). Even if we allow that anything below an average of 5 percent unemployment was full employment, there were just six full-employment years (1906, 1907, 1918, 1919, 1926, 1929). In short, any of the benchmarks support the view that there was almost always excessive unemployment in 1890–1929. Anything even close to full employment was rare in the estimates by the three scholars.[29]

In 1915 an anonymous author at the U.S. Bureau of Labor Statistics summed up the general situation this way: "unemployment is a normal condition in many industries carried on today." But many observers would not admit that "there just was not enough work for everyone in America." There were many reasons for joblessness. One that seemed new was a matter of policy in some large industrial concerns. Owners operated their plants at full capacity or not at all. Next to an idle steel plant, another was running twenty-four hours a day. Steelworkers were overworked or "chronically idle." When the breadwinner was idle, budgets were strained. There was no unemployment compensation, and in the Pittsburgh area, there weren't many jobs outside the mills; when men were laid off, the family ate less and wives begged for credit at local stores.

Of course, some people had it better. There was a broad duality to the whole labor market and to specific areas and businesses. In the primary or better sector, workers had more job security, less unemployment, and better pay. In the secondary market people were normally not paid well, changed jobs often, were often unemployed, and faced unpleasant working conditions. Merchants, office clerks, managers in larger firms, professionals, schoolteachers, federal employees, and employees of local electric trams and streetcars had more job security than other people. There were dual labor markets within many firms, including factories and department stores. More skilled and older employees had less turnover; younger, less experienced, or less skilled workers had more. Business sectors that faced significant seasonal challenges in their customer markets might employ a core of full-time permanent workers and a group of temporary or part-time workers whose numbers changed with the seasons. This was true of big farms in the West and Midwest that employed large numbers of migrant workers and of big department stores in the East. In 1913 an official investigation found that seven New York department stores had an average total labor force of 26,628, but hired 42,444 people a year to maintain that number. There were huge differences among stores: one store hired only 875 people to maintain a staff of 3,497 employees; another hired 12,159 to maintain a staff of 3,497.

Seasonal shutdowns, technological change, shrinking crafts, and general economic slumps caused layoffs. But workers often quit their jobs too, especially when business conditions were better and finding new jobs was easier. Labor turnover, which included workers quitting and bosses dismissing them, was high, even in nonseasonal businesses. In some shops, 80 percent of the work-force had not been on the job at least two years. The workplace reasons for rapid turnover included haphazard employment practices that meant companies hired people with the wrong skills and experience, the absence of training programs, and seasonal and cyclical layoffs. But some of the most important reasons can be summed up in five words: many jobs were lousy jobs. Low pay, insecure tenure, long hours, authoritarian foremen, and dangerous work that included poisonous fumes and murderous heat in the summer caused employees, even poor people living on the edge, to quit their jobs. How bad were workplaces? Industrial death rates in the 1910s were more than eighteen times as high as they are in modern times.[30]

While the causes were many, and some workers who quit their jobs found better ones elsewhere, they were out of work and without income during the search period. In that way, the extreme churning in the labor market meant more unemployment. And though some commentators might think this search process was benign—as they think much unemployment in modern times is frictional and not a problem—many of these workers did not find better positions. There was a huge demand for workers without high-level skills. And there was a huge supply of workers for low-wage, insecure jobs. Of males in manufacturing, mining, and other extractive industries, agriculture and forestry work, and transportation, almost ten million, or a third of the total, could be classed as unskilled or common labor. Many were poorly paid, often unemployed, and degraded by an economy that did not provide enough decent jobs. Some lived in filthy labor camps or seedy lodging houses. Often without work and without cash, they were cheated by municipal police courts, employers, and lodging house managers. An expert on these matters knew persons who, after a month of work, found that they were in debt to their employers for employment fees, post office fees, board, transportation, and hospital fees.

Until World War I, employers could count on an adequate surplus of common labor, and without much effort. Diggers, loaders, road builders, dockers, wheat harvesters, and many unskilled workers in factories and in construction spent a lot of time looking for jobs. Because there were plenty of recruits for many kinds of jobs, there was small incentive for employers to substantially improve compensation and conditions. In 1904, when meat packers were bargaining with the union over laborers' wages, they had this weapon: "3,000 to 5,000 transient laborers who gathered every morning at seven o'clock . . . asking for work, when not one tenth of their number could be employed." Among the ten million less skilled workers, there were plenty of quits but also fierce competition for jobs, especially among immigrants. The pool of low-skilled labor was "always oversupplied," so while there were a lot of job vacancies in better times, there were usually more job seekers than jobs.[31]

Scholars and employers began to talk more about labor turnover in the 1910s. As we have seen, high turnover was the norm in many businesses. In the logging industry, for example, it had not been unusual for employers to hire five men for every position every year. But in the 1910s, it seemed to be news that annual rates of turnover reached 400 percent at Henry Ford's modern Highland Park plant. And as the scholarly study of labor issues advanced, there were numbers to show how widespread the problem was and suggestions for fixing the problem. However, until the 1920s, most employers did not seem much concerned about turnover, and even in the 1920s, only a minority of businesses created personnel departments and rationalized hiring processes.

To wrap up the general argument of this section, here is a sample of occupations and economic sectors that tended to be associated with high turnover and high unemployment rates:

- **Great Lakes Shipping** had high unemployment in January, February, and March. Dockers and seamen filled nearby cities during the winter.
- In general, **Factory Workers** experienced a lot of turnover, but there were differences among factories, cities, and skill levels. In a stove-making plant in St. Louis, 50 percent of the employees had been employed five or more years. In a metal shop in Cleveland, only 16 percent. Most urban industrial labor markets were dual labor markets: a small group of workers held semi-permanent jobs, but most blue-collar jobs were unstable.
- **The Clothing Trades** and **Coal Mining** were affected by seasonal markets or fashion cycles. In the first half of 1903, unemployment often exceeded 20 percent in the clothing trades. In ninety New York shops in 1913, 4,858 workers we employed at some time over the year to maintain an average workforce of 1,435.
- In **Department Stores**, as in many other workplaces, there were internal dual labor markets: the top tier of female sales clerks had steady full-time work; below them, the part-time and less secure workforce ranged from as little as a tenth to as much as half of a store's staff.
- The jobs of **Migrant Farm Workers and Cannery Workers** were typically short-term.
- **Timber Workers and Ice Cutters** were thrown out of work by the wrong kind of weather or market ups and downs. So were laborers in **Construction**.
- **Railroads Engineers and Conductors** had a negligible turnover rate of 4.8 percent. But for **maintenance-of-way workers** the rate was 200 percent.

Employees on **local street railways** seemed relatively secure in their jobs. In one large company with more than three thousand employees, average years of service were more than seven.

- **Small Businesses and Small Farms** regularly failed. The memoirs and biographies of middle-class Americans often mention that a father's business failure thrust the family into poverty. This was a kind of unemployment that does not make it into our historical estimates.[32]

How Progressive Was the Progressive Period on Job Issues? (1900–1916)

The period was one of optimism about social reform and government activism. Some settlement houses played a part in reform movements, but few officers in the Charity Organization Societies softened their views. Philadelphia leader Mary Richmond asserted in 1907 that unemployment was strong "evidence of inefficiency or unwillingness to work." If you were unemployed, you were at fault. Records from a Connecticut social agency revealed negative attitudes. "Friendly visitors" expected poor people to be deferential, to dress properly, and to fit traditional roles. Charity workers were expected to exert control, not give material aid. Here are excerpts from visitor reports:

"Woman may have a mental defect," she cannot "line a coat."
A woman with tuberculosis should have gone to a sanitarium, but "if cured would surely return to immoral life." The investigator recommended no treatment.
"Treatment plan—get Mrs. C to be more moral."
Once a housewife accepted charity, "she gave up the right to make any decisions."[33]

But the long depression of the 1890s offered lessons. Some charity leaders had begun to grapple with economic realities. In 1895 Robert Treat Paine, president of Boston Associated Charities, wondered whether charity workers should continue to focus on individuals when it appeared that general causes like the depression were behind poverty, vice, crime, and disease. Edward Devine, Columbia University professor and general secretary of the New York Charity Organization Society, was also rethinking unemployment. In 1904 he claimed that even assisting people to find work would be harmful to their sense of self-help. Five years later, he decided that unemployment was rooted in impersonal factors like immigration and new machinery. Younger social workers began to think a little more about the root causes of homelessness, including unemployment. They were more likely than their elders to support handouts to the poor and less likely to brand needy people as deviants.[34]

Another sign of liberalization in the professional-intellectual class and the charity establishment was the settlement house movement. The most famous example was Jane Addams's Hull House in Chicago. There were a hundred settlement houses by 1900. Participants lived among the poor to help them and to learn from them. They tended to be less arrogant about the poor than charity society leaders and friendly visitors. The most advanced of them engaged in preventive social work by trying to fix social and economic conditions that caused poverty and disease. A number became politically active to address sanitation problems and unsafe working conditions. Settlement workers were leaders of middle-class progressivism on such working-class issues as unemployment insurance.[35]

Others in government, academia, churches, and organizations like the American Association on Unemployment (AAU) were learning to understand unemployment as an economic phenomenon. But many business leaders and many representatives of charity organizations still talked about unemployment as a matter of individual failure. AAU leader John Andrews concluded in 1911 that even professionals who were studying unemployment sometimes gave the impression that "we haven't any." After forty years of people being thrown around by massive economic forces beyond their control, "public opinion had not yet grasped fully the preponderant significance of industrial and economic factors as contrasted with the peculiarities of individuals as causes of unemployment."[36]

And among the minority who began to understand unemployment as the outcome of economic forces, few were ready to demand federal action to create jobs. Some experts thought that urban unemployment could be reduced if people were drawn back to the countryside, but millions of people were always moving to the cities because the country could not employ them. Another panacea, making the unemployed into more efficient workers, wasn't inherently a bad idea, but it could put others out of work. A third and fairly popular cure was to connect workers and jobs through labor exchanges or employment bureaus.[37]

A prominent advocate of this third approach was labor-relations scholar William Leiserson. He claimed that there was a shortage of skilled and efficient workers. What was needed was a system of government offices to match unemployed workers and job openings. Whether skilled workers were in short supply or not, government labor exchanges were a good idea. Millions of workers were at the mercy of unscrupulous private labor exchanges and contractors. Sometimes workers were conned into paying for jobs that did not exist. In 1912

American workers paid $15,000,000 to labor exchanges, some of which were criminal rackets. Efficient government-run labor exchanges had to be part of the nation's labor policy. But even the best-run exchanges could not actually create new jobs.[38]

There was also a little movement on a fourth reform, government unemployment insurance, led by people in the AAU. Businesses leaders were not supportive. Nor were Samuel Gompers and others in the American Federation of Labor; they had their own version of laissez-faire. Unions should achieve their goals through collective bargaining, not from government. But that position abandoned the majority of workers, who would not soon be organized by AFL unions, which were mostly for skilled craft workers.[39]

Efficiency and Soldiering: Workers Fought Unemployment by Direct Action

While scholars and reformers advocated for their special solutions, employees in and out of unions fought every day to preserve jobs from speed-ups, mechanization, and Taylorism. Engineer Frederick Taylor pioneered an effort to de-skill workers and increase managerial control of the work process. Employers and engineers bemoaned the fact that workers did not work as fast as they could—why were they so lazy?—but when a student named Stanley Mathewson visited worksites in the 1920s to get the answer, he learned that many workers were trying to preserve jobs and to keep the pace of the work reasonable. Employers pushed for more output per worker—speed-ups—and employees sometimes reacted in spectacular ways. In the huge strike of Paterson, New Jersey, silk workers in 1913, there were many grievances, but one was the effort of employers to force weavers to work on four looms instead of two. The weavers feared that the four-loom system meant more unemployment and a large army of desperate job-seekers who would be willing to work for less. That strike was defeated and employers pushed on.

Meanwhile, Frederick Taylor claimed to bring science to the class struggle. Through experiments and writings including his book, *The Principles of Scientific Management* (1911), he had been striving to undermine systematic "soldiering," that is, workers purposely doing less work than they were capable of doing in order to preserve jobs. One famous Taylorite method for breaking workers' control over the labor process was the efficiency expert, who walked around the shop with a stopwatch and a clipboard to discover just how fast workers could work. Workers tried to subvert the process by slowing down when the efficiency engineer came by. In industries where it was possible, workers who overproduced hid extra output in their lockers. On construction sites they worked more slowly to make the job last longer. Piece-work rates seemed a partial solution; workers would work faster because they could earn more. But Taylor knew that the piece-work system was flawed because managers always cheated. If workers produced twice as much in an hour to earn twice as much, managers cut the pay-rate so that, in the end, they were producing more but not earning more.

Over time Taylorism helped to erode workers' control on the shop floor, but probably more important were automation and mechanization, and most spectacularly the assembly line, an essentially simple way to erode crafts and limit worker control. But action by employees to preserve jobs continued. Over the twentieth century, unionized and unorganized workers strove to protect jobs and control in construction, on the railroads, in steel plants, and in many lines of work. Sometimes they succeeded. Sometimes they received bad press for protecting unneeded workers. In the railroad business it was called "featherbedding" when unions were able to preserve jobs that were not essential, but when good blue-collar jobs were wiped out, enough other good blue-collar jobs were not necessarily added elsewhere. When workers took extraordinary steps to preserve good jobs, they were acting with foresight and rationality.

Meanwhile, back in the Progressive era, in the 1912 presidential election, it looked like progressives and socialists might put unemployment insurance (UI) on the national agenda. The Socialist Party ran Eugene Debs, a strong candidate, and the party platform included a demand for UI. Settlement house leaders included a UI plank in the platform of the Progressive Party, whose candidate was Theodore Roosevelt. Unemployment insurance might have been discussed in Congress if the progressive and socialist tide had continued. In 1912 the two parties on the left won 33.4 percent of the vote. That was more than was won by the Republican incumbent, William Howard Taft, but Democrat Woodrow Wilson was elected with 41.8 percent of the vote. Wilson had welcomed union support, and he was more sympathetic to labor's needs than was the Republican candidate, but neither he, nor, for that matter, Samuel Gompers, wanted federal legislation to create government unemployment insurance.[40]

During World War I, the Progressive Party withered and socialist leaders either joined the pro-war side or opposed the war and went to jail. Over time some of the pioneering spirit of the settlement movement faded. Some houses became professional service providers. In the field of social and charitable service, the impulse to professionalize careers was strong. That could mean more college degrees and less political activity. Aspiring caseworkers were still taught in school that a person's culture and attitudes were everything. The helping process remained, as social historian David Wagner points out, "Not Alms, But a Friend," not money but character reform. But the reform side of social service represented by Jane Addams did not disappear. One of its offspring, Harry Hopkins, would manage New Deal relief policy and campaign for realistic and compassionate views of needy people; and in the 1930s, as well as the 1960s and 1970s, there was a radical wing of social workers that wanted to focus on remaking economic and social structures rather than repairing the psyches of the unemployed. But case work was still central to social work, and that often meant a focus on the flawed individual rather than flaws in the economy, even for clients who mostly needed work or cash, not counseling.[41]

One Step Forward, No More

A sign that some economists were moving toward systemic explanations of the causes of unemployment was economist Wesley Mitchell's *Business Cycles and Their Causes,* published in 1913. Mitchell demonstrated that the ups and downs of the economy were not accidents and they were not a matter of rising and falling levels of worker laziness. They were due to normal economic cycles, and the cycles were inherent in the modern money economy. Though Mitchell was more interested in the movement of prices than in unemployment, his work seemed to destroy the equilibrium assumptions that allowed other economists to deny that the inner motors of capitalism had anything to do with depressions and high unemployment. The new normal was an inevitable and continuing rise and fall of prices, production, and jobs.

Over time more experts understood that public works could promote recovery from depression, but very few of them committed to the radical idea that the federal government should take the lead. They pinned their hopes on states and cities, and often they did not ask for more spending but only that governments rearrange budgets so as to spend more in depressions and less in boom times.

In the years before war broke out in Europe, not much had changed in law and policy. More members of the professional-intellectual class had softer views of the unemployed, but it is doubtful that a "considerable part of the nation" understood that unemployment was involuntary and rooted in modern industry rather than individual psyches. The frequency of depressions was convincing more reformers that unemployment was both "periodic and chronic." But harsh policies for the poor and the unemployed were still common in this, the Progressive era. Public charity was stingy. New York City built a Municipal Lodging House for the Homeless in 1909, but male residents had to work in a stone yard to prove that they were not idlers. Unemployment activist Frank Tannenbaum had this to say about the house: "It's not fit for a dog. We can't get to bed there until 1 in the morning, and we have to get up at 4, then do five hours of work for three hours of sleep."[42]

World War I: Bigger Government and Fuller Employment

The United States slipped into depression in the winter of 1913, as the war in Europe disrupted markets. Members of a revolutionary union, the Industrial Workers of the World (the I.W.W., or Wobblies) put unemployment on the front page. In the spring of 1914, Frank Tannenbaum, then a twenty-one-year old busboy and Wobbly organizer, led demonstrators into New York City churches to demand food and lodging. The demonstrators were orderly, and at first they were given what they asked for. But anything linked to the I.W.W. was tarred by the press as dangerously revolutionary; the *New York Times* and other papers demanded repression. It is true that the I.W.W.'s long-range goal was to replace capitalism with worker control, and Tannenbaum had declared that everyone had a right to share in everything, and the way to get it was to take it. But I.W.W. practice was often moderate. On March 3, 1914, Tannenbaum led five hundred people to seek food and shelter in St. Alphonsus Roman Catholic Church. The priests refused and Tannenbaum agreed to leave; "All right, no hard feelings, cap. . . . We'll go away." After he failed to get the priest to shake hands, he tried to take his people out, but police blocked the way. They arrested 189 people for unlawful assembly, intent to riot, and disorderly conduct. Tannenbaum was sentenced to a year in jail and a $500 fine. Soon I.W.W. work among the unemployed ebbed. The Wobblies questioned how much was being won for the unemployed. Also, the economy adjusted to war and jobs became more plentiful.[43]

Wobbly agitation helped move more people to a better view of the unemployed and even won a public works project in San Francisco. Religious leaders were coming to understand that people needed jobs and that the churches could not provide them. A Merchants Association leader in New York urged people to take the problem of unemployment seriously and to understand that public demonstrations were the only way the unemployed could express their grievances.[44]

Entry into the war brought hefty increases in government spending, much of it deficit spending, and that pushed unemployment down to the lowest level of any year from 1890 to 1944. As immigration fell and the armed forces expanded, blue-collar workers enjoyed the freedom to choose from a multitude of job offers. It is true that price controls were ineffective and prices jumped 100 percent from 1914 to 1920. Many white-collar workers lost purchasing power to inflation. But demand for factory workers was so strong that, for many of them, wage advances outpaced inflation by 20, 30, even 40 percent. Full employment could be a wondrous thing. Also, partly owing to the demands of a war economy, government agencies even encouraged unionization, and the Bureau of Labor Statistics carried out a national family-budget survey to ascertain the real cost of living for workers. Also, the fledgling United States Employment Service was given a role as a labor exchange, although it had barely gotten started before the war ended.[45]

Soon, the positives of a full-employment economy would be overwhelmed by the negatives of hyper-patriotism. The anti-socialist and selectively anti-union repression of wartime and the red scare of 1918–1920 diminished the space for new ideas and action. The Wobblies had done the most to fight for the unemployed and really poor workers. But they were violently attacked by employers, conservative unions, and vigilante groups. Most Wobbly leaders were jailed and the organization was decapitated. So was the Socialist Party. The union movement as a whole doubled its numbers during the war but as the country entered the 1920s, unions still covered less than a fifth of the workforce and the labor-left was in tatters.[46]

. . .

To summarize this chapter, from 1873 through 1920, high unemployment was common, and business leaders and government did little to counteract it. For a long time, influential people denied the economic causes of unemployment. By 1920, there'd been major advances in technology and business organization, and giant increases in national wealth, but almost nothing at the federal level to deal with the scourge of the working class—unemployment.

CHAPTER 2

The Twenties and the Thirties

Boom, Bust, and New Deal

B etween the depressions of 1921–1922 and 1929, there was economic growth and there were substantial improvements in the way many people lived their lives. But prosperous periods often have plenty of unemployment, and the 1920s were no exception. Unemployment had not mostly disappeared, as some historians have said, and there was no safety net for households whose main breadwinner was out of work. In this respect, the 1920s were not so different from the late 1800s. Average incomes were higher and there were more cars and fewer horses on the street. But unemployment was a constant worry for millions of people, and governments offered virtually no help.[1]

The Great Depression was born out of the 1920s, particularly the lack of business regulation and the fact that a powerful business class faced workers who often had little bargaining power. Unions covered few workers, unemployment in many areas undermined employee bargaining leverage, and conservative judges often struck down minimum-wage laws. While working-class incomes increased, they grew less rapidly than labor productivity or the incomes of the very rich. An underconsumption crisis—not enough mass buying power—loomed over the economy late in the decade.

During the Great Depression and the crack-up of the old economic order, suffering was widespread, the anger and activism of employed and unemployed workers was often aggressive, and quite a few intellectual and political leaders moved to the left. These changes made government practices more humane and more realistic.

Ideas and policies began to change in five ways. The first advance was wider recognition that unemployment was not caused by the unemployed person. Until the 1930s, probably a majority of economists, politicians, and middle-class Americans echoed, consciously or not, the axioms of classical and neoclassical economics. The classicals argued that unemployment was not caused by anything internal to the system of supply and demand. It arose from things that interfered with free markets—government, unions, high wages, solar activity that caused trade fluctuations, and lazy workers. Usually the jobs were there; people needed to take them.[2]

In chapter 1 we learned that this view was challenged by unemployed people, by reformers and radicals, and by a growing number of scholars. Yet by 1921 the nation had not gone very far toward substantive anti-unemployment policies. There was support for regulating budgets so that governments spent more in recessions and less in good times. Commerce Secretary Herbert Hoover actually organized a conference to discuss responses to the 1921 recession, and the conference was a sign that a significant minority of American leaders believed that dogmatic laissez-faire was not enough. But people could not eat a conference or the research that it led to. When he was president during the Great Depression, Hoover stood fast against federal aid to the unemployed. Eventually the Depression and people's responses to it would sweep Hooverism aside.

The old view and the new can be summarized in the words of two American leaders early in the Great Depression. In 1931 John Edgerton of the National Association of Manufacturers asked a rhetorical question: if the unemployed failed to "practice habits of thrift and conservation, or if they gamble their savings in the stock market . . . is our economic system, or government or industry to blame?" On the other side, in January 1932, New York Governor Franklin Roosevelt asserted that "No one who is out of work today can rightfully feel that he or she is personally responsible for having lost his or her job."[3]

A second fundamental shift, which flowed from the first, involved the federal obligation to assist the unemployed with cash and jobs. Of course, it was important to understand that individuals did not cause their own unemployment—and as unemployment lines lengthened in the '30s, that became crystal clear. But if that recognition did not lead to concrete actions, what was the point? And if you left the task of providing assistance to private charities and local governments, as Hoover and others wanted to do, you were saying that you did not want people to get much help.

A third advance involved government's role as a job creator. It included government job programs like the Works Progress Administration (WPA) and advanced ideas about federal spending and borrowing to stimulate economic growth and job creation in the private sector. Already a little in the 1930s but spectacularly during World War II, heavy federal spending and huge budget deficits brought full employment.

We will pay special attention to New Deal public works programs because they offer lessons and inspirations for our time. There were positives and negatives about most New Deal job programs, but overall they were an advance for the people they helped and for reform thought. But the lessons to be drawn from New Deal job programs and also from Keynesian-style spending deficits would be fiercely resisted by conservatives.

On the question of government's duty to counteract inadequate economic demand in the private sector, it has been said that there was a Keynesian revolution during World War II. Keynes was not the only person who broke free of the paralysis of orthodox economics, but in his *General Theory of Employment, Interest, and Money* (1936), he offered unequivocal arguments for an activist budget policy. He argued that the capitalist economy did not always tend toward full employment. In fact, it could fall into a hole of high unemployment and get stuck there because, often, there was not enough economic demand to spur growth. Keynes argued and policy-makers in the United States in the late 1930s learned that government must spend to compensate for inadequate private-sector demand. And they could do it with borrowed money. Deficit spending was magical in the sense that it did not take money from taxpayers that would be spent anyway. It added, as though from nothing, more spending. The huge deficits of World War II brought truly full employment to America, and that seemed like proof for the efficacy of deficit spending. But the Keynesian revolution, as we will see in chapter 3, was only a half turn. Not until the 1960s did the first significant peacetime experiment in activist Keynesianism occur, and despite substantial success, many economists and politicians attacked deficit policy, even conservatives who were causing high deficits.

The fourth advance in the 1930s and early 1940s was that federal officials were able to construct a reliable monthly survey of unemployment. That was a big advance for the working class. It took the massive job crisis and creative employees in several government agencies, including the WPA, to generate a credible estimate of the unemployment rate. The history of that achievement is discussed in more detail in chapter 6.

In the fifth area, serious ideas about full employment began to sprout. For classical and neoclassical economists, full employment was happening all the time—or would be if outside influences did not intervene. Some intellectuals and many workers knew better, but full employment was rarely discussed and it was actually a rare occurrence except in wartime. Gradually, more scholars became interested in the business cycles. Marxists argued that advanced capitalism naturally generated catastrophic unemployment and also that capitalists would not tolerate full employment. But liberal non-Marxists developed the idea that policy could bring full employment. Examples were John Maynard Keynes in England in the 1920s and 1930s and William Trufant Foster and Waddill Catchings in the United States in the 1920s. However, not until the late 1930s and the 1940s did national politicians seriously discuss full employment. Government programs that gave millions of people jobs showed what government could do. Opinion surveys registered majority support for the idea that government should assure jobs to everyone who needed them. Spending and direct job creation in World War II showed that government could bring full employment. Franklin Roosevelt had said that people had a right to a decent job and that government might have to guarantee that right. He made the right to a job part of his second bill of rights in the 1940s. Fans of harsh economics and thin safety nets never gave up, and they came roaring back in the 1980s, but popular and scholarly ideas about why people were unemployed and what to do about it had changed forever in the '30s.[4]

Prosperity and Poverty in the Twenties

In 1919–1921, the red scare and a depression with 23 percent unemployment for blue-collar workers enhanced employer power. In the '20s all three presidents were Republicans who were more or less hostile to unions. After 1921 the economy grew and wages rose for many workers. Millions of homes got indoor plumbing and electric lighting. Auto registrations jumped from eight million to twenty-three million. These were significant changes, but many commentators and business representatives went a little crazy for capitalism. The economy, they claimed, had entered a "new era" and depressions were a thing of the past. Employers, one historian gushed later, "agreed to pay high pay rates and to give lavish benefits" in a policy called "welfare capitalism" that provided pleasant workplaces, grievance forums, and stable jobs.

Reality was not quite so rosy. Many employers who claimed to support high wages believed in "other employers (actually) paying high wages." While average real annual earnings for employees at all levels increased by a hefty 28 percent (1920–1929), millions of blue-collar workers received no increase. Building trades workers received large pay increases and white-collar workers recovered from huge losses to inflation in World War I, but unskilled railroad workers, steel workers, farm laborers, textile workers, coal miners, and many others fell behind. The gap between the rich and the lower half widened.

The twenties were a mix of progress and poverty. Perhaps half of all working-class households were poor. A man name Archie Chadbourne made $25 a week, which was about $1,300 for a full year's work (about $19,200 of purchasing power in our time). In his twentieth year as a truck driver for the same store, he felt that "Debt Is the Only Adventure a Poor Man Can Count On."

Chadbourne's personal anguish was linked to macroeconomic problems. Workers and machines produced more every year, and output advanced faster than average wages. Even with more installment credit, the economy would soon be able to turn out more goods and services than people could buy. Insufficient consumption spending meant less investment spending on raw materials, buildings, machines, and employees. That meant slower economic growth.[5]

Real Unemployment in the Jazz Age

Historian Ellis Hawley once claimed that unemployment all but disappeared in the 1920s. If you use the numbers for the civilian labor force in the U.S. Census publication *Historical Statistics of the United States* (1975), you might agree. But, in fact, there was a good deal of unemployment and "virtually nothing was done to protect against joblessness."[6]

One thing did change in labor markets in the 1920s. The rate of workers who quit factory jobs fell. High labor turnover, often fueled by frequent worker quits, had been the rule in the years before the war, especially in factories. That changed in the '20s. If less turnover means more job security, then there was more job security where there hadn't been much of it before. A defining characteristic of secondary labor markets was being modified.

But the rate of labor turnover, especially quit rates, has several determinants, and those interact in complex ways. Normally, lower unemployment means more quits, because employees are confident they will find better jobs. But employer labor policy, from cleaner workplaces and attentive supervisors to better pay, can help to bind workers to their jobs. Also, unemployment and job insecurity may be higher in the manufacturing sector than it is for the whole economy.

What was going on in factories in the 1920s? Did workers stay on the job longer because they felt more secure or less secure than before the war? The overall unemployment numbers were not very different. Nonfarm unemployment averaged 7.13 percent in 1900–1909 and 7.68 percent in 1920–1929. So unemployment rates before and after the war were quite similar, but worker quit rates fell noticeably in the 1920s, and that is not what we would expect. Why were factory workers less likely to quit their jobs in the 1920s if unemployment was not much higher?

While overall unemployment rates were not notably higher in the '20s, what was different was that key blue-sectors were shrinking or stagnant. There were about the same number of workers in manufacturing at the end of the decade as at the beginning, despite huge increases in total output. Job totals on the railroads and in mining were falling or stagnant. The movement of factories to the South may also have increased northern workers' sense of insecurity. As Douglas's numbers in table 2.1 show, blue-collar unemployment was quite high; in the first seven years of the decade, it never fell below 7 percent. A worker who was not prepared for retail or office work must have felt more insecure in the 1920s. That may explain why quit rates diminished.

A second reason for the lower rate is that at least a minority of large manufacturing firms took steps to reduce labor turnover. They created personnel departments that devoted resources to careful hiring and to keeping employees happy. Some firms created employer-controlled grievance forums for employees, raised wages or cut hours in highly publicized ways, and invested to make their workplaces more attractive. But these moves were probably not the main reasons for the sharp decline of employee resignations; the business reforms did not involve a majority of firms, and they were already contracting by the end of the '20s. The main factor must have been that unemployment for manual workers stayed high and that out-of-work blue-collar workers were less optimistic about finding jobs than they had been in the early 1900s when factory work and other blue-collar occupations were expanding.[7]

There was a big change in the '20s that should have contributed to fuller employment. Legislation cut the flow of immigrants from southern and eastern Europe. While immigration from Canada and Mexico picked up, the total foreign inflow was less than half what it had been in the prewar period. But other things maintained the labor pool. Migration from farm to factory stayed high, and owners and engineers made factories more efficient. Large increases in industrial output did not require increases in the factory workforce. Office jobs increased, but there seems to have been enough educated young men and women to staff them.

So, labor shortages were unusual and unemployment was common in many sectors. Coal miners lost hundreds of thousands of jobs, and the New England textile industry was dying. Industrialists enjoyed a labor surplus as advances in technology and the organization of production cast off workers and continually lifted the supply of people without jobs. The majority of the unemployed eventually found jobs, but few had substantial savings, and there were no unemployment benefits to pay the bills in the meantime.[8]

The cloud of unemployment hung over working-class households. Robert S. Lynd and Helen Merrell Lynd, in their deep study of Muncie, Indiana, which they called *Middletown,* thought unemployment was such a common problem that they made it the defining difference between the blue-collar working class and the business class of owners, managers, and clerical workers. Few in the business class were ever laid off; many in the working class often were. So, in this town, as undoubtedly in others, a hugely important aspect of dual labor markets—more job security in the primary market and less security in the secondary market—endured.

It is worthwhile pausing to delve into the unemployment numbers. There were many efforts by government agencies and scholars to estimate unemployment rates, but there was no comprehensive, reliable government survey until the 1940s. In the late 1920s, economist Paul Douglas carried out detailed investigations to calculate unemployment levels in manufacturing, transportation, the building trades, and mining. In 1964 economist Stanley Lebergott published his estimates for national unemployment rates. Table 2.1 shows Lebergott's numbers for the nonfarm sector in column A, and Douglas's calculations in column B, both for just the years of the twenties that Douglas studied.

It is fair to mention that instead of the population used in column A, one can use the rates for all workers, including people on farms. If you do that, you get astonishingly low unemployment rates for some years, including 2.4 percent (1923), 3.2 percent (1925), and 1.8 percent (1926). I am skeptical of those numbers and of our ability to count farm unemployment. The twenties were often years of agricultural depression, so it seems strange that when you include the farm sector in the unemployment numbers, unemployment rates fall. I believe it is better to use nonfarm numbers from Lebergott or something like them, along with Douglas's estimates for blue-collar workers. Lebergott's

Table 2.1   Two Unemployment Estimates for the 1920s

Year	A *Historical Statistics* (1975) (Lebergott) Nonfarm	B Douglas: Wage-earners in mining, transportation, manufacturing, building trades	C B/A
1920	8.6%	7.2%	0.8 times
1921	19.5%	23.1%	1.2 times
1922	11.4%	18.3%	1.6 times
1923	4.1%	7.9%	1.9 times
1924	8.3%	12.0%	1.4 times
1925	5.4%	8.9%	1.6 times
1926	2.9%	7.5%	2.6 times

Sources: *HS,* I, 126, and Douglas, 460.

numbers show four bad years and three good or very good years. Every year in Douglas's list shows high unemployment for blue-collar workers. Douglas's numbers may help us understand why factory quit rates fell in the '20s.[9]

The nonfarm numbers and Douglas's estimates show that unemployment was often quite high in the 1920s. So do case studies. In Chicago, 20 percent of unskilled and semiskilled employed workers lost six or more weeks of work because of layoffs or sickness over a year. In Muncie, Indiana, 24 percent of working-class men lost at least three months of work. In terms that are comparable to modern unemployment numbers, Muncie's working-class monthly unemployment rate was 17.5 percent.[10]

It would be nice to have Douglas's estimates for the last years of the twenties, but he stopped his research at 1926. Lebergott's unemployment figures were 5.4 percent, 6.9 percent, and 5.3 percent for 1927–1929—not depression levels but not full employment.[11] Labor leaders, social workers, and progressive politicians in those years believed that unemployment was often quite high. They observed "large scale unemployment" in every industrial center in 1928. In some places there were the usual mini-depressions owing to plant shutdowns, market shifts, retooling, and the normal surplus of workers. Liberal politicians in Congress, led by Senator Robert Wagner of New York, pressed for action, and President Hoover proposed a bill to set aside $3 billion for public works, but when the idea was denounced as socialistic, he backed off.[12] There were signs of change, but limited support for unemployment insurance or government job-creation programs at the federal level. Quite a few politicians were still in denial about unemployment realities, and for employers, unemployment was just right: not so high as to cause mass protest but high enough to undermine workers' bargaining leverage. Union officials worried about joblessness, especially among their members, but the labor movement represented relatively few workers.

So, the old order endured in the 1920s. There was less unemployment than in the 1890s, but there was still a lot of it, and about as much as in the early 1900s. While there was more job stability in the manufacturing sector than there had been before the war, workers' sense of economic insecurity may have gotten stronger because of somewhat limited opportunities in blue-collar occupations and perhaps also because the demands of the new consumerist culture were becoming more insistent.

It is true that the United States looked very prosperous to European observers. Some of them thought that every American had a car, but that was not yet true. And half the households in America did not have enough income for a decent American living standard. Working-class families whose main breadwinner was out of work for more than a few weeks faced malnutrition and demoralization. If they had set aside a few dollars for a rainy day, they might get by for a few weeks. But then things got tough. Some people sold their furniture. Renters moved to cheaper accommodations. People kept the heat off and ate less. Eventually, they pawned treasured possessions. A woman named Dorothy Dohancy hocked her wedding ring. The Sapellis pawned their little girl's communion ring to pay for Mrs. Sapelli's dental work. When they learned that the procedures would cost more than they received for the ring, Mrs. Sapelli, age thirty, had all her teeth pulled.

Despite unemployment conferences and more research, in terms of cash assistance, the 1920s were pretty much like the late 1800s. Agents of charitable organizations doled out material aid grudgingly. Some officials and social workers were sophisticated in their understanding of the economic roots of poverty and unemployment. But negative attitudes were still widespread. The taint of needing charity was one that some poor people tried to avoid. A Mr. Estrada could not find work. He hated charity, but his kids needed help, so he took food that was supplied by charity organizations, but he refused to eat it. This was life under the regime of laissez-faire for the working class that conservatives and moderates like Herbert Hoover advocated. Hoover was an outstanding example of a politician who talked about unemployment but did not want the federal government to do much about it.[13]

We know that hard times were the daily lot of many Americans in the 1920s, often because of unsteady work and low pay. We know it because researchers and reformers were doing the work. There were stories and statistics about unemployment in magazines, newspapers, and scholarly journals. But quite a few economists and politicians in the United States and in Europe too hung on to old ideas. In Britain unemployment was very high, but even pro-worker experts sometimes seemed more concerned about restoring the gold standard, cutting the national debt, and fighting inflation than about direct action to reduce unemployment. However, John Maynard Keynes was already writing about public works to promote jobs in the 1920s. And in America there were scholars who studied unemployment and wanted a reliable count of unemployment, and others who developed the field of business-cycle analysis. We just read about Paul Douglas's effort to estimate blue-collar unemployment. There were a fair number of people who began to understand that overproduction and underconsumption were problems that could cause more unemployment. Earlier I mentioned William Foster and Waddill Catchings, who believed that modern capitalism naturally faced underconsumption crises—not enough buying by consumers to propel more employment growth. So, some people were ready for a deep conversation about the dimensions, causes, and cures of unemployment. But the impact of new ideas on federal actions would be small until the Great Depression.[14]

The Crash and the Depression: No Incomes, No Homes

Between 1921 and 1929, there was enough unemployment to keep working-class income growth lagging behind productivity increases and potential output. That planted the seeds of an underconsumption /overproduction crisis. You can see this in one sector. From 1923 through 1929, average pay in manufacturing increased by 8 percent—a good record—but productivity jumped 32 percent. As in recent times, many of the gains from more efficient production flowed to owners and investors, and not enough to the working class. Some firms were so flush with money they began lending it in the stock market. That fueled speculative buying, which drove up prices and encouraged more speculation.[15]

It's true that stock-market gains encouraged optimism about the economy, created jobs in the financial sector, and stimulated spending by affluent households. But the bull market on Wall Street was based on risky credit mechanisms and unrealistic expectations. And affluent households did quite a bit of discretionary spending, which could be cut back in an emergency. That the stock market was unregulated didn't help either.

The Wall Street crash began in the fall of 1929. The Dow index was 381.17 on September 3, 1929; it would fall to 41.22 by July 8, 1932.[16] No one knows exactly why the crash came when it did. Perhaps stocks just got too expensive. Many things could have burst the bubble of overconfidence and overborrowing on Wall Street. Once the crash came and pessimism took hold, businesses and consumers who had a choice became cautious and cut spending, pushing the economy into a tailspin. In brief, inequality, lagging working-class incomes, and minimal financial regulation brought massive unemployment. Rigid ideas about federal recovery policy were a problem too. If business and consumer spending falls, unemployment climbs. Monetary authorities can make money available to stop bank runs and to encourage borrowing. And, as was well known in a general way, the federal government can spend more. Hoover seemed to understand some of this, but in many ways, he stayed old-fashioned and conservative, particularly in his fanatical opposition to federal handouts to the unemployed.

You can see the dimensions of the catastrophe in the unemployment rates that economist David Weir estimated for nonfarm private sector workers:

    1929: 4.05%
    1930: 12.4%
    1931: 21.7%
    1932: 31.7%
    1933: 30.2%

These numbers are shocking. At any moment in 1932 and 1933, almost a third of private-sector workers were out of work. In 1931 the unemployment rate for African American women was 58 percent in Chicago and 75 percent in Detroit. Many employed workers had their hours cut. From 1929 to 1933, U.S. Steel went from 250,000 full-time workers to no full-time workers.

The impact of unemployment and underemployment on daily living standards was horrific. Local and private sources of aid were totally inadequate, and federal sources were almost nonexistent: no unemployment benefits, no food stamps, no welfare system, no Social Security, and no Medicaid or Medicare. In 1933 half the population was very poor, often unable to pay for food and rent. One in four had virtually no income. When skilled steelworker George Patterson married his wife in 1931, he thought they had nothing to worry about. But the next year he worked only one day a month. By the time a son was born, the Pattersons were living with his in-laws. By then he could not afford to buy a bottle of milk for the baby.[17]

Lack of income led to homelessness. Left-wing radicals led the way in organizing demonstrations to get people back into their homes, but they could not reverse the trend. Almost every city had a Hooverville—a village of shelters made of junk on an empty lot. While thousands lived in Hoovervilles, two million people tramped, rode the rails, and lived in hobo camps. The Southern Pacific Railroad ejected 683,457 free riders in 1932. Where were these people going? Sometimes, just away from where they had been. Men deserted families they could not support; youngsters ran away so that relief checks would support fewer people at home. Some transients were looking for work; others wanted warm weather for outdoor living.[18]

Mellon and Hoover: Hard and Soft Laissez-Faire for the Working Class

How did business leaders and economic conservatives respond to the human crisis? Henry Ford was revered for bringing cars to the masses, but he was morally numb. He thought it was a great education for young men to ride the rails: "They get more experience in a few months than they would in years at school." Andrew Mellon, secretary of the Treasury in the 1920s, seemed clueless about people's misery and about how his tax cuts for the rich contributed to inequality and a shortfall in mass purchasing power. He thought laissez-faire was the best cure for depression: let businesses fail, real estate markets collapse, and people go without work. Hard times would force people to work harder and to live a "more moral life . . . enterprising people will pick up the wreck from less competent people."[19]

As hinted earlier, Herbert Hoover was more flexible in his thinking than these representatives of the old way. He'd been an energetic secretary of Commerce and called a conference to respond to the depression of 1921. Now he was president (1929–1933). A former mining engineer, he sometimes conceived of unemployment as a "technical problem" to be solved by efficiency engineers. Planners could use modern forecasting methods to smooth out the ups and downs of the business cycle and avoid high unemployment. The federal role must be limited, but the central government could gather reliable statistics, plead with employers for good behavior, and raise public spending by changing the timing of federal projects and encouraging state and local governments to spend on public works. But the substantive role had to be limited, especially when it came to direct federal aid to people in need. Hoover's views on poor people and the unemployed were, often, old-fashioned and heartless.[20]

Before 1929 Hoover's ideas had really not been tested, but in the early 1930s he confronted a job crisis that could not be ignored. Hoover urged local governments and private organizations to help the unemployed, but at the center of his social philosophy was the hair-splitting assumption that federal aid was demoralizing, but private and local aid was not. While this position got by in the mid-1920s, it seemed cruel in the Great Depression.[21]

Hoover did act. Late in 1929, he urged state and local officials to accelerate public works spending. He asked Congress for a small increase in federal spending on public works and tax cuts. Congress passed a billion-dollar veterans' bonus bill that Hoover opposed. Overall, there was more spending, in part because big budget surpluses had been predicted, so there was room for additional spending without incurring high budget deficits.

Meanwhile, Hoover urged employers to keep wages and thus purchasing power up. He liked non-compulsory approaches in which the federal government persuaded but did not compel. But once markets began to collapse, employers laid off workers and cut wages too.

Hoover also found scapegoats. He ordered the Immigration and Naturalization Service to expel more immigrants and political radicals. Hundreds of thousands of Mexicans and Mexican Americans were deported. As unemployment soared, Hoover claimed that local governments and private organizations like the Red Cross could take care of the unemployed and their families. He believed that federal income grants to the working class were a "most vicious" threat to liberty. He worried about the survival of individualism, but not about the fact that without federal help, millions of people were slaves to poverty, unemployment, and despair. He was dogmatic. He created unemployment committees, mainly, as one historian put it, in a "frantic struggle to keep the federal government pure from relief contamination." When Colonel Arthur Woods, head of the first committee, urged public works spending, Hoover refused.[22]

In January 1932, and under pressure to do more, Hoover and Congress agreed to a business-first recovery program. Under the Reconstruction Finance Corporation (RFC), a federal bank would make loans to financial institutions and railroads. The benefits were supposed to trickle down to the people. But the RFC did not reverse rising unemployment and falling incomes. Bankers acted selfishly—they were capitalists—using RFC money to shore up their assets rather than make loans to businesses. The RFC trickle-down failed.[23]

Later, Congress broadened the RFC to include $300 million in loans to the states for assistance to the needy. Hoover reluctantly signed this Emergency Relief and Construction Act (ERCA), but he still did not like federal welfare. Following his orders, subordinates rejected 240 applications and approved just three over three months.

Hoover believed, as did many people, including Franklin Roosevelt, that a balanced federal budget was essential, except in war emergencies. Some authorities thought that budget deficits would interfere with the cleansing effects of depression, or that they could spark inflation, or tarnish the reputation of America's credit. Also, federal borrowing, it was claimed, would make it harder for people to borrow. So, there were many reasons, in the traditional way of thinking, to balance the budget. But that got harder. Federal revenues fell as the Depression took hold, the deficit soared in 1931, and alarm spread. Hoover and Congress approved the Revenue Act of 1932, which included a giant tax increase. That reduced private incomes and private demand—the wrong thing in a depression. And, in any case, it was difficult to balance the budget in a depression when federal revenues from economic activity were declining. So, although the deficits were lower in 1932 and 1933, they were still high by traditional standards. Had they been higher, more jobs might have been created.[24]

The president and Congress were not doing much to halt the economic decline, and most of the time the Federal Reserve was not pumping enough money into the economy. The money supply shrank by 25 percent. Federal Reserve officials had reasons for not helping out more. At times they wanted to keep interest rates high to keep money flowing into the country and keep gold from flowing out. But high interest rates and the gold standard did not create jobs and income for millions of people being thrown out of work.[25]

Meanwhile, in 1932, unemployed vets demonstrated in the capital. In 1931 Hoover had vetoed a bill that would have allowed veterans to borrow 50 percent of a World War I bonus that was redeemable in 1945. Congress overrode him. In 1932 an army of twenty thousand vets converged on Washington to demand more of the bonus right away. Hoover and the Senate turned them down. Eventually, Hoover called out infantry companies and tanks, and General Douglas MacArthur drove the veterans out of the nation's capital. Hoover later recalled, "Thank God we still have a government that knows how to deal with a mob." That's what he said about unemployed veterans demonstrating for government aid.[26]

The Poor and Unemployed (1929–1932): Protests and Government Assistance

Across the nation, there was no way that private charities could take care of millions of people in desperate straits. Local governments and states were running out of money. Many people did not want their taxes raised to help the poor. In 1932 states and cities were giving an average *annual* grant of $27 per unemployed person. Some people received help from friends and relatives, and even landlords and storekeepers; but as unemployment spread, everyone had less to share. Shop owners went bankrupt because customers never paid their bills. It seemed that there was just one institution that could deal with the income shortage—the federal government.

Hoover pretty much stuck to his conservative guns, but some conservatives bent to reality. Chicago steel man and philanthropist Edward Ryerson had long defended private welfare, but eventually he sought money from the state of Illinois and from Washington. "I was bitterly opposed to federal funds. . . . But I realized the problem was beyond the scope of local government."[27]

Many of the unemployed were, especially at first, in shock. But as more people were thrown out of work, and as it became clear that high unemployment was caused by economic forces, not individual failures, more of them banded together to help themselves. Thousands of unemployed Californians, led by veterans in Compton in 1932, organized cooperative self-help groups to exchange goods and services and to forage from farmers and grocers. It was an inspirational experiment but it could not supply all of people's needs. Some unemployed cooperatives demanded government aid, and many cooperators worked for the election of socialist Upton Sinclair as governor in 1934. Sinclair promised to put people to work in idle factories and on idle land. It was a simple idea that made sense to people. But the opposition played the anti-communist card, and Hollywood studios threatened to fire people if Sinclair were elected. He lost by a significant margin.

Meanwhile, people fought, often under socialist and communist leadership, against evictions. On October 31, 1932, twenty-five thousand Chicagoans marched against cuts in relief payments. There were farmer protests to take back foreclosed properties. And, as we have seen, thousands of unemployed veterans marched on Washington. In June 1932, Mayor Anton Cermak of Chicago told Congress to provide federal relief or to send soldiers to control angry people. Working-class Americans in the streets and at the ballot box were toppling the pro-capitalist idea that laissez-faire was good enough for the masses.[28]

FDR

In the presidential campaign of 1932, Hoover faced the governor of New York, Franklin Delano Roosevelt. Roosevelt, too, believed in balanced budgets, but not dogmatically. On the campaign trail, he said that if spending to fight starvation required budget deficits, so be it. Roosevelt and his advisors were convinced that the federal government could end or soften the Depression. They weren't exactly sure how to do it, but Roosevelt promised to act boldly, and voters gave him a big victory.

Roosevelt was a man of enormous confidence. He was rich with old money but not as wealthy as robber barons like Ford and Rockefeller. FDR practiced noblesse oblige: those to whom much had been given had to give back. His battle with polio made him more compassionate about people's suffering and more willing to use government to assist them. It helped make him a founder of modern American liberalism.[29] As president, Roosevelt included conservatives and moderates in his administration, but liberals like Harry Hopkins, his relief boss, and Frances Perkins, his secretary of labor, led the way on unemployment and welfare policy. Another liberal influence was Roosevelt's wife. In 1905 Roosevelt married his fifth cousin, a niece of Teddy Roosevelt named Eleanor. The marriage proved shaky, but Eleanor was a tireless advocate for liberal policies.

New Deal Recovery Policy: The First R

The Democratic New Deal was a flood of experiments and programs. I'll sketch two R's—recovery and reform—and then concentrate on the third, relief and job programs. New Deal recovery policy aimed to get the private sector producing jobs and income. The approach was scattershot; some things were effective, some were not. The New Dealers began to directly create jobs, and they borrowed money. But it would take a while for some people to feel comfortable with deficit spending or big federal job programs.

Soon after Roosevelt's inauguration on March 4, the administration closed the banks to stop bank runs. After an experiment in which the president set the price of gold every day, legislation and presidential action established it at

$35 an ounce. That high level drew gold to the United States and expanded the money supply, which helped to lubricate economic activity.

Then came what was supposed to be the centerpiece of recovery policy, the National Industrial Recovery Act. The NIRA was a business-first approach; it focused more on overproduction than underconsumption. It aimed to cut production and keep prices up. But higher prices weren't good for consumers, especially if the NIRA did not substantially raise wages and mass purchasing power. The NIRA included the Public Works Administration (PWA), which would have helped more if officials had spent money faster to employ people. The NIRA also included minimum-wage regulations, which raised some people's pay. But employers resisted and some of them laid off workers rather than raise pay. Wages did turn up in 1934, partly due to New Deal spending, but average pay did not climb back to 1929 levels until 1940–1941. By then the NIRA was long gone. It had not done enough to raise incomes and consumption to fuel an investment boom.[30]

Something other than NIRA permission for corporations to act like price-setting monopolies was needed. There had to be more jobs, higher wages, and increased consumption demand. Even in the late 1920s, half of all consumers could not afford all their basic needs. When the Great Depression pushed unemployment and poverty way up, much more than half of the population had trouble paying their bills. More unemployed workers with no purchasing power created more unemployed workers in retail and factory work. Something had to break the vicious circle, and government-assisted cartels had not done it. Barring a surge in foreign purchases—and many other nations were in depression—a two-pronged federal policy to stimulate economic growth was necessary.

The Federal Reserve could expand the money supply and keep interest rates low, and the government could spend on a large scale to make up for the shortage of private demand. As to the latter, where could Congress and the president find the money? If it came from higher taxes on people with average and low incomes, little would be added to total demand, for such people spent most of their incomes anyway. Taxing the affluent and redistributing the income made sense, but the affluent classes had enough political influence to limit tax increases. That left deficits. Government could borrow money and spend it to stimulate economic growth and job creation. In this way government, would be putting idle money to work for the nation. As deficits added economic demand, and as buying power filtered through the economy, there would be a multiplier effect; an increase in jobs and working-class incomes would generate other jobs. This was a version of Keynesian demand-side economics. You did not have to be an economist to understand it. You did not have to sit on your hands and wait until Keynes published his masterwork in 1936. But you had to want to solve unemployment.[31]

Most economists, business leaders, and politicians, including Roosevelt, accepted the orthodox view that unbalanced budgets were dangerous. (If asked why, they offered plenty of reasons, including fear of inflation and high interest rates.) But Roosevelt and the New Dealers practiced a modest form of deficit spending, not because of Keynesian-style ideas, but because people needed help. Whatever the intention, new spending promoted economic recovery. The output of goods and services was 44 percent higher in 1937 than in 1933. Job totals increased by eight million. That was substantial but not enough. Full recovery required more spending.[32]

But there was pressure inside and outside the Roosevelt administration—and in FDR's head—to balance the budget, and sometimes it succeeded. Even though nonfarm unemployment was still a whopping 21 percent in 1937, Roosevelt cut spending on job programs. At the same time, new Social Security taxes began withholding money from paychecks. The federal budget was balanced for the year ending July 1, 1938, resulting in more unemployment and a new recession. That led to a crisis of faith for anti-deficit liberals and more confidence for pro-deficit liberals like Harry Hopkins and Marriner Eccles, chairman of the Federal Reserve. FDR, seeming to join the deficit-lovers, emphasized that "government had to make definite additions to the nation's purchasing power." The economy improved, but that did not end debates about spending and deficits.

Soon, war needs overcame opposition. For the biggest war in history, the president and Congress were not going to debate whether it was bad to borrow money to support the troops. In 1943 the federal deficit was ten times the average annual deficit in the thirties. The outcome was something unusual: a general labor shortage and full employment. Cause and effect seemed clear: large federal deficits and massive spending eliminated unemployment. Would that lesson become common knowledge for the American people? More later.[33]

The Second R: Boosting Spending Power and Promoting Economic Security

In 1935 Congress passed the National Labor Relations Act to provide a fair process for those who wanted independent unions. Many thought, too, that unions would raise incomes and purchasing power and thus fight depression. Also passed in 1935 was the Social Security Act. It included a contributory government old-age pension system, which would ease unemployment by paying people to leave the workforce. The background motives were that elders were increasing their numbers, that men over sixty-five had huge unemployment rates, and that most people who retired from the workforce did not have enough saved for a comfortable old age. The Social Security Act also included a new federal program for widows with children—the origin of the American welfare system.

Finally, the act included provision for unemployment benefits. This meant that an unemployed person might be less distressed and a little less poor. It meant more purchasing power in depressions and it could provide a boost to wages and efficiency because it allowed unemployed workers to search longer for jobs that fit their skills and desires. Unemployment benefits thus counteracted to some degree the effect of higher unemployment on pay, which was normally to push wages down or at least keep them from rising much. With unemployment benefits, there were fewer jobless people who had to take the first job offered, no matter how low the wage offer. Much the same can be said of the Fair Labor Standards Act of 1938. The FLSA established a federal minimum wage, over-time pay, and restrictions on child labor. If the wage provisions were kept up to date, they would help to lift the bottom of the wage ladder. The other regulations could improve labor markets for adults by limiting child labor and penalizing employers who made employees work overtime rather than hire new workers.

The Third R and the Big Job Programs

Now we focus on New Deal relief and job programs: the Civilian Conservation Corps (CCC), the Public Works Authority (PWA), the Federal Emergency Relief Administration (FERA), and the Civil Works Administration (CWA), all begun in 1933, and the Works Progress Administration (WPA), created in 1935. Twenty million people went through these programs, and the nation's physical and cultural infrastructure was vastly improved. Except for the PWA, the agencies acted with speed. There were negatives, including the exclusion of women and racial segregation, but on balance the programs were a plus. The following sketches can help us think smartly about how to achieve fuller employment in our time. They show that it is possible for federal officials to manage large job programs efficiently.

The Civilian Conservation Corps (CCC)

FDR was inaugurated on March 4, 1933, and on March 21 he sent a bill to Congress to create a corps of young people to work on nature conservation. Two weeks later, the administration was setting up the CCC. Most enrollees were young men, eighteen to twenty-five, out of work, unmarried, and U.S. citizens.

The program also employed World War I veterans and thousands of "Local Experienced Men" whose knowledge of forestry was invaluable.[34]

Women were excluded, African Americans included. CCC legislation forbade racial discrimination, but southern states refused to enroll many or, in Georgia, any African Americans. Pressure from CCC administrators changed that, but often the black share of CCC jobs was less than 10 percent, well below the black share of unemployment. CCC director Robert Fechner actually segregated more units, but there was vicious racism in local communities, even against all-black units. Los Angeles park commissioners refused space at Griffith Park to a black unit, claiming that ordinances in surrounding cities barred "negroes" after sundown. Still, in 1941 there were seventy-one integrated units, mostly in New England. Many African Americans would remember their CCC experiences as positive ones. Their economic situation had been desperate, and the CCC gave them temporary jobs, skills, and a little income.

CCCers were required to send $25 of their monthly $30 earnings to their families. They received room, board, uniforms, medical and dental care, and schooling; forty thousand learned to read or taught others to read; some studied forestry; others took academic courses in psychology, sociology, and speech. Some trained as auto mechanics and truckers.[35]

Environmental experts have criticized the CCC for upsetting ecological systems and making wilderness areas so attractive as to draw crowds and automobiles that generated pollution. But the CCC spread conservation ideas, sparked a debate about how to care for the forests, and began to reverse the causes of the Dust Bowl. In years past, millions of acres of fertile soil had been destroyed by uncontrolled timber cutting. That brought huge dust storms. Now "Roosevelt's tree army" planted two billion trees to promote soil conservation. CCCers built six million little dams, forty-five thousand bridges, eight hundred state parks, and untold campgrounds, picnic areas, ski trails, and sanitary systems. They created sixty-eight thousand miles of fire breaks, and spent seven million days fighting forest fires. Forty-seven corpsmen lost their lives battling fires.

The total cost of the CCC was $3 billion, but the benefits to young men and to the landscape were immeasurable. Almost three million people went through the program. The CCC was "exceptionally popular" and probably the best loved of all New Deal programs.[36]

The Public Works Administration (PWA)

The PWA was designed to create jobs and promote recovery by pumping up the depressed construction sector. Normally the PWA did not directly employ construction workers; the work was performed by other government agencies and private contractors. Employees did not have to come from relief rolls; unions often provided skilled workers. In 1933 hourly wages averaged forty-five cents for unskilled workers and $1.10 for skilled workers. A skilled PWA worker getting 120 hours a month could keep his family out of poverty, but an unskilled worker's family would fall below even a 1930s poverty line of about $1,000.

The PWA contributed to thirty-five thousand projects, including 384 airports, 295 court houses, the Boulder (Hoover), Grand Coulee, and Bonneville Dams, the Triborough Bridge and Lincoln Tunnel in New York City, the Hetch Hetchy Reservoir in California, and Skyline Drive in Virginia. The PWA's achievements were impressive, but the agency was overly cautious. Secretary of the Interior Harold Ickes, who ran the PWA, set up a division of investigation to ferret out fraud and waste. Well and good. But the PWA was spending too little; it employed only 631,000 in 1934. The number of unemployed persons in America was 11,340,000.

The PWA's social record was mixed. Most Americans considered heavy construction as men's work, and PWA officials made no effort to challenge that bias. As to race, Ickes's African American advisors actually developed affirmative action plans. For example, regulations stipulated that 40 percent of all wages paid to unskilled workers in Detroit went to blacks. Of forty-nine public housing projects that the agency built, fourteen were for blacks and seventeen were for joint occupancy by blacks and whites. African Americans would occupy one-third of PWA public housing units. That was progressive for the time, but it was counterbalanced by the agency's general commitment to promoting racially homogeneous neighborhoods, even if that meant remaking communities where blacks and whites lived side by side.[37]

FERA and the CWA (1933–1935): Federal Welfare and Direct Job Creation

In May 1933, Congress passed the Federal Emergency Relief Act (FERA), allotting $500 million, mainly for direct relief, that is, "welfare." Recipients were means-tested by social workers who made home visits to decide whether people were truly needy. That was old-style relief, but FERA included two advanced principles. The first was that no money was to go to private charities; their record of generosity was not good, as we've seen in chapter 1. The second was simply that the federal government was now in the business of giving handouts. Of course, conservatives were irked. Governor Eugene Talmadge of Georgia thought castor oil was a better cure for poverty. Governor Charles Martin of Oregon declared that no able-bodied jobless person should get any government aid. But these kinds of people were now challenged at every level, by protesters in the street and by Washington liberals, including FERA head Harry Hopkins.[38]

While government policies became more forward-looking, benefit amounts were stingy, and FERA required the states to contribute funds, so poor states offered meager benefits that left people poverty-stricken. Mississippi gave households $11 a month. New York's $33 a month was better but it too meant, barring other income sources, extreme poverty. Local authorities could exclude out-of-state migrants, but the FERA created hundreds of work-relief camps for them. FERA had many other projects, including a program to hire jobless teachers into nursery schools for underprivileged children; construction projects; and "women's work": sewing, canning, nursing, and making statistical surveys.[39]

It soon became clear that the FERA and the PWA weren't making enough of a dent in the unemployed population. In autumn of 1933, Hopkins told the president that he could create millions of jobs fast. And he did. In the Civil Works Administration (CWA), federal officials had more control over spending and hiring. Many CWA workers were not paid with FERA welfare dollars, so they were not subject to control by social workers, and employees earned twice as much as FERA workers: $600 a year for unskilled labor and $1,500 for skilled workers. CWA workers were more likely than FERA workers to think of themselves as employees than as charity cases. Higher pay made for better morale.

In two months, Hopkins had enrolled four million people in the program. CWA workers constructed no dams but they built or improved 500,000 miles of roads, forty thousand schools, and thirty-five hundred playgrounds and athletic fields. They responded to flood disasters and drained mosquito-breeding swamps. They painted murals on public buildings in Texas and Oklahoma. Kodiak Eskimos replenished the snowshoe rabbit population. Thousands of women sewed mattresses and underwear for those on relief. CWA employees worked at museums, repaired tattered books, and began the Historical American Buildings Survey.[40]

There was corruption, and Hopkins and Roosevelt worried that support for the New Deal would fall away if it were not controlled. They invited complaints. The CWA had 130 employees investigating abuse and the PWA had 100 working on CWA issues; investigators referred 77 cases for prosecution, resulting in 22 convictions.[41]

On equality issues, both the FERA and the CWA lagged. For example, females composed only 12 percent of the FERA relief rolls and only 5 percent of the CWA; both fractions were far below women's share of the labor force. Married women faced discrimination. Females earned less and were more likely to be subjected to means tests. Blacks, too, often received lower pay.[42]

In spite of these blemishes, the CWA was a remarkable achievement. It lifted morale and pumped up local economies. Why then was it so quickly dismantled? Local merchants favored the CWA because it created more shoppers, but industrialists, construction contractors, and plantation owners hated anything that interfered with their control over workers. The CWA offered workers an alternative to rock-bottom wages in the private sector. Conservatives complained that CWA employees produced nothing useful, but they really feared the opposite: that government programs that produced mattresses and canned goods for free distribution to the poor were the first step toward large-scale government production—in other words, socialism.[43]

For his part, Roosevelt thought the CWA was too expensive and he feared that CWA workers were developing an entitlement psychology about federal work programs. At other times FDR talked about people's right to a job, but Hopkins and Roosevelt shut down the CWA on March 31, 1934. Too bad. The CWA had poured millions of dollars into the stream of consumer spending. It boosted Christmas sales, and brought a little happiness to millions of families. It lifted morale; many CWA employees did not feel that they were on welfare. Some used their first checks to pay down debts, but most bought things. An Iowa woman purchased a dozen oranges. "I hadn't tasted any for so long that I had forgotten what they were like." On payday workers cleaned out the shoe stores in Columbus, Ohio. The CWA helped people get through a New England winter when temperatures hit fifty-six degrees below zero.[44]

The WPA

If anyone thought that the CWA was the last big federal work project, they were mistaken. In 1934 left-wing radicalism was surging, as evidenced by Huey Long's Share the Wealth movement, Upton Sinclair's EPIC campaign in California, and three victorious strikes, including one by West Coast dock workers. Nonfarm unemployment was still 33 percent. One Pennsylvanian wrote to Eleanor Roosevelt: "The forgotten man is still forgotten . . . the new deal and the N.R.A. has only helped big business." Democratic electoral gains in 1934 brought a two-thirds majority in the Senate and a 3-to-1 margin in the House. Many new members of Congress were more left-wing than the president. All across the land people were pushing for radical action.

Leftists and liberals wanted a jobs program. Roosevelt agreed, and in April 1935, Congress provided the money. FDR appointed Hopkins to run the Works

Progress Administration (WPA). The plan was to hire 3.5 million employable heads of household currently on federally subsidized relief rolls. "Unemployables," such as severely handicapped people, were supposed to receive help from federal and state welfare programs.

In the end, WPA workers constructed or repaired 572,000 miles of rural roads, 67,000 miles of city streets, 122,000 bridges, 4,000 airport buildings, 24,000 miles of sewers and storm drains, 12,800 playgrounds, 36,900 schools, and thousands of other structures ranging from armories to fish hatcheries. They worked in adult and nursery schools; 200,000 WPA workers helped victims of a massive flood in the Ohio River Valley. WPA nurses and doctors made nine million home visits; a school lunch program fed hundreds of thousands every day. WPA librarians delivered books to the backwoods by car, boat, and horse.[45]

There were programs in music, theater, art, and writing, which employed artists and offered art to the public for free or almost free. The music program was run by Nikolai Sokoloff, who disrespected jazz, black church music, brass bands, and pop tunes, but those genres were produced, along with operas and symphonies. The Federal Writers' Project employed Saul Bellow and Ralph Ellison, as well as people of less talent who also liked to eat. The writers created state travel guides and collected oral histories about slavery. Painters and sculptors produced work that was seen by two million people at the New York World's Fair. WPA murals, some influenced by Diego Rivera and Clement Orozco, decorated public spaces.

NATIONAL YOUTH ADMINISTRATION

In June 1935, Franklin D. Roosevelt created the National Youth Administration under the WPA. It was run by Harry Hopkins's assistant, Aubrey Williams. Williams appointed well-known educator Mary McLeod Bethune to head an Office of Negro Affairs to make sure that black youth got their share. Over eight years, the NYA helped 4,500,000 young people. The NYA paid high schools and colleges to hire students for on-campus jobs—work-study, it was called later. That gave youngsters income and kept them out of overcrowded labor markets. For youth who were not in school, the NYA created job programs that mirrored the WPA. In 1939 Roosevelt ordered the NYA to train machinists and other skilled workers for defense industries.

The most controversial arts program was the Federal Theater Project, run by Hallie Flanagan. Participants included Orson Welles, Arthur Miller, Canada Lee, and Burt Lancaster. There was racial segregation but not exclusion. Sixteen black units were formed, and Welles directed a black version of *Macbeth*. Flanagan created Living Newspapers, agitational dramas about farm problems, unions, and utility monopolies. Audiences were large, but the leftism and racial liberalism of the productions angered conservatives. The House Un-American Activities Committee (HUAC) ran a witch hunt against radicals, and the FTP was shut down in 1939.

The WPA itself lasted until 1943. It boosted morale and provided income to millions, improved the nation's infrastructure, and enriched the culture. On the whole, it was efficiently run. Of course, there were problems. There were irritations for artists, including time sheets and local censorship crusades. Managers often had trouble matching skills and jobs. The agency's first goal was to employ people, not make a perfect match. The WPA needed training programs.

There was labor conflict in the WPA and it was not necessarily a negative. Employees wanted more hours and better pay. Roosevelt decided that WPA workers had the right to unionize but not the right to strike. But strike they did. After all, everyone was doing it, from factory workers to drugstore clerks. One thing that upset WPA workers was job insecurity. WPA enrollment numbers gyrated wildly. In June 1936, the agency had 2.3 million employees; in September 1937, only 1.5 million; at the end of the next year, 3.2 million.[46]

Anti-communism hurt too. In 1939 the witch hunts that were destroying the Federal Theater Project led to the requirement that all WPA workers swear a loyalty oath. Later, they had to sign affidavits that they were not communists or Nazis. Most signed, but 429 employees were fired, including Charlotte Long, who refused to sign. She thought the requirement was un-American. She lost a job that paid $68.90 a month.

At times, WPA officials in Washington tolerated political corruption when it benefited New Deal candidates. Some local politicians monopolized access to WPA jobs and told employees how to vote. FDR invited complaints, and the WPA employed sixty people investigating fraud, extortion, forgery, and, later, "pernicious political activity." They sent 2,215 cases to the attorney general for criminal prosecution. After its own investigations of 17,352 complaints, the WPA disciplined or dismissed 4,496 persons. In 1940 a House committee could not find a single serious irregularity in WPA affairs that had not been investigated.[47]

But there were more serious issues than corruption. Did WPA workers earn enough? Did WPA jobs really lift morale? Did the WPA advance women and minorities? Did it serve enough of the unemployed? And finally, did the WPA and other New Deal programs help to advance modern ideas about unemployment, full employment, and government obligations?

Pay rates varied by skill, region, and city size. Monthly hours were often limited to 130, because total earnings were not supposed to be so high as to keep a WPA worker from accepting private-sector employment. Average monthly pay was around $55 a month, or $660 a year. That was double the average check for non-work relief, but definitely poverty-level.

As to morale, one WPA worker was proud that "I'm no longer a 'case'; I'm an employee." Another said that his kids disrespected him when he was unemployed, but when he got a WPA job, "I'm the breadwinner of the house and everybody respects me." Officials reported that WPA employees faced them with a "less cringing" posture than those on direct relief. If we measure WPA morale against some utopia of enough jobs with good pay and secure tenure, it loses. It was intended to be unattractive enough to "encourage in every possible way the separation of its employees" and their reemployment in the private sector. But if we judge the WPA against straight relief or the demoralization of being jobless and cashless, it looks better. It paid wages, improved morale, and maintained work discipline.[48]

On the question of whether the WPA promoted minority interests, the answer is mixed, at best. Southern blacks without special skills received as little as $21 a month; that was extremely low. But the WPA and other programs gave blacks more than any administration since Lincoln's, and it was one reason African Americans changed political loyalties from Republican to Democratic.[49]

Women's 13 percent share of the WPA rolls in 1938 was half their fraction of the labor force. The rule was one WPA job per family, and it usually went to the man. When one state project was found to have too many female employees—more than 16 percent of the total—women were fired. WPA practice was typical of a chauvinist nation in which school districts refused to hire married women and a prominent intellectual thought it was okay to suggest that sending working women home would solve the unemployment crisis. If the WPA gets a C- for African Americans, it gets a D for women.[50]

Finally, did the WPA employ enough people? The WPA normally employed two to three million every month, averaging 28 percent of the unemployed. The administration claimed that the WPA only left out unemployables who could be aided by welfare programs. But millions of employables were left out of everything. Roosevelt won a huge election victory in 1936; but the worst of the Depression seemed to be over, and business leaders, conservatives, and the press revved up attacks on relief programs. On the left, unemployed movements exerted less force, as leaders entered government or obsessed about organization, rather than disruption. So, there was less pressure to help people left out of the WPA and welfare programs for the handicapped, the aged, and dependent children. Many left-outs received local relief or no assistance at all. In ten southern states, families received $10 a month. In New Jersey, some people were given nothing but a license to beg. That's how bad it was without a WPA job. While the idea of full employment and the right to a job had entered the national conversation, it was often overwhelmed by other concerns and by strong opposition.[51]

Were American Ideas and Institutions Too Backward to Meet the Unemployment Crisis?

American culture was sometimes held back by excessively individualistic ideas, but were national institutions so underdeveloped as to retard the development of an efficient modern welfare state? Perhaps not.[52]

For example, job programs created in the CWA and the WPA are outstanding examples of what could be accomplished by talented leaders of good will. Despite the fact that extreme versions of self-help individualism warped the culture, New Deal innovations created millions of jobs and hundreds of new programs. Innovation and action were fueled by the enormity of the crisis, the boiling discontent of farmers and workers, and the flexibility and compassion of FDR, Secretary of Labor Perkins, Hopkins, and thousands of skilled managers from the public and private sector who had the desire and the skill to run new programs.

Hopkins was a prime example. During Roosevelt's tenure as governor of New York, Hopkins put eighty thousand people to work. In 1933 he turned down an offer of a $25,000 salary at Macy's Department Store to work for $8,000 as chief federal relief administrator. Hopkins had a degree from Grinnell College and real-life education as a social worker in a New York settlement house, where he learned to reject nasty stereotypes about the poor. As a New Deal official, Hopkins preferred to offer the unemployed jobs, but he preferred welfare to nothing.

Hopkins was a genius at getting programs off the ground. In the first days of November 1933, he discussed a new job plan with the president. On November 9, Roosevelt signed an executive order to establish the CWA. Hopkins had announced his intention to start paying people in two weeks. The Treasury Department said it could not be done, but Hopkins relied on the largest federal disbursing system in existence—the Veterans Administration—and Roosevelt ordered federal agencies to drop everything else. The Bureau of Printing and Engraving went on three shifts and blank checks were sent by special delivery and airplane to distribution centers. On November 23, the CWA paid a million workers. That was just three weeks after Hopkins and Roosevelt had discussed the plan and two weeks after the CWA had been created.

Hopkins was not unique. There were thousands of dedicated public servants in hundreds of agencies and organizations working to improve people's lives. Many had college degrees and experience in government, business, social work, nonprofits, engineering, and scientific management; a fair number, including Harold Ickes, were Republicans. It turned out that the country had a treasury of talented and committed individuals willing and able to run dozens of new government programs serving millions of needy people.[53]

American Values and Policy: What Changed?

Events of the 1930s altered many people's attitudes about unemployment. In the 1800s, influential Americans showed little sympathy for beggars, the homeless, and the unemployed. Ideas began to change, but slowly. Then catastrophic levels of unemployment in the '30s, and the fact that the Depression pushed middle-class workers down into the ranks of the unemployed, caused a major shift. Radical protests and progressive officials in Washington encouraged people to think that they had a right to income and jobs. But there was no clear idea of what full employment would require or what level of unemployment would be, in effect, full employment.

Americans were divided. Government job programs remained a battle-ground. In one 1939 opinion survey, 23 percent picked "Relief and the WPA" as the worst things the Roosevelt administration had done; 28 percent picked "Relief and the WPA" as its greatest accomplishments. In part, these numbers reflected class differences: the have-nots liked New Deal job programs more than the haves did. Overall, most people were favorable toward the WPA and agreed that government should guarantee that everyone who wanted a job got one.

But many people were ambivalent about government programs and, apparently, other people's work ethic. It did not help that the press was obsessed with the idea that government jobs were a "boondoggle," make-work that produced nothing useful. A fair number of people who agreed that government should guarantee jobs weren't sure that the unemployed had a *right* to such jobs. In mid-1937, when unemployment was still very high, the percentage of Americans who believed that an individual could find work outside the WPA jumped to 55 percent, up from 24 percent in January. When skilled workers in New York City went on strike, most people thought that they should be fired. So, the unemployed in government job programs were often not thought of as real workers with a full panoply of rights.

People's views about class position and individual success still seemed unrealistic. Unionization spread and so did anger against capitalists. But in 1939, half of the respondents in one survey claimed to be middle class, and only 10 percent admitted to being in the working or laboring class. Only 37 percent of factory workers said that employer and employee interests were different. Most agreed that the future was bright and that they would enjoy more opportunities than their parents. These views came while unemployment remained very high.

Self-help individualism had deep roots in America. It hampered the insight that owners and rich people profited not just from their own talents and hard work, but from exploiting people who worked under them. Also, as events were collectivizing institutions and attitudes, the media blocked people's appreciation of what was happening. The American movie industry was run by capitalists; of four thousand movies produced in 1933–1941, only eleven showed unions or other working-class organizations. This occurred at a time of remarkable advances for unionization.[54]

In the postwar years, general prosperity, consumerism, conservatism, and anti-communism constricted people's thinking about poverty and unemployment. So did historical amnesia. CCCers had their reunions, but many people did not want to think much about the Depression years. Amnesia meant less support for the poor and minorities, many of whom were stuck in their own depression. By the late 1960s, some workers who were doing okay showed less sympathy for those who were not, especially if the losers were people of color, female, and poor.[55]

Unions, social justice groups, civil rights organizations, and local branches of the Democratic Party supported cooperative ideas and worker rights and offered alternatives to capitalism's harsh ethic of competitive struggle. But many labor and liberal organizations were wrong on race and gender issues, and many embraced consumerism in ways that encouraged individualism. In the 1950s, some of them were enthusiastically anti-communist, and that left little space for people to argue for such cooperative and quasi-socialistic ideas as people's right to a decent income and a decent job. There was a turn to the left in the '60s and early '70s, but an aggressive conservative-business push-back in the 1970s and 1980s organized against new values. Usually, though a majority of the American people agreed with the general idea that the federal government should provide jobs for the unemployed, they were less enthusiastic about helping one another through their central government than were the people of Denmark, Scotland, Sweden, and France.[56]

Unemployment Lessons from the 1920s and '30s

First, periods of prosperity may look very prosperous, but they often have a dark underside. The years between 1922 and 1929 were free of depression and had apparently low unemployment and substantial increases in average incomes. It was, some said, a new era, without depressions and on the way to eliminating poverty. But those years included plenty of hidden unemployment and widening income inequalities. The imbalance between consumption power and productive capacity helped to turn the stock market crash into a Great Depression. Something like what happened in 2008. One lesson is that we don't learn our history lessons.

Second, Americans are often cynical about their own power and about federal incompetence. There has been plenty of the latter: the response to Hurricane Katrina, the lack of planning for postwar Iraq, the botched rollouts of Medicare D and Obamacare. But the New Deal showed that government officials can create millions of jobs very quickly. New Deal job programs were flawed but they lifted millions. They were victories for the people. Demonstrators in the streets and voters put pressure on the central government. Unionists, civil rights organizations, liberals, and radicals fought for jobs and for programs that cushioned people against loss of work and income. The resulting programs weren't perfect, but they made life less brutish and that was a huge achievement.

Furthermore, the achievements of left-wing radicals and liberals—people often maligned in America—in government and in the streets, promoted huge advances for human dignity and human welfare. People were helped when they desperately needed it. Attitudes toward the poor and unemployed became less vicious. Unemployment insurance, union protections, job programs, and Social Security meant a better life for many people. And radical activists and average folk began the long struggle to institutionalize the idea that people have a right to a decent job. In 1944 President Roosevelt talked about a new bill of rights and it included the right to "a useful and remunerative job." However, although there was broad support for people's right to a job, exactly what that meant in practice would always be a battle.[57]

Third, in recessions and depressions, the federal government needs to spend heavily and run large deficits. It failed to spend enough in the 1930s, and when spending was cut back in 1937, a new recession began. Something similar occurred during the recent Great Recession in 2008. In the recent slump, government spent enough to keep the country from falling off the cliff into a depression, but not enough for a robust job recovery. That was partly because Republicans obstructed just about anything President Obama proposed, including budget deficits that the experts knew could fight depressions and recessions.

Fourth, it appears that there was not enough education among the population on the value of targeted budget deficits to fight recessions and promote job creation. Do progressive Democrats do enough to educate people about the utility of deficit spending and about the story of government job programs that have worked? It does not appear so.

Finally, we can debate and learn about specific matters of large importance by studying the WPA and other New Deal job programs. First, should government programs be based on the assumption that, since there are really enough good jobs in the regular economy, new government jobs should be temporary ones, a helping hand until people can get back to the regular economy? Will programs run that way end up sending too many people into lousy positions at Wal-Mart, Target, McDonald's, and a thousand other such places? Second, fighting the discriminatory isms—racism, sexism, ageism, and others—has to be central to job creation programs. In the 1930s, oppressed minorities suffered more in the regular economy and they got less from government job programs. In our time, that contrast should be reversed. People who get the shaft every day deserve special consideration and then some to assure they don't get the shaft in new government job programs.

CHAPTER 3

Full Employment

Experiments and Battles (1940–1974)

During World War II, easy credit and deficit spending brought full employment and ended the Great Depression. Problem solved and Keynesian lessons learned forevermore? Not really. Most economists now understood that large deficits could be used to reduce unemployment, but conservatives in Congress defeated a full employment bill in 1946. There would be no agreement that higher spending and larger deficits should be an at-the-ready tool to bring full employment. Many conservatives still believed that if government stayed out, there would be full employment, or at least the right amount of unemployment. Business leaders claimed that the private sector normally provided enough jobs, and they worried that full employment strengthened employee bargaining power. That was why they sometimes liked recession. The Federal Reserve usually took a conservative view of things, too. Federal Reserve chair William McChesney Martin famously said in 1955 that it was the Fed's job to take away the punch bowl just as the party was warming up; that meant that the Fed could limit wage and job growth.

The Keynesian lessons of World War II were contested rather than widely accepted. But growing programs like Social Security and huge increases in the defense budget made federal spending a large part of the economy. It had been equal to 3.4 percent of GDP in 1930. It was 17.8 percent in 1955.[1] Keynesian ideas had not won out in the 1940s, but personal savings from wartime, new social programs, and defense spending kept the economy humming along. Urban deindustrialization was underway in the 1950s, but many white male workers did well in the late '40s and early '50s.

Then, higher unemployment and slower economic growth in the late 1950s and early '60s provoked debate about the causes of unemployment and spurred the first Keynesian tax cut to promote job growth. High spending and deficits to support the war in Vietnam also helped. Overall it seemed that Keynesian methods had succeeded. Unemployment fell and stayed under 4 percent for four years.

But business leaders and conservatives were wary of big federal deficits, because they feared government influence over the economy, worried about inflation, and did not like it that low unemployment increased employee leverage. In the late '60s, higher inflation rates, rising wages, and falling profit rates led to a government-engineered recession in 1969–1970. Before it had much effect, Republican president Richard Nixon ramped up federal spending to boost his chances for re-election. He also installed a system of government controls to dampen wage and price increases. The rate of inflation fell a bit but real wages increased in 1971–1972. He won re-election, began lifting controls, and switched back to the recession method of controlling wages and prices.[2]

Unemployment soared and real wages fell three years in a row (1973–1975). But inflation, driven more by surging oil prices than wage hikes, accelerated. This was stagflation—high prices and high unemployment. And it was the beginning of the end of three decades of steadily rising real wages.

Meanwhile, a group of scholars and politicians—I call them Dissenters—came to believe that even with substantial increases in federal spending and deficits, civil rights laws, and War on Poverty programs, there would be millions of people without jobs. It was apparent that even with "full employment" in the second half of the 1960s, crowds of African Americans who rioted in Detroit, Newark, and other cities were partly motivated by unemployment or underemployment in lousy jobs. Some Dissenters thought the government would have to create its own job programs, as it had in the '30s.

World War II: Really Big Deficit Spending Brings Really Full Employment

Massive federal spending during World War II pushed the unemployment rate for civilian workers down to 1.2 percent in 1944. Seven million civilian and nine million military jobs were added in three years. But where did the spending money come from? Some came from adding average earners to the tax rolls and some from raising the marginal tax rate on rich people to 94 percent. But much was borrowed from individuals, financial institutions, and the Federal Reserve, and the total amount was very large. From 1933 through 1940, budget deficits were less than $3 billion almost every year; in 1943 the deficit was $55 billion.[3]

There were also negative lessons or cautions from the full-employment war economy. Although wartime full employment was marvelous, it was not utopia. Employers and government officials believed that full employment empowered workers. The war period began as a good time to switch employers for a better deal, but in 1943 the U.S. War Manpower Commission froze workers in essential jobs. It was also a good time to strike, but union leaders agreed to a no-strike pledge, employers made a no-lockout promise, and government agencies supported union membership, which jumped from nine to fifteen million.[4]

Government agencies also put a lid on pay increases. As demand for workers pushed wages up, the War Labor Board declared in 1943 that wage increases would be limited to a total of 15 percent for the duration of the war, regardless of inflation. This rigid "Little Steel" formula incited many small strikes and big ones in coal mining. The strikes provoked legislation that authorized the federal seizure of struck plants and jail time for strikers. But there was also progressive action on inflation. Federal price controls and an army of volunteers helped keep inflation down, despite a booming economy. After rising 23 percent (1940–1943), consumer prices advanced only 4 percent (1943–1945). That was a remarkable achievement—more than full employment but little inflation. We should study that experience.

Full employment had a net positive impact on women, minorities, and poor people in general. A million African Americans migrated from southern farms and villages to industrial centers for better jobs and a little more freedom. Some employers still refused to hire blacks, and whites sometimes attacked black workers. But black workers increased their numbers in manufacturing by 600,000. Overall, full employment rescued millions of people from no jobs or bad jobs. Real average annual incomes jumped 71 percent (1940–1944). It was notable that the incomes of the poorest fifth of the households grew twice as fast as those of the richest fifth. This was the opposite of what would happen in later decades.[5]

Did Spending Lessons from the War Years become Permanent?

New Deal and wartime experiences spread support for permanent programs to ensure full employment. In the last years of the war, many politicians and 68 percent of the people agreed that government should guarantee work for everyone who needed a job. In his "Second Bill of Rights," President Roosevelt included the right to "useful and remunerative jobs." The Republican presidential candidate in 1944, Thomas Dewey, stated that government should provide enough jobs so that every man and woman could earn a decent living.[6]

Experts were predicting a postwar depression with eight million unemployed when Democratic senators James Murray of Montana and Robert Wagner of New York introduced a full employment bill. The 1945 proposal assumed that private enterprise could not assure full employment, so the federal government should borrow and spend to create jobs. The NAACP, the YWCA, the National Catholic Conference, unions, and other liberal organizations supported the bill. Business leaders, big farmers, conservatives, and many Republicans opposed it. Business leaders claimed, even after the Great Depression, that when business was left alone, unemployment was rarely a problem. They also argued that full employment was inflationary.[7]

On September 28, 1945, the Senate passed, by seventy-one to ten, a bill to ensure that all Americans, even those with "full-time housekeeping responsibilities," had access to decent jobs. But conservatives fought back, and they soon had several things in their favor: Depression breadlines had not returned, a strike wave incited anti-labor feeling, and anti-communism heated up. Opponents could attack full employment as socialism, tyranny, and anti-Americanism, not to mention the death of free enterprise and individual initiative. The House defeated a strong jobs bill; the final bill did not require that government borrow and spend to create jobs. Republican senator Robert Taft told supporters that "there is no full employment bill anymore." Pro-worker Keynesian deficits had been defeated.[8]

More Jobs, but No Full-Bodied Keynesian Revolution

From 1945 through 1956, the economy performed well enough that unemployment was rarely a major issue. When World War II ended, government spending fell. Nine million people were released from the military in one year. Yet there was no depression. A tax cut helped, but so did the fact that federal spending stayed high by historical standards. Also very important, there was a lot of catching-up to be done in the private sector after the rigors of depression and war. Americans had padded their savings during the war. Now consumption spending rose by $14 billion, and investment by $21.6 billion. Foreign competitors were in ruins and net exports jumped by $9.8 billion.[9]

Still, there is an employment puzzle. Ten million federal jobs were cut in one year, while other jobs rose only by 2.7 million. But unemployment increased only from about 2 percent to 4 percent. Why so little? First, about 2.6 million women workers were forced out of their jobs or decided to go home. Second, some older workers and some teens left the workforce. Third, millions of veterans took advantage of federal benefits to enter training programs or college and stay out of the labor market. The president of the University of Chicago, Robert M. Hutchins, sneered that colleges would become "educational hobo jungles. . . . Education is not a device for coping with mass unemployment." But it was. Benefits kept veterans on the sidelines and supported training and education that would make them attractive to employers.[10]

So, despite cuts in government spending and a wavering commitment to budgetary activism, the United States avoided a postwar depression. Government spending fell but stayed larger than it had been in the prewar period. And wars—Korea, Vietnam, and the cold war—added hugely to economic demand. While few American leaders wanted "a full-bodied, Keynesian *civilian* deficit-spending policy for maintaining high employment," many were comfortable with high military spending, Social Security, and, sometimes, passive Keynesianism, which held that government must not worsen recessions by cutting spending or raising taxes to balance the budget.[11]

How Good Was the Job Situation in the 1950s?

The economy of the 1950s was often strong, although perhaps not as wonderful as we imagine; economic growth would be better in the 1960s. People increased their buying, but less than in the '60s (14 percent versus 35 percent). But real employee incomes increased by 27 percent and income inequality did not widen. There was poverty and near poverty—40 percent of families earned less than $5,000 a year (the equivalent of about $47,000 in 2019)—but millions of people seemed to be climbing out of poverty. The first two postwar recessions (1949, 1954) were short. Spending on the Korean War pushed unemployment down to 2.9 percent.[12]

Did the experience of the 1950s prove the virtues of limited-government, free-market policies? Hardly. Government jobs grew twice as fast as private-sector jobs, and dozens of large federal programs bolstered consumer spending. These included defense programs, unemployment insurance, the G.I. Bill, government-insured mortgages, Social Security, and Aid to Dependent Children. The number of people on welfare and Social Security jumped from two to eighteen million (1945 through 1960). Incomes from these programs supported economic growth and kept recessions from turning into depressions. And defense spending soared. While consumers spent 7 percent more each year, defense expenditures increased 22 percent a year from 1948 to 1956! The United States was becoming a welfare-warfare state.[13]

Over the decade, civilian nonfarm jobs increased by 27 percent, close to the 31 percent surge of the 1960s. In both decades, the war years were, by far, the winners as job-creators. Nonfarm jobs grew 19.4 percent in 1950–1955, the era of the Korean War, but only 9.6 percent in 1955–1960. During the Vietnam War, nonfarm jobs increased 19.5 percent (1965–1970), but they had grown only 9.9 percent in 1960–1965. Large-scale, war-induced spending was an effective job creator.

In addition to higher spending in the '50s, the working-age population was not growing much. There were actually fewer twenty-five- to thirty-four-year-olds at the end of the decade than at the beginning, so in some areas there must have been less competition for jobs. Because of that and unionization, males increased their real weekly earnings by 25 percent. Women gained, but less so. There was demand for female workers, especially in office and retail work, but a rising supply too; the number of women in the labor force jumped 33 percent.[14]

There were also improvements as black Americans moved north. In 1949 the poverty rate for southern black families was 75 percent; in 1959 the rate was 32 percent for northern black families. But northern manufacturers were already sending jobs away from strong union and urban centers, and they were spending heavily on automation. Deindustrialization was underway. The workforce in motor vehicle production fell 15 percent in the 1950s. Automation and plant closures were a problem. They stopped making Packards after 1958. The city of Detroit lost 136,000 manufacturing jobs (1947–1963) in this, the golden age of the American automobile. These changes had an outsized impact on African Americans, who had only recently gained a foothold in northern factories.

Laid-off black workers and older workers had a hard time finding new jobs. The young suffered too. The shrinkage of entry-level jobs seemed a kind of silent firing to some job-seekers. Sluggish economic growth in the late '50s made things worse. Detroit's African American population was in depression. Thousands gathered every day on Detroit's Eight Mile Road in a "slave market" for day labor.[15]

Until the late '50s, the overall unemployment rate was pretty low. Times were generally good for union workers and for employees in government, public utilities, finance, insurance, and real estate. Not much was said about the uncounted unemployed, but some scholars and politicians paid attention to structural unemployment: dying industries, automation-induced job loss, people with low skills, and racial discrimination. Others, including Keynesians, believed that the economy was just not creating enough jobs and that the overarching cause was not enough aggregate economic demand.[16]

Both structural and aggregate factors were important. In 1958–1961, two recessions raised unemployment and caused more deindustrialization. In the '50s there were job losses in the depressed coal mining areas of Appalachia and southern Illinois and in factories in Pittsburgh, Detroit, Chicago, and East St. Louis. Industrialists were cutting jobs, automating more, and running away from militant unions. Armour Meatpacking closed twenty-one factories and displaced fourteen thousand workers. In East St. Louis, the company shut a plant that had employed forty-five hundred. Armour donated the out-of-date building to the city rather than pay taxes on it. The ruins are still there. Armour opened smaller plants in new locations. Some employees were offered transfers, but it was hard to move if you could not sell your house in a declining neighborhood. Unions did not often use mass actions to keep plants open; they did make deals in which current workers accepted automation in return for income guarantees.[17]

As good jobs vanished, some individuals felt helpless. After the Packard shutdown, one guy asked: "Where will this old man look for a job? I am too old for a job, and too young to retire." A jobless miner said he was "one of the lucky ones. I only have to wait twelve years till I get my Social Security."[18]

A Senate committee toured the country to hear from displaced workers. On December 1, 1959, in Evansville, Indiana, committee members met fifty-year-old Elmer Ragsdale, tossed out with five thousand other workers when Chrysler closed a factory. Elmer had twenty-four years with the company. The committee also heard from James Alderson, who said that when you tell employers that

> you're 61 years of age . . . they seem to look at you and say . . . you ought to have better sense than to ask and they will tell you if you are over 50, there's no need talking, so I think they should bring the old-age pension down and give it to people where people won't hire you. . . . (There is) discrimination against older people . . . why? Because Eisenhower wants to play golf. He is not interested.

It was hard to be old and laid off. But the unemployment rate was actually higher for younger workers. While forty-five- to fifty-four-year-olds averaged 4.9 percent unemployment in 1959, twenty- to twenty-four-year-olds averaged 11 percent. A Detroit journalist talked to young people who wanted older workers "chased out of these mills."[19]

The Keynesian Turn in the 1960s

There is no doubt that people were unemployed because of discrimination, deindustrialization, and other structural causes. But there is also no doubt that overall job growth was too slow in the late '50s and early '60s. The official unemployment rate never fell below 5.5 percent in all the years from 1958 through 1963. Over time, liberal Democratic presidents in the 1960s, John Kennedy and Lyndon Johnson, developed programs for different kinds of unemployment: government budget policy to spur economic growth and increases in job totals, as well as special programs to educate and train the poor and the unemployed and to ensure fairness in hiring. Here we focus on aggregate approaches that worked on the whole economy, including Keynesian-style budget deficits and the general tax cut of 1964.

Recessions in 1957–1958 and 1960 were caused in part by slower increases in consumer and government spending, including defense spending, which had been falling as a share of the total federal budget since 1954. Anti-Keynesian thinking was also a factor. The economy hit bottom in the first quarter of 1958 but then began to grow. Republican President Eisenhower, an economic conservative and one who prioritized inflation-fighting, restrained spending, and the budget year starting July 1, 1959, ended with a small surplus. That meant the federal government was not adding extra spending stimulus to the economy. This was one reason there was a second recession in 1960.[20]

The recessions, deindustrialization issues discussed in the last section, and high unemployment were part of the reason Democrats added congressional seats in 1958. Congress passed aid packages for depressed areas, but Eisenhower vetoed them. Despite evidence of painful outcomes in deindustrialized areas, the nation did not have special assistance programs for those left behind by economic change. Eisenhower rarely mentioned jobs, and Republicans argued that inflation was "the gravest potential obstacle" to growth. The annual rate of inflation was 3.3 percent and 2.8 percent in 1957 and 1958, but in every other year from 1952 through 1965 it was less than 2 percent. Underlying inflationary pressures did not seem to be very strong.

The Democratic Party Platform in 1960 promised aid for depressed areas and displaced workers and also efforts to stimulate economic growth. But the winning presidential candidate had not promised to spend borrowed money to fire up economic growth. In January 1961, when John Kennedy was inaugurated, unemployment stood at 6.6 percent. Yet he "pledged allegiance to the balanced budget." Lessons from World War II had not changed the public conversation much.

But out of the limelight, Keynesian economists, especially the head of Kennedy's Council of Economic Advisors, Walter Heller, were working on the president. And events seemed to be pushing economic policy in Keynesian directions. Tensions over the Berlin Wall and the Cuban Missile Crisis caused an upturn in military spending, and Heller convinced the president not to propose tax increases to pay for the new spending. The result was a kind of backdoor military Keynesianism that added to the federal deficit. Meanwhile, another crisis would add pressure for new incentives for corporate America. In April 1961, the president had proposed substantial tax credits for new business investment. A year later, on May 28, 1962, the stock market crashed and that raised fears about a new recession. President Kennedy gave a speech at Yale in which he seemed to go over to the Keynesian cause. In October the investment credits were passed into law, but Walter Heller wanted something more: broad income tax cuts and federal deficits, or at least no significant budget surpluses. His ultimate goal was not simply a little more economic growth or the avoidance of recession, but maximum economic growth to achieve full employment. His working assumption was that economic underperformance was a chronic, not a temporary condition.[21]

While the tax plan worried some business leaders and conservatives, quite a few corporate leaders were supportive of a plan that would reward them very richly. And the tax plan was not really radical, although the idea of tax cuts and frank advocacy of deficit spending in non-recessionary times seemed unusual. But the method of generating deficits was a conservative one, so much so that socialist Michael Harrington, who had recently written about poverty in *The Other America,* called the program "reactionary Keynesianism." For deficits could have been created not by tax cuts that favored the affluent and corporations, but by new government spending on income-assistance programs, direct-job creation, urban reconstruction, and a dozen other things that directly aided the lower half. Furthermore, if there had to be tax cuts, they could have been given only to middle- and low-income earners.

But Heller and the administration chose the politically easier method of general tax cuts. Even then, the specters of more government management of the economy and too much debt irked conservatives in Congress. President Johnson had to agree to balance the budget in the first year of the new tax regime, although deficits had been part of the original plan.[22]

In February 1964, the corporate tax rate was lowered from 52 percent to 47 percent. Personal tax rates were cut from a range of 20 percent to 94 percent to a range of 15 percent to 70 percent. The rich got a bigger cut than the poor. But the results seemed very good. Real Gross Domestic Product was up 5.8 percent in 1964 and 6.5 percent in 1965. An economy that had grown by 13.5 percent over 1956–1961 would grow by 33 percent over 1961–1966. Job totals had increased 2 percent a year in the early '60s; they jumped by 4.9 percent in 1965.[23]

Were the peacetime Keynesian tax cuts a success? The answer is, "Yes, but." Job growth was strong in 1965 and 1966. But spending on the Vietnam War was soon growing very rapidly and that would help to push unemployment below 4 percent for four years. Without war spending, inflation problems might have been more manageable. But there may have been less job creation. In general, it is best to view the 1964 tax cut as one of four stimuli that also included investment credits for businesses, an easy money policy at the Federal Reserve, and high spending on the war in Vietnam. Certainly, the effect of the combined causes was striking. The civilian labor force grew by eight million people from 1965 to 1969 and unemployment stayed below 4 percent for four years. The boom even added jobs in industries that had been cutting employees; the number of production workers in motor vehicle manufacturing jumped 26 percent. More federal spending, including a lot of deficit spending, had a positive impact on structural unemployment.

While prices and wages usually increased rather slowly, rising inflation could eventually threaten the Keynesian growth program. In 1958 economist A. W. Phillips had argued that when unemployment was high, wage increases were low, and when unemployment was low, wage increases were high. That seemed to mean you could not have low unemployment and low inflation at the same time. But American Keynesians had believed they could manage spending and tax policies to get to a point on the Phillips curve that combined lowish unemployment of 3 to 4 percent with moderate inflation of 3 to 4 percent. Additionally, the Kennedy administration had designed voluntary guideposts to restrain prices and to limit wage increases to the rate of productivity increases. A machinists' strike in 1966 scuttled the guideposts, but increases in the rate of inflation were mild considering that tax cuts and military spending pushed unemployment below 4 percent for four years. The annual inflation rate was still only 4.7 percent in 1968—on the high side, but a low price to pay for a nearly full-employment economy.[24]

White House economists had hoped to act on inflation before 1968, but President Johnson wanted to maintain spending levels on Vietnam and social programs—both guns and butter. And he did not want blowback from raising taxes; the war was already hugely unpopular. So, a tax increase that was supposed to cool the economy did not come until 1968. Had it come sooner, there might have been less inflation. But also, probably less job creation.[25]

A more important issue than inflation involved morality; a lot of new spending went for the murderous war in Southeast Asia. It did not have to be that way, either to protect Americans from Communism or to create jobs. More deficit spending on park development, roads and bridges, Head Start, city beautification, local health clinics, affordable housing, and a dozen other projects would have been infinitely better.

The Jobs Will Be There; Fix the Workers

In the Kennedy-Johnson years the main cure for unemployment was aggregate—tax cuts and easy credit to stimulate the whole economy. But there were also programs for specific structural problems, including civil rights laws to ensure that minorities were treated fairly in the hiring process, and anti-poverty programs to improve people's skills and attitudes.

Already before the War on Poverty (WP), the Manpower Development and Training Act (MDTA) of 1962 addressed structural unemployment caused by technological change and plant closures. The idea was to train people for high-tech jobs. But as the economy picked up, displaced workers found new jobs on their own, so MDTA began to serve underprivileged youth. Because trainees often lacked the educational background for advanced training, MDTA offered remedial subjects and then vocational training in auto mechanics, food services, office work, and health services.[26]

Over six years, 600,000 people completed an MDTA course. Studies evaluating the program came up with widely different conclusions. One study showed that graduates did worse than a control group whose members had not been in the program, and another concluded that the program improved graduates' earnings by $1,000. It was difficult to say whether the MDTA did what it was supposed to do. At times it seemed that while MDTA raised school and skill levels, people were being trained for occupations where there was no shortage of applicants.[27]

Soon the MDTA was eclipsed by the War on Poverty. A variety of concerns and impulses in the late 1950s and early 1960s led to the creation of an agency and many programs for a direct assault on poverty. Experts on America's cities were worried about juvenile delinquency and urban decay. It looked like the economy was not reducing poverty rates fast enough, and the civil rights movement put the spotlight on economic disparities. In 1962 Michael Harrington's book, *The Other America: Poverty in the United States,* portrayed varieties of poverty with great feeling and helped to focus disparate concerns on fighting poverty. Within two years, Congress passed and the president signed legislation to create an agency with the authority to create anti-poverty programs. The WP ran many useful programs including Head Start and Neighborhood Legal Services, which aimed to make opportunities and the legal process a little less unequal. There were also, on a parallel track outside the WP, Medicaid and Medicare, which would vastly enlarge access to health care.

Many people, including poor people, found employment as staff members in Head Start and other WP employment programs, but the goal of most WP job programs was not about direct-job creation but job preparation. However, some legislators, people in the Labor Department, and also leftish thinkers like Harrington had wanted job creation. They suggested that there be an additional five-cent tax on cigarettes to pay for jobs. But Johnson and his advisors believed that if their tax cuts worked, the private sector would create enough jobs.[28] So, WP employment programs focused on job preparation rather than job creation. An example was the Job Corps. It moved young people from slums and rural backwaters to residential campuses for remedial education classes, social skills development, and vocational training for clerical work, welding, cooking, auto-body repair, and similar occupations. Some kids were school dropouts; some had criminal records. It was not easy to get them to study. Two-thirds of Job Corps enrollees never finished the program. Those who finished earned wages that were similar to those earned by people who had been accepted into but had not entered the program.[29]

Of course, young people needed knowledge and skills, but a bigger problem was that even in a booming economy there were still not enough good jobs. When one employer advertised for workers in Scranton, Pennsylvania, ten thousand people filled out job applications without even knowing the name of the company. Only four hundred were hired. In 1966 there were fifty-seven thousand applications for fifty-seven hundred slots at GM's Lordstown plant. These events occurred at a time when the official unemployment rate was low. Perhaps the official count was missing many people.[30]

If Unemployment Was Under 4 Percent, What Was the Problem?

Lyndon Johnson wondered why more people did not have jobs when unemployment was under 4 percent, which his economists thought was close to full employment. His Department of Labor (DOL) was discovering that real unemployment was higher than headline rates. But there would be no big jobs program even as thousands of economically distressed African Americans rose up in riots and protests in Newark, Detroit, and a dozen other cities.[31]

Many African Americans experienced a Great Depression every day, even while the nation had low unemployment numbers. In a special survey of the "slums" in 1966, DOL experts combined four groups to create a "subemployment rate": 1) those normally counted as unemployed; 2) part-timers who wanted full-time work; 3) discouraged job seekers who had quit looking for work, including an estimate for people often missed by government surveyors; and 4) non-elderly employed people who earned below-poverty incomes. Total subemployment averaged 34 percent. Excluding people who had jobs (category 4), the subemployment rate was 22.4 percent. It was not news that unemployment was high in poor communities, but conventional estimates had the rates at 6 to 11 percent.[32]

So, the first subemployment survey showed that there was a much bigger problem than previously thought. It could support a different War on Poverty in which the federal government directly created millions of jobs. Of course, subemployment information could be used another way. One could blame rampant unemployment on broken families, lack of skills, and a bad work ethic. That argument was half of Daniel Patrick Moynihan's *The Negro Family* (1965). In the subemployment study DOL analysts seemed to agree, claiming that the causes of subemployment were "*personal* rather than *economic*," not lack of jobs, but lack of skills and education, and also police records, drug addiction, disability, and hopelessness. Yet these analysts also offered economic explanations. Personal problems might be the *result* rather than the cause of people being unemployed. People might stop searching for work because they could not find good jobs; young people might choose to work in the drug trade because it paid better. The analysts noted that many of the subemployed wanted to work and were willing to train. A Philadelphia training program had a waiting list of six thousand. An Oakland job fair attracted fifteen thousand but placed only 250 in jobs. Perhaps more should have been done to create good jobs and less to rehabilitate unemployed poor people.[33] It seemed clear in the late '60s that high levels of federal spending were not trickling down in the form of enough jobs for millions of urban and rural poor people. It seemed, too, that 4 percent unemployment was not full employment. A group of dissenting liberals began to coalesce around the idea that government had to directly create new jobs, as the WPA and the CCC had done in the 1930s. More about that later.[34]

Inflation, Nixon, Stagflation (1969–1976)

This period began a major turning point in the history of job policy, wages, and worker power. Rising prices and wages led to an income surtax in 1968. The budget year ending June 30, 1969, ended with a surplus. Government was causing a recession. Economic growth was negative in several quarters during 1969–1970. The unemployment rate rose and stayed around 6 percent during 1971. Price inflation fell but it was still 4.4 percent in 1971. Despite higher unemployment, union workers won substantial wage increases in 1971 and 1972. The recession method of suppressing wages and prices had not yet worked well enough. Owners wanted stronger action to stop wage advances. But at that time Nixon did not want a bigger recession. He was getting ready for his re-election campaign, and believed that he lost the 1960 election to Kennedy partly because Eisenhower (Nixon was his vice president) had refused to spend the economy into a boom. But could Nixon spur economic activity with easy credit and higher federal spending without causing wages and prices to take off? He thought so. In August 1971, he instituted a rather un-Republican system of government wage-and-price controls. That helped keep inflation under 4 percent in 1972, even while economic demand increased. Wages were controlled, profits weren't, and workers did not like that. But as it turned out, real wages still increased in 1972 and 1973. That was not what business leaders had hoped for.[35]

After he won a second term, Nixon began to remove controls, and prices exploded. In 1974 they jumped 11 percent, and that wiped out real wage increases for many people. Nixon and his advisors returned to the recession-method of dealing with wage-and-price increases. It was the B-side of Keynesianism: federal spending and deficit plans were cut and the Federal Reserve restricted credit. While world oil prices and some other causes of inflation were beyond direct control of the U.S. government, much higher unemployment, it was hoped, could reduce wages, consumer demand, and price inflation. And a big enough recession might shift a little more power away from labor and toward capital.

After Nixon resigned over Watergate in August 1974, his successor, President Gerald Ford, also emphasized inflation-fighting rather than job creation. Unemployment reached 9 percent in May 1975, the highest level since the 1930s. But prices were rising at 9 percent. Americans were facing high unemployment and high inflation, and that was not supposed to happen. Someone called the combination stagflation. Whatever it was called, the twin impact of high inflation and high unemployment was part of a historic reversal from three decades of wage increases.[36]

Over the course of the 1970s and 1980s, many conservatives, a fair number of centrist Democrats, and many economists, including some who worked for President Jimmy Carter in the late '70s, came to believe that high unemployment was the best way—perhaps the only effective way—to limit wage and price increases. Additionally, some conservatives thought that a little more misery for some of the people was no big deal. In 1972 Nixon's secretary of the Treasury, Texan John Connally, told Congress that many jobless people were not primary wage-earners; they were women, blacks, and young people, people who usually had high unemployment rates. The jobless rate for adult family heads was only 3 percent, so "we can't be carried away by an unemployment figure of say, 6%." President Ford's Council of Economic Advisors, led by Alan Greenspan, announced that unemployment should not fall below 4.9 percent and perhaps never below 5.5 percent. It was rumored that Greenspan really wanted even higher levels of unemployment to be the norm. This kind of thinking foreclosed alternative approaches to inflation and sacrificed workers to the cause of stable prices. It had extra back-up in the Phillips curve and in a more fatalistic version of the same thing, Milton Friedman's "Natural Rate" below which unemployment could not fall without igniting inflation. Soon that would get a fancy name—the Non-Accelerating Inflation Rate of Unemployment—and an impressive acronym—NAIRU. But it came loaded with questions about just what the NAIRU number was and whether it was a humane way to control inflation.[37]

Much of this was in the future. And presidents like to be re-elected and they know that high unemployment can be political suicide. President Ford, a conservative who initially made inflation-fighting a priority, agreed to tax cuts and more spending to stimulate the economy as election time neared. Budget deficits were very large but perhaps not large enough or well-targeted. Unemployment fell a bit but was still 7.7 percent just before the election. Jimmy Carter defeated Mr. Ford. Could Carter's team find ways to create jobs without higher inflation? Would economists exert themselves to find ways to combine low inflation, rising real wages, and enough good jobs for all?[38]

New Views of Job Markets on the Left

A small group of liberal politicians and social scientists were developing a complex view of labor markets. These Dissenters doubted that capitalist markets always tended to produce enough jobs; some of them thought the official unemployment rate omitted many truly unemployed persons; some argued that job markets were structured to hurt certain social groups more than others; and some doubted that scattershot federal spending increases could bring truly full employment. The Dissenters included sociologist Ivar Berg, anthropologist Elliot Liebow, liberal senators like Gaylord Nelson of Wisconsin, congressional staffer William Spring, and economists Bennett Harrison, Barry Bluestone, and Michael Piore. Some of their research showed that there was not one labor market open to all, but a dual labor market. Entry into the primary sector of better-paying, more stable jobs was partly fenced off by racism, sexism, classism, hyper-credentialism, and craft-union exclusion. Some individuals, regardless of skills, were less likely to get primary-sector jobs and more likely to get jobs with poor pay and frequent unemployment. Their situation was "rooted less in individual behavior than in the character of institutions and the social patterns that derive from them."[39]

Many of the Dissenters were also convinced that there simply were not enough jobs. William Spring said that if you have one hundred applicants for ninety jobs, "ten people are going to be unemployed. They will probably be the ten with the poorest ratings on whatever scale is being used, education, skill, age, work experience . . . or race. But the basic problem . . . (is) the lack of jobs."[40]

An opportunity for a new job policy had arisen when unemployment hit 6 percent in 1971. Nixon and the Democratic Congress agreed to the Emergency Employment Act, which authorized a Public Employment Program (PEP). PEP allocated $2 billion dollars for a two-year pilot program to create local and state government jobs. At its peak, PEP supported only 185,000 people—less than 1/25 of the average monthly number of unemployed. It was an "amazingly puny" effort, but it was the first direct job-creation program since the 1930s.[41]

A second opportunity came in 1973 when Republicans and Democrats passed the Comprehensive Employment and Training Act (CETA). CETA was supposed to eliminate duplication in federal training and manpower programs and give more control to the states—satisfying Republicans. It would create public service jobs in high unemployment areas—satisfying Democrats. At first, enrollees were drawn from the structurally jobless—those who were said to be jobless because of skill deficits and social handicaps, not job shortages. But as the program got going, the economy went into recession, and job shortages spread and were clearly a general problem. In December 1974, Congress added money for state and local government jobs. CETA then served not only those who often had trouble getting hired, but people thrown out of work by recession. Initially, 300,000 were enrolled.[42]

Conservatives for Unemployment

While one group of liberals pushed for direct job creation and studied the failures of job markets, some conservatives fought for higher unemployment to restrain wages and prices; eventually quite a few liberal economists and business leaders would agree. While recessions could be risky for businesses, some executives might accept a large but quick economic shock if it helped to bring inflation under control. Some also thought it would be a bonus if unemployment weakened unions and employee bargaining power.

A leader in the fight to use unemployment against inflation was conservative economist Milton Friedman. He claimed that his theory showed that the need for high unemployment was just a matter of economic reality. There was a "natural" rate of unemployment below which we could not go without sparking uncontrollable inflation and, eventually, more unemployment. We'll see more about this worldview and NAIRU in the next chapter.[43]

Here, we take note of common attitudes and theories that shored up theories like Friedman's. One we have seen. Young people, minorities, and women tended to have higher unemployment rates, but, it was claimed, they were not the "real" breadwinners, and we should not worry about them. Some of them, it seemed, just had a preference for more time away from work, or, as some called it, leisure. Married women, for example, moved easily in and out of the labor force as their desires and needs changed. Other economists, equally bewitched by the choice factor in classical economics, agreed that unemployment was not a painful experience caused by large economic forces; it was a decision by the jobless person, sometimes to take a vacation, sometimes to invest in their future by searching for new jobs. How about "discouraged workers," people who gave up the job-search because they could not find a job?

This group's existence could support the idea that there was real unemployment among those outside the labor force. But according to some job-search economists, discouraged workers weren't discouraged at all; they too had simply decided to take a vacation from work and even from the search for work.[44]

Of course, many economists understood that there were other kinds of unemployment than voluntary unemployment. Most economists who were close to the center, whether liberals or conservatives, believed that recessions caused more unemployment (cyclical unemployment), and also that there was an irreducible level of unemployment owing to the fact that it took time for people who wanted a job to find one (frictional unemployment), and the fact that job-seekers might lack the skills for available job slots or they might be in places that were losing jobs rather than gaining them (structural unemployment). There was some truth in each of these positions, but there was also, normally, the huge assumption that jobs were there and so, normally, there was no real shortage of jobs. The frictional passage was relatively pain-free.

But clinging too closely to the frictional story blinds us to many realities of unemployment. The fact is that many job seekers classed as unemployed do not find jobs. Sometimes they drop out of the labor force and out of the unemployed category because their life-plans change, sometimes because there aren't enough jobs or enough decent jobs. If demand for workers were really booming, there would be less official unemployment, less frictional and structural unemployment, and less hidden unemployment. While many mainstream economists accept that frictional and structural unemployment are about people who are looking for jobs, they assume that, normally, the jobs are there and that the frictionally unemployed at least are almost not unemployed—they are just about to find jobs. But many don't find jobs. Normally, more people exit the unemployed category by dropping out of the labor force than by finding jobs. The frictional narrative, which assumes an easy passage from unemployment to employment, is profoundly misleading about the situation that many people confront, namely, not enough half-way decent jobs.[45]

CHAPTER 4

Low Unemployment + Low Inflation

Can't Be Done, Is Done (1975–2000)

"Plenty of Workers Waiting in the Wings"

Table 4.1 says a lot about jobs, wages, and power.[1]

The second column was one cause of the first. High unemployment and more job seekers helped to keep wages down in the later period. But why was unemployment higher in the second period? The big answers had to do with population, politics, and policies. First, rapid increases in the working-age population and broad social changes expanded the pool of workers. Baby boomers were flooding into the labor market. Many more women took jobs, seeking more independence or more income for their families, or both.

And over time, the number of immigrants from Asia, Africa, and especially Latin America ballooned. As economic conditions worsened and threats to

Table 4.1   More Unemployment = Lower Wages

	Average Real Hourly Pay Total Change	Years When Unemployment Averaged 6% or Higher
1950 to 1975	+53%	3 of 26
1975 to 2000	−5%	16 of 26

Sources: *Economic Report of the President, 1984* (Washington, D.C.: U.S. Government Printing Office, 1984), table B-38, p. 264; and *Economic Report of the President, 2016* (Washington, D.C.: U.S. Government Printing Office, 2016), table B-15, p. 418. Wage data are for production and nonsupervisory employees in private, nonagricultural jobs.

personal safety increased south of the border, more people were motivated to come to the United States, and changes in U.S. laws generally meant more of them would be undocumented or illegal immigrants. In 1964 the bracero program, which began during World War II and brought as many as 445,000 farm workers a year into the United States, was eliminated. The following year, the Immigration and Naturalization Act ended the national-origins distribution of immigrant entry, which had favored those from western Europe. But for the first time, it put restrictions on entry from the Western Hemisphere and instituted single-country limits of twenty thousand a year. These two changes would mean more illegal immigrants.[2]

Another cause of the bad news about wages in table 4.1 was the class war on workers. Conservatives and business leaders were in charge, but some conservative Democrats and neoliberals went along with efforts to limit union power and cut government income supports for workers. And more experts, including liberals, were willing to support high unemployment to fight price and wage inflation. This was a switch, after it had appeared that activist policies to bring full employment had gained much support in the 1960s and early 1970s. The attack on full employment was bolstered by ideas that sounded scientific: first, the "natural" rate of unemployment (NRU), and then the non-accelerating inflation rate of employment (NAIRU). These ideas allegedly expressed basic economic laws that meant that the rate of unemployment must not be allowed to get too low.

Another important change in the '70s and '80s can be summarized as a shift from the War on Poverty to the War on the Poor. Police repression of poor people and people of color had always been a problem, but the War on Drugs and the incarceration mania that accompanied it multiplied the dangers. In the thirty years after 1980, the number of American felons and ex-felons increased from five million to twenty million people. By 2010 one-third of all black males were felons or ex-felons.[3]

The Nixon-Ford Recession and the Demand for Higher Unemployment

Inflation became a pressing problem in the '70s, and many politicians and economists shifted their priority from full employment to low inflation. High inflation seemed tenacious, even in periods of high unemployment. The combination of high unemployment and high inflation was not supposed to happen. Someone dubbed it stagflation, and it seemed to contradict the Phillips Curve idea that you could have at least one of two good things: low inflation or low unemployment. In periods of stagflation, you got neither.

In the '70s, two main government policies were used to fight inflation. Strategy one was a surprise from Republican President Nixon: government controls on wages and prices. Strategy two was well known—Eisenhower used it in 1960—and that was spending cuts and a Federal Reserve clampdown on credit to slow economic growth and raise unemployment. Lower business activity and rising unemployment meant less demand for goods, services, and labor, and that was supposed to limit wage and price inflation.

As mentioned in the previous chapter, when Richard Nixon became president in 1969, prices were rising about 5 percent a year. A mild recession in 1970 cut inflation, but not enough. However, the president did not want a deeper recession. On the contrary, he hoped to stimulate job creation and business activity for his re-election campaign. But an economic boom could boost inflation. So, in August 1971 the president surprised the country by announcing a system of government wage-and-price controls. In time, they reduced inflation even as the economy grew. But neither business nor labor were happy with controls. After his re-election, Nixon lifted controls and prices soared. In 1974 consumer prices jumped 11 percent. Underlying causes included big increases in grain and oil prices around the world, but workers' wages were a prime target of some inflation-fighters.[4]

So, it was back to strategy two, but more of it. Presidential advisor Herbert Stein later described the policy in bland generalities: "Demand would have to be restrained by fiscal and monetary policy and the resulting unemployment and other pain would have to be accepted until inflation was substantially eliminated." Government spending and credit would be tightened to bring a recession. That was clear. But which income groups would suffer most was not much discussed by the champions of higher unemployment.[5]

Stein's position was an old one but it was gaining new scholarly support. As previewed in chapter 3, right-wing economist and American Economic Association president Milton Friedman claimed in the late '60s that there was a "natural" rate of unemployment. If unemployment fell below the "natural" rate, inflation would accelerate. In other words, anyone who messed with economic laws risked runaway inflation. Accordingly, government should keep unemployment pretty high all the time, especially if the rate of inflation were rising.

Oil prices did not seem important to Friedman, and his ideas about workers' psychology seemed contrived. He must have reasoned to his natural-rate idea not from research but from his bedrock belief: unregulated markets good, activist liberal government bad. Friedman normally opposed Keynesian deficit spending, and he thought that the Federal Reserve should put money-supply growth on automatic at a low but steady rate. Governments should stop tampering with the economy and rely on "natural" market forces to create the right number of jobs. But that could mean long periods of depression. In 1974 Friedman declared that we had to live "with an abnormally high unemployment rate for the next five to eight years." Again, not much about the fact that higher unemployment hurt some people—minorities and most working-class Americans—much more than CEOs and economists.

Over the course of the 1970s and 1980s, many conservative politicians, the Federal Reserve, and many economists, including liberals, joined the high-unemployment movement around the idea of the non-accelerating inflation rate of employment. Several aspects of NAIRU were questionable, but the idea was linked to basic supply-and-demand principles: keep economic demand down and unemployment up and there will be less income, less buying and investing, and less inflation. If inflation rates were accelerating, unemployment would have to stay high.

In the mid-1970s, President Gerald Ford's Council of Economic Advisors, led by conservative Alan Greenspan, announced that unemployment must not fall beneath 4.9 or even 5.5 percent. In private they may have been thinking 6 or 7 percent was necessary. In 1976 a *Fortune* magazine writer claimed that unemployment had been *"too low for the past twenty-eight years."* In the late '70s, economists began the Orwellian project of relabeling bad stuff: whatever amount of unemployment was necessary to control inflation—in other words, NAIRU—would be considered full employment. So, full employment was defined not in terms of how many people needed jobs but in terms of how much unemployment was necessary to control prices and wages.

The 1974–1975 recession was caused, in part, by restricted government spending and tighter credit. Unemployment reached 9 percent, the highest level since the 1930s. The rate of inflation fell from 11 percent to below 6 percent in 1976. That was a big change but still pretty high after the worst recession in decades. And prices were soon rising again. One might have concluded that Americans needed higher unemployment for a longer time, or that other means of controlling inflation should be explored.[6]

One could conceive of several strategy-three anti-inflation policies, including new ways to control oil prices and limit oil consumption. While across-the-board government controls on wages and prices were hard to manage and often unfairly administered, as recent experience had shown, one economist suggested selective controls on businesses that acted like monopolies. Or one might try collective bargaining in which unions and management exchanged nonmonetary goods and agreed to restrain wages and prices. This might have been a good idea except that conservatives and business leaders wanted a war on unions. Union leaders tried to make nice with owners, but to no avail.

Some business leaders and economists were coming to believe that a deep recession along with a campaign to weaken unions was the way to limit inflation, expand corporate power over workers, and increase profit margins. Owners did not like what recessions did to their customer base, and they did not want a long one, but most of them did not mind that high unemployment weakened unions. Many economists, especially conservatives but liberals and centrists too, came to support the recession-solution to high inflation, and the idea that harsher medicine than was applied in 1970 and the mid-1970s was necessary. From this viewpoint, the trouble with the 1974–1975 recession was that politicians flinched. The recession had been big, but not big enough. President Ford, who replaced Nixon in 1974, began by making balanced budgets and inflation-fighting his priorities, but he wanted to be elected president in 1976, so he backed off and agreed to anti-recession measures: tax cuts, easier credit, and unemployment benefits extended to sixty-five weeks. As was normal in recessions, federal revenues fell and spending rose, and that meant higher budget deficits—in fact the highest since World War II. So, deficits promoted economic recovery before inflation had been fully tamed. While the Nixon-Ford recession was the worst since the 1930s, it was not deep enough to permanently reduce inflation. And it wasn't scary enough. A year later, 82 percent of jobholders did not think they would lose their positions in the near future. If high unemployment were to limit wage demands, that would have to be changed.[7]

Was Being Unemployed Too Easy?

In the playbook of some conservatives and centrist liberals, unemployment needed to hurt more if high inflation were to be conquered. There had to be more of it and the unemployed must receive less government support. A cluster of ideas that might be labeled the New Unemployment Theory bolstered the argument that unemployment was too easy and that much of it was voluntary. In part, this was a revival of the nineteenth-century assumption that there was normally little involuntary unemployment—just lazy or ill-prepared people. Events of the 1930s and the 1960s had expanded the influence of the alternative worldview that the unemployment problem resided in the economy rather than in people's psyches. But the old view had not died, and its influence began to spread again in the 1970s and 1980s. There were several aspects to the new unemployment position, but crucial was the idea that many of the unemployed chose to be unemployed and that government programs made unemployment an attractive choice. New unemployment experts ignored systemic economic causes for higher than normal unemployment. Here's more about key elements:

- *Business Week* ran a piece entitled "A Million Jobs with No Takers." People were unemployed because they wanted to be. They enjoyed idleness, or they had chosen not to get the right skills and schooling, or they chose to stay at home with their children. But the jobs were there.
- More of the unemployed were women and youth, people not firmly attached to the labor force. They went in and out of the labor force, had low skills, and weren't breadwinners. Why worry about them?
- There was a serious recession in the mid-1970s, but there was not much real hardship—nothing like the Great Depression. But there was pain in this, the worst recession since the '30s. It was true that more of the unemployed had working spouses, unemployment benefits, and savings than in the past, but being unemployed was not a picnic for most people, especially if they had dependents and especially if they were not affluent and hadn't much money saved.
- It was a soft life on food stamps and unemployment benefits. But actually, benefits left many people in poverty, and many of the unemployed did not receive benefits. But conservatives wanted more pain. Economist Martin Feldstein proposed to tax unemployment benefits in order to force people back to work sooner and at lower wages.[8]

The new unemployment model ignored the normal tendencies of capitalism, such as overproduction crises that led to recessions, and wide income inequalities that were immoral and economically inefficient. It erased the miseries that afflicted many unemployed people. At times it melded with the view of some observers that social change and higher government benefits were eroding the work ethic. This particular bias ran up against one large fact. In the 1970s, '80s, and '90s there were huge increases in the number of people working or looking for work. The counted labor force grew by fifty-one million. More women, baby boomers, and immigrants entered the labor force.

It is true that if we pay attention to individual stories from the 1970s, we find some confirmation for the new unemployment position, especially for more well-to-do people. Mark Rinaldi, a twenty-three-year-old, lived with affluent parents in a Connecticut suburb and received unemployment benefits that helped him turn down "crummy" jobs. Sandy Biggest, a bored housewife, wanted a job, but nothing paying less than $15,000 (about $57,000 in 2019). Robin Landau, age twenty-four, received more income from her parents and unemployment benefits than she earned "busting my ass" at work. Dick Franco and his wife, an unemployed cellist, had their unemployment claims transferred from Vermont to Massachusetts, and moved to Boston for the music scene. Franco was writing a novel and did not want a regular job.

The Francos reflected artists' values and perhaps also ideals of the '60s counterculture. But most of the unemployed were not hippies or artists. Many female workers were heads of household and had to work, and others supplemented their partners' earnings to lift their families out of poverty. Though it was easier for people to be unemployed than it had been in the 1890s or 1920s, many people suffered. An elevator operator was automated out of his job. He became demoralized and stayed home with his dog, watching television and sleeping. Another fellow was laid off after three years of taking phone orders for a steel company. At first he was optimistic about finding work; then he despaired: "There is nothing I can do. I've become a has-been. I've gone from being comfortable to being hungry . . . it's too painful to discuss."[9]

Unemployment could be a shattering experience. Giorgio Ricupero, an electrical engineer, recalled that "the initial phase is very bad. You're very down. You think you're good for nothing. You feel a lot of resentment for the company." He gave up hope of finding a job in his specialty. Al Salvatore had not been thrilled about making public relations films, but when he lost the job, he "felt terrible . . . very insecure, very scared." Grace Keaton never learned why she was fired from her publishing job, but she was devastated. She sent out dozens of résumés. It was especially depressing when the Sunday want ads came out. She "knew it was hopeless from the beginning."

It was not always easy to find work. There were fewer jobs than job seekers, and always discriminations—racial, ethnic, gender, age-based, and other kinds too. Vietnam veteran Anthony Pastorini had trouble finding a position and finally had to take a junkyard job cutting up old cars. But the yard lacked safety precautions, and when he was almost blown up, he quit. African Americans still faced discrimination. Mississippi welfare officials told a black woman with an M.A. that they did not hire blacks, and post offices in Mississippi allegedly did not hire blacks except as letter carriers. Older people complained about hiring bias. Over time the War on Drugs would mean many more people with prison records.[10]

Most of the unemployed worried about money. An unemployed clothing worker with three kids and two mortgages was receiving $48 in weekly benefits, minus what he made working two hours a day as a bartender. Farm worker Juan Camacho, his wife, and four children, received $37 a week. Even with food stamps and welfare assistance, the family fell below the poverty line. Jim Hughes, an unemployed welder, needed a lawyer to help get unemployment benefits. Meanwhile, his family lived on $224 a month from welfare. At times there was no money to put gas in the car or to buy food stamps. "We just went without. We didn't eat . . . three or four days at a time."[11]

In short, new unemployment advocates painted half a picture and sometimes pushed an intentionally harsh agenda. Some researchers were just trying to understand the behavior of people searching for work, but others were conservative propagandists who had little sympathy for the unemployed (especially if they were people of color) and wanted more unemployment rather than less.

If NAIRU Was Flawed, Why Did Many Experts Support It?

NAIRU—non-accelerating inflation rate of employment—had a kernel of truth and many flaws. Truly low unemployment normally encouraged higher pay. But the links from lower unemployment to higher wages and then to price inflation were not simple and often not studied. In modern times, rising wages have rarely been the main cause of rising inflation in the United States. Economist James Galbraith thought he had a better index than NAIRU: NAIROP, or the non-accelerating inflation rate of oil prices.[12]

But if parts of NAIRU were debatable, especially as an explanation for the beginning of inflation surges, as a cure for high inflation it seemed the way to go for many influential people. Very high unemployment meant less economic demand and less upward pressure on prices. And although high unemployment carried many risks for American businesses, it was also a powerful tool in the growing conservative-business campaign to diminish worker power and limit wage growth. *Business Week* said that Americans had to be convinced to get by on less "so that big business can have more." Weakening unions was one method; so was higher unemployment.[13]

But why did quite a few non-conservative, non-business economists and politicians go along with a program that would disproportionately hurt people who were not affluent? I imagine that for many of them a bigger recession was the method that seemed most likely to succeed at lowering inflation rates. Perhaps another reason was that many economists were conservative about markets in fundamental ways and NAIRU seemed like a way to nudge markets to do their work. NAIRU was not exactly laissez-faire; it required decisions and actions by government agents. But in some ways, it was a return to pre-Keynesian austerity economics: stop using government spending and easy money to generate full employment, and let unemployment rise to bring prices down. Quite a few American economists, and not just conservatives, had excessive respect for capitalist markets. Some of them may have thought that limiting government spending and tightening credit were the best ways to let markets work their magic on price inflation.

There is a parallel case in the area of trade. Many liberal economists, sometimes thought to be friends of the working class, were uncritical supporters of "free trade" treaties like the North American Free Trade Agreement (NAFTA). They believed that in the long run everyone would benefit because freer markets promote competition and efficiency, and that must be good. Similarly, in the case at hand, while high unemployment might require government intervention—for example, the Federal Reserve raising interest rates—the method could be thought of as facilitating freer market operations in the form of a recession or, if necessary, a sizable old-time depression to cut economic demand and thus inflation. Whatever the reasons for the ease with which quite a few liberal economists supported programs that harmed workers, few of them spent much energy thinking about alternative ways to limit inflation.[14]

Humphrey-Hawkins: The Battle for Full Employment

As discussed in the last chapter, a handful of liberals in the late '60s began to suspect that War on Poverty programs and scattershot deficit spending were not enough to bring truly full employment. They pressed for direct job creation. In 1971 Democrats in Congress convinced President Nixon to agree to the Public Employment Program (PEP), which supported 185,000 jobs. In 1973 the Comprehensive Employment and Training Act (CETA) added more public jobs for the unemployed. CETA numbers were still low, but some liberal supporters hoped for a larger program of jobs at decent wages. Led by Representative Augustus Hawkins from Los Angeles and Senator Hubert Humphrey of Minnesota, supporters of a serious full-employment program included professor Bertram Gross, a creator of the 1946 full-employment bill, Leon Keyserling, one-time chair of President Truman's Council of Economic Advisors and a steady proponent of full-employment policies, and sixty-nine mostly Democratic senators and representatives. Hawkins introduced the first version of his bill on June 19, 1974. It included a legal government obligation to provide a job for everyone. There would be significant revisions before the Humphrey-Hawkins bill became law in 1978. In the final version, there was not much left about the government's obligation to ensure jobs for everyone, nor of the idea of direct job creation by the federal government.[15]

The first version of Humphrey-Hawkins, the Equal Opportunity and Full Employment Act, obligated the federal government to ensure full employment, and it gave priority to full employment over inflation control. It was to bring full employment in part by utilizing existing federal policies to maximize economic growth, but also by new spending on direct job creation for those who were not being lifted by economic growth. The United States Employment Service, which helped people find work, would be renamed the United States Full Employment Service, and it would house a Job Guarantee Office to make certain that everyone who could not find a job would get useful and rewarding employment. The office was to be supportive of groups that often suffered discrimination, including racial and ethnic minorities, the disabled, veterans, and older workers. The first Humphrey-Hawkins bill did not set a numerical goal for the level of unemployment that might be considered virtually full employment. Rather, full employment was to be achieved by making sure no one who wanted to work was jobless. To add punch to the federal obligation, the law provided that an individual who was not finding a job and not getting help from the federal government could grieve and even sue in district court. Full employment was to be achieved five years after passage. The act also provided funding to study ways to limit inflationary pressures without increasing unemployment.

Humphrey-Hawkins had four main versions. The fourth became law as the Full Employment and Balanced Growth Act of 1978. This final version was cluttered with statements on private-sector job creation and on the importance of a balanced budget. The latter made little sense when full employment might require deficit spending to spur job creation. Above all, missing from the new law was the idea that government had an absolute obligation to provide jobs and that people should have some recourse if neither the private sector nor government would employ them. It might be seen as a plus that the law included numerical goals. Unemployment was to be reduced to 4 percent by 1983 and lower after that. Inflation was to be reduced to 4 percent by 1983 and, amazingly, 0 percent in 1988.

Opponents of earlier versions had objected to the central planning aspects—too much government intervention, too much socialism—but the final version seemed to have more planning and reporting mechanisms than the first version. The president was to announce goals on employment, unemployment, inflation, and other key indicators including output, incomes, balancing the budget, and limiting federal spending. Throughout the final bill, it was apparent that full employment was not the top priority. As further evidence of that point, jobs directly created by the government were to be implemented only as a last resort and not until two years after the law's passage.

In the years ahead, the employment goals of Humphrey-Hawkins would not be met, and it does not appear that people in the Jimmy Carter and Ronald Reagan administrations considered that the law obligated them to do anything to bring full employment. With a strong mass movement to defend its best points, even the weak law could have made a difference. But there was not enough of a movement. Between 1979 and 1989, annual unemployment stayed under 6 percent only three times, and it exceeded 9 percent in 1982 and 1983. Inflation came down in the 1980s, partly owing to the Volcker-Reagan high-unemployment recession of 1981–1983, the worst slump since the 1930s. Outside periods of very high unemployment, there was usually no large-scale full employment movement after the 1970s.

Even without a strong Humphrey-Hawkins, there was significant job growth. The number of people wanting to work zoomed upward. Ten million jobs were added between 1977 and 1980 when Jimmy Carter was president, and twenty million between 1983 and 1990. But these were not enough to provide full employment or decent wages for a ballooning labor force. Real wages fell or stagnated in the 1980s.

Even if Humphrey-Hawkins had come with stronger full-employment guarantees, the political climate was changing in ways that were antithetical to full employment. More American leaders were choosing inflation-control over job-creation. Economists were using versions of NAIRU to define full employment not as jobs for all but as the level of unemployment at which price inflation was steady and modest.

There were organizations that worked for Humphrey-Hawkins and continued to be committed to full employment, including the Congressional Black Caucus, the United Auto Workers, the United Electrical Workers, and the Full Employment Action Council co-chaired by Coretta Scott King and Murray Finley, head of the Amalgamated Clothing and Textile Workers Union. In support of Humphrey-Hawkins, the National Council of Churches had taken the lead in mobilizing at the grassroots. In 1977 a million and a half people were involved in actions across the country for a Full Employment Action Week. So, there was a well of support in the country for full employment.

But some union leaders were tepid supporters. AFL-CIO leaders had pressed successfully to remove from Humphrey-Hawkins the government's legal obligation to provide a job and the job-seeker's right to sue for a job. Also, union leaders believed that Nixon's program had controlled wages better than it controlled prices, and they pressed successfully to delete anything about wage-and-price controls. They may have been right about the way the controls worked, but removing them meant that anyone who was worried that low unemployment caused more inflation would not support a strong bill. One such person was liberal economist Charles Schultze. He had worked for full employment in the Johnson administration, but in hearings on Humphrey-Hawkins, he told the Senate that anything below 5.5 percent unemployment was inflationary. Then, as chief economist for President Carter, Schultze led the administration's effort to deemphasize the full-employment goals of Humphrey-Hawkins. Labor economist and soon-to-be Secretary of Labor Ray Marshall argued ingeniously that it was high unemployment that was inflationary because it meant less output—normally that meant higher prices—but his unorthodox views had little impact.

One might have thought that stagflation in the mid-'70s would have provoked deeper rethinking than it did. Stagflation severed the simplistic Phillips relationship between low unemployment and high inflation. The Phillips curve predicted that high unemployment meant low inflation, but stagflation brought high unemployment and high inflation at the same time. For the most part this anomaly did not end the domination of the Phillips curve and similar straightjackets in textbooks and government policies. Rather, the curve was revised upward. As NAIRU, it still meant that higher unemployment should mean lower inflation, but new economic patterns that favored inflation—automatic cost-of-living increases, for example—might mean that unemployment rates had to be much higher to limit inflationary surges. The principles behind the Phillips curve and NAIRU were the same and there were flaws in each. But NAIRU gave a semi-scientific gloss to harsh unemployment cures for inflation and it helped to exclude other options.

In any case, even if low unemployment were not an adequate explanation for rising prices in the 1970s, it could still be true that very high unemployment, by limiting wage increases and cutting consumer demand, could be a remedy for high prices, no matter what the original causes of the inflation were. And the Volcker-Reagan recession of 1981–1983 worked. Wages fell, and inflation rates did too. There would be nothing close to full employment until 1999–2000.

Indeed, by the late '70s, prominent conservative experts were embracing the end of a full-employment ideal that meant what it said. As inflation picked up in 1977–1978, William Fellner of the conservative American Enterprise Institute wanted "7% unemployment for up to three years . . . there is no other way." In the *Wall Street Journal*, Herbert Stein, one-time Nixon advisor, thought we should just decide that 7 percent unemployment was full employment. To support the relabeling, he used "everybody-knows" arguments: everyone knew America had to import workers to get lettuce picked, and it was "common knowledge that people with jobs are not working. Try to get waited on in a department store." In a way his malicious equation of high unemployment with full employment was prescient. By the '90s and still today, many economists and often the Federal Reserve equate NAIRU, the level of unemployment they imagine is necessary to keep inflation under control, with full employment, regardless of how many people cannot find jobs at reasonable wages.[16]

Perhaps one reason that NAIRU captured university economics departments and the Federal Reserve was the absence of a large enough left-wing/social democratic/worker movement whose members believed instinctively and without reservation that full employment was a human rights issue and had to be implemented. Such a movement could have supported more leftish and socialist economists. Leaders, members, and scholars in such a mass movement had to believe that it was evil to make millions of middle- and low-income workers pay the price for low inflation by losing their jobs. Of course, there were groups that kept the fires burning for full employment, including liberals and leftists and liberal members of the United Church of Christ and other churches. Some of them helped to found the National Jobs for All Coalition in 1994. And there were a lot of labor-liberals around the country—many of the 21,757,000 union members qualified—but they weren't mobilized as a mass force for full employment. Many union members were not even being educated about their own organizations or about the labor movement as a historic force for good. Some were being turned into conservative Republicans by the racist and nationalist appeals of politicians like Richard Nixon and Ronald Reagan.[17]

In the later '80s and the 1990s it seemed that the liberal-left lagged in organization, funding, and self-confidence, while the conservative-business coalition spent more and became more assertive. The Coors family and other right-wing groups subsidized think-tanks and propaganda machines such as the Heritage Foundation and the American Enterprise Institute. These organizations generated arguments for the war on government regulation, minimum wage laws, unions, and aid to poor people and the unemployed. They fostered a climate in which it was acceptable to make fun of poor people and the unemployed. They helped to elect Ronald Reagan.

Mainstream businesses became more right-wing and more aggressive, too. In 1972 John Harper of ALCOA and Fred Burch of General Electric formed the Business Roundtable to organize executives against unions and liberalism. Company bosses learned to be ready to descend on Congress at a moment's notice, and they hired more lobbyists. In 1968 General Motors had three lobbyists in Washington; in 1979, twenty-eight. Although Democrats controlled the Senate, the House, and the Presidency in the late '70s, some liberals became less liberal, and conservatives could rely on a growing number of right-wing Republicans and the old guard of conservative southern Democrats.[18]

As a result, conservatives won four important victories against full employment and worker power in the late 1970s. First, government's obligation to bring full employment was removed from Humphrey-Hawkins. Second, business lobbies and conservative politicians turned back efforts to add bite to federal laws that were supposed to protect unions and union organizers. Third, conservatives and the mainstream press revved up the attack on public service jobs in CETA. Earlier, Nixon and other Republicans had won the battle to limit federal control of the program, but local governments fell down on the job and there were mistakes and corruption in the program's administration. In 1978, when CETA was up for reauthorization, the press had a field day. *Reader's Digest* published a report on a CETA-supported effort that was guaranteed to rile the public: "a nude sculpting workshop . . . in which naked men and women ran hands over one another's bodies." The *New York Times,* the *Washington Post,* and Democratic senators Byrd of West Virginia and Eagleton of Missouri joined the frenzy. CETA's success at employing the unemployed and helping people transition to private-sector jobs did not receive much attention.

Congress mandated new federal controls over CETA, and local officials spent many hours filling out forms. One administrator begged for relief, if only to save Oregon's forests. Congress restricted CETA jobs to the poor and the long-term unemployed. While it was imperative to ensure that poor people were being helped, restricting CETA to the poor made it seem like a welfare program, and that weakened public support. The number of CETA jobs was cut from 725,000 to zero in 1981. That was a big conservative victory—and just as a recession pushed unemployment up to 10 percent.

And that brings us to the fourth victory, this one for conservative austerity economics. In 1978 President Carter appointed Paul Volcker to head the Federal Reserve, with a mandate to take strong measures against inflation. Volcker did, and the result in 1981–1983, as we shall see, was the worst unemployment since the 1930s.[19]

Supply-Side Economics

Ronald Reagan, who would become president in 1981, had promised something better than a giant recession. While conservatives like Herb Stein and Reagan (privately) wanted more unemployment, others were crafting a voter-friendly message to advance conservative goals. Journalist Bruce Bartlett, author Jude Wanniski, and Congressman Jack Kemp argued that the right kind of tax cuts could bring more jobs without causing higher inflation or higher budget deficits. They thought they had found a way around NAIRU, which assumed that high unemployment was essential to controlling inflation.

Their solution was something called supply-side economics, and it turns out that there was not much more to it than the vague hope that labeling tax cuts supply-side would improve the production and supply of goods so that they could be cheaper, or at least that prices would not go up much. Whereas Democratic tax cuts in the 1960s allegedly stimulated only the demand or buying side, which pushed up prices, the new tax cuts were supposed to work on production and work effort—the supply side. Viewed broadly, the supply-side program of tax giveaways and social program cuts was part of an international conservative pushback against economic security and a basic minimum of economic equality. Margaret Thatcher in the U.K. was a leader of this cause.

In retrospect, it is hard to see why people believed that supply-side could accomplish everything that was promised. But from that point in U.S. history, it was a cardinal principle of conservative Republican politics to push for tax cuts for businesses and the affluent, regardless of their value to economic progress. Supply-side was the rationale, but there was nothing particularly supply-side about the Reagan tax cuts in 1981. Most of the program involved across-the-board reductions that favored the rich but gave something to most taxpayers. That meant more consumer demand, although supply-siders talked as though demand-economics were a bad thing. Some supply-siders claimed that huge tax cuts for the rich would provide savings for supply-side investments that would make production more efficient and less costly. The rich would get much richer, but inflation could be controlled without a major recession. But there was no guarantee that rich people would not use their new money to buy Old Master paintings, build mansions, or construct factories abroad. A real supply-side program would have rewarded capitalists only for investing in technologies that made the work process more efficient while also adding jobs.

One highly questionable assertion thrown out by supply-siders was that tax cuts would make employees work more because they'd get to take home more income. That was a possible outcome, but it was also possible, as research had showed, that people would work less when they had more pay. In any case, it was not clear how more work hours from employees solved anything about inflation or productivity except to make an argument that sounded vaguely supply-sidey.

Finally, there was the deficit problem. Conservatives said they hated deficit spending, but the supply-siders were proposing a very large tax cut. That would mean less revenue and higher deficits. Why would conservative Republicans support that? For several reasons. Many of them then and later loved tax cuts much more than they hated deficits. Also, they liked to use budget deficits as an excuse to chop away at liberal income programs, which they disliked more than deficits. Finally, there was the unfortunately named USC economist Arthur Laffer. He came along with a bit of flimflam to give cover to a tax-cut plan that was likely to make federal deficits soar. Laffer argued that at a 0 percent tax-rate on income, the government would collect no revenues; the same was true of a 100 percent tax rate by which government took all earned income because no one would work. Laffer then asserted that the United States was close to 100 percent taxation; tax rates were so oppressive they put a damper on economic activity and tax revenues. He then asserted that Reagan's proposed tax cuts would ignite such an explosion of business activity that total tax revenues would soar, even though rates were lower. But there was no evidence that he was right about where tax rates were on the Laffer curve. In the years after the big 1981 cuts, Reagan and the Congress had to raise taxes several times because of soaring federal deficits.

That was later. In 1980 the tax-cut program appealed to many Republicans, and it could be sold to the public as a cure-all; it would cut taxes, cut inflation, increase government revenues, and create jobs. What's not to like? And the tax-cut program had more appeal to voters in the 1980 presidential election than the anti-inflation program that some conservatives and many economists favored. These people included presidential candidate Ronald Reagan, Federal Reserve Chair Paul Volcker, and Republican economist Herbert Stein. Their solution, not always admitted in public, was to create a really big recession, cut business investment, raise unemployment, and cut economic demand. Wages would stop climbing, more people would be unemployed, and more would have less income, and that meant less upward pressure on prices.[20]

What Really Cured Inflation?

Reagan joined the supply-side camp in 1978. It meshed with his desire to cut taxes and social programs. In the 1980 presidential election he trounced Jimmy Carter, and Republicans captured the Senate for the first time in twenty-eight years. Reagan and the Republicans, with help from some Democrats, enacted legislation to cut personal income taxes by 23 percent over three years. The marginal rate on the rich, which had been over 90 percent during Eisenhower's presidency in the 1950s, was immediately cut from 70 percent to 50 percent.

Did the supply-side medicine cut inflation and boost production? Mostly not. The key weapon in cutting inflation was Federal Reserve action to jack up interest rates and cause the worst recession and the worst unemployment crisis since the 1930s. Business and consumer demand fell. In 1981, 1982, and 1983, unemployment averaged 7.6 percent, 9.7 percent, and 9.6 percent. While some

Reaganites worried about the political backlash, others were honest about the fact that bankruptcies and unemployment were not the problem; they were part of the cure. President Reagan apparently held privately to his belief that the country needed to suffer "two, three years of hard times to pay for the binge we've been on." Behind the scenes, he supported Volcker.

But people got angry. Soaring unemployment helped the Democrats increase their House numbers by twenty-six in 1982. Congress passed a $4.9 billion-dollar public works program, and Volcker lowered interest rates. There were huge budget deficits, caused by the recession, the tax cuts, and massive increases in military spending. That kind of spending had Keynesian results: it promoted economic recovery and job creation, although not higher wages. But conservatives were not supposed to like deficits, so the Reaganites railed at the Democrats for deficits that Republican policies were creating.[21]

The Volcker-Reagan recession brought inflation down from 13.5 percent in 1980 to 3.2 percent in 1983. That was a victory, but not for supply-side theory. High unemployment, lower demand, and weakened employee organizations helped tamp down prices and wages. But why didn't inflation surge again when business and consumer spending picked up? For one thing, world petroleum prices started falling in 1982. Also, at times a stronger dollar made American exports more expensive and destroyed American jobs, but it also made imports cheaper and helped to lower prices. Finally, high unemployment during the recession and in the recovery period and attacks on labor unions reset the balance of power between owners and employees. Many employees were beaten down. If they fought back, they got no protection from the Republican White House or the National Labor Relations Board. Reagan set the tone by firing striking unionized air traffic controllers in 1981. Real wages fell and stayed down in the 1980s. Thus began an historic reversal from the wage gains of previous decades. As the balance of power shifted further toward capitalists, employers became more callous. An auto company employee in the early 1980s recalled that his office was next door to a man who had worked for the company since 1955. "He was the oldest employee in the company. . . . On a Friday afternoon at 4:30 they fired him. He had . . . lived and breathed his work. He was in charge of all . . . the parts warehouses. They decided to consolidate the warehouses and figured he would be unnecessary. So they just fired him. . . . He was in his office and he was crying."

Meanness was in, compassion out. Headhunter John Wareham, writing in the *New York Times,* thought it was a joke to ask how an employer could be certain to hire a "genuine incompetent." The answer was to hire "other people's rejects," people "whose present employers don't want them around anymore." In other words, the unemployed were defective. Other experts recommended laying off older workers. They couldn't keep their skills current, could they? The *California Management Review* offered advice on "How to Fire a Friend."[22]

Some people were extra desperate for jobs, as funding for food stamps, welfare, and unemployment benefits were trimmed. The Reaganites were social Darwinists about worker-friendly programs. Although liberals in Congress resisted, vital programs were cut. Reagan wanted to slash food-stamp funding by 51 percent from its projected level; in the end it was cut 14 percent. Reagan wanted to cut welfare by 29 percent; he got 14 percent. For unemployment benefits, eligibility rules were tightened and federal funding was cut 20 percent. While 76 percent of the officially counted unemployed received benefits in the 1975 recession, only 45 percent did in 1982.[23]

Always bolstering employer power was the surplus of workers. Unemployment stayed above 7 percent for seven years (1980–1986). That was NAIRU with a vengeance. Also, millions of people were not looking for work and were not counted as unemployed, although they were ready to work. The labor glut kept real wages down. In 1980 the average worker earned $8.26 an hour; in 1988, after inflation, only $8.07. More income went to the rich, more to business, and less to workers. Recessions, low wages, and government program cuts added eleven million people to the poverty population (1979–1983) and increased the poverty rate to 15.2 percent, its highest level since 1965. That shows how supply-side medicine failed the people.[24]

The War on Unemployed and Poor People

Job totals increased strongly in the Reagan period, but not spectacularly. Table 4.2 presents a comparison.

The Reagan era had begun with rising unemployment. In 1989, just before the next recession, unemployment was still 5.3 percent, and when government said 5.3 percent, real unemployment was more than 10 percent. For blacks, even their official rate was 11.4 percent and for Hispanics 8 percent. Jobs had increased but so had the population wanting to work. The female labor force grew by more than eleven million (1980–1989) and the immigrant workforce expanded very rapidly.

Labor demand varied around the country. In Santa Ana–Anaheim (California), Boston, and other areas, demand for workers was strong. In other places there were plant shutdowns, pay cuts, and speedups to squeeze more work out of employees. Well-paid union workers were tossed out. General Motors continued to close plants in Detroit. Chrysler shuttered five Detroit plants after receiving a federal bailout.

Table 4.2   Percentage Increase in the Nonfarm Workforce, Eight-Year Administrations

JFK-LBJ	January 1961–January 1969	29%
Nixon, Ford	January 1969–January 1977	16%
Carter	January 1977–January 1981*	26%
Reagan	January 1981–January 1989	18%
Bush I	January 1989–January 1993*	5%
Clinton	January 1993–January 2001	21%
Bush II	January 2001–January 2009	1%
Obama	January 2009–January 2017	9%
Trump	January 2017–January 2019*	13%

*Bush I and Carter four-year records are doubled to make them roughly comparable. Trump's two years are quadrupled. I calculated the percentages in table 4.2 from total jobs in the Current Employment Statistics (CES) of the BLS.

Some decline in the U.S. share of world manufacturing was inevitable as other countries caught up. But political decisions made things worse. Reagan and his successors had no desire to save factory jobs or limit cheap imports. The manufacturing share of the labor force shrank from 30.5 percent (1969) to 25.2 percent (1979) then to 20.3 percent (1989). Here are shocking numbers for the years from 1981 to 1989, the Reagan presidency:

Total nonfarm jobs: +16,131,000
Manufacturing jobs: −582,000

The shrinkage of good blue-collar jobs across the Midwest meant lower living standards and disillusionment for many people. Minorities were hit hard. Half of the black males in heavy manufacturing in the Great Lakes region lost their jobs.[25]

Reagan was unsympathetic. In January 1982 at a press conference, in the midst of the worst recession since the 1930s, he asserted that newspaper help-wanted ads supported his claim that there were plenty of jobs. But many such jobs were part-time positions or very low-wage jobs or not jobs at all. In the real world, Rick Baron was laid off from a $13 *an hour* job in Peoria, Illinois in 1981. He was driving a cab for $10 *a day*. As layoffs at Caterpillar in the early 1980s climbed to 20,000, the social costs were "staggering": wife battering, child abuse, runaways, severe depression, alcoholism, drug abuse, suicide, and homelessness. Sacked after twelve years at Caterpillar, Rick Gillam told a reporter: "If my kids get sick, we couldn't pay it. We'd have to sell the house. How's that for the American dream?"[26]

In 1990 a professor recalled that he had dropped out of college in the 1960s to work in the steel mills. He made "good money . . . got myself an apartment and had all these things . . . (now) you'll get a job at Burger King . . . you can't get married and support anybody if you only work at Burger King." But many conservatives and business leaders wanted the Burger King economy, and they were getting it: more low-wage jobs and less job security. For conservatives, business leaders, neoliberal Democrats, and Federal Reserve officials, too, low pay was not part of the problem; it was key to low inflation and higher profits. During Reagan's eight years, the minimum wage was not raised once.[27]

While the number of good jobs for non-college-educated workers was shrinking, there was also something equally terrible: a new War on Crime and Drugs. It was, in large part, a war on racial minorities. It's true that some African Americans and Hispanics committed crimes, and there really was a crack cocaine epidemic, but the War on Crime and Drugs created millions of new young criminals out of people who hadn't been doing anything wrong or who would not have been arrested if they'd been white. Young men of color were hassled, entrapped, and arrested for lesser amounts of drugs than whites could use with minimal risk of arrest and less chance of conviction. Minority youth were more likely than whites to be arrested for trivial causes, more likely to get poor legal representation, and more likely to be convicted. They were more likely to be shot by police than whites were.[28]

Conservative intellectuals did the most to push toxic narratives of black youth and the need for police repression. But liberals joined in. Journalist Pete Hamill characterized the entire population of nine million poor African Americans as an underclass trapped by drugs, disease, alcohol, welfare dependency, and crime. This underclass was the "most dangerous fact" of daily life in America. Really? How about the shortage of good jobs, or racist ideas emanating from President Reagan and his Justice Department? Bill Moyers, once secretary to President Lyndon Johnson and now revered as a liberal sage, offered *The Vanishing Family: Crisis in Black America* in 1986. This television documentary focused on several black women on welfare and a man who lived off them. Of course, such people existed, but they weren't typical of black poor people. And what were the real causes of black poverty? One was the shrinkage of good jobs accessible to African Americans. Another was racism. A better documentary would have been *Bad Jobs, Vanishing Jobs: the Real Crisis in Black America*.[29]

Good journalists wrote about working-class African Americans who did the right thing and were barely making it. In the *Los Angeles Times*, Barry Bearak wrote about Gilbert Maxwell. He had worked for ten years at a Georgia shrimp factory. He had been promoted to the cleaning crew, which paid $10,800 a year, but he was still $3,400 below the poverty level. Kenneth Jones had a white-collar job at Amtrak that paid almost $30,000, but he was laid off. Most non-affluent people wanted to work and to succeed. As a journalist put it, they shared "the dreams of an industrious nation. . . . They are people like us."[30] There were millions of stories like these, especially for African Americans but for others too. Opportunities for a middle-class lifestyle were shrinking. Average real wages were falling, the rich were getting richer, and think-tank propagandists and misguided or malicious journalists diverted people with tales about a dangerous black underclass.

The racist incarceration mania that was the War on Crime and Drugs served as a way to blame the victims of an increasingly harsh economy for their situation. And it left millions of casualties. By 2010 one in three African American men was a felon or ex-felon. National unemployment was often high, black unemployment was even higher, and a lot of black men weren't even looking for work because they'd tried and given up, or had not even bothered to try. So, they weren't counted as unemployed. They were ostracized for having criminal records and in some cities, parolees and other ex-prisoners were harassed by police forces that behaved like occupying armies in black neighborhoods. Normal life was impossible under such conditions.[31]

It's true that after the Reagan-Volcker recession, job totals increased (1983–1989), but there weren't enough good jobs. Average real wages at the end of the Reagan growth period were 13 percent below where they had been in 1973. And before anything like full employment had been attained, there was a new recession. The unemployment rate climbed to 7.5 percent in 1992. George Bush's secretary of the Treasury said it "was no big deal": we'd pull out of it again. Meanwhile, the authors of mainstream economics textbooks ignored the goal of full employment, replaced it with NAIRU, and claimed that a lot of unemployment was simply a choice made by unemployed persons.

The causes of the new recession included some of the usual suspects: business overinvestment, lax regulation of the financial sector, too much income going to the richest people who did not consume enough of it, and the Federal Reserve's preference for low inflation and slow wage growth over full employment and higher wages. Federal Reserve Chairman Alan Greenspan had raised interest rates to fight inflation, and so unemployment climbed. Job growth eventually picked up, but people were worried. Journalists wrote about a jobless recovery. Greenspan was aware of people's "deep-seated concern," but the Fed's NAIRU policies were one cause of the problem. Inflation hurt workers, but unemployment hurt many of them much more. Greenspan was called the maestro, but sometimes he mostly played one tune: "Fight Inflation."[32]

Pros and Cons of the Clinton-Greenspan Economic Boom

The 1992 election, pitting Republican President George H.W. Bush against Democrat Bill Clinton, occurred while people were still feeling the recession. A sign in Clinton's Little Rock campaign war room shouted this: "IT'S THE ECONOMY STUPID." Clinton ran against a bad economy and won. But he was no left-winger. He'd been active in the Democratic Leadership Council, which was founded to make Democrats more electable by making them more conservative, or neoliberal. Once in office, Clinton deferred to Greenspan, who convinced him that if federal budget deficits got out of control, he'd raise interest rates, and that could bring a new recession. Clinton convinced Democrats in Congress to approve a modest tax increase on the rich to help balance the budget, and he agreed to shelve his campaign promise to spend $50 billion for job training, public infrastructure, and other programs to create jobs and improve productivity. In the years that followed, Greenspan often kept his side of the bargain. Interest rates stayed down and that encouraged investment. He was ever on alert for hints of rising wages and ready to raise interest rates to cool the economy. But despite strong job growth in 1992, 1993, 1994, and after, real wages stayed down until 1997, when a period of significant increases began.

Meanwhile, like many economists and every American president in modern history until Donald Trump, Clinton was an enthusiastic supporter of international free-trade treaties, which eased the export of American jobs. Clinton fought for the North American Free Trade Agreement among Canada, Mexico and the United States. NAFTA added to other factors including automation that helped to shrink the relative size of the manufacturing sector. In the United States in the 1990s, there was a 50 percent increase in construction jobs and professional and business services, but virtually nothing in manufacturing. Reputable studies have suggested that NAFTA caused the loss of a million American manufacturing jobs. America's trade deficit in goods went from $132 billion in 1993 to $447 billion in 2000.While NAFTA boomed Mexico's industrial sector, it allowed large international firms to wipe out many Mexican small farmers.[33]

Clinton also showed his neoliberal free-market credentials by supporting cuts in the welfare rolls and devolving control to the states. These things hurt poor people and sent more of them into the labor force, adding to the worker glut. Under Temporary Assistance for Needy Families (TANF), as welfare was renamed, the rolls were cut in half. Politicians boasted that cutting welfare helped "people on welfare to become self-supporting," but most people shoved off welfare stayed poor. Sometimes "all we're doing is taking the (welfare) poor and making them . . . the working poor." Many of the working poor still required government assistance.[34]

To his credit, Clinton secured more government assistance for low-wage workers. He and the Congress expanded the Earned Income Tax Credit and raised the federal minimum wage to $5.15. These improvements were welcome but did not by themselves do enough to reverse twenty years of low pay. A minimum-wage employee working two thousand hours would now earn only $10,300. That was far below the federal poverty line of $17,463 for two adults and two children in 2000.[35]

In the later 1990s, experts were amazed that unemployment fell to 4.5 percent while inflation stayed low—just 1.6 percent in 1998. Were the Phillips curve and NAIRU finished? Could we have full employment and low inflation? Investment analyst Maureen Allyn said, "You just sit there scratching your head and wondering how we could do this." At the end of the chapter, I will suggest why it seemed possible to have low inflation and low unemployment. Here we should sample workers' stories to get a realistic view of late 1990s job markets. Certainly, it was easier to find work. One weekend, Noralee Gay faxed 250 resumes to employers. On Monday and Tuesday, she received thirty-three calls, and by the end of the week she had real job offers. A club for unemployed professionals and executives had 250 members in the early '90s but only thirty in 1998. Minority unemployment was at its lowest level since the government began keeping good records in 1972.[36]

There may have even been spot labor shortages. People with computing degrees were in high demand. The governor of Iowa and two dozen business leaders traveled to California to ask ex-Iowans to come home. In Tennessee, Whirlpool managers allowed Muslim employees to maintain religious practices at work in order to hold on to them. Staffing services recruited disabled workers. Marriott had recruiters driving around Orange County, California, pitching hotel jobs in front of the courthouse and at the corner taco stand: "If you or someone you know needs a job, our address is on top."

But worker shortages are often a relative matter. If labor shortages had really been widespread, there should have been a bigger wage jump. And there were wage increases, and very low-skilled workers got some of them. Demand for workers was strong in the late '90s and pay was growing. But even when it was more difficult to attract workers, some employers tried to avoid wage hikes by offering shopping discounts, softball fields, and free transportation. Frank Salizzoni of H&R Block asserted that "We have not been pressured to increase pay for workers because of the labor shortage." An Orchard Supply Hardware store was down to twenty-nine workers from sixty, but managers still wanted hirees to accept a poverty wage of $8 an hour. When the Census Bureau offered $14 an hour for temporary positions, there were plenty of applicants. A young man named Conrad Bell was happy to focus on his studies until H&R Block offered him $11.54 an hour and a flexible schedule to answer tech questions on the phone. Quite a few employers were no longer accustomed to working hard to find the right employees, and the press and employers talked too loosely about labor shortages; but in the late '90s, there really was high demand for workers, and that showed up in higher pay. In the years of 1995–2001, real hourly wages for rank-and-file employees increased every year and by a total of 7.7 percent. That was the best period for real wage growth since 1964–1973. As we will see, the good news did not last. From 2002 through 2018, there were just four years in which real wages increased by at least 1 percent—2002, 2015, 2016, and 2018.[37]

Real unemployment, including those who wanted jobs but were not counted as unemployed, was still high and workers' sense of job security was pretty low. There were many layoffs, millions of people just outside the labor force ready to jump in, and millions of part-timers who wanted full-time work. At the height of the boom in 1999–2000, job totals were increasing by 300,000 people a month, indicating high demand for labor, but also a plentiful supply of workers. Economist Brad DeLong wrote, "We seem to keep finding the bodies to hire."

Official unemployment fell down near 4.0 percent. The results felt good to many workers but not to all. In all growth periods, some companies are adding and some are subtracting, but in the 1990s the subtractions were more numerous than expected. Some companies went on hiring sprees; others trimmed their staffs or closed up shop. In 1999 five plants shut down in Farmington, Missouri; one was bike-maker Huffy, which sent jobs overseas. Millions of dollars in public subsidies and the defeat of a union organizing campaign could not keep Huffy in Missouri. The shutdown hurt people like Sherry Sutton, who had been earning $10 an hour. Clinton's economists admitted that the speed at which jobs were being wiped out was high for a period of prosperity. Greenspan admitted that despite apparently low unemployment, workers felt insecure about their jobs, and that kept wages down. At 444 large companies, the fraction of workers who feared job loss more than doubled over 1986–1996 (20 percent vs. 46 percent). Union workers rarely felt confident enough to strike.[38]

The open war on workers was permanent. Investor-shareholders demanded job cuts to pad profits. Slashing payrolls in good times made for a new euphemism: "downsizing." Chainsaw Al Dunlap earned his reputation by firing people at Scott Paper and Sunbeam. Even skilled workers had trouble. In the Silicon Valley, machinist Finn Runge was laid off six times in two years. Michael

Pachter, ARCO's director of strategic planning, got wind of big layoffs, took a generous severance package, and left. He learned that "you should watch out for yourself and not count on corporations to take care of you." The idea that a loyal, well-paid workforce promoted productivity, creativity, and service went out with the trash.[39]

National poverty rates fell close to record lows in the late 1990s, but higher levels of poverty were common in many parts of the country. In Los Angeles County, new jobs often paid less than $25,000, especially for workers in restaurants, child care, and light-manufacturing shops. Compton, California, and South Central Los Angeles had been scarred by decades of capital flight and the 1992 riots. People were moving back and so were a few big retailers. But there were still many abandoned stores, piles of trash, and idle adults on street corners. Unemployment was 11 percent and the poverty rate 33 percent in Compton in the late 1990s.

In New York City, immigrants and people kicked off welfare flooded labor markets. The governor's economist, Stephen Kagann, claimed that "Employers are very hungry for people. What hungry employers do is bid up wages." But many people did not see much improvement. In the Bronx, a fifty-eight-year-old woman named Gloria Pye worked fifty-five hours a week at $7.19 an hour, trying to pay for hypertension drugs and missed rent payments. Andres Pulinario, a Dominican immigrant, earned $5.27 an hour at a Bronx meat-packing plant. His fifteen-year-old daughter worked twenty-five hours a week at a supermarket. "Sure, I worry that it will hurt her in school, but what can you do? Some months it's difficult trying to pay the rent on time."[40]

It was a bad economy and a good one. Much of the increased income created by workers was grabbed by the top 1 percent. Executive pay jumped from eighty-five to 326 times average pay (1990–1997). On the plus side, there were enough new jobs and job mobility that many young adults who had not finished high school were doing a little better. The poverty rate fell to 11.3 percent in 2000, close to the record low of 11.1 percent in 1973. And the job boom and the lowest unemployment in years did lift people. Adelicia Bermudez, a twenty-three-year-old high-school dropout and mother of two, got a job. The day after she interviewed with an insurance business, she was hired at $9 an hour, and the next morning she was at work. Sprint finally opened an office in the center of Kansas City. After seventeen years on welfare, Carla Williams was earning enough at Sprint to buy her first car, get married, and stash $20 a week in the company 401(k). But it was easy to see the job ladder taken away. Shanna Wicks had been among 780 people on welfare hired by Packard Bell at $5.25 an hour at a new assembly plant in Sacramento, California. She was promoted several times and was earning $12.50 an hour in 1999. Then came an industry slow-down, and Packard Bell laid off three of every four former welfare recipients.

Meanwhile, a group of once prosperous adults including managers, skilled technicians, and well-paid factory workers were left behind by recessions, defense cutbacks, deindustrialization, and downsizing. Pundits and scholars had often stereotyped jobless African Americans as the "hardcore" unemployed. Now they accentuated the negatives about older workers: such workers, it was said, were worth less because their skills weren't up to date and, apparently, could never be. A Stanford University sociologist noted that many employers considered that once an applicant passed fifty, he was less flexible and had fewer years of service to give the employer; hence, he was a less desirable employee.[41]

Although many people still needed jobs, Fed Chairman Greenspan worried that the economy was growing too fast for the available pool of workers. In 1999 he began to raise interest rates. Yet hiring continued at a brisk pace. Wages rose but there were still quite a few people ready to go to work. While Greenspan was beginning to act in ways that would limit job growth, he did not put his staff to work on anti-inflation methods that did not require more unemployment. And he did not campaign against the most egregious inflation of his time, the soaring incomes of the top 1 percent. Nevertheless, given that he was very conservative, Greenspan did pretty well, allowing unemployment to fall below 5 percent, even when colleagues told him not to. But the range of his thinking on wages and inflation was narrow and, ultimately, class-biased in ways that favored the 1 percent at the top. That was the norm for Federal Reserve chairs.[42]

The End of NAIRU? Recapping the 1990s Boom

What was behind the low-inflation job boom of the late '90s? It seemed to disprove NAIRU, for there was very low unemployment, low inflation, and significant wage increases.

Unlike most strong growth periods in the decades after World War II, this one was not propelled by Keynesian-style deficit spending. Actions by Clinton and Congress, and economic growth too, reduced annual deficits. There was even a budget surplus at the end of the decade.

Second, many people, including Clinton and Secretary of Labor Robert Reich, talked up the importance of education and job training, but advances in that area had little to do with the '90s boom. School years and skill levels had been rising over three decades as wages fell and unemployment rose. Two-thirds of new jobs did not require a college degree or advanced training, and still don't.

Third, one source of the Clinton-Greenspan boom was essential. When Greenspan thought wages and prices were under control, he kept interest rates down. Easy money contributed to wealth creation on the stock market, more business investment, and more spending all the way around. The downsides were soaring personal debt and overinvestment in dot.com businesses and real estate. Stock values were out of kilter too, increasing by ten trillion dollars. The 1990s boom was, in part, a financial bubble—inflated prices for stocks and other assets and very high debt levels. It was not a good model for the next century.

Finally, economic success in the 1990s required that price increases stay moderate. But how could that happen if spending was rising and if higher demand for workers and lower unemployment pushed wages up, and consistently faster than prices? How long could that go on? There seem to be several answers. First, there were a number of anti-inflation forces at work. Labor productivity rates increased in the late '90s. Higher productivity meant employers were getting more per hour out of every worker and that could support higher pay. At the same time, the continuing flood of cheap imports and lower oil prices kept consumer prices down even as demand was growing.

Another explanation is that real unemployment was higher than the official figures showed, and so workers' bargaining leverage, while improved, was still weaker than official unemployment rates indicated. There were still many people ready to work. Even in a boom year like 1997, four thousand people applied at the Roosevelt Hotel in New York City for seven hundred mostly low-wage jobs. Throughout the decade, immigrants supplied millions of new workers, and there were eleven million more women in the labor force in 2000 than in 1990. When the government said unemployment was 4 percent, things were much better than usual, but real unemployment was still probably around 10 percent. Furthermore, many employers were quick to threaten to send jobs abroad, and they did send them away.

Finally, add the fact that unions covered a shrinking fraction of the workforce and you have another explanation for why the lowest unemployment since the 1960s did not bring more than 8 percent in total real wage increases over the boom years of 1995–2001. It's true that 8 percent was the best record of any group of years after the 1970s. But it was only half as good as it ought to have been. There was something true about one aspect of NAIRU: even in a job boom, if real unemployment, counting hidden unemployment, were quite high and the non-employed labor supply still quite large, and if union power represented a relatively small number of workers, employers would not have to offer very large increases in real wages to attract new workers.[43]

CHAPTER 5

Low Pay, Great Recession
(2001–2018)

The worst economic slump since the 1930s began in 2007. It was deep and long. The official business cycle dating committee announced that economic recovery started in June 2009, but the key indicator for most people, unemployment, stayed high for a long time. It reached 10 percent in October 2009, and was still above 7 percent in 2013. And these rates did not include people who wanted jobs but weren't searching for them because they believed they weren't there.

Government spending brought the country back from the abyss of a Great Depression, but recovery programs did not reverse long-term ailments: four decades of mostly stagnant real wages; a large population of uncounted job-wanters; and extreme unemployment differentials for different classes and social groups, notably African Americans, whose rates were always twice as high as the national numbers. You might have thought that the Great Recession would give a boost to those who wanted permanent repairs for the economy and deliver a rebuke to those who wanted less regulation, fewer programs for workers and the poor, and more money for people who already had most of the money. But while there were new movements for better wages and against inequality and a few new regulations in the Obama years, there would be no second New Deal for workers and almost nothing to reverse inequality trends.[1]

The Great Recession wiped out $16 trillion in wealth, but corporate profits, stock prices, and the wealth holdings of rich households recovered faster than did job growth, average incomes, and the assets of working-class households.

For the richest 1 percent, the recession was a brief intermission in their long campaign to acquire more money. The 1 percent had captured 12 percent of all pretax income in the 1960s. In the 2010s, they garnered 20 percent. The poorest 50 percent of the households went from earning 20 percent of all pretax income in the 1960s to earning just 12 percent in the 2010s.[2]

This chapter covers the 2001 recession and recovery and the Great Recession, its causes, and the recovery period. It does so with two focuses. First, there are numbers and people's stories about the severity of the crisis. Second, there is analysis of the policies, ideas, and interest groups that caused the recession, retarded recovery, and stymied efforts to deal with the long-term deficit of good jobs. Without understanding what happened and why, it is difficult to form realistic positions about what should be done for the future. Broadly speaking, the Great Recession was the outcome of a forty-year business-conservative-neoliberal campaign to cut taxes on the rich, cut regulations on businesses, and keep American workers underpaid and underemployed. The campaign succeeded. Lacking adequate incomes for a reasonable down payment on the American dream, millions of workers overborrowed, and bankers and people in government encouraged them to do it. The result was a disaster that many experts said could not happen.

Jobless Recovery, Lagging Wages, and the Debt-Bubble Boom (2001–2007)

Job creation had surged in the late 1990s and, as we have seen, real wages rose more strongly than they had in decades. Unemployment and inflation were both low. But Federal Reserve officials began to worry that "inflation risks would rise if the labor market were allowed to tighten further." In June 1999 the Fed started raising interest rates to slow down business activity and demand for labor. Soon, the boom in the tech sector and in commercial real estate faltered and the associated stock bubble burst. As a recession began in the spring of 2001, the Fed reversed course and began cutting interest rates to spur economic activity.[3]

The expansion of 2001–2007 brought neither the best of times nor the worst. Poverty rates did not fall as much as they normally do in growth periods. Manufacturing jobs had begun to fall in 1998 and they declined by 2.2 million between January 2001 and January 2007. Millions of people who were not under the government's extra-low poverty lines were still really poor. But money was cheap, home buying boomed, and real estate prices soared. Some people learned to buy and sell homes quickly to make a killing on rising prices; others refinanced their mortgages to get more cash. Things got crazy. House-flipper Marshall Whittey was raking in the money, and he "bought a new truck just 'cause I didn't like the color" of the old one. But tens of millions of people were poor or almost poor. Single mom Dorothy Thomas earned as much as $22 an hour, but living in a nicer neighborhood with good schools for her daughters was often beyond her income. She maxed out her credit cards and could not pay her car registration or the ticket she got for the expired registration. Her vehicle was impounded, she could not get to work, and she lost her job as a hospital administrator. She became homeless.[4]

Debt is vital for economic growth, but very high debts laid on people of modest incomes can be hazardous. Personal debt was growing 8 percent a year in the early 2000s, twice the rate of the 1990s. The financial bubble around housing was paying off for banks and for millions of homeowners. But homeowners had to be earning enough to make their mortgage payments. They had to be able to sell their homes if they found that they could not afford their mortgages. Prices had to keep rising so that owners' equity was rising; equity was collateral for refinancing mortgages and borrowing money for consumer purchases. It was a fragile structure, but experts assured the public that home prices would not fall.[5]

But economic fundamentals were not strong enough to support such a vast expansion of risky personal debt. The real wage of the average employee did increase but only by a total of 3.5 percent from 2000 through 2007. And that period included four years with no increases at all. Median family income in 2007 was less than it had been in 2000. Meanwhile, lobbyists working for corporations, rich people, and conservative causes made things worse. The Bush tax cuts of 2001 and 2003 favored affluent households. The richest 257,000 taxpayers already had more money than they could use, but they were handed a cash pile that equaled the total tax break of eighty-five million people at the bottom. The new cuts were a handout to those who ruled the economy; the cuts did not come with sound arguments about their necessity for job growth, and, unless you believe that everything people can grab belongs to them, they lacked moral purpose.[6]

The trickle-down theory that tax cuts for the rich meant good things for workers was questionable at best. After the Reagan and the Bush tax cuts, there were no unusual bumps in business investment. The annual trade deficit would double between 2001 and 2006, and three million factory jobs were lost in 2000–2007, even before the Great Recession. Private-sector employment sank in 2001–2004. Although an increase in government jobs helped, observers talked about a jobless recovery. Eventually the unemployment rate fell below 5 percent. But many people did not bother to look for work. Profits were growing

14 percent a year, but automation, outsourcing, more temporary workers, and less unionization meant harder times for many workers.[7]

These were problems that ruling business and political elites did little to address. For many business leaders they were solutions, not problems. At the Federal Reserve, Alan Greenspan wasn't pushing to raise pay for the average worker. He often interpreted rising wages as a threat rather than an opportunity for less risky economic growth. To keep the economy from overheating, he raised interest rates seventeen times between July 2004 and July 2006. For Greenspan and other conservatives and neoliberals, rising wages were often a problem, but super-inflated executive compensation packages were just fine.

The long-term stagnation of average wages did not just happen on its own. Business, conservative, and centrist/neoliberal leaders wanted it that way. As mentioned, Greenspan often used rising wages as a portent of higher prices. Other economists backed him up; it had been a matter of faith in the profession that low unemployment meant high wages and accelerating inflation. Surprisingly, in the late '90s, Greenspan went against the numbers attached to NAIRU, but he never threw out the core idea. Nor did other economists. In January 2007, the usually level-headed Mark Zandi of Moody's Investment Service warned that we had reached full employment, and that jobs and wages were growing so fast they would start an inflationary surge. But inflation rates were not particularly high and the housing boom was already cooling. Real wages increased an average of a half a percent a year (2000–2007). Although demand for labor was supposed to be high and official unemployment, at 4.4 percent in March 2007, was thought to be close to full employment, it really wasn't. There were twelve million job-wanters on the sidelines. In January 2006, 24,500 people lined up for 375 jobs at a Wal-Mart near Chicago. That doesn't look like a full-employment economy.[8]

A Scam Economy: The Housing Bubble of 2001–2007

The Great Recession that began in 2008 was rooted in a mostly unregulated financial sector, and an extremely unequal distribution of income. Over the years, affluent households, and especially the top 1 percent, were taking a larger piece of the national income pie. The pie got bigger, but for most members of the working class, the pieces did not. Real wages for the vast majority of employees went up and down a bit over forty years, but they ended in the 2010s about where they had been in the early 1970s.

Consistently growing real incomes for a hundred million workers would have been a sounder basis for economic growth. But instead of less inequality,

Americans got a huge bubble of private debt. As managed by the Federal Reserve, more private debt was the nation's main job-creation policy. Coming out of the 2001 recession, the Federal Reserve pushed interest rates way down. Borrowing was cheap. Democrats and Republicans talked up homeownership. People wanted to own their own homes, even if they had low incomes. Some of them made "harebrained decisions." But bankers, who were supposed to guide them, were con artists. They had united "around high-risk mortgage lending as their primary cash crop." Fraud was common.[9]

The mortgage problems that beset home buyers included these:

- In 2005, 43 percent of new buyers made no down payments. That seemed like a gift but it came with higher interest rates and bigger mortgage payments.
- Subprime loans came with higher interest payments for people with poor credit and limited incomes. Some subprime loans should never have been made because lenders lacked evidence of borrowers' earning power. But loan-agents received bonuses for selling riskier loans. They even pushed subprime loans on people who qualified for regular mortgages.
- Many borrowers did not understand what they were getting into. Some could not read English and lenders had reasons not to help them understand what they were getting into. Lending agents could earn up to seven times as much for subprime as for prime mortgages, so they took advantage of unsophisticated borrowers.
- Adjustable Rate Mortgages—ARMs—began with low interest rates, but if other rates went up, ARMS went up. In 2004 Greenspan claimed that people were wasting money if they did not have ARMs. But when he raised rates in 2004–2006, he raised mortgage bills.

It is true that borrowers should have been smarter. They should have researched what they were doing, and they should have been more cautious. But most people did not have the time or the skills to figure out the small print. They were getting bad advice from professionals who had no sense of responsibility for their less knowledgeable clients. Government regulators and many politicians did not help. Here are four examples.

- Some government regulations had been eliminated, others were unenforced, and financiers created new instruments and new labels to evade regulation. The Federal Reserve could have regulated more, but Greenspan believed businesses would regulate themselves.
- Bankers bundled mortgage loans and sold the bundles to others. The bundles were used as collateral for bonds; investors bought the bonds and

depended for earnings on homeowners paying their monthly mortgage bills. Connections and responsibilities got murky.

· Credit agencies that rated the risk-level of mortgage bonds were paid by the banks that were selling the securities. In effect, bankers were buying high ratings. Imagine that students could pay their teachers to get A's in all their classes.

· Investors could buy insurance (credit default swaps) to protect themselves in the event that homeowners could not make their mortgage payments, but nothing assured that insurers were not underfinanced and liable to collapse if many homeowners defaulted. One such insurer, AIG, would require a massive infusion of federal money after the crash.[10]

Business First, Wages Last: Bad Economic Ideas

Why weren't politicians and financial leaders more cautious? First, the debt-boom was hugely profitable for bankers and others who offered or invested in mortgages. Second, business and political elites were reckless because of the climate of opinion about what was right and efficient. Economists, Wall Street executives, conservative Republicans, and Clinton Democrats exaggerated the virtues of lightly regulated capitalism. They believed in a set of ideas that added up to a business-first ideology. These ideas rationalized carelessness about the banking system and indifference to the fate of half of the population that had to deal with poverty and economic insecurity and lousy jobs. Here are some of the most important business-first ideas.[11]

The Great Moderation: Recessions are rare and mild. Conservative economist Robert Lucas declared that the "problem of depression-prevention has been solved." Some claimed that balanced budgets were the key to prosperity, but except for the Clinton years, this was not often true.[12]

Efficient Markets: Prices generated in financial markets are the best estimate of the real value of investments. How did we know? Greenspan claimed that "hundreds of thousands of informed investors" could not be wrong, could they?[13]

Trickle-Down Economics: Policies that benefit the rich benefit everyone; tax cuts favoring the top 1 percent bring more jobs. But if wages stay low and one in five people are poor or nearly poor, where's the trickle down?

Business Bosses Need More Power, Workers Less: Conservatives, centrists, and even some liberals accepted that owners and managers should thoroughly dominate employees. Wages and hours laws, safety regulations, and laws protecting the right to unionize were often unenforced. The conservative-business campaign that began in the 1970s to reduce busi-

ness regulations and worker-friendly programs had been partly successful. Bankers were at liberty to do as they pleased. Employees received little
government support for unionization and higher pay. But one consequence
of disempowering employees and quashing wages was that millions of
workers had to assume too much debt to buy a home.

Privatization: Most of what government does is inefficient and harmful.
Government regulations hinder growth, and firms can police themselves
because it is in their interest to do so. But what if business leaders are
obsessed with short-term profits, apathetic about the harm they inflict on
people, and unconcerned about the risky economic instruments they are
creating?

The Official Unemployment Rate Measured All the Truly Unemployed: But if
that were so, why didn't full or almost full employment send inflation rates
soaring in the late '90s when unemployment was under 5 percent almost
every month from 1997 through 2001? What happened to the NAIRU assumption that low unemployment would ignite inflation surges? There
were several explanations, but one of the most important was not often
applied to the NAIRU riddle, and that was that actual unemployment was
quite high. There were millions of people who we would normally expect
to be working, but who did not show up in the official numbers as searching for work. The slow job recovery of the early 2000s received comment,
and the left-outs were discussed by journalists and studied by scholars,
but their existence did not have much impact on broad assumptions about
the limitations of the official unemployment count. In part that was because there was a bag of explanations that removed such people from the
category of being unemployed. One was that such government benefits as
disability payments encouraged people not to work. Another was the assumption that not working was a choice. This was part of the equipment of
many search theorists, whether conservative or liberal. It was a fundamental assumption of many conservative economists. And obviously, there is
some element of choice in not taking a job that will not support a decent
living standard. It is true that if more people would work for five dollars an
hour, there would be more jobs. But people should be able to find jobs that
provide a decent living. That side of the equation is underplayed and in its
most extreme formulation, choice theory led to the conclusion that even
in recessions, unemployment was just "a voluntary decision by workers to
take time off until conditions improve."[14]

The takeaway from this last point is that many economists and policy-makers, especially but not only conservatives, were in active denial about the extent
of real unemployment. This meant that the United States would not solve its

long-term job shortage problem—not in 2010 when even official unemployment was very high or in 2015 when official unemployment was falling. In 2016 Donald Trump appealed to many of the workers who were being left behind even as the economy was reaching officially low levels of unemployment. But he hadn't a clue about real solutions, and he belonged to a party dominated by Tea Party social Darwinists. More about them later.

The Great Recession Begins

The financial sector crashed in 2008. The immediate cause was that people had mortgages they could not afford. In 2006 home prices began slipping. As prices fell, homeowners lost equity and the collateral they needed to refinance for lower monthly mortgage payments. Meanwhile, adjustable rate mortgage resets raised monthly payments. Ben Bernanke, Greenspan's successor at the Fed, was a scholar of the Great Depression. He told Congress that the subprime crisis would do little damage to the economy. But economist Nouriel Roubini showed that 30 percent of all employment growth was dependent on the housing boom, including construction workers, real estate agents, and bank employees. If the housing market crashed, the whole economy would collapse.[15]

By 2007 Fed officials were worried. They began cutting interest rates to promote lending and spending. But many authorities stayed confident. In January 2008, a financial expert in the House of Representatives, Massachusetts Democrat Barney Frank, claimed that the economy was "more prone to bubbles but less prone to severe recession."[16]

Banks before People

On September 15, 2008, Lehman Brothers, an investment house with massive debts, was allowed to crash. President Bush's Treasury secretary, Henry Paulson, thought this was the way to go—let the market do its work. But the event shattered confidence on Wall Street. Banks stopped lending and investors rushed to buy U.S. Treasury bills that offered low interest but high safety. Unemployment reached 7.2 percent in December. Was a 1930s-style Great Depression on the way?[17]

As the world financial system teetered, Secretary Paulson changed his mind about the glories of the free market and letting big banks collapse. With support from Fed Chair Bernanke, Paulson, who came from Goldman Sachs, a leader in creating risky mortgages, gave Congress and the American people an ultimatum: provide the banks with billions of dollars in aid or take the blame for driving the world economy over the cliff.

An ethical policy for the banks and the people would have included provisions for breaking up the biggest banks. If some banks were "too big to fail," as people said in defense of federal subsidies, then they were too big to exist. Also, an ethical plan required that bankers offer assistance to troubled homeowners, perhaps by reducing mortgage payments. Paulson's initial idea for the Troubled Asset Relief Program (TARP), which the Congress passed as the Emergency Economic Stabilization Act on October 3, 2008, might have helped in this respect. Paulson wanted the federal government to purchase bad assets from the banks in order to improve their financial position and to encourage them to ramp up lending again. The TARP law specified that government was to act to protect home values, college accounts, and other personal assets and to preserve homeownership. Under Section 109 of the law, the secretary was "to maximize assistance to homeowners." But rather quickly officials decided that the task of buying and managing bad assets to help homeowners as well as bankers was too difficult. That approach was jettisoned in favor of federal investments in bank stock, and thereafter not much was done for homeowners. Key people in the Bush and the Obama administrations did not rate the troubles of homeowners as a priority. Tim Geithner, Obama's chief advisor on the bank crisis, worried much more about the banks—he knew them intimately from his time as head of the New York Federal Reserve—than he did about homeowners losing their homes. He and colleagues in the administration believed that the failure of one large bank would cause much more chaos than if a million homeowners defaulted. And a segment of the general population did not want to help homeowners. When the announcement came that Obama wanted to use bailout funds to help poor and minority homeowners facing foreclosure, CNBC commentator Gene Santelli went into a tirade that helped birth the Tea Party.

TARP included several programs. One of the most important invested federal funds in banks and other financial institutions to prevent a cascade of business failures and to encourage the banks to start lending again. TARP money also went to prop up auto companies. Banks and other companies that received capital infusions eventually paid back most of what they received from the federal government. But presidents and legislators did not use the leverage they possessed to require assistance for home buyers. Nor did they push efforts to prosecute criminals. Obama's Justice Department succeeded in going after little people committing small crimes, such as four people in Tacoma who made false statements on loan applications and five Californians who engaged in bid-rigging at a foreclosure auction. But the Department of Justice did not arrest and charge the bosses of big banks whose employees deceived inexpert clients, or companies like AIG that failed to set aside sufficient reserves to cover most emergencies. The ties between the big bankers and political leaders in both parties were close. There was a revolving door between the financial and the political sectors in terms of personnel and money. Party wasn't an issue. Bush's secretary, Henry Paulson, came from Goldman Sachs, and Goldman Sachs contributed one million dollars to Obama in 2008. Lawyers working for the banks and lawyers working for the government were the same kind of people at different stages of their careers. Their children went to the same prep schools; they inhabited the same social set, a network that did not include representatives of average families who were losing jobs and homes.[18]

TARP was just one of several programs to rebuild the financial sector and restart economic growth. The Federal Reserve cut interest rates to zero and sent trillions of dollars as loans and bond purchases to dozens of institutions. The amounts were staggering, but so was the problem. Bernanke learned fast to open the Fed's money faucet, and eventually he put low unemployment back on the Fed's priority list, along with low inflation. But the Fed did little to aid drowning homeowners. As people lost jobs and home values sank, household wealth fell by $17.6 trillion—a 25 percent decline in two years. Becoming poorer, people tried to limit their buying; employers had no reason to hire workers when their customer base was shrinking. But fewer employees meant fewer people with incomes to buy stuff. It was a vicious circle.[19]

More money in circulation and lower interest rates were insufficient to bring recovery in the midst of a severe crisis of confidence and huge declines in wealth and income held by the people. The economy was stuck in a hole of inadequate private demand. An obvious solution was for the federal government to borrow and spend more, and/or also to cut taxes for those who would spend new money. Deficit spending would put more income into the economy than it took out. But it mattered very much whose taxes got cut and where the new spending went. Economist Mark Zandi, who served as advisor to presidential candidate John McCain, estimated that extending the Bush tax cuts and cutting corporate taxes meant less economic demand than additional federal spending on food stamps, unemployment benefits, and infrastructure.[20]

Obama's Stimulus Program: Pros and Cons of ARRA

In 2008 President Bush's tax rebate program gave middle- and low-income families up to $1,200. That was not enough to stop the recession in its tracks. As Barack Obama took office, his team developed a large spending package to send to Congress. Most Republicans joined Senator Mitch McConnell and Representative Eric Cantor in a campaign to ridicule the stimulus plan and the president. Of course, it is standard in party politics to make the other party look bad, but Republicans took this approach to a new level during a crisis that threatened the world with a second Great Depression.[21] Only three Republicans voted for the bill. But it passed and Obama signed the American Recovery and Reinvestment Act (ARRA) on February 17, 2009. ARRA provided $787 billion for two years. Here are important elements of ARRA; most were effective and many were worker-friendly:

- "Making Work Pay," a $116 billion cut in taxes on lower and middle incomes. That promoted consumption power.[22]
- Green America: tax breaks for renewable energy, green workers, and energy efficiency. This initiative included $50 billion for rail transit, $11 billion to improve the electricity grid, and money to add electric vehicles to the federal fleet.
- $86.8 billion for Medicaid, and $53.6 billion to help school districts save jobs. This was probably the most focused and fastest-acting job-saver in the whole bill.
- Money to prevent homelessness, $20 billion more for food stamps, a one-time $250 extra payment to Social Security and SSI recipients and disabled vets, and more for Head Start and Pell Grants.
- For the unemployed, there was $40 billion to extend benefits beyond twenty-six weeks and to increase the weekly amount by $25. There was money to pay 65 percent of COBRA bills for some of the jobless.
- There wasn't much for homeowners facing foreclosures, and during Obama's first term, "federal efforts to support the housing market (were) . . . missing in action."[23]
- When we recall 1930s job programs, we often think of infrastructure projects. ARRA had some, but not enough; $105 billion went to road and bridge projects, improving Defense Department facilities, developing high-speed trains, repairing harbors and federal buildings, computerizing medical records, and extending broadband and wireless access. These things spurred job growth and improved economic efficiency. But more should have been spent. Obama's people had decided they could not get more than $800 billion for two years, so they did not try to get more.[24]

Did the stimulus program and Federal Reserve money policies work? ARRA created or saved several million jobs and helped keep the economy from falling into a Great Depression. But ARRA spending was only 2 to 3 percent of a $15 trillion-dollar-a-year economy. Table 5.1 (later in this chapter) shows how far behind Americans still were in December 2012. They needed bigger deficits and more federal job programs. They really needed a second New Deal to end the recession and to fix long-term job and wage problems. Republican opposition to anything Obama wanted was one reason spending was too small and there was no New Deal. Also, Obama's team should have tried harder to build support among voters and in Congress for long-range job programs that responded to the recession crisis and the long-term deficit of good jobs. But many Democratic advisors and national politicians held conservative ideas about the value of budget deficits and high wages. They identified less with workers than with bankers—and quite a few were bankers.[25]

The Tea Party and Some Democrats against Full Employment

Conservative politicians attacked Obama for increasing federal debt. It was a matter of faith and tactics for many conservatives that federal debt was risky—although not a problem if the cause were a tax cut that favored the rich, as we would see later with Trump and a Republican-controlled Congress. Republicans liked to scare people about deficits as a way to motivate cuts in federal programs that helped the working class. In reality, there wasn't much evidence that annual deficits or the total accumulated debt hurt economic growth. Or that deficits caused inflation, as was claimed in the 1970s. Federal debt was soaring but inflation stayed low.

The deficits in Obama's early budgets were in accord with what most economists had learned from Keynes and from history. But the anti-debt campaign heated up in 2010, even though unemployment stayed high. This was standard operating procedure for Republican right-wingers: if Democrats were for it, they were against it. But independent minds and leaders who should have known better joined in. Deficit spending was saving the country from a big depression, so it is not clear why centrists and liberals joined the campaign. Some mainstream economists and political centrists like Thomas Friedman at the *New York Times,* Peter Orzag, Obama's budget chief, and Robert Rubin, a Wall Street tycoon who had been Bill Clinton's Treasury secretary, began to obsess about deficits. Obama even created a committee of deficit-o-phobes and he seemed to believe at times that cutting deficits was more important than cutting unemployment.[26]

But probably the most dogmatic foes of budget deficits and of federal spending for the poor and the unemployed came from a new formation in the Republican Party called the Tea Party. Some rank-and-file Tea Partiers were worried about losing what they had. A number had been deindustrialized out of good jobs. Neither party had done much to help people, especially those without college degrees, who had lost high-quality jobs. Every Democratic president pushed for free-trade treaties that eliminated good jobs.

Most Tea Partiers were not poor and were not deindustrialized workers, but many of them hated liberal ideas and modern America. They hated the first black president; they railed against federal authority (for example, federal control of federal lands); they feared or hated immigrants, poor people, and, apparently, foreclosed homeowners; they demonized food stamps and other programs that helped poor people. At times, Tea Party members seemed willfully uneducated about economics and power. They rarely criticized capitalists and the rich. They benefited from the donations of wealthy conservatives, such as the Koch Brothers, who wanted to cut Social Security and Medicare—programs that many Tea Party supporters were happy to have.[27]

Increased federal spending and massive budget deficits had fueled job creation in World War II, in the 1950s and 1960s, in the Reagan years, in 2003–2005 when Bush's deficits topped $300 billion a year, and in 2009–2013. But Tea Partiers and other Republican conservatives had learned from Ronald Reagan to stay off the reality train and to attack Democrats and liberals, especially on deficits, even as they themselves demanded big tax cuts that would increase deficits. Ranting about deficits excited conservative voters, kept Democrats off balance, and kept job-creation programs small.[28]

Coping

Even as the economy improved in 2011, 2012, and 2013, poverty rates stayed high; in 2011, 46,247,000 Americans—15 percent of the population—were poor, even using low government poverty lines. That was ten million more than in 2006. In September 2012, twenty-seven million people were either officially unemployed, part-timers who wanted full-time jobs, or people who wanted work but had not recently searched for it.[29]

Unemployment meant lost income, homelessness, and high levels of stress and even despair. The recession caused fifteen hundred suicides per year. More people had to live in shelters, tents, and battered cars and trailers. Near Ann Arbor, Michigan, a village of thirty tents was occupied by people who had no jobs or earned too little to pay rent. The city of Ann Arbor's shelters were jammed. In Santa Barbara, California, car-sleeping was common. A few brave souls lived under Las Vegas in storm drains that occasionally filled with rushing water.

Many people had been poor before the recession, but many who had not been poor were now scrambling to come up with carfare to get to a job interview. They had to decide where to get that aching tooth pulled: by the questionable dentist around the corner who charged $25.00, or students at the university dental school that charged $97.00.[30]

People adapted and learned. Kris and Jim Fallon were earning $100,000 when both lost their jobs. Jim found three months of work out of state, and Kris used food banks. "I never understood why there were so many food pantries and why people couldn't just get on their feet and get going, but now that I'm in it, I fully understand." Food pantries were one way to survive. More important was the food stamp program, which was reaching forty-seven million people in 2012. For many conservatives, food stamps were evil, perhaps because they wanted to believe that most recipients were black and because they thought poor people weren't trying hard enough.[31]

Obviously, more people needed assistance during the recession, but the welfare system had become stingier in 1997, and its name was changed from Aid to Families with Dependent Children to Temporary Assistance for Needy Families. The rolls were supposed to grow when more people needed help, but they did not grow much. However, more people were able to use federal social insurance programs. There was a 21 percent increase in applications to the Federal Disability Insurance program in 2009, and 200,000 extra people applied for Social Security.[32]

Coping: Unemployment Benefits, Finding a Job

A major coping aid for the unemployed was unemployment insurance (UI). States collect UI taxes from employers and establish benefit levels. In the post–World War II era, every state came to guarantee at least twenty-six weeks of benefits. Starting in the 1950s, the federal government added extra benefits in hard times. In the Great Recession, people in high-unemployment states could receive UI for up to ninety-nine weeks.

UI helped people pay their bills, and nudged them to get a job because it required a job search. But it provided them time to search for something half-way decent. UI also added spending power to the economy. By one estimate, $157 billion in benefits stimulated $300 billion of economic activity in 2011. But right-wing Republicans loved to hate UI. Iowa Representative Steve King called UI benefits "welfare for people that won't work." Texas congressman Blake Farenthold claimed that UI encouraged laziness. Chris Edwards, an economist at the conservative Cato Institute, thought that cutting benefits could cut unemployment because it would force workers to reduce wage demands or move to North Dakota, which was adding jobs in the oil business.[33]

People were moving to North Dakota, but job additions in that state were a drop in the national bucket. Nationally the number of Americans looking for work was six times the number of job vacancies. That's why the number of people out of work for twenty-seven weeks or more multiplied five times. The total exceeded six million in 2011.[34]

For most people, being unemployed wasn't easy. When ex-manager Mollee Harper exhausted her benefits, she had to get by with food stamps, selling household items, pulling weeds, and caring for a dying old man. People getting UI went on Craigslist to offer to organize your garage, mow your lawn, change a faucet, drive you to the airport, or assemble your Ikea furniture, for ten dollars an hour.[35]

A third of the unemployed were not getting UI, and others received meager benefits. Weekly payments were as low as $186 in Mississippi, and the national average was $293. For many people, that was not a big incentive to stay home if jobs were available. In one study, people on UI took only a week or two longer to find work than people who did not have UI. Meanwhile, UI lifted 3.3 million above the poverty line (2009), and it allowed job-seekers more time to find better positions that paid more and suited their interests. That might reduce the employers' turnover expenses.[36]

Before the economic recovery was completed, conservatives cut benefits. Soon, seven states guaranteed fewer than twenty-six weeks of benefits. In Florida a Tea Party governor and legislature compelled applicants to pass a forty-question online test of math and reading skills. As a result, the initial rejection-rate of UI applications in Florida tripled.[37]

Jobs and Budget Battles (2010–2012)

These years of economic recovery from the recession were taken up with bitter political struggles over spending and stimulus programs. The job recovery was slow for several reasons, but one reason was Republican resistance to adequate spending for job programs. In December 2010, President Obama was able to convince some Republicans to agree to a temporary reduction in the employee Social Security tax from 6.2 percent to 4.2 percent. That added $1,000 a year to the average family's buying power. Also, the Bush tax cuts were extended through 2012, but because they were tilted toward the affluent, they added less to general demand than they cost in lost tax revenues.[38]

It seemed impossible to push larger stimulus programs through the Congress. Obama proposed an American Jobs Act that included infrastructure spending, a Social Security tax cut, and extended unemployment benefits, but he only succeeded with the last two items, and only for two months. Early in 2012, Congress agreed to extend both until the end of the year.[39]

In the 2012 presidential contest, Republican Mitt Romney presented himself as a job-creating capitalist, but Democrats maintained that his kind of in-and-out investor capitalism meant job cuts. Romney wanted less government regulation, a five-trillion-dollar tax cut, an end to Obamacare, the popular name for the Affordable Care Act, and less Medicaid. Obama took credit for the federal bailout of the auto industry; he tied Romney to Bush policies that caused the recession; and he talked up his tax-the-rich plan. Obama won.[40]

Soon, the president and Congress confronted a "fiscal cliff." Some tax cuts were set to expire, and that meant less private spending power. Also looming were automatic spending cuts if the annual deficit was not reduced enough. These cuts had been legislated in 2011 to convince conservative Republicans to allow the total federal debt to rise enough to cover authorized expenditures. Now, Republicans hoped to use a crisis of spending cuts to cut government spending more. The real peril—the fiscal cliff—was that federal spending and federal deficits would fall too fast and send the economy back into a recession. Eventually, Obama and Democrats got a tiny tax hike on the rich and permission to raise the debt limit. But consumers had less money in their pockets when the Social Security cuts ended.

Though unemployment rates were falling and the stock market rebounded, demand for workers remained rather anemic. Young people with college degrees were still having more trouble than usual finding regular jobs. The number of state and local government employees had been cut by 760,000; 70 percent of the losers were women; 20 percent were black. Not much was done to rebuild state and local governments. It was normal for right-wing politicians to attack government workers and government services, but their attacks here meant slower job growth.[41]

Whatever the specifics and causes, job totals at the end of 2012, the year in which conservatives and neoliberals wanted to cut federal spending, were still terrible. The pre-recession peak would not be attained again until May 2014. Job totals then reached new highs almost every month, but were never enough to make up for the job deficits of the whole period of January 2001 through January 2018. Baby boomer retirements helped cushion average sluggish job growth of about one million additions a year, but not enough.[42]

Table 5.1 Total Nonfarm Employees in the Great Recession and the Recovery

Pre-Recession Peak	January 2008	138,422,000
Recession Low	February 2010	129,715,000
Mid-Recovery	December 2012	135,088,000
Pre-Recession Peak Surpassed	May 2014	138,533,000

These are CES totals, accessed on April 3, 2019.

Did the Great Recession Shatter
Business-First/Free-Market Dogmas?

Did thoughtful conservatives and neoliberals reconsider their faith in unregulated private markets after the crash? Some did; many did not. At the University of Chicago, federal judge and faculty member in the university's law school, Richard Posner, urged people in the Economics Department to back off their opposition to government regulation and deficit spending. Most refused. Eugene Fama, who had developed the efficient-markets idea that contributed to the crash, saw no reason to change. Robert Lucas still believed that largely unregulated markets were good self-regulators and that workers chose to be unemployed rather than accept low wages. A Lucas letter to the unemployed would have been short: "It's your fault."[43]

Most Americans understood that UI, Social Security, Medicare, and food stamps were vital protections against the harsh outcomes of capitalism. Occupy Wall Street pushed inequality issues to the forefront in 2011–2012, and fast-food workers began striking for higher pay in the fall of 2012. But it was not clear how far Democrats were willing to go to fight economic inequality. It took a while for many of them to push for a hike in the federal minimum wage, which was still $7.25 an hour. Many Democratic politicians received donations from big bankers and other business leaders. And the American people had mixed attitudes. Some were dazzled by wealthy executives who were picking their pockets. Better-off members of the employee class, including some retirees on Social Security and Medicare, feared that they would have to pay the bill for programs that served the whole population. A majority of older people did not support the Affordable Care Act.[44]

Bad Jobs in the 2000s: The World Made by McDonald's,
Wal-Mart, Uber, and Amazon

Net job additions in the 2000s were low. In twelve years under George H.W. Bush and Bill Clinton starting in January 1989, 25.6 million jobs were added. In the next twelve years, under George W. Bush and Barack Obama, 2.6 million jobs were added. In the 2010s, job creation improved, as expected in an economic recovery period, but the average annual increase for all the years from January 2000 through January 2019 was 1,030,000. That is pretty shabby and helps explain why there are still so many potential workers on the sideline.[45] And the average quality of new jobs was low. Wages did increase, but not fast. From 2000 through 2018, real wages increased a total of 12.9 percent. That rate

Table 5.2 Real Hourly Wage of Private-Sector Nonmanagerial Nonfarm Employees (in 1982–1984 dollars)

1970:	$8.72
1972:	$9.26
1980:	$8.26
1990:	$7.91
2000:	$8.30
2008:	$8.56
2012:	$8.73
2019:	$9.37 (April)

Economic Report of the President, 2013 (Washington, D.C.: U.S. Government Printing Office, 2013), table B-47; and table A-2 from BLS monthly reports called *Real Earnings.*

of increase was less than 1 percent a year, and the 2019 wage was not much above where it had been in 1972.[46]

Of course, there were good jobs. Even Wal-Mart had to pay pharmacists $100,000 a year. Software developers could make $90,000 a year, and utility workers were generally paid well. Radiologists earned $448,900 in 2010. Harvard professors averaged $193,800. But most college teachers earned much less. Half of them were temps and it had been that way for decades.

In the 2000s, more workers were like Uber drivers, who were treated as independent contractors. The designation usually meant no company contributions to pensions, Social Security, Medicare, workers' compensation, or unemployment insurance. In short, it meant less sharing of expenses and more risks for employees. The sharing economy, the gig economy—these seemed to be euphemisms for changes that made life harder for employees. Some people liked the change; it seemed to give them more control over their work. But a significant number took irregular jobs because there weren't enough regular jobs with decent pay, security, and benefits. In many labor markets, employers had extra bargaining power because they had weakened government protections for employees, because there were a lot of people needing jobs, and few workers had unions.

In areas where there had once been good jobs for persons of average education, job totals declined. In the 1960s the manufacturing workforce had been 30 percent of all nonfarm workers, but in the 2010s it was just 8 percent. There were a relative handful of new factory jobs that required modern skills to run and repair sophisticated machines, but these positions were part of an automation process that eliminated millions of other jobs. Manufacturers repeatedly claimed that they could not find skilled workers, but many of them did not want to pay their new-skilled workers much above Wal-Mart wages, so it is unlikely there was really much of a shortage.[47]

While factory work shrank as a part of the economy, two other areas—the retail and the leisure-and-hospitality sectors—remained large. They employed twenty-nine million—one in five workers and more than twice as many as the manufacturing sector. In 2017, for retail sales workers, median hourly pay was $11.24, and for food and beverage servers, $9.81. Most employees did not work full time and most were poorly paid. Fifty-nine-year-old Linda Archer, a cashier at a McDonald's, earned $8 an hour and made $10,000 a year.[48] After five years, Costco workers could earn $42,000, but Wal-Mart workers at the same level earned only $18,000. It was hard to find retail jobs that provided a family wage, decent benefits, reasonable schedules, and real careers. Clerks at North Face were paid barely more than the minimum wage and had to sell $30,000 worth of merchandise to get their bonus—a $25 gift card good only at North Face. Department stores like Macy's were shrinking, while huge warehouses serving online buyers were opening around the country. Some of them employed almost as many robots as human beings.[49]

In the grocery business, the national average for cashiers, union and non-union, was $11.43, totaling $23,774 for full-time, year-round work. In many stores, most employees were not full-time and did not have guaranteed hours or predictable schedules. Even in union shops, quite a few employees were poorly paid and part-time, and not just teenagers. In three Orange County, California, stores of three unionized grocery chains, 80 percent of the staff was part-time. A majority of workers in large New York City stores were part-timers or temps. Fresh and Easy, a quick-shop grocery store, typically hired no full-timers. You might be a good worker but get scheduled for only twenty-eight hours a week at $10.90 an hour. That was $16,000 a year.[50]

Bad jobs were also common in many very large businesses, some of which were thought to be cutting-edge enterprises. But at Amazon, Staples, Apple, Dell, Office Depot, and Wal-Mart—the top six online retailers—cheap, fast shipping was extracted from the minds and bodies of warehouse workers and independent drivers. Big retailers pressed for low wages and often farmed out labor relations to contractors who routinely broke the law. The whole distribution process was called "logistics," but at times it seemed to be about sweatshops—literally, because warehouses sometimes heated up to 115 degrees, and figuratively, because bosses strove to squeeze more labor out of workers. In some warehouses, people earned as little as $12 an hour to race around with scanners that told them where to find an item and how long it should take to get it; in others, a handful of workers earned $20 an hour to manage machines that did the heavy lifting. In some cases, workers weren't even getting legislated minimum wages. There was nothing new about this, but wage theft was one of the nastiest aspects of the so-called underground economy. As many as five million low-wage workers were cheated out of their legal minimum wage. Service workers, younger workers, women, people of color, and part-time workers were all more likely than others to be victimized by wage theft.[51]

Another expanding area, health care, steadily added jobs, but many were not well-paid. The labor supply was usually ample for the demand. Of six occupations projected to add the most positions in 2012–2022, four were in the health field, but of those four, only one, registered nursing, averaged more than $25,000 a year.[52]

The tech revolution generated good jobs. Highly skilled, lucky people got rich. Computer and math occupations tended to have the most employees with high wages. But older engineers and technicians struggled to find work while tech companies lobbied for the admission of cheaper immigrant workers to fill labor "shortages." Some tech fields were glutted. There was gold in software and app development, but many prospectors did not strike it rich. The Bureau of Labor Statistics' *Occupational Outlook Handbook* claimed that app developers were earning $87,790 a year, but many were earning hardly anything. A man named Ethan Nicholas made a million dollars; but after Shawn and Stephanie Grimes cashed in their 401ks to buy equipment, they earned only a few thousand dollars for a couple of apps. Meanwhile, there were new micro-mini-jobs—"crowd work"—online. Some of these jobs lasted just a couple of minutes and paid as little as $2 an hour. The work included taking surveys, creating titles for porn films, writing product descriptions, and transcribing insurance claims. People liked working at home, but workers were classified as independent contractors and were unprotected by labor laws. Employee organization was difficult. Amazon had a site but claimed it was not the employer, just a facilitator of thousands of contacts between crowd workers and real employers.[53]

2018: State of the Nation

Nine years after the recovery from the Great Recession began, there was a lingering sense of unease and even pessimism among millions of Americans who were poorly paid or left with no jobs in the wake of corporate flight and insufficient economic demand. Workers, supportive unions, and some liberal politicians reacted to the shortage of good jobs by organizing to make bad jobs a little better through minimum-wage legislation. They succeeded in cities and states around the country. But quite a few politicians and scholars across the political spectrum seemed to think that if more Americans got a college education, new jobs for the college-educated would magically appear. But many with college degrees were not finding jobs that fit their level of education.

The constriction of economic opportunities in rural America and in ruined cities helped Donald Trump win the presidency, but in his first two years as president he did little to stimulate the creation of good jobs. He promised to bring back coal, which was a cruel deceit, for coal was terrible for the environment and for underground miners and it could not compete with low-priced natural gas. His signal achievement for left-behind workers was to highlight the damage done by trade treaties, but his tariff program utilized a giant scythe when it needed small hoes and rakes. Many American producers found that they could no longer acquire vital elements for their production process, and some faced retaliatory tariffs.[54] By and large, Trump excelled at managing a media circus that was packed with lies and made his core supporters feel good. But there wasn't much in the way of good jobs for those white workers without college degrees who helped him win key states.

The president and Republicans in Congress and in the states strove to abolish Obamacare and cut the Medicaid rolls. The Republican tax-cut legislation of 2017 eliminated the Obamacare mandate that taxed people who did not enroll themselves in the program. But Democrats, with the help of Senator John McCain, defeated the effort to abolish Obamacare. In the elections of November 2018, opposition to Obamacare had become a liability for many Republican candidates.

Medicaid, significantly expanded under Obamacare, was one of the largest providers of rehabilitation services for white opioid addicts in depressed economic areas from the Rust Belt into the Deep South—areas that voted mostly for Trump. The opioid epidemic had other causes but an important one was the obliteration of local economies. It seemed to be news that many white people were newly addicted to opioids and heroin, and that more of them were dying. And the indicators were not just in the drug epidemic. In a swath of states from Ohio south into Alabama and Mississippi, a rising number of young white people were applying for disability benefits. Some were very disabled and some only partially disabled and able to perform some jobs, but they were using the federal disability program as a form of long-term unemployment insurance.

For minority groups, prospects were a mixed bag. For black people, unemployment was the lowest ever since data were first collected in 1972. But the black rate in March 2019 was still 6.7 percent and twice the white rate of 3.4 percent; and many more African Americans were actually unemployed but not included in the official unemployment count. Homicide rates were very high in Baltimore, Chicago, and other cities. Police still killed young black men almost with impunity. And young black people killed each other too. In Chicago's poor black neighborhoods, 30 percent of men ages fifteen to twenty-four were not at work or in school. For the nation as a whole, it was not the best of times or the worst, but conditions in African American communities in Chicago, Detroit, and Flint, Michigan and for whites in Beaverton, Alabama, Ashtabula, Ohio, and Montgomery County, Ohio, were dire. These left-behind people were not rare exceptions to a story of prosperity for all, but extreme indicators of the failures and sins of immoral and incompetent political and business leaders who caused and allowed extreme inequality and grinding insecurity for half the population.[55]

The Final Score for 2001–2018

A deep, nasty recession and a slow job recovery. In 2016, 2017, and 2018, the economy was reaching what seemed to be full recovery by conventional standards, but real pay for rank-and-file workers was still low and about where it had been in 1972–1973. Journalists and economists endeavored every month to find evidence that real wage growth was finally taking off, but there was not much of a take-off. Real wages advanced by 1 percent or more a year just five times over 2001–2018. (Those good years were 2001, 2007, 2009, 2015, and 2016.)

The opioid epidemic was an indicator of deep economic problems. There were still higher than expected numbers of people outside the labor force, for example, people in the prime working ages of twenty-five to fifty-four. At the federal level, little was being done to remedy the long-term deficit of relatively secure, full-time, and decently compensated jobs.

· · ·

This ends the first part of the book, the history of unemployment and bad jobs since 1870, as well as American efforts to deal with or ignore the problems. The reader should now understand that there has almost always been too much unemployment in America and know about some of the things that can provide enough jobs. Chapter 6 explains the official unemployment rate and offers details about the underestimation of unemployment. Chapter 7 evaluates explanations for why we usually have a lot of unemployment. It is important to highlight the reasons why we have too much unemployment if we are to get less of it. Chapter 8 discusses federal programs that can create enough good jobs that pay a living wage, and it confronts the political and cultural barriers to full employment.

PART II

Real Numbers, Explanations, Remedies

CHAPTER 6

The U.S. Unemployment Rate

Development and Debate

For most adults who can work, a job is the way they obtain income to buy life's necessities. Often, it provides them with a sense of worth. With reliable unemployment statistics, those who govern and the people they govern should be able to have a rational discussion about how to ensure that there are enough decent jobs for all who need them.

We can debate the methods used by the Census Bureau and the Bureau of Labor Statistics (BLS) to produce unemployment numbers, but we should not forget that the development of generally reliable unemployment numbers was a major achievement for the American people. Aside from their practical and policy uses, credible unemployment numbers nudge people to understand the systemic nature of unemployment. The frequent publication of numbers about unemployment and related issues may help people understand that the ups and downs of unemployment reflect impersonal processes and big economic events rather than the rise and fall of mass laziness. This view might be called the systemic or social narrative of unemployment.

In the 1930s Depression, when unemployment was the dominant fact of everyday life for millions of people, and when liberal, union, and socialist forces grew strong, the social narrative gained ground. But the older, voluntarist market view, never died. It was potent in the late 1800s and early 1900s, receded in the Great Depression, but gained new support again in the late 1970s and 1980s. In our time, there are a fair number of die-hard traditionalists, including a Nobel prize winner and many Tea Party/Freedom Caucus members, who think that even in big depressions, a lot of unemployment is voluntary. However, many conservative economists are more sophisticated than their counterparts in the late 1800s. They understand that the economy can crash and throw people out of work, and also that there are other kinds of unemployment, including structural and frictional, that are not chosen by the unemployed person, or are only partly voluntary. Still, for many conservatives—politicians and economists—the reality and the gravity of being unemployed and unable to find a job, especially one that pays the bills, is underappreciated, and the causes of significant unemployment rarely include the possibility that capitalism normally and naturally generates a significant amount of unemployment, in part owing to extreme income inequalities that limit mass consumption. Even for moderate conservatives, the causes of unemployment seem to lie in things that warp the natural goodness of the system, such as wage and price rigidities, some of which come from liberal benefit programs that make it too easy not to work, and from high minimum wages and union contracts that raise pay levels so much that employers cannot afford to create jobs. In this view, the economy would normally produce a balance between supply and demand and full employment too, were it not for inessential rigidities and extrinsic imperfections.[1]

Learning to Count Unemployment: It Wasn't Easy

The United States did not get dependable unemployment numbers until the 1940s, seventy years after the first high-unemployment depression. Why did it take so long? Partly because of the underdevelopment of statistical methods and government bureaucracies, but also because many politicians, scholars, and charity-organization leaders resisted the idea that unemployment was caused by economic factors and not by character defects. As seen in chapter 1, mainstream economists assumed that in "a competitive economy there could be no long-term unemployment." A related reason for the lag in developing unemployment numbers was that influential Americans—for example, business owners, the Supreme Court, political conservatives—did not want the expansion of federal power that might follow if research showed that unemployment was frequent and systemic.

But by the early 1900s, more scholars and government officials were studying unemployment, and how to count it. In 1915 and 1916, the Bureau of Labor Statistics (BLS) surveyed urban households and began to collect job totals from manufacturers. The Census Bureau collected information about the number of working people in different occupations in the censuses of 1880, 1890, 1900, and

1910. The 1910 effort included modern questions about unemployment, but the results were not published. Some people at the bureau were not convinced that counting the unemployed was part of their mission. Unemployment questions were omitted from the 1920 census.[2]

During the 1921 depression, Secretary of Commerce Herbert Hoover organized a national unemployment conference to consider ways to minimize unemployment. Hoover and others recognized the need for a reliable count, but a committee he appointed could not agree on how to do it. When the economy improved in 1922, the urgency of unemployment issues seemed to wane. Some people who wanted solid numbers gave up the battle to get them. But others labored on. The Hoover conference generated serious publications, including some about counting the unemployed, and there were other efforts too, including community studies, union and business estimates, and a detailed analysis by economist Paul Douglas, which we read about in chapter 2.[3]

Unemployment did not disappear in the 1920s. There were no depressions between 1921 and 1929, but there were reports of high unemployment around the country. In 1927 Senators Robert Wagner of New York and David Walsh of Massachusetts got the Senate to pass a resolution ordering the Bureau of Labor to survey unemployment and to study methods for a regular tally. The first survey results seemed to Wagner a flagrant underestimation. A prominent scholar of unemployment and the business cycle, William Berridge, concluded in 1928 that regarding existing numbers on unemployment and other key indicators, there was still no "*direct* evidence worthy of serious consideration." Pressure built for accurate information, especially after the stock market crash in October 1929. In January 1930, President Hoover used BLS job totals reflecting a 4 percent increase due to holiday hiring to bolster his claim that the Depression was almost over, but he was criticized. In New York, Frances Perkins, an authority on labor questions, told the press that Hoover was deceiving the public and making life more miserable: "Mother will be mad when father comes home and says he can't get a job . . . the President said that employment is going up."

The crash and agitation by liberals like Wagner helped to get unemployment questions into the 1930 census. In June Secretary of Commerce Robert Lamont announced the results: between 2.3 and 2.5 million people were unemployed. That amounted to a 5 percent unemployment rate, which seemed low for a troubled economy. In the public debate that followed, it emerged, in the words of one historian, that "officials had no clear conception of how to count the unemployed when they planned the census." The Census Bureau's expert on unemployment, Charles Persons, resigned and told the press that the numbers were wrong. The *Pasadena Labor News* discovered that of seventy-six local people who had been surveyed, only eleven had been asked the unemployment question. In short, the government count was deeply flawed. People began to pay more attention to an insurance company poll of 200,000 policy holders, which came up with a 24 percent unemployment rate.[4]

What would it take to get credible unemployment numbers? First, political support and funding for well-designed surveys. Second, the Census Bureau and the Bureau of Labor Statistics had to recruit more up-to-date statisticians. Third, a clear definition of being unemployed, one that did not cause confusion for the surveyors and the surveyed.

The Great Depression made unemployment a matter of life-and-death interest. New Deal agencies, businesses, unions, and workers wanted credible numbers. But President Franklin Roosevelt, who supported government assistance to the unemployed, was not enthusiastic about an improved unemployment survey. Authoritative numbers might show that his New Deal was not doing enough to reduce unemployment. However, Roosevelt supported a broad effort to modernize government statistics, and that was a plus for unemployment studies. Also, as the New Deal expanded, legislators wanted accurate numbers on which to base their decisions about, for example, how farm subsidies would be divided up and how much funding was needed for the unemployed. These impulses helped to drive modernization at the Census Bureau and the BLS. Also, planners in the Works Progress Administration (WPA), which supervised thousands of projects for the unemployed, wanted accurate information and the WPA had personnel who could design employment surveys.

In the executive branch, there was a lot of activity around modernizing government statistics. Secretary of Labor Perkins, who knew about the 1930 counting fiasco under Hoover, claimed that the BLS was "padded with untrained and uneducated people." In her first month as secretary, Perkins asked the American Statistical Association to create an Advisory Committee to the Secretary of Labor (ACSL). The president of the American Statistical Association, Stuart Rice, claimed to find at the Census Bureau "the moldy remains and dried bones" of the past. Roosevelt's early presidential actions included the appointment of a new census director, and approval of a Central Statistical Board to oversee numbers reform.[5]

In 1933–1934, the Central Statistical Board, the BLS, and the ACSL directed a three-city sample carried out through the Civil Works Administration, a federal job program that appeared in chapter 2. In 1937 Roosevelt gave in to congressional pressure and agreed to an experiment involving WPA workers and the Census Bureau. But he shunned responsibility, insisting that the survey cards state that "The Congress directed me to take this census." In this "Enumerative Check Census," letter carriers delivered a postcard survey on unemployment to all residential addresses and helped people who needed assistance filling out the forms. Experts were worried about the reliability of the sample, so specially trained postal workers engaged in direct interviews with a sample of the population. This follow-up indicated that the postcard survey missed 30 percent of the unemployed. WPA personnel performed a new survey on a national sample of sixty-four counties in December 1939. They were advancing on procedures and definitions: data would be acquired every month and by direct interview with a sample of the population, and people would be counted as unemployed if they did not have jobs but had actively searched in the previous week. Surveyors would not ask, "Are you unemployed?" but rather "Are You at Work?" If not, "Are You Actively Seeking Work?" If you did not have a job but were looking for one, you were considered unemployed.

The WPA was working on a *Monthly Report on the Labor Force,* based on a sample survey of twenty thousand households. The agency made its first unemployment report for April 1940. America's modern unemployment count began here. The Census Bureau included an unemployment section in the 1940 census, and the results were close to what the WPA was getting. That gave WPA experts confidence that they were on the right track.[6]

As war mobilization began and unemployment declined, the WPA was phased out. In 1942 the Census Bureau took over the monthly survey and increased the sample to twenty-three thousand units. In 1948 it was named the Current Population Survey. In 1959 the Bureau of Labor Statistics took over analysis and publication; the Census Bureau still collected the information. By then the sample covered thirty-three thousand households. Today, it covers sixty thousand households.

It is a testament to the simplicity and utility of the survey that its essentials have lasted. Often government experts and officials have revised the employment survey and occasionally even responded to critics.[7] Perhaps the most important issue for some critics revolves around the question of whether the official unemployment rate includes all who are truly unemployed.[8]

So How Do They Count the Unemployed Today?

Several approaches might be used to count the unemployed, but some obvious choices don't work. Federal officials do not base national unemployment rates on the number of people receiving unemployment insurance benefits

You'll find monthly unemployment rates and other useful numbers, such as unemployment rates for women, African Americans, Latinos, Asians, veterans, and the disabled, and the duration of unemployment spells, at BLS.gov. This information appears every first Friday of the month as *The Employment Situation* for the previous month.

(UI). Many jobless people are not eligible for UI and others have used up their benefits. The percentage of the unemployed who get benefits has ranged from roughly 30 percent to 70 percent, so the number of UI recipients is not a stable measure of unemployment.

Using another method, government employees could survey employers about their payrolls. In fact, the Bureau of Labor Statistics does that, but the survey of establishments does not tell us how many people do not have a job and want one, and it leaves out the farm sector and the self-employed. It counts the rise and fall of jobs in the surveyed organizations, not unemployment.

Third, government agencies could survey the entire population of the United States every month. But that would be very expensive, and also, as the BLS guidebook explains, "people would soon grow tired having a census-taker come to their homes every month, year after year." More practical and less expensive is a sample of the population.

So, every month, twenty-two hundred trained and experienced employees of the United States Census Bureau interview people in sixty thousand households. These households are supposed to add up to a representative sample of the population. Some of the surveys are done in person; some by phone. Answers to interviewers' questions used to be written on large paper schedules, but they are now entered nightly into laptops and sent to the Census Bureau's main computer. The results are turned over to the Bureau of Labor Statistics. They constitute the Current Population Survey (CPS) from which unemployment rates are calculated. Normally, on the first Friday of every month, the bureau releases employment and unemployment information for the previous month.[9]

The survey covers all occupations except active military service; it covers everyone sixteen and older except those in institutions (correctional, long-term nursing, and the like). The self-employed, government workers, farmers and farm workers, citizens and noncitizens, are included. The interviewers do not ask household members to judge whether they are unemployed; rather, they ask about their activities: whether they worked for pay in the survey week (the week in which the twelfth of the month falls), and if not, whether they searched for work in the previous four weeks. People are then divided among three categories:

Employed: people who had a paid job in the survey week, even if they worked only one hour.[10]

Unemployed: people who had no job in the week of the survey, were available for work, and searched for a job in the previous four weeks. Acceptable job searches include contacting employment agencies, friends, relatives, and employers, and sending out résumés. Reading about job openings and taking job training programs do not qualify.

The Employed and the Unemployed make up the labor force. The unemployment rate is the number of unemployed divided by the labor force. Table 6.1 gives a recent example.

Out of the Labor Force: Those who are not employed and are not searching for a job are not part of the official labor force. However, we have information about some people who say they want a job, but have not recently searched for one. They numbered 5.1 million in April 2019. The majority of them said they had not searched for work at any time in the twelve months prior to the survey; 454,000 of them were classified as "discouraged" workers, which meant they had searched sometime in the past year, were not currently searching, and stated that the reason they were not searching was that they believed they would not find a job. I believe that the number of discouraged workers is much larger than the BLS reports. In the Great Recession, possibly the most discouraging job market since the 1930s, the government never found more than 1,318,000 discouraged workers. That is partly because the really discouraged, those who had not searched at least once for a job over the year, did not fit the narrow requirements of the category.[11]

Table 6.1 The Official Labor Force in April 2019

The employed:	156,645,000 + the unemployed: 5,824,000 =
The labor force:	162,469,000

5,824,000 unemployed divided by the labor force of 162,469,000 = a 3.6% unemployment rate.
Source: BLS, *Employment Situation—April 2019.*

Debates and Revisions

Over the years, the official unemployment rate has often been debated. Federal agencies have not ignored criticisms, but they have been cautious. Disputes have ranged from hysterical and highly partisan to the serious and highly technical. In the late 1950s, things got rather heated. Employment had not recovered from the 1957–1958 recession; in fact, the economy sank into a second recession before full recovery. This became part of a conversation about above-average unemployment. Was the reason a lack of total economic demand or a specific cause, such as worker skill deficits or a long-term contraction of manufacturing?[12]

One pundit decided that the problem was simpler: the government was lying. In the *Reader's Digest,* James Daniel claimed that government personnel were conspiring to exaggerate unemployment to "push Uncle Sam into new federal spending programs and new controls over the economy." Daniel's position was extreme but not unique. Other conservatives, too, wanted a lower unemployment count because they believed that most people could find a job and because higher unemployment justified more government spending and that was a threat to "free enterprise." Daniel's assault was not a serious analysis, but it may have been one factor that led to a scholarly review of the government's methods. But not much changed at the BLS.[13]

In the later 1960s and in 1970, there were experiments that might have brought major revisions. In 1966, led by Secretary of Labor Willard Wirtz, the Department of Labor carried out a survey of inner-city "subemployment" that generated very high numbers. This subemployment survey added part-timers who wanted full-time work, discouraged job-seekers who had stopped searching, an estimate for people typically missed in government surveys, and non-elderly employed people who earned below-poverty incomes. As discussed in chapter 3, the new estimates were two, three, and even four times the official unemployment rate for inner-city neighborhoods. But this pioneering effort to get a more realistic count of the unemployed and underemployed was not institutionalized. There was one similar effort, linked to the 1970 census, but nothing after that. Higher unemployment rates were not something presidents cared to sponsor.

But the numbers debate continued in the 1970s. In 1973, when official unemployment was 5.7 percent, scholars Bertram Gross and Stanley Moss claimed that the real unemployment rate was 25 percent when you included discouraged workers and millions of others who would seek work if there were enough jobs. In the recession of 1974–1975, the editors of the socialist *Monthly Review* claimed that real unemployment was one and a half times the official number.

Around the same time, social scientists Frank Furstenberg and Charles Thrall challenged the government's definition of being unemployed. They suggested that searching for a job and a stated desire for work were not adequate criteria because American culture was warped by a job rationing ideology. Some people who might need work did not even bother to search because they thought they did not deserve a job.[14]

Critics also attacked from the other side, claiming that the official count missed people with jobs. The underground economy included a variety of illegal and off-the-books activities, for example, people employed as serious criminals, people doing legal jobs who did not report all their earnings, and people receiving disability benefits while secretly working. The underground sector existed because people wanted to hide something, so its size was and is a matter of conjecture. In recent decades it may have been the equivalent of 5 to 10 percent of the total economy.

In the 1970s and '80s, some critics elaborated on their view that the level of unemployment was exaggerated because some people hid their work. Persons receiving unemployment benefits and working on the side would say they were not working but looking for work—and thus were labeled as unemployed—for fear of losing their benefits. The critics claimed that there were thousands of criminals employed in the numbers rackets and loan sharking who were not surveyed. In short, many employed workers were missed. Some of these critics seemed to assume that only employed workers inhabited the hidden or underground economy, but there was a large underground labor force of people needing work but not counted as unemployed.

Also, some questioners did not make an effort to understand the survey. The official survey did not ask about unemployment benefits or other social programs. Though it is possible that some respondents feared that the surveyors might report their responses to legal authorities, it was made clear that the survey was strictly for statistical purposes and no names would be revealed. While it seems reasonable to assume that undocumented immigrants would fear contact with any federal agency, the survey asked no questions about legal status. Finally, it seems likely that fearful immigrants and real criminals would simply refuse to participate in the survey. The rate of refusing to participate was rising, although it was still just 2.5 percent in 1982.

Finally, the basic math of the issue does not seem to support the idea that the unemployment rate would have been significantly lower in the 1970s and 1980s or would today be lower if underground activities that are allegedly not included were included. One critic of the official count, Peter M. Gutman, admitted that adding his guesstimate for the unemployed who were actually working and not telling surveyors they were working would lower the unemployment rate by .5, or half a point in April 1978. And here is a broad math hypothesis for October 2017, using the assumption that there is a vast uncounted army of workers out there. In that month the official labor force was 160,000,000, there were 6,520,000 unemployed, and the unemployment rate was 4.1 percent. If there were an uncounted underground army of employed workers as large as sixteen million, and if every single one of them were included in the count, the unemployment rate for the labor force of 176,000,000 would be 3.7 percent. That is not a huge impact and it is less than the effect of adding uncounted unemployed workers to the unemployment rate, as we shall see.[15]

While officials at the Bureau of Labor Statistics took note of some challenges, they did not change fundamental methods. In 1976 the Commissioner of Labor Statistics, Julius Shiskin, created a table with seven different unemployment categories, representing "differing bodies of opinion about the meaning and measurement of unemployment."[16] In the 1990s, BLS staff came up with U-6, a simple alternative rate that added part-timers who wanted full-time work and discouraged workers. U-6 did not replace the official rate, but it is there in every monthly employment report for those who want it. In October 2018, when the official unemployment rate was 3.7 percent, U-6 was 7.4 percent. Meanwhile, members of an independent organization, the National Jobs for All Coalition, believed that a more accurate rate for October 2018 was 9.5 percent. Some of us often use the higher numbers, but most journalists and economists rarely do, except in recessions, when they want to emphasize how grim the job situation is. In better times, when the official unemployment rate is 4 to 5 percent, many observers accept that the economy is essentially at full employment and rarely bother about the hidden unemployed.[17]

Three Cases of Hidden Unemployment, or Why 4 Percent Unemployment is really 10 Percent and Not Virtually Full Employment

Case 1: Every month millions of people want a job but are not searching for one. In hard times there may be more than seven million non-searching job-wanters; when jobs are more plentiful, there may be only five million of them. If the United States had real full employment, there would not be so many non-searching job-wanters.

These people offer various explanations for why they are not searching for a job. A significant minority say the reason is that they believe they cannot find a job. Others say they are ill, disabled, in school, or have family responsibilities.

I think some of the people in these groups would actively look for work if there were more half-way decent jobs nearby. The non-searchers are not counted as unemployed, but many of them really are. Some are passive searchers. If something good comes their way, they will go to work, although they had not been counted as unemployed or looking for a job.[18]

Case 2: If something around 4 percent unemployment were virtually full employment in 2017 and 2018, average wages would have been on a sustained climb, even without more unionization or higher minimum wage laws. But while the dollar amounts (sometimes called nominal or money wages) many workers were taking home increased in some months, they rarely increased more than prices. Even though inflation was rather low in these years, it was high enough to wipe out most increases in the paychecks of average workers. For example, from January of 2017 through January of 2018, real (after-inflation), hourly wages for rank-and-file workers rose 1/10 of 1 percent. Essentially, not at all.[19]

If there had been real full employment, there would have been real labor shortages and employers would have had to raise pay more than they did. Workers in places that have raised their minimum wages have seen increases and some occupations ranging from security guards to truckers and store clerks have gotten raises at times, but on average, there has not been a substantial, general, and sustained upswing in real pay. Most employers can find the workers they need without raising pay much more than prices are rising. That implies that the official unemployment rate is not a reliable indicator of the size of the real available labor force.[20]

Case 3: There is a specific group of people not in the labor force—not working and not looking for work—about which much has been written. For several decades journalists and economists have studied the "exodus" of prime-age men from the labor force. In the 1950s the percentage of men 25 to 54 years old who were working or looking for work was as high as 97.8 percent. In 2011–2018, it was under 89 percent. There are millions of adult men who, it seems, are not even trying to find work. Their behavior can be used to rail against government benefit programs and the erosion of the work ethic. Half of the people in this group take pain-killers, ranging from aspirins to opioids. Some spend a lot of time watching television. A conservative narrative is that these men have been allowed to flee the world of work for a life of self-indulgence.[21]

But some of these people really are ill or disabled and should not be working; a relatively small number receive federal disability benefits. Some are discouraged and demoralized about job markets and don't try to find work. Some have probably tried to find a job but have prison records, which sharply lowers their odds of getting work. But quite a few of these dropouts would go to work if their situations changed or if employers in their regions were really short of workers. In fact, quite a few of them do go to work and the number who do so has recently been rising as labor markets have improved. Also, an underlying assumption for many who discuss this problem is that these men are permanent dropouts, now and forever. But about a third of the increase in non-participation since 1977 has been due, researcher John Coglianese discovered, to "in-and-outs"—men who drop out briefly, live off partners or parents, and then return to work.[22]

I believe more prime-age male dropouts would be working if jobs were reasonably rewarded. One analyst made the point succinctly: "if you want more people in paying jobs, pay them better." If there are few jobs or only bad jobs, not working looks better. A job that pays $10 an hour for 20 hours a week yields $10,400 a year before deductions. If you are disabled and lucky enough to get federal disability benefits, you receive, on average, $1,166 a month, or almost $14,000 year. That still leaves you poor, but it's better. And you are able to enroll early in Medicare. The point here is that when decent work is hard to find, the alternatives look better. The dating of the drop-out phenomenon adds force to the argument. The decline in labor force participation became significant in the 1970s. That was also when average wages began to stagnate and good blue-collar jobs really started to disappear.[23]

· · ·

To summarize the three cases, there is a large near-by labor force of people who are not currently searching for work, but who are virtually in the same situation as the unemployed who are looking for work. They are the hidden unemployed and their numbers would be much smaller if there were more good jobs and real full employment.

If the United States Had a Fuller Unemployment Count, Government Might Have to Provide More Jobs

There is no legal requirement that the U.S. government guarantee full employment, nor is there an official full-employment benchmark. Government agencies sometimes increase unemployment, for example, to fight inflation, or by promoting unrestricted free trade. A substantive federal obligation to guarantee full employment was rejected by Congress in legislation passed in 1946 and 1978. One result of living in a society that does not guarantee work is that some jobless people do not believe that they deserve a job, and they may not tell surveyors that they want one.[24]

In the end it is impossible to know with precision how many people outside the labor force actually want to work until the United States has affordable child-care, decent sick-leave policies, decent wages, and real full employment for a sustained period. I've written more about full employment in other chapters, but, in brief, to get full employment, government can guarantee jobs to all who want them, and it can revise procedures to create a new unemployment rate that is more realistic about how many people need work. But if the BLS sticks with current methods, the official rate of unemployment would have to stay at or below 2 percent for a long time to approximate full employment. Since World War II, annual unemployment rates have never been under 2 percent and, in fact, they have almost never been under 4 percent.

What Would a Better Official Unemployment Rate Look Like?

If Americans had more realistic unemployment rates, politicians would have to pay more attention to unemployment. More realistic estimates of unemployment might look like the BLS alternative rate or the National Jobs for All Coalition rate (see table 6.2). The official BLS rate covers those who have searched for work in the four weeks leading up to the survey week. The BLS alternative adds part-timers who want full-time work and a small group of discouraged workers. NJFAC adds to the BLS's unemployed group, part-time workers who want full-time work and people who say they want jobs, but are not actively searching for one.

Either the BLS's alternative unemployment rate or NJFAC's amplified number would be a more realistic gauge of unemployment and worker availability than the official rate. But what are the chances of getting either of these as the main monthly number? Officials at the BLS are wedded to their central assumption: if you have made no acceptable job search in the weeks before the survey, you are not unemployed. Meanwhile, few politicians care about a more accurate count. Except when it is politically advantageous—for example, when they are running against an incumbent liberal administration—conservatives don't care

Table 6.2   Three Unemployment Rates, April 2019

BLS official unemployment	Rate: 3.6%
BLS alternative unemployment (U-6)	Rate: 7.3%
NJFAC unemployment	Rate: 9.3%

Sources: BLS, *Employment Situation—April 2019*; and njfac.org, "The Full Count."

about upward revisions of the unemployment count. And many Democrats aren't very advanced on the issue. Also, business owners like the hidden labor surplus, which means plenty of job applicants and lower wages.

It is also crucial that few mainstream economists, liberals included, seem to care about more inclusive numbers. Economists of varied political sympathies desensitized themselves to the negative aspects of unemployment in the 1980s and early 1990s when they supported high unemployment to fight wage and price inflation. They helped to win acceptance for the notion that unemployment of 6 or 7 percent was a positive goal. As we have seen in chapters 3 and 4, these high unemployment rates, justified as the Non-Accelerating Inflation Rate of Unemployment (NAIRU), even came to be used as full-employment rates. But they had nothing to do with a level of unemployment that signaled real full employment. And, as mentioned, there has never been an official determination of a full-employment rate in the United States. Defining full employment is a question of who has the power to define it, and mainstream economists and, perhaps, business interests, have disproportionate influence. Average Americans have rarely been asked to contribute their views. There is not one working-class seat in the Cabinet or on the Federal Reserve Board.

CHAPTER 7

Why So Much Unemployment?

What really causes high unemployment? If you ask six people, you may get six answers: the unemployed don't want to work; they don't have the right skills or enough education; they face employer discrimination; immigrants are taking jobs; corporations are sending jobs out of the country; and there is too much government interference in the economy. While there may be truth in some of these, none is an adequate, comprehensive explanation for excessive unemployment in the United States. I believe that the best explanation is that business leaders, conservatives, many economists, and even some liberals don't want high-wage full employment.[1]

To emphasize the point: the lack of jobs and especially good jobs are outcomes that can be changed. They are the result of human decisions and actions. Many factors contribute to the job shortage. These include globalization, racism, neoliberal trade policy, automation, and shrinking business sectors (manufacturing, brick-and-mortar retail outlets). But above all, elites have done little to create enough good jobs in the public and private sectors in order to counteract negative forces, in part because they thrive on some of these forces. In the past the Federal Reserve has slowed economic growth before real full employment was achieved. The federal government and the multinationals do little or nothing to reemploy workers and repair communities that are devastated by trade treaties and disruptive industrial change. Tax cuts usually send more extra income to the top rather than spreading it around to the mass of consumers.

Real full employment and real assistance to declining communities require mass political action to get substantive programs. Without massive pressure and militant champions, not much can be expected of liberals and conservatives who uncritically love free trade and technology or fake populists who promise to save factory and mining jobs by putting more income into the bulging pockets of the superrich.

We Usually Have Too Much Unemployment, Even in Good Times

If we use a 4.0 percent unemployment rate as an index of virtually full employment, we find that after the 1960s, the United States has had only three years of full employment (2000, 2018, and 2019). And, as explained in other chapters, 4.0 percent is not really full employment. There were, even in 2018 and 2019, millions of people on the sidelines who were ready to work but were not included in the unemployment count. Their large numbers are one reason why real wages have not taken off, even in what many observers believe is a red-hot economy. In general, excessive unemployment is with us all the time and we do have something to explain.[2]

The Unemployed Are Lazy, and They Are Too Picky

One claim about unemployment is that people are lazy. This was a common view in the 1800s and was still around in the 1980s when President Ronald Reagan claimed that newspaper want-ads offered a lot of jobs. But analysts showed that many of the offers were paper thin. Some were for extremely part-time jobs (school bus drivers to work two or three hours a day). Others weren't job offers; they were entrepreneurs selling door-to-door sales kits. Fewer real jobs were being offered than it appeared, and most genuine offers were quickly filled.

Not many people focus on newspaper want-ads anymore, but attacks on the unemployed continue. In the Great Recession, when it seemed obvious that being unemployed was beyond the control of the unemployed, conservatives attacked them as freeloaders and fought to limit unemployment insurance because benefits made it too easy for people to refuse a job. But many of the unemployed on benefits weren't living high on the hog, and most could not get by for very long without a job. The average weekly benefit was $300, and many of the unemployed received less or nothing at all.[3]

It is true that job seekers are sometimes careful about which jobs they pursue. But that's a plus if they find jobs that fit their interests, talents, and budgets better than the first job offer. It is true that some people have said good-bye to jobs that pay sub-poverty wages, have dropped out of the labor force and the unemployment count, and found other ways to get by. But is it picky to have qualms about working at a job that brings in less than $20,000 a year?

The critical fact here is not that job seekers refuse to take jobs; it is that there are always more people ready to take jobs than there are jobs. In 2005, a prosperous year, eleven thousand people lined up for four hundred jobs at a Wal-Mart store. In the fairly mild recession of 1991, 350 applied for one janitorial position paying about $16 an hour (in 2019 prices) at a church in Maryland. In 2012 sixteen hundred people applied for sixteen low-wage jobs at a Maryland ice cream packer. As the economy recovered slowly in 2012, thousands of workers at Wal-Mart, McDonald's, and other companies that lived off needy workers demonstrated for higher pay and unions. But millions did not. Some were grateful for $8.42 an hour. One of them declared that the availability of low-wage jobs showed that Wal-Mart "really cares for the working class in this country."[4]

A final point about the laziness charge. It is obvious that the rise and fall of the unemployment rate follows the rise and fall of general business conditions, not arbitrary changes in people's desire to work. Unemployment did not soar in the Great Depression or in the Great Recession because millions of people suddenly decided to take a vacation.

Not Lazy, but Untrained: The Skills Argument

Another common explanation for excessive unemployment is that Americans lack skills and education. Centrist politicians like this argument and so do quite a few economists. It is easier to talk about skills than to pass legislation that creates good jobs. Rich bosses at Facebook and Microsoft complain that there's a dearth of skilled American workers, but sometimes they are just angling to import technicians who will work for less than citizens do. Other organizations have done the same. In the spring of 2015, Southern California Edison had employees training their replacements, immigrants in the United States under the H-1B program that allowed the importation of skilled workers for jobs where there were no workers. There's obviously something wrong with these immigration policies and employer behavior.[5]

But don't more skills pay off for workers? We know that more schooling, higher incomes, and lower unemployment go together. The more education you have, the higher your income and the less likely you are to be out of work. In the race for better jobs, it usually makes sense for individuals to acquire more education and relevant skills. So, what's wrong with the skills-and-school explanation?

More skills and education don't mean less total unemployment and don't lift the whole working class. Individuals with more education do better than those with less, but large segments of the working class as a whole don't advance. The share of the workforce with four-year college degrees increased from 20 percent in 1979 to 34 percent in 2010, but real wages for two-thirds of the workforce were about where they had been in the 1970s.[6]

In fact, millions of people are overeducated for their jobs. Employers' skill requirements have not risen more rapidly than the supply of skills. Twenty of thirty occupations predicted to have the largest numerical growth over the next ten years require nothing more than a high school diploma. Yes, there is need for nurses and programmers, but there are many more slots for home health-care aides, customer-service representatives, sales clerks, construction laborers, janitors, fast-food workers, and restaurant workers. Before, during, and after the Great Recession, quite a few college grads were taking jobs below their educational qualifications. Sometimes they were bumping less-educated people who were qualified for jobs at Starbucks and the Olive Garden. In some cases, college grads had less unemployment simply because low-wage employers had the luxury of hiring them for jobs that did not require college-level skills.[7]

Millions of Americans are improving their school and skill levels all the time. When it looks like special training will pay off, many people go out and get it.[8] But many U.S. employers do not expend resources to train employees. And at times they can be so picky about selecting job applicants that they exclude good prospects. Technology helps them. Internet postings have vastly increased the number of applicants, but employers use filters to eliminate whole categories that include competent applicants. Unless their labor needs are dire and unemployment is very, very low, they may reject, out of hand, the long-term unemployed, older workers, people with prison records, and African Americans.[9]

But if it is true that the American population is not, on average, under-skilled and under-schooled in relation to employers' needs, and if unemployment is always excessive, why do we read about shortages of nurses and welders, and about factory owners who cannot find people to run automated factories? Of course, there are sometimes real shortages and training bottlenecks. But many shortages are fabrications used to disguise the fact that employers don't want to pay enough to attract the people they need. Also, employers and trade association representatives love to blame other people and institutions—the schools especially—for the sorry situation of American workers.[10]

So, although employers must pay much more for very special skills and unique personalities, they are resistant when it comes to an adequate wage for modest skills. Sometimes they do pay more and something good happens. Late in 2016 a California garlic grower said he was short fifty workers. Early in 2017, he raised wages and promised they would eventually reach $15. Result? No labor shortage and a waiting list of 150 applicants. But the opposite strategy of complaining about worker defects rather than paying workers a wage that will quickly attract them is common. And so is deception. In 2012 an official of the National Association of Manufacturers claimed that there were hundreds of thousands of openings for skilled workers. But this is a sector that has discarded millions of skilled and trainable workers, and now sometimes tries to pay skilled workers fast-food wages. In 2012 starting pay for a skilled employee at Gen-Met, a metal plant outside of Milwaukee, was $10 an hour.[11]

To summarize this section, a lot of talk about skill shortages seems to scapegoat workers and suck up oxygen that should support the discussion about creating more good jobs. My point is not that people should not get the general and specific schooling and training they need to get decent jobs. It's that a lot of them have done so, but with meager results. School and skill deficits do not explain why average wages are about where they were in the 1970s. Americans need more good jobs, and there won't be more of them simply because more people get college degrees and specific training.

A Disproportionate Share of Total Unemployment Goes to African Americans

Do racial, ethnic, gender, and other kinds of discrimination and stereotyping cause more unemployment? Yes and no. Some groups (at different times Latino immigrants and women) get hired because they work for less. But many African Americans are rejected because of racist stereotypes and, sometimes, because Latinos are thought to be easier to manage. Also, both Latinos and African Americans have been hurt by the link between unemployment and criminal activity. More unemployment can actually lead to more criminal activity, but arrests and imprisonment can, in turn, make it harder for people to secure regular jobs. African Americans, in particular, have been especially victimized by the Reagan-Bush-Clinton war on drugs. That crusade meant more people in prison and more job-seekers with prison records.

Adding to the problem is that corporations underinvest in African American communities; also, black workers who live in or near white communities may not even hear about good working-class jobs because black job networks aren't well connected. White networks—Uncle Joe tells Bobby about a laborer's job and puts in a good word with the employer or the union—may not seem racist, but when the networks are all white, they mean fewer jobs for African Americans. That means more black unemployment, but it may not mean fewer total jobs in the economy.

The barriers to black people's employment success are many. Hiring discrimination is real. Experiments involving white and black applicants with the same skill-sets have shown time and again that employers discriminate against blacks. Such tests also show that employers eliminate people with criminal records in the time it takes to do an online search. So, blacks face racial discrimination and they are more likely to have criminal records, partly because they are more likely to be harassed, arrested, and convicted than are whites.[12]

So, black unemployment is high, twice as high as white unemployment because of the high levels of joblessness in America and because racism channels an extra dose to black people. But robust demand for labor can make a difference. If we had sustained full employment, if real wages always rose, if there were less racism and more programs to counsel job seekers and employers, employers would hire people whom they normally filter out, including African Americans with criminal records. Black imprisonment and unemployment rates would fall. The history of the late 1980s, 1960s, and 1990s is suggestive.

Black unemployment exceeded 20 percent in the early '80s recession. The recession destroyed millions of good jobs, including factory positions held by blacks; the recovery had not pushed the overall official unemployment below 5 percent or black unemployment under 10 percent before a new recession arrived in 1989–1990. In the '80s, President Reagan stoked racism by insulting poor people (when he attacked welfare queens, listeners knew that he often meant black people) and appointing Justice Department lawyers to sabotage civil rights enforcement. So, racism, too many bad new jobs, and the fact that unemployment stayed high through the 1980s limited economic advances for black people. White poverty rates were 10.2 percent in 1980 and 10 percent in 1989, but African American rates stayed much higher, at 32.5 percent and 30.7 percent.[13]

The 1960s were different. A combination of low unemployment and antiracist policies yielded some progress for African Americans. National unemployment stayed below 4 percent for four years. The ratio of black-to-white male unemployment fell from 2.5 (1957) to 1.8 (1970). The fraction of black-to-white female income rose from under 60 percent to over 80 percent. There were still many unemployed and poorly paid black people in the 1960s, but robust job creation, rising wages, and less discrimination made a difference.

White poverty rates in 1959 and 1969:   18.1 percent and 9.5 percent
Black poverty rates in 1959 and 1969:   55.1 percent and 32.2 percent[14]

After the 1960s, there wasn't another truly strong period for working-class African Americans until the late 1990s. Black poverty declined from 33.1 to 22.5 percent (1993 and 2000), white poverty from 12.2 to 10.5 percent. The Clinton-Greenspan boom pushed the national unemployment rate down to 4.0 percent in 2000—the best year from 1972 through November 2017. Until December 2017, the best month for African Americans was April 2000, when their rate fell to 7.0 percent. It is worth adding here that in 2018 and 2019, generally good labor markets pushed black unemployment rates to their lowest levels since the numbers were first collected in 1972. This was a real plus, but black rates were still more than twice as high as white rates (6.7 percent vs. 3.1 percent), and black poverty rates were still, at last count, 21 percent, more than twice white rates.[15]

Although neither the 1960s nor the late 1990s (or the late 2010s) were perfect, and the sources of some booms (Vietnam War spending and a financial bubble) were objectionable, those years showed that low overall unemployment and more positive attitudes could lift poor African Americans. But extreme income inequalities and much joblessness persist decades after the civil rights victories of the 1960s. Why that is so is an important question. Certainly, racism is comforting and intellectually useful to many Americans. Millions of white people felt good thinking that President Obama had not been born in America, and many worked for Donald Trump's election. Also, letting black people suffer depression levels of unemployment is useful to those who run the country. That unemployment for minorities is much higher than for whites makes the high unemployment generated by the economy more acceptable to whites. If the distribution of unemployment were reversed and whites had higher rates of unemployment, there would be more agitation to fix unemployment. As it is now, black unemployment can be rationalized by racist ideas—blacks are lazy and they are spoiled by government programs, so they don't have to work—and by seemingly neutral explanations that blacks have fewer skills and less education.

Does Heavy Immigration Cause More Total Unemployment?

Probably not as much as we might think, especially if immigrants are desperate for work. When a lot of immigrants flow into job markets, they help to keep wages down, and that may encourage job creation in some sectors. But competition from cheaper new immigrants can harm native-born workers, including the children of earlier immigrants and African Americans. Among people without a high school diploma and in the same ethnic group, unemployment for native-born workers is five points higher than for foreign-born workers. Why is that so? Perhaps native-born workers are less willing to work for very low wages at unpleasant jobs, and are less attractive to employers who want pliable workers. Whatever the reason, low-wage immigrants raise unemployment a bit for their U.S.-born sisters and brothers and for other poor people.[16]

Does Globalization Cause Unemployment?

Globalization adds to total unemployment, especially in the short run, and it has helped employers disempower workers and clamp down on pay and benefits. Some transfer of work to other countries was inevitable after World War II as Japan, Germany, and other countries rebuilt and offered quality goods at lower prices. But the wholesale exportation of good jobs to low-wage countries, especially in manufacturing, was also business policy, a weapon in the war on workers at home. Corporations offered their employees a choice: lower pay, lower benefits, and less job security, or no jobs. This take-it-or-leave-it policy was part of a campaign that was enthusiastically supported by conservatives and, in many of its aspects, by neoliberals like Bill Clinton. In fact, every president in modern times until Donald Trump has been enthusiastic about trade treaties that make it easy for capitalists to send jobs overseas.[17]

And the United States lost a lot of factory jobs. But is that why total unemployment stays high? Despite globalization, from December 1970 to December 2007, for example, the total number of nonfarm jobs almost doubled, from seventy-one million to 138 million. But while there were many more jobs, there were not enough for everyone who wanted one, and not enough good jobs. A continuing labor surplus, enlarged by job exports and employers' threats to close up shop, weakened workers' resistance power, and helped keep the lid on real wages.[18]

While job exports usually did not change official unemployment rates very much, they did reduce the number of good jobs open to workers of average skills, they added to the number of hidden unemployed people, and they decimated many communities. Clearly, the impact of globalization on factory workers has been severe. Manufacturing employees were 30 percent of the nonfarm American workforce in 1955. Now they're just 8.5 percent. Automation has been a major factor, but sending jobs abroad was also important. Researchers have estimated that NAFTA cost a million factory jobs and the opening to China cost two to three million more. Fewer decently paid factory jobs is a large backstory to the decline of African Americans' position in northern industry, the hollowing out of Detroit, Youngstown, and a dozen other factory towns, and rising rates of drug addiction and early mortality in white working-class communities. Many people left town to find jobs elsewhere, but many could not. Government did little to nothing to create good jobs for people of low education—black or white—in areas devastated by job loss. Free-market bias, for the most part the operational mode of most business leaders and leading politicians of both major parties, was one reason why globalization's results were fatal for some communities.

Government can do more; the private sector does not provide enough high-wage full employment. But it is naive to think that government can bring back enough factory jobs to equal their relative weight in the 1950s. We'd have to add thirty-one million factory jobs and that is not going to happen. But we could have more factory jobs. Robots and other forms of mechanization have been important in shrinking the factory workforce, but automation does not explain the $600 billion trade deficit in manufacturing. That deficit means we are buying more factory goods from outside the United States than we are selling. In the very best of cases it may be possible, through selective tariffs and restrictions on currency manipulation that some countries deploy to make their exports cheaper, to halve the $600 billion manufacturing trade deficit. That could add several million factory jobs.[19]

Several million good jobs where they are most needed could make a difference. If these jobs offered decent pay and benefits and union protections too, think what they might do in Baltimore, on the south side of Chicago, in opioid-ridden deindustrialized counties of Ohio, and a hundred other depressed urban and rural areas.

Are Robots Destroying Jobs and Raising Unemployment Rates?

Over the last century and a half, new technologies and new work methods have eliminated millions of jobs, first in agriculture and now in manufacturing. Globalization is one reason that the factory workforce is shrinking, but another is automation. Obviously, more jobs have been added in other sectors than were lost in those two sectors. But many new jobs in the retail, restaurant, and health sectors aren't well-compensated.

In the 1950s, experts predicted the end of work, but since then, the number of workers has doubled. Now experts are again sending out dire warnings. Some predict that most of the jobs we have now will be gone in forty years. But have we entered an era in which the total number of jobs has begun a long, permanent decline? Is everything going to be automated? Clearly, machines are getting smarter. A 2015 movie called *Ex Machina* was not too far off the mark. It featured robots that could do everything—cook, have sex with humans, and kill their masters. Manufacturers claim that we already have cars and trucks that can drive themselves without killing people. Programming itself may be taken over by other programs. Already, advanced warehouses employ relatively fewer people than in the past. Instagram and WHATSAPP are worth billions of dollars but may have relatively few employees.

But is a massive job collapse underway? The total number of American jobs has recovered from the recession and is at an all-time high. If we wanted to get to real full employment—2 percent unemployment is the official rate—in 2020, we'd need ten million jobs to accommodate those in and outside the labor force who want to work. Is automation an important reason why we are not there? Or is the reason that extreme economic inequality gives a relative handful of extremely rich people more money than they know what to do with—trillions are hiding overseas—while the public sector and the poorest half of all households lack spending power that would stimulate job creation on a grand scale? The latter seems more important right now.

Skeptics about the robot revolution have argued that robots should be more efficient than human beings. If they are taking over, we'd expect that efficiency levels in the workplace would be rising. But productivity growth is not high. Perhaps the reason is that many of the forms of automation that futurists talk about—self-driving cars, for example—are not yet in place.

Whether or not more automation in the future will cause a lot of permanent unemployment, Americans should be discussing how to create good jobs, raise compensation for the lower half, and, eventually, reduce the average work week. If we had effective federal job programs in place, we could be generating high-wage jobs, and we would be more prepared if robots took over too much work. If robotization eventually generates permanent mass unemployment, some kind of guaranteed income will be essential if people are to afford the basics and if we want to avoid a collapse of consumption spending and a great, great depression.

In a sane society, we might be discussing the benefits of a much shorter work week. More of us might be thinking about quality-of-life issues. Do we want to be examined by robot doctors and nurses and do we want our children and older people to be cared for by robots? Will some of us continue to like the idea of leaving the house to do our shopping and being waited on by a human being with whom we can chat?

But above all, we should be debating the fundamental economic issues. We should begin to find ways to spread the work we have, cut the normal work week, raise pay rates, and redistribute income downward so that shorter hours do not mean less total income for non-affluent workers, but more. Also, while most capitalists don't care much about the long-range health of the societies they work in, they ought to be in serious discussion about what they will do for a customer base if robots cut the workforce in half and leave many people with no or little income. For the most part, capitalists are racing to automate.

The summary point of this section is that we don't yet seem to be in a truly transformational period of automation, but we may be soon. In any case, we should be fixing problems that are here and well-known. Doing so will help to prepare us for an over-automated future. We know that average pay is low and that many people who work are poor. A higher minimum wage and new federal job programs are vital right now. If robots cut too many jobs, government programs will be in place and ready to expand.[20]

Do High Wages Cause More Unemployment and Fewer Jobs?

Many business owners and conservatives answer yes to both questions. As I suggested earlier, a plentiful supply of workers willing to work cheap may encourage job creation in some locales. But many workers cannot and won't work cheap enough—eight or nine dollars an hour or even less—to keep more jobs at home. More broadly, it is clear that while average pay has stayed low for decades, Americans have rarely had anything like full employment since the 1960s. That is, they have not gotten the alleged benefit of keeping pay down—enough jobs.[21]

The U.S. economy has generated a lot of jobs in the last half century, but never enough and certainly not enough good ones. And far from solving unemployment, low average pay caused massive unemployment just a few years ago. In the early 2000s, people with not enough income were encouraged by bankers to assume unsustainable mortgages, and the result was the worst unemployment crisis since the 1930s. Not a great recommendation for low wages as a job creator.

The negative outcome of low pay on employment is evident in other ways. There is, for example, the long decline in labor-force participation by prime-age males. (See chapter 6.) There are several explanations, but one is crummy pay. People who can find other sources of income sometimes stay home. Low wages, which are touted by conservatives as a job creator, often cause less involvement in the labor market.

Perhaps these points make sense to the reader, but the next one may not. Higher minimum wages don't cause much job loss. Why not? Surely, if legal minimums go up, owners have to raise prices. That could drive customers away and that means job loss. But is that the reality of gradual increases in minimum wages? If the national minimum wage of $7.25 were raised, say, 10 percent a year for ten years, would prices soar and millions of jobs disappear? A recent review of scholarly research found that a 10 percent annual increase in the minimum wage was associated with a 4 percent increase in food prices but only 0.4 percent for all prices.

State studies have also shown that higher minimums have not caused much job loss. One reason job loss was not large is the simple fact that some new minimums were still so low that they lifted relatively few people. But there were other explanations for why employers did not have to raise prices much. Employers do not have to increase pay for their better-paid workers when they lift low-wage employees. Also, better pay makes employees more loyal and productive. That means less turnover and lower hiring costs. Wal-Mart, a low-wage leader, decided not long ago that lousy pay meant lousy workers, messy stores, and unhappy customers. The company raised pay a bit and had positive results.[22]

In short, quite a bit of research shows that the unemployment effects of moderate annual increases in the minimum wage are small and that higher minimums can benefit businesses. And the positive effects on the working poor are substantial. A couple of dollars more per hour for someone earning nine dollars an hour is a big deal. And it means more consumer spending and that creates more jobs.

One final point. Criticisms of higher minimum wages suppress the role of income concentration among the affluent and the rich. As wages rise, consumer prices would have to be raised less if owners, investors, and the rich grabbed less income. Also, though rich people spend a lot on themselves, it's not enough. They save too much. We can help them spend more. A couple of years ago, the average annual income of the 1.4 million households in the top 1 percent was $1,264,000 and the income of the whole group was $2,000,000,000,000. Most of these people do pay taxes, but not enough and even less after the 2017 Republican tax cut. Americans should be going in the opposite direction. More taxation for those who can afford it. If we could get $200,000,000,000 more from the top 1 percent—about 10 percent of their income—we could pay twenty million full-time workers an extra five dollars an hour for a year. Or fund jobs for three million workers in a new WPA.[23]

Do Higher Taxes Mean Fewer Jobs and Tax Cuts More Jobs?

Some people think so, but at least for large businesses, it is likely that many other issues are more important factors behind job creation. Labor costs that are higher than those in less developed nations, the price of real estate, and, in some businesses, the availability of well-educated workers are key factors. Several years after the Reagan tax cuts in 1981, a lot of jobs were created. But many were low-wage jobs and job increases were not markedly different from what we'd expect in a recovery from a big recession. And the cuts did not keep more basic economic activity at home. The trade deficit increased six years in a row (1982–1987).

Most important, it is unlikely that the main reasons for high levels of job creation in the 1980s were lower tax rates for companies and individuals. A bigger reason was Keynesian deficits. The huge Reagan tax cuts meant huge federal deficits, and so the government was pumping a lot more money into the economy than it was taking out. But Keynesianism was linked to liberalism, and so Reagan and other Republicans railed against the deficits that were generating the economic growth they took credit for.

Most major job booms since the Great Depression can be linked to deficit spending. This is true on a grand scale of World War II, the Korean War, the War in Vietnam, and the Reagan era. The outstanding exception was the Greenspan-Clinton boom of the late 1990s. In 1993 Clinton and Democrats in Congress raised taxes a few points on rich households. That did not limit job creation. In fact, there was enough demand for labor in the late '90s that real average wages rose 8 percent (1995–2001)—the best record since the 1960s and early '70s.

In fact, conservative tax-cutting fervor often has had little to do with job creation. Increasingly it's a matter of rewarding big political donors. New tax breaks legislated in the George W. Bush presidency in 2001 and 2003 tilted overwhelmingly toward the rich and the affluent. It does not appear that the tax breaks added much to job creation. The recovery from the 2001 recession was sluggish and there was much talk of a "jobless recovery." From January 2001 through January 2005, government employment increased but the private sector lost 821,000 jobs. More startling, the number of production and non-supervisory employees in manufacturing fell by 2.2 million. But federal budget deficits increased and that added to the factors prodding economic growth. Eventually job creation picked up and unemployment fell to around 4 percent. But the number of people out of the labor force was higher than expected, and real hourly wages after 2002 rarely increased much. The Bush tax cuts added to income inequality, average wages stayed down, and more people took on risky loans to buy a piece of the good life. That wobbly system came crashing down in 2008. When President Trump and the Republican Congress gave corporations and rich people even more money in 2017, few Republicans even bothered to make fact-based arguments to the effect that more breaks for the rich would mean more good jobs.

Tax cuts aimed at average consumers are likely to have a larger impact on economic growth than those aimed at corporations and rich people, and the Obama recovery plan included such tax breaks as well as direct job-creation programs. But there was not enough federal spending to fill the void of inadequate private-sector spending—in part because of Republican obstruction—so jobs recovered at a slower than normal pace for recovery periods. But job numbers increased almost every month, right into the presidency of Donald Trump.

While there were troubles in job markets—in particular the dearth of good jobs—Mr. Trump created a largely fictional picture of the economy he inherited from Obama. He was right about the loss of jobs, especially in manufacturing, and the fact that Democrats had not done enough for left-behind communities. But his own policies would not do anything about the problem of lousy wages and his administration acted in ways that further disempowered workers. Republicans claim to love the white working class but they are dead-set against promoting unionization and they usually oppose legislation to raise the minimum wage. The all-purpose Republican economic program involves more deregulation for businesses and tax cuts slanted toward the rich and corporations. So, in 2017 Republicans enacted cuts on personal and corporate rates that offered some dollars for average households but huge benefits for rich people and corporations. Cutting the corporate rate was supposed to draw trillions of dollars back from foreign lands and overall stimulate job creation. But early surveys show that officers of large corporations planned to use most of the money for other things than job creation; one top priority was stock buy-backs, which lifts stock prices and makes many rich people richer for doing nothing. As of late 2018, there was little evidence of an extra bump in job creation beyond the year-to-year increase in job totals that had been established over the course of the long recovery from the Great Recession. As to real wage growth, 2014 was excellent at 3 percent and 2015 was better than nothing at 1.2 percent. In 2016 and 2017, whether under Obama or Trump, real wages went nowhere. In 2018 there was a 2 percent bump, but will the increases continue for several years this time?[24]

Do We Have Too Much Unemployment Because Government Interferes with Markets in its Efforts to Fight Depressions and to Provide Worker Protection Programs?

If laziness, skill deficits, discrimination, globalization, high taxes, and high wages are wrong or inadequate explanations, why don't we have full employment? It's a puzzle, especially because the general benefits of full employment are many. Real labor shortages lift wages and help to turn bad jobs into good jobs. The labor power of millions of people who weren't working is put to use. Poverty rates fall, minorities do better, retail sales increase, and so do government revenues. As people earn more, the Social Security, disability, and Medicare trust funds get richer. Wanting full employment seems like a no-brainer.

But many conservatives and some neoliberals want to march back toward the days when government did little to relieve the pains of unemployment and poverty. Perhaps they imagine that before liberal government programs, the nation usually had full employment. Chapters 1 and 2 have shown that was not true. And it is a fact that the economy does better than it did in the days of laissez-faire. Prior to the beginning of substantial programs for workers in the New Deal and substantial government efforts to promote economic recovery, the number of months of economic growth and months of decline were about equal in number. In the postwar period, from 1945 through 2009, with a big government in the mix, the number of months in which the economy grew were five times the number of months in which the economy shrank.[25]

If Government Can Be Effective, Why Aren't Americans Closer to Full Employment?

The broad answer is that powerful groups don't want full employment, or they do not like the methods that can bring it, or they don't want to be taxed to support more good jobs, or they don't want to expend resources to devise programs that limit such possible side-effects of truly full employment as higher inflation. Although the personnel in the following groups are not monolithic in their beliefs, these groups often fill out the army that stands against real full employment.

Some employers are wary of truly full employment. Firms that sell to the public and their investors want more customers with spending money, but usually not if that requires higher taxes to support government job programs. Most employers want a more than ample labor supply. They don't want really full employment because that makes it easier for employees to get wage increases. Most capitalists don't want real full employment.[26]

Most Republican conservatives—now most of the party—seem to believe that unemployed persons and poor people don't need financial assistance, or only for a very short time. Needy people need tough love or no love at all. More people must be compelled to work, no matter the compensation. Free-market politicians may be true believers but they also get a lot of money from anti-government extremists like the Koch brothers. The 2017 Republican tax cut was more about rewarding donors than creating jobs. The average conservative man and woman may feel, as Arlie Hochschild argued, that minorities and immigrants unfairly jump to the head of the line and that the federal government is helping them do it. Some of them might view large government job programs as just another way that the federal government rewards undeserving people. But their views are more fluid than those of Republican politicians. Many average Republicans have come around to support the essentials of Obamacare, although congressional Republicans and President Trump spent many hours trying to destroy it. The rank-and-file liked Trump's promises of more jobs for coal miners and factory workers and a major infrastructure program, but they must be getting disappointed on that front. Republican political leaders and party activists tend to be more conservative on economic and health issues than their constituents. Furthermore, partisanship is intense in the Congress. Most Republicans, even those who are not in the extremist Freedom Caucus, may not support major federal direct-job creation programs, especially if they are proposed by Democrats. Republicans did not support a stimulus package when the economy was about to go over the cliff in 2009.[27]

Many Democrats in Congress have not made real full employment a priority. There have been exceptions, like Representative John Conyers and people in the Congressional Black Caucus and other progressive formations, but most Democrats in the past accepted that the official unemployment rate was the real rate. It was typical of Democratic centrists that the 2016 candidate, Hillary Clinton, seemed indifferent to the unemployment problems affecting many regions of the country. Things may be changing. In 2019 the House of Representatives has more progressive Democrats and some of them understand the need for good-job legislation.

Most conservative economists and many mainstream liberal economists after the early 1970s have not made truly full employment a priority. Most liberal economists accepted the non-accelerating inflation rate of unemployment (NAIRU), and that meant higher unemployment. Many conservatives and some liberals were willing to believe the nonsensical proposition that whatever the level of NAIRU or the natural rate (NR), that was, by definition, full employment. For some economists, the idea of full employment has almost no independent existence anymore. You can see this erasure in a widely used text by the conservative-centrist economist, Gregory Mankiw. In *Macroeconomics* (2016), the concept of full employment is barely mentioned. There are two references in the index—that's all—and they are not about defining full employment. Standing in for full employment is the NR (Friedman's Natural Rate), which seems to be the equivalent of NAIRU, although the latter is not mentioned often. How do we know what the Natural Rate of Unemployment is? Is it derived from careful analysis of prices, wages, and unemployment levels? Not here. Here it is the average of many months of unemployment rates. Thus, the natural rate for May 2005 is the average of unemployment rates in the ten years before and the ten years after that month. So, we don't have to make an effort to judge how many jobs we'd need to fully employ everyone who needs and wants a job.

A few liberal economists have questioned the validity of NAIRU and the Natural Rate, and there's always been a group of left-liberals and Marxists who rejected it. But if there were a full-employment job-creation program being discussed in Congress tomorrow, some liberal economists and most conservatives would find reasons to oppose it. Many would say they feared excessive wage and price inflation, but few would exert themselves to fight for other ways to limit inflation than by restraining job growth.[28]

Among investors, bankers, and Federal Reserve officials, goals vary by group and time. Big players in the stock market like low interest rates and cheap money, strong economic growth, and even modestly rising wages, which can boost consumption and generate higher profits and dividends. They don't mind a little inflation and they like some job growth, but too much of each may cause the Federal Reserve to raise interest rates, and many investors don't want that. When unions are weak and the labor force has plenty of jobless people, financiers are happy with an official unemployment rate below 5 percent. If real wages rose for several years, some of them might want less economic growth and even a recession.

Bankers are wary of full employment to the extent that they think it comes with inflation; higher inflation reduces the real value of the loan repayments owed to them and brings uncertainty about Federal Reserve policies. Generally, bankers like economic growth—more customers—but not too much growth. Most of them probably think the best strategy for the Federal Reserve is vigilance about wages and prices and minor adjustments to interest rates in order to nurture growth but not real full employment.[29]

In recent decades, Federal Reserve chairs have sometimes acted vigorously to keep unemployment high. In the late 1970s, President Carter appointed Paul Volcker to lead the Federal Reserve's all-out war on inflation. Volcker delivered a big recession with 10 percent unemployment in 1981–1983. The recession helped to trim inflation and it destroyed millions of good jobs, some of them permanently. Alan Greenspan, appointed Fed chair in 1987, was ever on the alert for signs of high labor demand and rising wages, so he sometimes raised interest rates to slow economic growth just as it was lifting pay for low- and middle-wage workers. It was said that he "would rather have higher unemployment than run the risk of inflation . . . he wants a certain proportion of Americans to be unemployed permanently." But for a man whose bedrock views were very conservative, Greenspan restrained himself at times, and he allowed unemployment to fall to 4 percent in the late 1990s. Janet Yellen, who became Fed chair in 2014, began raising interest rates in very small steps, but at times she seemed aware that there was significant unemployment despite the low official unemployment rate. Her successor, Jerome Powell, has been cautious about raising interest rates, and he could be restrained about it because inflation rates have stayed low. So, low interest rates have been one factor in prolonging the economic boom that began with recovery from the Great Recession. As emphasized many times in this book, the official unemployment rate is not the whole story about jobs and joblessness, but an official unemployment rate of 3.9 percent is quite low and has been extremely rare in peace-time since 1948.[30]

Finally, rich and affluent Americans have money and influence, but most aren't concerned about unemployment. It rarely hits them, and if they are business owners, they benefit from the general surplus of labor (and it's nice to employ gardeners and maids who have to work for peanuts). They may have no deep contact with the unemployed, and when they meet the working poor, they don't really understand them. Powerful persons who interact with the less powerful tend to be less compassionate than the less powerful are. Less powerful people face more insecurity on the job and off. They may feel they have to show that they are concerned about their employer to hang on to their jobs. Also, affluent persons may be inclined to think that the poor are poor because they lack skills or talents. After all, aren't the rich rich because they are more intelligent? Finally, wealthy households don't suffer much from recessions. Their unemployment rate is often negligible and, surprise, having a lot of money makes economic problems less urgent. If you have five million dollars and lose one million, you still have four million for a decent living and seed money to generate more wealth. Already by 2012, the richest 5 percent of households had recovered their 2007 income levels while the poorest 20 percent were still 10 percent below their 2007 levels. During the Great Recession banks got more help than people who couldn't pay their mortgages.[31]

· · ·

In sum, these are the groups that stand against government programs that could directly create enough good jobs to bring truly full employment. Some people in these groups are not against full employment. I've described general tendencies. The big point is that excessive unemployment is not necessary; it is something that influential people allow to happen or cause to happen.

A Mini-History of Resistance to Full Employment

A short review of the history of unemployment and full employment will put more flesh on the bones of the topics in the last section.

Excessive and even catastrophic levels of unemployment were the norm in past periods that featured non-interventionist economic policy. From 1870 through 1930, with low levels of government regulation, capitalism generated six major depressions, several smaller slumps, and excessive unemployment in many prosperous periods. With heavy immigration thrown into the mix, the robber barons usually had a large labor surplus to work from and they usually dominated the bargaining game with employees. Wage growth there was, but it was limited and the rich grew very rich. As scientists and owners revolutionized production on farms and in factories, potential output raced ahead of business needs and mass purchasing power. More railroads were built than were needed. Consumer items could be produced in excess of mass spending power. Even in the better times between the depressions of the 1870s and 1890s, whiskey producers were operating at only 40 percent of their capacity and there were "too many stoves and not enough people to buy them." In the late 1920s, there was no need to hire people to build more auto factories.[32]

Why weren't fundamentals fixed? Was it lack of economic knowledge that kept capitalists from raising wages and politicians from experimenting with programs to counteract depressions and high unemployment? If so, it was a convenient form of ignorance. Recall from chapter 1 Coxey's plans for government-funded job programs and frequent protests by the unemployed for government assistance. It was not difficult to think that government could create jobs. But most business leaders, most economists, and many upper-middle-class persons did not want solutions to depressions, even if some capitalists and some middle-class owners and employees went down in depressions. Scapegoating poor people and unemployed workers was better than government regulation and government spending on job creation. Nasty ideas about the unemployed bolstered the authority of robber barons like Carnegie and Rockefeller and captains of charity like Josephine Shaw Lowell.

So, Americans had too much unemployment, and it was not because of strong unions or minimum wage laws. Nor was it because influential people just happened to have bad ideas, or because economists had not yet discovered the secret formula for full employment under a rock. For some people in the nineteenth century and still today, religious ideas supported the view that the sins of the poor were the reason they were poor. But also, not fixing the unemployment problem paid off in cash for capitalists and was in line with economists' dearly held dogmas. For owners, an unprotected and insecure working class was more easily exploited. Also, substantial government intervention to counteract depressions and to give income to the unemployed threatened the legitimacy of capitalists' right to rule, for it acknowledged that capitalism could not maintain high employment, contrary to free-market dogma that said unregulated capitalism naturally tended toward full employment.[33]

As depressions piled up in the late 1800s, conservatives and capitalists continued to claim that when millions were without food or shelter, the solutions were personal and individual, not political and systemic. People should have saved more in better times to provide for hard times. Why did they have to "eat and drink up their earnings as they go?" Could it be that they had nothing left for savings after normal expenses? Not so. They just weren't trying. People suffered when there was no work because, said the president of the University of Wisconsin, they had been wasteful and extravagant. They were laid off not by employers and economic conditions but by their own failure to make themselves indispensable. This was the kind of nasty economics people of privilege thought they could get away with back then.[34]

A change of tone was apparent around the turn of the century. The depressions of the late 1800s began to erode old dogmas. Some scholars tried to understand unemployment, and settlement house workers showed empathy for the poor. But the new attitudes had little impact on government policy. In the 1920s federal policy was not so different from what it had been in the late 1800s. Unemployment was still a dark cloud over working-class communities, and it was unrelieved by government assistance programs.[35]

Meanwhile, the rich took a bigger piece of the income pie, so inequality increased and mass consumption could not keep up with the always increasing productive capacity of the world's leading economy. In the 1920s, capitalists won the class struggle over income shares too well, and the result was a catastrophic loss of jobs and income in the 1930s.

Solutions to the Great Depression did not come quickly. President Hoover did more than previous presidents, but not much. As we learned in chapter 2, he was stubbornly opposed to direct federal aid for the unemployed. Franklin Roosevelt expanded credit and spent on welfare and job programs. Roosevelt's New Dealers, led by Harry Hopkins and Frances Perkins, urged Americans to stop blaming the poor and the unemployed for their situations. The New Dealers restarted job creation, but they weren't able to end the depression. Then World War II raised government spending massively and a lot of it was deficit spending. War made Keynesianism non-debatable for a while. Deficit spending supported sixteen million new military and civilian jobs in 1940–1943. That meant full employment and real labor shortages.

At the end of the war, the lessons of the 1930s and '40s seemed clear. Americans did not have to have high unemployment. They could cushion people against unemployment with federal job programs and unemployment insurance. And they could increase federal spending to ensure full employment. But many leaders did not like the methods or the results. In the same way that leaders had chosen not to learn in the late 1800s, many of them now resisted the lessons of the recent past about government job creation and deficit spending.

In the years that followed, Americans benefited from passive Keynesianism, which owed less to anti-unemployment policy than to rapidly increasing federal budgets, especially for the military. Unions and limited growth in the labor force helped many workers secure higher wages and benefits. Cultural norms and progressive taxation meant that the 1 percent did not siphon off as much spending power as they do today.

International competition was not a major threat. Government-assisted capitalist markets and military spending worked for quite a few people. But in the late 1950s, economic growth slowed. Economists debated whether stubbornly high unemployment came from structural change in particular industries and regions or insufficient aggregate demand. Both approaches shaped liberal responses in the 1960s, but Keynesian tax cuts to increase total demand were the most important, and their effect was amplified by spending on Vietnam. Tax cuts and spending increases pushed unemployment below 4 percent for four years—a unique record in the post–World War II era. But economists and business leaders worried about wage and price inflation. And nearly full employment gave employees enough bargaining power that their compensation took a bite out of profits. Profit rates for nonfinancial businesses fell from 13.7 percent to 8.7 percent (1966–1973).[36]

For capitalists, workers were too powerful, and for conservatives there was too much liberal government—the War on Poverty, minimum-wage laws, support for unions, federal spending, and monetary programs that stimulated job growth enough to increase employee bargaining power. In the 1970s, conservatives and business leaders mobilized to cut regulations and programs that served the poor and working class, in order to restore profit margins. Higher inflation and rising foreign competition were real, but they were also propaganda points. Unions, high wages, full employment, and government spending were blamed for inflation and trade deficits. Business leaders, scholars, and politicians—and not always just conservatives—came to accept that high unemployment was the best way to control wages and prices and, for some leaders, the way to tip the balance of labor-capital relations further toward capital. The Volcker-Reagan recession of 1981–1983, with the worst unemployment since the 1930s, traumatized many workers.

So, although in the late 1930s, the early 1940s, and the 1960s Americans learned a lot about how to bring fuller employment, important interest groups did not like the effects of full employment. In the 1800s, they had not wanted to learn how government should fight unemployment; in the late 1900s, they did not want to fight inflation in ways that did not raise unemployment.

From the late 1970s through the early 2000s, capitalists won many battles in the class war. Union density declined. The rich became far richer while real wages stagnated. Gross income inequalities meant that one propeller of job growth—the purchasing power of the lower 90 percent—was less than it should have been. Instead of better pay for workers, bankers found new, risky ways to lend back to the people the billions they had extracted from them in the workplace and at the cash registers. They sold mortgages to people who could not afford them. The rickety structure came tumbling down in 2008. Official unemployment hit 10 percent and declined very slowly.

Adequate government stimulus spending and direct job creation, as well as more income to the working class, would have brought fuller employment. But conservatives resisted and some liberals, infected with timidity and orthodox economics, did not fight back much. Many Tea Party supporters who were not affluent were blinded by racism, economic stress, and anxieties about an immigrant takeover of America. Few of them knew about the real causes of depressions and poverty. Many of them resented food stamps, Obamacare, government spending for the unemployed, and—when Democrats did it—government spending to stimulate job growth and anything they thought might raise anyone's taxes in order to help people in need. So, they lined up with the most reactionary elements of the richest 1 percent and against full employment. They lined up to have their pockets picked.[37]

Americans have almost never had truly full employment—whether in the 1890s or the 2010s—because powerful interests benefit from less-than-full employment and extreme income inequalities. Many people who would benefit from government-directed job creation programs support politicians and donors who don't want such programs. As 2019 began, there were still millions of jobless people outside the labor force, but not much was being done at the national level to hook them up to jobs, or lift the pay of millions of working poor people.

CHAPTER 8

Real Full Employment

Where Capital Fails, How Government Can Succeed

Wage growth has been terrible since the 1960s and job growth has been on-again-off-again since 1980 (as table 8.1 makes clear). It's been rare after the '60s to have strong job growth and strong wage growth at the same time.[1]

The Great Recession was a catastrophe for millions of people in the United States, but it did add energy to movements organizing against income inequality and for higher wages. Occupy Wall Street had a big impact. Unions and low-wage workers demonstrated. Around the country, state and local governments began to raise their minimum wages, sometimes to levels that had once seemed unattainable.

During the recession, everyone was talking about unemployment, but as the economy improved and the official unemployment rate fell, less was said about the need for job creation. It is true that Donald Trump promised to bring back jobs in the mines and factories and to add millions of infrastructure jobs; but after more than two years, he had presented no realistic plans for adding a significant number of good jobs. The Trump administration fought to pull back from trade treaties, but it used tariffs in a ham-fisted way that often ended up hurting American farmers by inciting retaliatory tariffs and American manufacturers who depended on foreign sources for parts of their production process. In 2017 there were tax cuts favoring rich people and businesses but not much for the average worker. Bush's tax cuts in the early 2000s leaned the same way; working-class incomes grew slowly or not at all, and that was one reason so

Table 8.1   Report Card on Real Wages and Job Growth, Five-Year Periods, 1950–2015

	Wages	Jobs
1950–1955	A+	A
1955–1960	A	B
1960–1965	B+	A
1965–1970	C	A+
1970–1975	F	B+
1975–1980	FF	A+
1980–1985	FF	D
1985–1990	FF	A
1990–1995	FF	D
1995–2000	C-	A
2000–2005	F	F
2005–2010	F	FF
2010–2015	D	B

Total five-year growth in wages and jobs graded thusly: 10% or more = A, 8%-9% = B, 7% = C, 6% = D, under 6% = F, decline = FF. For jobs, CES nonfarm totals at BLS.gov, measured January to January; for example, figures for 2010–2015 compare January 2010 to January 2015. Real wages from various years of the *Economic Report of the President,* including 2016, table B-15, 418.

many people assumed mortgages they could not really afford. The end result was the catastrophic employment collapse in the Great Recession.

Americans need to turn bad jobs into good jobs by raising wages and benefits, and they need to create more good jobs from the ground up. While the official rate of unemployment was under 4 percent in the spring of 2019, there were almost sixteen million people who wanted a job or wanted to move from part-time to full-time work.[2] In 2019 Americans did not have full employment or enough good jobs. Here is what real full employment might look like in ten years if job programs began soon:

What Real Full Employment Might Look Like in 2029

- The federal government guarantees a job for everyone who needs one. That ensures full employment. At real full employment, the official unemployment rate is at or below 2 percent.
- Securing a new job takes only a month or two. There are real labor shortages and employers routinely raise wages to attract workers. Job-seekers have much more bargaining power. Before the new job programs, even in better times, observers could rarely find evidence of significant wage gains,

and so they had to be excited about real wage increases of 1 percent. Now, real wages are increasing 2 to 3 percent a year.

- The economy adds 300,000 to 400,000 jobs per month, instead of 200,000. Sound impossible? As mentioned, there are about sixteen million people who want jobs or are part-time workers looking for full-time jobs. Many of these people are not counted as unemployed and looking for work, but they are. In the past, the majority of the people who found jobs every month weren't in the labor force the month before.

- The federal minimum wage rises every year. It is $20 an hour in 2029. Because of fuller employment and high demand for workers, most employers have to pay more than that. The actual average working-class wage, which was $23.10 in January 2019, is $35 in 2029. Even after inflation, the purchasing power of that wage is up by about a third.

- The national unemployment rate of 2 percent pretty much holds true across the land. There are specific programs for communities that were left behind by the job boom of the 2010s. Thanks in part to the focus of the National Full Employment Trust Fund in the Humphrey-Hawkins 21st Century Full Employment and Training Act (HH21), and similar programs, a disproportionate number of jobs are going to areas with extremely high levels of joblessness. Jobless rates for young African Americans in Chicago and poor whites in Appalachia are falling fast. Lifting people in these areas is a work in progress, and has been least successful in rural counties with few people. But experiments in bringing jobs to the countryside or helping people move to job-rich areas are underway.

- Full-employment America includes a dense network of social services to facilitate employment, including universal, affordable child care and federal training programs linked to real jobs. Affirmative action is broadly conceived and enforced. Minorities, poor people, and residents of hollowed-out communities really have a chance to get decent jobs. Federal policy and government-supported citizen-groups help ex-prisoners find work. Employers are required to accommodate people with disabilities, and because there are labor shortages, they are more willing to comply than in the past.[3]

- From 1970s onward, the private sector thrived on low wages and a labor surplus. That is one reason why real full employment required direct government job creation. Now, in 2029, the federal presence has spread. There are thousands of new public- and private-sector projects funded and supervised by the federal government. They range from new parks, better bridges, and clean water projects to more and better Head Start schools, more green-energy businesses, and high-speed broadband for rural areas and tribal lands. Some projects are supervised by the Department of Labor or by the new Department of Public Infrastructure. There is attractive signage identifying many federal projects.

· Job quality is improving in terms of employee involvement and opportunities for advancement. As compensation improves, there is more discussion about reducing the standard forty-hour work week.[4]

Methods That Look Good on Paper But Don't Add Many Good Jobs

ADDING FREE-TRADE TREATIES OR REPLACING OLD ONES WITH HIGH TARIFFS WON'T HELP MUCH

International agreements such as NAFTA were alleged to promote jobs at home and abroad. But factory workers lost millions of good jobs to low-wage producers around the world. As a conservative economist put it, contrary "to what many economists had promised . . . the rise of Chinese exports . . . held down the wages of some parts of the American middle class."[5] The United States has to trade with other nations, and less-developed nations need to sell to richer countries, but people don't have to believe it when neoliberal and conservative free-marketers assert that freer trade is always a plus for workers. On the other hand, the connections between American-based production and overseas suppliers is complex and intricate. A heavy-handed laying on of new tariffs, especially on China and Europe, as the Trump administration has been doing, is unlikely to add much to the number of U.S. factory workers. American producers who currently need foreign parts, materials, or craftsmanship may find them in countries that aren't under heavy new tariffs. Also, as the United States raises tariffs on some countries, those countries retaliate with their own tariffs.[6]

WORK HARDER, PEOPLE! AND GET SOME SKILLS!

Wouldn't we have more jobs if people tried harder and if they upgraded their skills? Mostly not. Despite conservative rants about lazy workers, most people want to work. At least four million part-time workers want full-time jobs. Low-wage workers must deal with employers who cheat them out of their daily wages and misclassify them to avoid overtime rates. Yet they keep going to work.[7]

But don't workers need more skills and schooling? It is true that an individual with more skills and education normally does better. Apprenticeship programs linked to jobs—"learning by earning"—may be effective. More tuition-free colleges would offer low-income people specific and general skills that can help them get better jobs. Also, training funds should be included in federal

Table 8.2   More Education, Same Wages

	1980	1990	2000	2010	Total change
% of adults 25 & over w/4-year degrees	16.2	21.3	25.6	29.9	84.0%
Real Wage (1982–1984 dollars)	$8.26	$7.91	$8.30	$8.78	6.3%

Sources: School data from various years of the U.S. Bureau of the Census, *Statistical Abstract of the United States.* Wages from *Economic Report of the President, 2013* (Washington, D.C.: U.S. Government Printing Office, 2013), table B-47.

job-creation programs, as they are in the Humphrey-Hawkins 21st Century Full Employment and Training Act (HH21). But training and education should not be thought of as an alternative to creating more jobs with better pay. After all, there are more Americans with college degrees than in the past, but that isn't lifting the working class as a whole. Table 8.2 shows a general disconnect for a recent thirty-year period.[8]

IF WORKERS WERE CHEAPER, WOULD THERE BE MORE GOOD JOBS?

Table 8.1 showed that low wages were often accompanied by episodes of low job creation. Also, while low pay may bring jobs to some sectors, as a national trend, it means households cannot afford an American standard of living, except by assuming too much debt. In the early 2000s, that meant millions of risky loans and that set the stage for a major shrinking of job totals in the Great Recession.[9]

WHY NOT GIVE SUBSIDIES AND TAX CREDITS TO EMPLOYERS WHO HIRE THE UNEMPLOYED?

Some experts favor subsidies to businesses for every unemployed worker hired, but studies of the effectiveness of this policy aren't encouraging. Such programs are usually aimed at hard-to-employ workers. The jobs are often temporary, and a fair number of employers get rewarded for hiring that they would be doing anyway. It's true that some disadvantaged people, including people with baggage (for example, ex-offenders), sometimes get a job that leads to a permanent position, but many employers cut positions when the subsidies end, and workers are jobless again. On the whole, Enterprise Zone programs and similar efforts to reward capitalists for investing in poor communities have not helped poor people much.

There is also a complex ethical question here. Is it good that government does so much to subsidize employers who pay poverty wages? The Earned Income Tax Credit (EITC), Medicaid, food stamps, and other programs already make it easier for employers to pay low wages. Quite a few Wal-Mart employees survive by using Medicaid and food stamps.

We should not get rid of the EITC, Medicaid, food stamps, and similar programs—people need them now—but when it comes to job creation, policymakers should focus on creating jobs with decent wages rather than programs that subsidize low-wage employers and rich investors. We should be creating millions of regular jobs with good pay. And not just for the poor. A program open to the broader working class includes more people who need decent jobs, and it is politically stronger. Of course, the needs of people in groups with extra-high unemployment, and people with negative baggage should receive priority. Ex-offenders may need psychological counseling. Some people will need wrap-around support services, including skills improvement, help with child-care, and someone to talk to about unsympathetic supervisors. And affirmative actions are essential to reduce discrimination, and especially institutionalized racism in job markets. But job programs must not be limited to the very poor and underprivileged; others need jobs or better jobs, and a program that includes non-poor participants is less easily eliminated than one that serves only the poor.[10]

WHY NOT RELY ON MONETARY AND FISCAL TOOLS THAT WE HAVE EXPERIENCE WITH?

The Federal Reserve has often kept interest rates low to encourage economic growth and job creation. But when unemployment falls too much, Fed officials begin to worry about wage and price inflation. They sometimes raise interest rates to curb job growth before full employment is reached. It's true that when inflation was low in the late 1990s, the Fed usually kept interest rates down, and that spurred job creation. Wages actually began to rise for low-skill workers. Normally, the Fed likes a little of that, but not too much. Lately, the Fed hasn't had much wage or price inflation to worry about, so it has not needed to raise interest rates very much in the cause of slowing the economy and restraining inflation. But in the long run, it is not a reliable friend in the battle for full employment and decent pay.

A final point. Even when the Federal Reserve supports easy credit, a fair amount of new money does nothing to create jobs. Easy money may finance good jobs, bad jobs, or no jobs. It may finance new jobs in San Francisco rather than Harlan County, Kentucky. It may travel to another country. The same is true of tax-cut money.[11]

We know that increased spending, tax cuts, and budget deficits powered economic growth and job additions in the liberal '60s and in the conservative '80s. But tax cuts that give the game away to corporations and rich people don't generate enough good jobs. The Reagan boom was not very effective at lifting people out of poverty and it never got close to full employment. The George

W. Bush tax cuts did not bring much of an extra bump in new jobs and higher wages. By one estimate, the Bush cuts were 1/15 as effective as direct job creation would have been.[12] During the Great Recession, Moody's Analytics economist Mark Zandi argued that spending on Food Stamps, unemployment insurance, and infrastructure would stimulate more job creation than Bush-style tax cuts that favored the rich and corporations.[13]

Rich people and corporate planners are skilled at finding alternatives to spending on good jobs in the United States. They send capital abroad to hire cheaper workers, and they stash billions of dollars in low-tax havens overseas. Many of them invest heavily in job-killing automation and some buy companies with tiny workforces. In 2014 Facebook paid $19 billion for the WHATSAPP messaging company that had fifty-five employees. CEOs get bonuses and cheers from Wall Street for cutting jobs and limiting employee compensation. Many companies used new money from the Republican tax cut of 2017 to fund stock buy-backs, not to fund new jobs. In general, as a job creator, tax cuts for the rich are iffy at best. More money is thrown out there, but the recipients can do whatever they want with it. It is more efficient for the federal government to spend directly to create good jobs in the public and private sectors.[14]

Can the Federal Government Manage Job Programs?

If we agree that the private sector won't create enough good jobs, and if we agree that hail-Mary tax cuts and low interest rates aren't sufficient, then direct job creation is essential for real full employment. But are government officials up to the task? We have had stunning failures of government management, including the response to Hurricane Katrina and the rollouts of Medicare D and Obamacare. But federal officials don't usually mess up, and business leaders bomb all the time. A quick review of the historical record is instructive.[15]

In the first sixty years of the modern American economy (1873–1933), capitalists failed to provide the majority of the population with a decent living. In the long term, average incomes increased, but periods of advance were punctuated by painful depressions. The worst one began in 1929, and it stimulated reforms on a grand scale. Starting in 1933, the federal government began to offer income and job programs for the poor and unemployed. In chapter 2 we learned about the CCC, the WPA, the PWA, and CWA. The WPA typically had two to three million people working at hundreds of jobs, from road repair to child care. The PWA funded and supervised public infrastructure projects carried out by private firms. By the end of the '30s, the PWA had built something—dams, airports, bridges, schools, post offices—in 3,068 of 3,071 American counties. In this agency and others, government officials were effective administrators.[16]

In the war and postwar eras, the federal government played a vital role in economic adaptation and innovation. Government employees helped win the war, training millions of troops and workers and directing the war economy. Over the years, the National Institute of Health helped to create dozens of new drugs, and defense spending stimulated job creation and also contributed to innovations that gave birth to Silicon Valley. Touch-screen technology was developed in government labs in the United States and Europe. In the 1960s, liberal politicians responded to civil rights activism by passing landmark legislation. They also created Medicare and Medicaid and improved Social Security. By and large, these programs worked. Later programs helped, too. Obamacare endured a rough opening, but within a couple of years, twenty million uninsured Americans had health insurance.

And we know that large corporations fail all the time in matters of economic efficiency and ethics. Big financial concerns failed massively in the run-up to the Great Recession. Dozens of rich companies, including Facebook and credit-reporting companies, have not protected people's privacy rights. It is true that public-private institutions, such as the Federal Reserve, enabled bad behavior by not regulating enough, but bankers themselves fought regulation, and many of them showed little concern about the health of the economy or even of the banking system. It is true, too, that government did more to save the bankers than to help people losing their homes. But there is little doubt that the Federal Reserve's money policies and Obama's stimulus package kept the economy from falling into a great depression.[17]

Finally, it is worth remembering that some public-sector SNAFUS reflect private-sector incompetence. Governments hire private experts who aren't always very expert. By contrast, one of the simplest and least privatized programs, Social Security, works well.

All that being said, we do seem to have a management problem. Why don't we have enough competent administrators in the public sector? One reason might be that we don't pay top managers enough. Another is that politicians are always in kill mode. Republicans routinely demonize people in government service. That makes public service less attractive for good managers. Finally, Bush, Obama, and other presidents are often too busy raising money to manage their own managers. Public financing of political campaigns would help, but don't hold your breath.

What Kind of Job Programs?

Some job programs can be managed by existing federal departments, and some can be funded and supervised by the Department of Labor and a new Department of Public Infrastructure (DPI).

The DPI exists only as an idea, but such a department would make infrastructure work a priority. For several years now, a modern Humphrey-Hawkins bill has been introduced in the House of Representatives as H.R. 1000, and recently it had twenty-nine representatives sponsoring it. It proposes to reduce the official unemployment rate to 4 percent in the short term and to continue reducing joblessness thereafter to get to real full employment. Full employment will be guaranteed in the sense that everyone who needs a job and cannot find one elsewhere will get a job at fair compensation. To create more jobs, the government will increase investment in public infrastructures, but it will also use the trust fund to directly create millions of public-service jobs. The Department of Labor will make grants to state agencies, Indian tribes, local government agencies, educational institutions, and nonprofits. The grants can cover a wide range of activities, including: construction or rehabilitation of residences and public facilities to encourage energy efficiency; expanded social services, including training and job networking for disadvantaged youth; augmentation of Head Start and similar programs; renovation of parks and other public spaces; expansion of Work-Study programs; and supplemental labor for infrastructure projects that are receiving state and federal funds. The grants are to focus on areas of high joblessness, high poverty rates, and high rates of vacant and abandoned properties. HH21 will be financed by a small tax on securities transactions.[18]

HH21 is one model of a full-employment program. But whatever the specifics, federal agencies ought to follow three guidelines. First, not all government-created jobs are good for society or workers. A million-dollar investment in fossil fuels generates only 5.3 jobs, raises global temperatures, and makes extreme weather events more likely. A million-dollar investment in clean energy adds seventeen jobs and staves off climate disaster. Investments in education (twenty-seven jobs) are better than military spending (twelve jobs). Economist Robert Pollin estimated that shifting $330 billion out of fossil fuels and military spending and into education and clean energy projects could add 4.8 million jobs; that's because the latter are less capital- and more labor-intensive.[19]

Second, some government-created jobs will disappear when they are no longer needed, but the goal of full-employment policy, in my opinion, ought to be the creation of permanent jobs in many areas, from Head Start to water recycling and infrastructure maintenance. Some employment experts propose plans only for recessionary periods or for underprivileged Americans, but other Americans need good jobs too and in prosperous times. Some people will cycle out of the public programs as wages rise elsewhere, but we should not follow the WPA model and make wages and hours so stingy as to force workers back into the private sector as soon as possible. Pay levels should match the best in local markets, and if the programs started today, there should be an absolute minimum wage of $15 an hour. Critics today attack $15 as too lavish and a threat to job creation, but $15 an hour is just over $30,000 a year. That's poverty for anyone with family responsibilities and even for single people in high-rent areas. The policy goal for new good jobs should not be to tide people over at poverty-level wages on make-work projects until they can transition to "real" jobs in the private sector. And government should not be labeled "the employer of last resort." The rhetoric is deadly and so is the idea. Working at Wal-Mart or running around like a rat in an Amazon warehouse are last-resort jobs. New federal jobs should involve useful work that needs doing and is justly rewarded. Many of the jobs will be permanent positions.

Finally, our goal should not be that everyone is working all the time. Enough jobs and better compensation will make it easier for individuals to take a break from work, whether the reason is to take care of a child or an ill person, or write a great American song or novel.

There are hundreds of possible job programs, but here are specific examples:

More Buses. In many cities, we can expand alternatives to the automobile to slow global warming and ease congestion. Trains and trams may pollute less than buses, but they are expensive to build and maintain. Buses are easy to add and they can use cleaner fuels. We could create thousands of jobs and reopen automobile factories in dying neighborhoods if we sharply increased the number of buses in service.[20]

Infrastructure Spending. A Department of Public Infrastructure can partially fund and supervise private contractors in construction and repair projects. It is widely acknowledged—President Trump once talked about a trillion-dollar program—that many of the nation's bridges, roads, schools, dams, levees, airports, water pipes, and other physical structures are in bad shape. Many waste energy. Bad roads damage vehicles.

A big push on infrastructure does not force administrators into areas where they have no experience. Governments and contractors are doing this kind of thing every day. But the DPI would supervise a large increase in spending. How large? In 2017 the American Society of Civil Engineers gave U.S. infrastructure a D+ and estimated that there was a ten-year $2 trillion investment gap. If all levels of government together increased infrastructure spending by $200 billion a year, we'd have smoother roads, cleaner water, safer bridges, and four million new jobs.[21]

When we talk about bridges and roads and water systems, we may forget humbler structures that need work. Many public schools need repair and modernization. If you have recently visited a public school in a low-income neighborhood, you know this. In the last two decades, spending on school upkeep has lagged. It would take an additional $300 billion to bring schools back to their original condition and more money to upgrade facilities for the twenty-first century. Other entities have to help, too, but the federal government should take the lead. But where will the money for the federal contribution come from? President Trump has not invested much effort in this area, but he and his staff have proposed to privatize more infrastructure. Democrats and important business groups, including the U.S. Chamber of Commerce, support an increase in the gas tax, which has not been raised in twenty-five years. But conservatives who dominate the Republican Party oppose that strategy. In the fall of 2017, Republican Senate leader Mitch McConnell helped push through Congress tax cuts that favored the rich and increased the federal deficit by trillions of dollars. But he said he would not support infrastructure repair if it added to the deficit. It seems likely that an adequately financed program that does not give too much away to private companies will not be enacted while Republicans control much of the government.[22]

Day Care and Head Start. If you ask working mothers whether they are happy with their current day-care arrangements, many, including some who are not poor, say that the high cost of quality care is a cloud over their lives. There are tax credits, subsidies, and Head Start for some families, but not enough for everyone. Quality care is expensive. A comprehensive system of first-rate care will create more child-care jobs and allow parents to work outside the home with confidence that their children are safe.

We can begin with Head Start. We should raise eligibility cut-offs, which are stuck at the poverty line. A family of four with total income over $25,750 a year is not normally eligible for Head Start. If we get more people into Head Start, we create more Head Start jobs. We can also lift the profession of Head Start teacher. A majority of Head Start teachers have a B.A. in early childhood education, but their salaries recently averaged only $37,000.[23]

Greening the Economy adds jobs and slows the drift toward environmental catastrophe. The possibilities are endless. Some neighborhoods—low-income areas of Los Angeles, for example—need more parks, picnic grounds, and park workers. Building, expanding, repairing, and running parks means jobs for landscapers and recreation leaders. More greenery and less concrete means cooler temperatures. Members of youth conservation corps can be hired for some of this work. With incentives from state and federal governments, local governments can modernize and beautify medians and town centers. Rooftops of more commercial and government buildings can be planted with greenery or loaded with solar panels. Research on renewable energies, including wind turbines, solar panels, and electricity storage batteries received $70 billion in Obama's stimulus package. That gave a boost to renewable businesses despite the highly publicized failure of Solyndra.[24]

Onshore and Offshore Wind Power. Iowa, Texas, Kansas, and South Dakota are leading producers of wind-generated electricity. More can be done, especially offshore. Currently there is just one water-based installation; it is in Rhode Island and it is small. A Great Lakes wind farm could generate 250,000 megawatts of electricity—enough to power a hundred million homes—and thousands of jobs constructing and maintaining the machines. Such projects face opposition from those who love fossil fuel, but others have concerns too. People along the shore worry that turbines will ruin their view. Shippers fear accidents, and bird lovers worry about migrating flocks. But the Great Lakes are huge, and there must be spaces for large wind farms.

Important to maintaining momentum in the wind industry are tax credits and other subsidies that entrepreneurs can rely on when making long-term plans, and also federal policies that require withdrawal from fossil fuels. The latter means keeping the EPA's Clean Power Plan, which mandates that states reduce carbon emissions from existing power plants.

However, it is unlikely that manufacturing windmills will be a major source of jobs in the United States. The Danish firm Vestas has five thousand employees stateside, but American and other foreign firms have few. G.E. is a leader in the field, but some of its plants are overseas. In 2017 there were only twenty-five thousand American employees in the manufacturing sector of the business. Most American jobs will be in construction and maintenance.[25]

The Weatherization Assistance Program (WAP) was created in 1976 to help low-income households make their homes energy-efficient. The program was small until Obama's stimulus package added $5 billion. The expanded WAP had a bumpy start. The Department of Energy had overall supervision of the program, but state agencies and local nonprofits were asked to manage more money. Democratic legislators required that WAP pay decent wages, but the Department of Labor was slow to organize more than eighteen thousand bits of wage information for six job categories in every U.S. county. Many agencies and nonprofits refused to start work until they had certainty about wages.[26]

Early on there were problems with workmanship. Republican Darrell Issa's House committee issued a report with full-color photos of bad work. But WAP improved. Thousands of individuals received training and income, households spent less on fossil fuel, and people were warmer in winter and cooler in summer.[27]

By the time the stimulus money for WAP ran out, an additional million homes had been weatherized. Today, millions of homes could be eligible for WAP subsidies. A $10 billion-a-year program would be four times as large as Obama's, but measured against positive outcomes, it would be a bargain, and it would cost infinitely less than Republican tax-cut programs that favor the rich and guarantee no new jobs.

More Affordable Housing is a widely recognized need and filling it would bring more good jobs. Getting there requires government action to limit the destruction of affordable residences and expand subsidy programs for renters. It also requires federal investments in constructing affordable housing. The National Housing Trust Fund became law in 2008, but did not receive funding until 2016. It takes a billion dollars of Trust Fund investment to generate fifteen thousand construction jobs, but the fund received less than a fifth of that amount.[28]

More Factory Jobs? Some green programs create factory jobs, but we cannot bring manufacturing employment back to the glory days. Due to low wages abroad and more automation, we do not require as many factory workers as we once did. As noted in chapter 7, we simply cannot add the thirty million factory jobs we'd need to get back to the relative size of the 1950s factory workforce. Through selective tariffs and less currency manipulation by foreign powers, the United States might reduce the $600 billion trade deficit in manufacturing and add several million manufacturing jobs. That won't get us back to the '50s, but it would be wonderful to have even a million new jobs offering good pay, decent benefits, and union protections on the south side of Chicago, the north side of Milwaukee, in coal areas of West Virginia, and in down-and-out areas of Fresno, Cleveland, Baltimore, Detroit, Philadelphia, St. Louis, Indianapolis, and the state of Mississippi. These areas are among the poorest places in the nation.[29]

Replenish the Ranks of Public-School Employees. Many public schools need more teachers, teachers' aides, tutors, librarians, counselors, physical education and art teachers, and nurses. Spending to hire more staff for public schools is a quick way to create jobs.

Preserve and Reform the Affordable Care Act (ACA), also known as Obamacare. Despite conservative assertions, there is not much evidence that employers decided not to grow their businesses because of the mandate that all but small businesses provide health insurance. Nor did employers disrupt their organizations by shifting employees from full- to part-time to limit the reach of the mandate. The big-picture is that the ACA is something of a model centrist job-creation program. First, it subsidizes useful activities that improve the quality of life for millions of people. Second, in a saner political atmosphere than the one we inhabit today, the ACA would have broad appeal, even to centrist-conservatives. It showers billions of dollars and much decision-making power on the private sector, and it includes mandates that were once championed by the very conservative Heritage Foundation and by Republican Mitt Romney when he was the governor of Massachusetts. Third, the left should be happy that the ACA uses progressive taxes to take dollars from the rich to expand health care and create new jobs. And that brings the fourth point: the ACA gave an expanding job sector a shot of adrenaline, adding as many as 500,000 additional health-care jobs. Repealing the ACA's Medicaid expansion provision would have disastrous effects on health-care access for low-income Americans, and it would wipe out hundreds of thousands of jobs, some of them in poor rural areas.

On the negative side is the fact that the ACA did little to control costs. And as a job program, the ACA creates many good jobs but also many not very good ones. A $15-and-rising federal minimum wage would be a start here, as elsewhere.[30]

The Money Question: Can Americans Afford a Large Jobs Program?

How large should new spending be? As an example, $200 billion a year could generate three million jobs that pay $50,000 a year, and leave money for taxes, workers' compensation, materials, and tools. Can we afford $200 billion? Your answer depends on how badly you want to live in a society with more good jobs. The Republican tax bill of 2017 gave at least a trillion dollars to the affluent minority, will add hugely to budget deficits, and increases rather than moderates income inequality. The point is that the money is there for many good things, and the question of how to spend it is a political question.

Keep in mind that government-created jobs generate other jobs in businesses that supply workers with tools and materials, and also that new workers spend more than they did before and that adds jobs too. Also, more jobs with decent pay means higher federal tax revenues, more money going into the Social Security and Medicare Trust Funds, and fewer people needing food stamps. However, it is true that additional revenues will not be enough to pay for all the new expenditures. So where will we get the money? The modern Humphrey-Hawkins bill funds up to six million jobs a year from a tiny tax on stock and bond transactions. We can get another $200 billion a year for major infrastructure projects by taking in taxes 1/10 more of the annual incomes of the richest 1 percent of all households. They're all millionaires. Finally, the government can borrow. It's for a good cause. Americans have often had to accept deficits to fund tax cuts for the rich and corporations. Why not for jobs?

The important point is that it's not lack of money but class interests and political opportunism that explains why elites have not taken steps to bring full employment. Elite Americans are doing just fine with the way things are now. They won't do the right thing without powerful movements disrupting business as usual and demanding good programs.

In a moment we can discuss how political structures and political attitudes constrain or support the process of getting to real full employment. But before that, one more item that has been used against full employment needs evaluation, and that is the inflation bugaboo.

Will Full Employment Cause Inflation to Soar?

For decades, most economists believed that the Phillips curve and similar economic models, such as NAIRU, meant that we could not have low inflation and low unemployment at the same time. Mainstream theory argues that when workers are in high demand for an extended period, they will get wage increases, and that will force employers to raise prices.

The inflationary effects of low unemployment and higher wages are thought to be higher if labor productivity is not rising much; higher productivity raises worker output per hour and makes it easier for employers to raise pay. But that is not a sure thing. Americans have experienced long periods of rising productivity with no or few advances in real wages. Labor productivity increased 80 percent over 1979–2009, but wages increased very little. The top 10 percent and especially the top 1 percent grabbed most of the benefits of rising workplace efficiency.

More broadly on the question of the relationship of unemployment and inflation, in the last few decades, the United States has, in violation of Phillips and NAIRU theory, combined low unemployment and low inflation, and in one case real wage growth. In the late 1990s, as we saw in chapter 4, unemployment was low and real wages rose, sometimes in small steps but consistently. The average rate of inflation for 1996–2001, however, stayed under 3 percent. In the last ten years, the official rate of unemployment has fallen to numbers lower than any peacetime years since the late 1940s. Clearly, it is possible to combine a low official unemployment rate and a low rate of inflation. Furthermore, the late

'90s seemed to show that you could also have sustained increases in real wages without a lot of inflation.

Does this solve the problem of inflation at full employment? Not necessarily. In the late '90s and in the 2010s there was more unemployment than was counted by the official rate. Employment wasn't as full as most mainstream writers thought. The Bureau of Labor Statistics publishes a fuller rate called U-6 that includes part-timers who want full-time work and a small number of people who want a job. This number still underestimates the number of people who want a job, but it supports the point. When official rates were 4 percent or less in the late '90s and the 2010s, U-6, one estimate of real unemployment, averaged 8.2 percent (1996–2001) and 10.3 percent (2013–2018). In other words, even at what is conventionally defined as full employment—around 4 percent—there is still a large labor force of people uncounted and ready to work. That means fewer wage increases.[31]

This argument implies that if federal job programs brought real full employment at decent wages, there might be inflationary pressures to the extent that higher wages translated into higher prices via higher labor costs and high consumer demand. However, there are ways that employers can avoid big price increases when they have to pay their rank-and-file employees more.

In my dream world of a just society, owners, especially of large concerns, would skim less than they do now. That would leave a little more money for rank-and-file pay raises without raising prices. In this same world, investors and managers could accept a lower rate of profit but strive to increase the mass of their profits by selling more stuff to consumers who have more income to spend. Even in the real world, as mentioned in chapter 7, owners and managers have strategies to moderate price increases that are realistic and possible. They employed some of them as cities and states have raised their minimum wages in recent years. Employers may save something from having lower turnover costs and a more efficient, more loyal workforce. Also, while raising the pay of rank-and-file workers, owners need not give the same increases to more highly paid employees.

Finally, government agencies can take steps to fend off significant inflation. Full-employment programs can be structured to allow for adjustments if inflation rates surge. This option was included in one version of the Humphrey-Hawkins 21st Century Full Employment and Training Act. Along the same lines, new employment programs should include funds for scholars and activists to devise anti-inflation programs that do not lay off workers and limit wage increases. As inflation sped up in the 1970s, very few economists worked on softer solutions. The brutal recession of 1981–1983 was a more certain cure for inflation, and it meshed with the aggressive campaign of conservatives and owners to disempower workers and ruin unions. Other countries with a stronger sense of WITT (We're In This Together) have, at times, had positive experiences with more humane solutions, and we should learn from those instances. The United States surely has more expert economists than any other country in the world. More of them need to study how to get to a full-employment, high-wage, low-inflation economy.[32]

Do Conservative Institutions and Ideas Doom Big Federal Job Programs?

Do most Americans still believe so strongly in self-help individualism that a federal jobs program is dead on arrival? Actually, no. In recent polls, there has been broad support for Social Security and Medicare, growing support for Obamacare, approval for higher minimum wages, and support for government job programs. It's true that individualistic attitudes on policy issues endure, not only among right-wing extremists in the Republican Party but also among average folk, especially when they think that other average folk are getting special favors from government. The Tea Party (now the Freedom Caucus in the House) was catalyzed in part by a business commentator's rant against plans to give federal aid to troubled homeowners during the Great Recession. For years Republicans have battled to take health insurance away from millions of people; and in most southern states and some in the Great Plains, Republicans blocked the expansion of Medicaid made possible by Obamacare. But popular support for Obamacare has grown, and extreme individualism seems stronger among conservative elites than average voters.

Normally, most Americans favor left-liberal economic and benefit programs. A 2010 survey found majorities for federal involvement to protect the environment (61 percent), reduce poverty (81 percent), and ensure access to health care (52 percent). Backing for Medicare, Social Security, and Unemployment Insurance ranged from 91 percent to 96 percent. For food stamps it was 82 percent. In March 2013, support for federal job creation programs, including the use of government money to fund infrastructure work, garnered majorities of 70 percent or more. In five southern states where Republican governments rejected the Medicaid expansion under Obamacare, 62.3 percent of the people wanted the expansion. Republicans tried to repeal Obamacare in 2017 and 2018, but on this issue and other key issues, Republican politicians and conservative donors were more right-wing than many of their constituents. In November 2018, voters in two conservative states, Arkansas and Missouri, passed minimum-wage increases. In three conservative states—Utah, Nebraska, and Idaho—activists working with union support persuaded voters to pass ballot measures to increase Medicaid access.

It may be that there is more hostility toward poor people in America than in other rich democracies. A fair number of elite conservatives are proud to broadcast the message that being poor is a sign of failure, that adequate government benefits for poor people is bad policy, and that politicians should cut benefits whenever they can. In that atmosphere, even people who need assistance sometimes "feel guilty for taking it and resent the government for providing it."[33]

But many people cherish the achievements of Rooseveltian liberalism from the 1930s (such as Social Security) and Johnsonian liberalism from the '60s (Medicare and, increasingly, Medicaid). However, the United States seems to lack a deeply rooted social-democratic worldview of the kind that is common elsewhere and that treasures government social-welfare programs. Such programs have been under attack in Europe in recent years, but popular devotion to government benefits remains strong in France, Germany, Scandinavia, and elsewhere. It is less automatic for Americans to think, "We're In This Together" (WITT) than it is for Swedes, Danes, Netherlanders, and Israelis. Americans have more YOYO ("You're On Your Own") in their hearts, even though they live in a complex web of dependencies. Many influential Americans have not seen it as their duty to educate people about cooperative values and about how much all of us depend on each other and on luck. In fact, as right-wing Republicans began to win elections in the 1980s, some Democrats began to push for benefit cuts and balanced budgets. President Bill Clinton asserted that the era of big government was over. He signed off on deep welfare cuts. Even today, according to one political pundit, Democrats are "often terrified of defending government."[34]

Democrats are better than Republicans on many issues, including climate change, student debt, and gender equality, but too many are missing in action on bread-and-butter economic issues. Out of political caution, affection for capitalism, the need for campaign contributions, the influence of anti-government neoliberalism among advisors, and facing a relatively small union movement pushing progressive programs, in recent decades some Democratic politicians have not been out front with an enthusiastic defense of old programs and new ones that help working-class Americans.

But this situation may be changing. As a symptom of change, several Democratic contenders for the presidency in 2020 have offered programs for federal direct-job creation. Whether these people remain steadfast is an open question, but the Democratic Party is changing in ways that support progressive economic programs, including job creation and a decent minimum wage. The November 2018 elections sent more Democrats and more progressives to the House of Representatives. These progressives, still a minority, will have to push hard to get their party to support economic programs that do something substantial about poverty, low pay, gross income inequalities, and depressed regions and locales that have been left behind for years. Top Democrats, including presidential candidates, need pressure. They will often be tempted, by advisors and political calculation, to move to the center. Obamacare, for all its shortcomings, was a major achievement and contained many progressive features. And Obama sometimes fought for higher taxes on the very rich. But he was a lukewarm leader on raising the minimum wage, and he went along with the obsession about federal deficits pushed by his neoliberal advisors. In 2016 candidate Hillary Clinton would agree to support only a $12 minimum wage—not $15, which had become the banner goal of wage movements.[35]

Big-money donors were given a boost when the Supreme Court in *Citizens United* (2010) removed virtually all limits on political contributions. Billionaire conservative donors like the Koch brothers and Sheldon Adelson spend lavishly to defeat Democrats, limit voting rights, and undermine progressive economics. But Democrats also receive large donations from business interests and bankers. There is a cozy relationship between financial firms like Goldman Sachs and their friends in the Democratic Party. Wildly irresponsible bankers, many of them supporters of the bank deregulation that contributed to the Great Recession, served in Obama's administration.

However, while many leading Democrats are not very leftish, most are susceptible to progressive pressure. Almost no leading Republicans are. The Republican Freedom Caucus in the House, the Koch brothers, and President Trump strive to undo hundreds of laws and regulations that offer protection to workers, consumers, and voters. Former Republican House Speaker Paul Ryan favors Ayn Rand's gospel of selfishness. Racist policies that were once the number-one priority of southern Democrats live on, sometimes subtextually, sometimes openly, among southern Republicans. That fact binds disaffected white people to the Republican Party. But more of these people than we think want expanded access to Medicaid, free college education, and a higher minimum wage. In 2018 the Democratic populists who supported such things seemed to be gaining power and influence.[36]

America is becoming more multiethnic, and that favors Democrats, but the structure of the Senate and heavily gerrymandered House districts favor conservatives. The Republican Party won the House of Representatives in 2014 even though Republican candidates received three million fewer votes than

Democrats. In 2018 many things, including economic discontent and disaffection with President Trump, helped Democrats win the House by a wide margin. But not the Senate, where representation favors rural, conservative areas and small-population states. Two senators represent thirty-five million Californians and two represent 1/70 of that number (520,000 people) in Wyoming.

Obviously, these structural barriers aren't determinative. Democrats did win the House of Representatives in 2018. At times in the 2000s, Democrats have wasted opportunities, owing in part to a centrist ideology and style. Neither Al Gore nor John Kerry, who ran for president in 2000 and 2004, respectively, were strong voices for progressive pro-worker positions. The financial crash in 2008, soaring unemployment, and the threat of a worldwide depression opened the door for a fundamental turn on economic policy. But the Obama team did not walk through the door. There was Obamacare but no second New Deal. Also, partly because of liberal cushions like unemployment insurance, the effects of the economic crisis were not severe enough to unleash huge movements that could exert massive pressures for a second New Deal. There was little to no Democratic leadership in the White House or the Congress for permanent job programs or even for raising the federal minimum wage, which, at $7.25, was an insult to workers. Within a few years of saving the economy through large-scale deficit spending, Obama came to support the idea that budget deficits hurt the economy. This is the anti-deficit position that Republicans use against Democrats, while they themselves pass giant tax cuts for the rich that send federal debt levels soaring.

The Great Recession did not bring a second New Deal but it did help activists and scholars who were fighting against income inequality. Wage struggles spread. Before the recession, no one would have predicted that fast-food workers and Wal-Mart employees would be demonstrating and even striking for $15 an hour. But they were. In 2011 the Occupy Wall Street movement put the inequality scandal on the front page. Several labor unions (notably the Service Employees International Union and the United Food and Commercial Workers) supplied money and personnel to publicize the disgrace of working poverty and the need for higher wages at very profitable companies in America, including McDonald's, Wal-Mart, and Amazon. Socialist Bernie Sanders, who ran for the Democratic presidential nomination in 2016, did the most among American political leaders to keep inequality and job issues at the forefront.[37]

Obama's attorney general failed to go after the banker-criminals who created the conditions that led to the Great Recession. In 2016 Donald Trump played to anti-business sentiment by talking about draining the swamp, but he stuffed his cabinet with conservatives and Wall Street bankers, a number of whom, including Treasury Secretary Steve Mnuchin, got rich off the miseries of foreclosed Americans. But Trump's presidency fired up progressive opposition. Since the day after Trump's inauguration, there has been an outpouring of opposition on the part of women's organizations, unions, civil rights groups, immigrant groups, people worried about losing health insurance, and more. On several occasions, angry constituents showed up at congressional town hall meetings to lambast Republican politicians. Disabled people flooded the halls of Congress to protest against health insurance cuts.

Added to the possibilities opened by these new movements is the fact that for decades formations in or close to the Democratic Party have supported full-employment programs. These include the Congressional Black Caucus, the Congressional Progressive Caucus, the Congressional Full-Employment Caucus, and some trade unions. Members of the National Jobs for All Coalition helped to write H.R. 1000, and they educate people and politicians about the necessity of direct-job creation for real full employment. Around the country there are thousands of organizations that will support good-jobs programs. Centered in North Carolina and led by Reverend William Barber II, there was the Moral Monday movement and now the Poor People's Campaign, which battles racism, poverty, and inequality. In 2016, in a largely white rural area in the same state, Brigid Flaherty and Sharon Cullins founded Down Home North Carolina and began to connect with residents about low wages, lack of health care, and the opioid epidemic. Meanwhile, at the top of the left-liberal movement, Senators Sanders, Sherrod Brown, Elizabeth Warren, Alexandria Ocasio-Cortez and her so-called Squad, and other outstanding progressive politicians consistently speak for working-class Americans.

Potentially the largest organization for progressive working-class politics is the union movement, but it constitutes just 11 percent of the workforce—a smaller proportion than at any time since the early 1930s. Many unions support the minimum-wage movement and some of the most progressive organizations donate real money to pass minimum-wage initiatives. Some support full-employment programs. But while most unions support Democrats, they are often stiffed by Democratic presidents. When Democrats had control of the presidency and Congress in recent years, there was no increase in the federal minimum wage and minimal effort to put teeth into labor laws that are supposed to protect union organizing. Unionists opposed most "free-trade" pacts, and many Democrats in Congress agreed, but every Democratic president championed trade treaties like NAFTA that hurt the working class. Once thought of as the party of the working class, Democrats have not done much to rescue the working-class from the ravages of globalization, automation, banker fraud, and the money-grab by the top 1 percent.[38]

Prospects for a second New Deal with federal job-creation programs would be helped by a double renewal of the union movement: many more union members, and more political pressure for progressive economics. In some states and cities, unions are still a potent force. For example, members of the Culinary Workers Union in Las Vegas were hugely influential in electing Democrats in 2018, and unions have played a crucial role in the progressive movement in California. As mentioned, union resources have helped the $15 minimum-wage movement, But the national membership numbers seem daunting. Fewer than 10 percent of private-sector workers are in unions. It may be comforting to know that in the late 1920s a labor expert predicted the demise of the union movement. That was just a few years before the largest surge in union history.

Republican Party economics are neoliberal/conservative to the max: deregulate, cut taxes for businesses and rich people, slash the Medicaid and food stamp rolls, and so on. There is a neoliberal element in the Democratic Party, but Democrats who are critical of corporate interests will have a larger voice in the party in 2019 and 2020. And this reflects important realities about the United States. Most Americans are not neoliberals. Majorities did not like the 2017 Republican tax-cut giveaway to the rich, they want a higher minimum wage, and they are supportive of jobs programs. In 2018 there were no progressives running in the Republican Party; in the Democratic Party, dozens of newly elected members were progressive and some even identified themselves as socialists, including Alexandria Ocasio-Cortez, newly elected from New York City to the House of Representatives. Progressive forces can push key programs that could actually begin to solve working poverty, gross income inequalities, and joblessness, especially in poor urban neighborhoods and left-behind rural communities that have not, over many decades, been lifted by general economic growth and tax breaks for rich investors. It would be wonderful to see some of these communities thrive.[39]

Notes

Abbreviations

BLS   Bureau of Labor Statistics
CES   Current Employment Statistics (omitting the farm sector)
ES   *The Employment Situation* (at BLS.gov)
ERP   *Economic Report of the President*

Introduction

1. Obama's Affordable Care Act was a progressive achievement that soon made life better for many millions of Americans, but its features were close to what moderate Republican policy had been not long before, in states such as Massachusetts. It did not replace private insurers with one government insurance company, as had Social Security and Medicare, nor did it do much to control prices. But the program did compel people to join, it included progressive features in its taxation and subsidy plans, and it allowed for a huge expansion of Medicaid. For ideological, financial, and partisan reasons, Republicans strove to replace Obamacare with nothing.

2. Officially unemployment fell below 4 percent in the spring of 2018 and stayed there for the rest of the year. The nonfarm sector added 2.6 million jobs in 2018. The economy was providing a lot of jobs, although not enough good ones, and there were plenty of people on the sidelines who were ready to work. In December 2018 the unemployment rate increased because people came off the sidelines to look for jobs.

3. The real-wage lag did promote a fair amount of discussion about what might explain it. Few of the discussants gave up on the official unemployment rate, but a couple of them finally decided that the official rate was not measuring all the unemployed, and there wasn't really full employment, and that was one reason that wages weren't rising faster. See Ben Casselman, "Why Wages Are Finally Rising, 10 Years After the Recession," *New York Times,* May 2, 2019, accessed at nytimes.com on May 3, 2019; and James Pethokoukis, "5 Questions for Adam Ozimek on Unemployment, Wage Growth, and Productivity," October 22, 2018, accessed at aei.org on May 3, 2019.

4. See the clip from a June 24, 2010, *Rachel Maddow Show,* "Republicans to Unemployed: You're Spoiled, Drug-Taking Hobos & Animals, Who Shouldn't Breed," accessed at youtube.com on May 23, 2012; Lauren Kelley, "The 10 Most Hateful Quotes About the Poor and the Unemployed," accessed May 23, 2012, at news.change .org/stories/the-10-most-hateful-quotes-about-the-poor-and-unemployed; Ross Eisenbrey, "Some Ugly Views About the Unemployed Among Congressional Republicans," December 22, 2011, at epi.org/blog/ugly-views-about-the-unemployed-by -congressional-republicans, accessed December 24, 2011.

5. Not only are general tax cuts for businesses and rich people inefficient as job creators. Even tax cuts that require direct investment in underprivileged areas don't result in many added jobs. This issue is discussed a bit more in chapter 8.

Chapter 1. Discipline for the Unemployed; Laissez-Faire for Business

1. Louise Bolard More, *Wage-Earners' Budgets: A Study of the Standards and Cost of Living in New York City* (New York: Henry Holt 1907, Arno Press Reprint, 1971). Also, *Historical Statistics of the United States: Colonial Times to 1970,* Part I (Washington, D.C.: U.S. Bureau of the Census, 1975), 164–65, 224; hereafter as *HS*; and William Burton Hartley, *Estimation of the Incidence of Poverty in the United States, 1870–1914* (Ph.D. diss., University of Wisconsin, 1969), esp. 132, 205. Showing that annual real earnings fell for blue-collar workers over 1890–1915 is Paul Douglas, *Real Wages in the United States, 1890–1926* (Boston and New York: Houghton Mifflin, 1930), 468 and table, 392–93. Also, U.S. Senate, 64th Congress, *Final Report of the Commission on Industrial Relations* (Washington, D.C.: Government Printing Office, 1916), 22, 36, 103; hereafter as *CIR*.

2. Amy Dru Stanley, "Beggars Can't Be Choosers: Compulsion and Contract in Post-bellum America," *Journal of American History* 78 (March 1992): 1265–293; Dorothy Ross, *The Origins of American Social Science* (Cambridge, U.K.: Cambridge University Press, 1991), esp. 3–171; and Henry May, *The Protestant Churches and Industrial America* (New York: Harper Torchbooks, 1969). On recent versions of the nineteenth-century view, Lisa Mascaro, "Rep. Ryan Calls for Cuts in Anti-Poverty Programs," March 4, 2014, A7; and Michael Muskal, "Critics Denounce Kansas Limits on Welfare Fund Use," April 17, 2015, A19, both in the *Los Angeles Times*. One article is about a state that gave needy families $400 a month, but whose legislators felt the need to forbid recipients from using the money for concert tickets, lingerie, and cruises.

3. Sumner quotation, 480, "The Forgotten Man" (1883), 465–95, in Albert Galloway Keller, ed., *The Forgotten Man and Other Essays* (New Haven, Conn.: Yale University Press, 1943). Also, Sidney Fine, *Laissez Faire and the General Welfare State: A Study of Conflict in American Thought: 1865–1901* (Ann Arbor: University of Michigan Press, 1964 pbk. of 1956 original), 79–91.

4. For two paragraphs: Helen Ginsburg, *Full Employment and Public Policy: The United States and Sweden* (Lexington, Mass.: D.C. Heath, 1983), 7; Fine, *Laissez Faire,* 48–53, 62, 322–29; Russell A. Nixon, "The Historical Development of the Conception and Implementation of Full Employment as Economic Policy," in Alan Gartner, Russell A. Nixon, and Frank Riessman, *Public Service Employment: An Analysis of Its History, Problems and Prospects* (New York: Praeger Publishers, 1973), 9–27, esp. 15–17; John A. Garraty, *Unemployment in History: Economic Thought and Public Policy* (New York: Harper Colophon Books, 1979), 121,141; Joseph Dorfman, *The Economic Mind in American Civilization: 1865–1918,* III (New York: Augustus M. Kelley, 1969 reprint of New York: Viking Press, 1949), 127, 472.

5. Mina Julia Carson, *Settlement Folk: Social Thought and the American Settlement Movement, 1885–1930* (Chicago: University of Chicago Press, 1990); Ross, *Origins of American Social Science,* esp. 3–171; May, *Protestant Churches.* Blaming foreign influence for labor strife was E. L. Godkin, editor of the *Nation,* in Leon Litwack, ed., *The American Labor Movement* (Englewood Cliffs, N.J.: Prentice Hall, 1962), 54–57.

6. Robert Bruce, *1877: Year of Violence* (Chicago: Quadrangle Paperback, 1970 reprint of 1959 original); Kenneth L. Kusmer, *Down and Out on the Road: The Homeless in American History* (New York: Oxford University Press, 2002), 35–72; Paul T. Ringenbach, *Tramps and Reformers, 1873–1916: The Discovery of Unemployment in New York* (Westport, Conn.: Greenwood Press, 1973), 3–35, esp. 10–12; *1877: The Grand Army of Starvation,* a film by the American Social History Project (1984); Herbert G. Gutman, "The Failure of the Movement by the Unemployed for Public Works in 1873," *Political Science Quarterly* 80 (June 1965): 254–76, esp. 257; Samuel Rezneck, "Distress, Relief, and Discontent in the United States During the Depression of 1873–1878," *Journal of Political Economy* 58 (December 1950): 494–512.

7. Gutman, "Failure of the Movement"; 256, 260, 270–74, two quoted phrases on 270; Rezneck, "Distress," 499, 503–5; Kusmer, *Down and Out,* 51–52; Foster Rhea Dulles and Melvyn Dubofsky, *Labor in America: A History,* 5th ed. (Arlington Heights, Ill.: Harlan Davidson, 1993), 110; Fine, *Laissez Faire,* 322–29.

8. Four paragraphs: Frank Tobias Higbie, *Indispensable Outcasts: Hobo Workers and Community in the American Midwest, 1880–1930* (Urbana: University of Illinois Press, 2003), 12; Ringenbach, *Tramps and Reformers,* 15–17, and passim; Gutman, "Failure of the Movement," n29 on the investigators who found nineteen of twenty people unworthy; Walter I. Trattner, *From Poor Law to Welfare State: A History of Social Welfare in America,* 5th ed. (New York: Free Press, 1994), 91–94; Rezneck, "Distress," 500–501; David Wagner, *What's Love Got to Do with It: A Critical Look at American Charity* (New York: The New Press, 2000), 46–68. For an early modern society that offered more exten-

sive relief than others, see Jonathan I. Israel, *The Dutch Republic: Its Rise, Greatness, and Fall, 1477–1806* (New York: Oxford University Press, 1995), 123–24, 353–60. Barry J. Kaplan, "Reformers and Charity: The Abolition of Public Outdoor Relief in New York City, 1870–1898," *Social Service Review* 52 (June 1978), 202–14, shows that as charity reformers cut aid, the Tammany Hall machine gave more.

9. Ringenbach, *Tramps and Reformers*, 17, for Wayland quotation, and 22–23; Kusmer, *Down and Out*, 43–50.

10. Bruce, *1877*; Dulles and Dubofsky, *Labor in America*, 112–16 (quotation, 114).

11. The *New York Times* is quoted in Rezneck, "Distress," 510. Godkin and Beecher in Litwack, *American Labor Movement*, 53–57. Beecher earned $100,000 a year (about $2 million in 2019), the highest salary for any American clergyman. He also endorsed consumer products and was paid for editorials favorable to the Northern Pacific Railroad. See David Herbert Donald, "True Soap Opera," *New York Times Book Review*, January 9, 2000, 9, review of Richard Fox's *Trials of Intimacy*.

12. "Russell Conwell Sanctifies Wealth" (1915), 10–11, in Leon Fink, ed., *Major Problems in the Gilded Age and the Progressive Era* (Lexington, Mass.: D.C. Heath, 1993); Beecher quotation in Litwack, *American Labor Movement*, 57. There were state laws to regulate child labor and mine safety, and, sometimes, hours of work for women. Some states began widowed-mothers pension plans and workers' compensation programs. But minimum wage laws were often nullified by conservative judges.

13. John A. Garraty, *The New Commonwealth, 1877–1890* (New York: Harper Torchbook, 1968), 128–78, 201; Robert Hunter, *Poverty* (1904), in Peter d'A. Jones, ed., *Poverty: Social Conscience in the Progressive Era* (New York: Harper Torchbook, 1965), 29. Samuel Rezneck, "Patterns of Thought and Action in an American Depression, 1882–1886," *American Historical Review* 61 (January 1956): 284–307, esp. 284, 289.

14. Gerald T. White, *The United States and the Problem of Recovery after 1893* (Tuscaloosa: University Press of Alabama, 1982), 23, 25, n15 on 122; and Udo Sautter, *Three Cheers for the Unemployed: Government and Unemployment Before the New Deal* (Cambridge, U.K.: Cambridge University Press, 1991), 14–16.

15. Charles Hoffman, *The Depression of the Nineties: An Economic History* (Westport, Conn.: Greenwood Publishing, 1970), 47–112, 194; Carlos C. Closson Jr., "The Unemployed in American Cities," *Quarterly Journal of Economics* 8 (1894): 168–217, 453–77, esp. 175–89; Douglas, *Real Wages*, 460; David R. Weir, "A Century of U.S. Unemployment, 1890–1990: Revised Estimates and Evidence for Stabilization," *Research in Economic History* 14 (1992), 301–46, esp. 341. Weir's 17 percent was for the nonfarm private sector.

16. Closson "Unemployed in American Cities," 178, 192–93; Harold U. Faulkner, *Politics, Reform and Expansion, 1890–1900* (New York: Harper Torchbook, 1963), 163.

17. *HS*, 126, has nonfarm unemployment at 12.6 percent in 1900. Also, Charles Hoffmann, "The Depression of the Nineties," *Journal of Economic History* 16 (June 1956): 137–64; Hoffmann, *Depression*; Faulkner, *Politics, Reform, and Expansion*, 141–62; David Whitten, "Depression of 1893," at Robert Whaples, ed. EH.Net Encyclopedia, August 14, 2001, accessed May 18, 2019.

18. White, *Problem of Recovery*, 21; Theda Skocpol, *Social Policy in the United States: Future Possibilities in Historical Perspective* (Princeton, N.J.: Princeton University Press, 1995), 234–35. Alexander Keyssar, *Out of Work: The First Century of Unemployment in Massachusetts* (Cambridge, U.K.: Cambridge University Press, 1986), shows that in Massachusetts, in every depression from the 1870s through the 1920s, unions demanded public works. Note also that federal budgets usually had surpluses, so there was money to spend.

19. For two paragraphs, Kusmer, *Down and Out*, 58 for quoted phrase; White, *Problem of Recovery*, 31 and note 14 on 122.

20. Faulkner, *Politics, Reform, and Expansion*, 163–81; Samuel Rezneck, "Unemployment, Unrest, and Relief in the United States during the Depression of 1893–1897," *Journal of Political Economy* 61 (August 1953): 324–45, esp. 329, 339; Keyssar, *Out of Work*, 229–31; Closson, "Unemployed in the Cities," 190–91.

21. White, *Problem of Recovery*, 23; Dulles and Dubofsky, *Labor in America*, 129. On Gompers's ambivalence about strategies, see Bernard Mandel, *Samuel Gompers: A Biography* (Yellow Springs, Ohio: Antioch Press, 1963),121–25, 183–85. Also see Irwin Yellowitz, "The Origins of Unemployment Reform in the United States," *Labor History* 9 (Fall 1968): 338–60. Kusmer, *Down and Out*, 58–66, shows that as conditions deteriorated for railroad operating crafts in the 1890s, workers became more sympathetic to free riders.

22. Cleveland supported repeal of the Sherman Silver Purchase Act, which required government to buy and coin silver. Repeal meant less money in circulation. Faulkner, *Politics, Reform, and Expansion*, 162, 265. Soon, new gold mines opened in Australia, South Africa, and Alaska. There was also a new cyanide extraction process for low-grade ores. Cleveland and McKinley each thought that the right position on tariffs was vital, while federal aid to the unemployed was wrong. Cleveland wanted to cut tariffs and McKinley did not.

23. The main federal welfare program at the time served older or disabled war veterans. In 1912 a veteran could get as much as $360. See Hartley, *Estimation of the Incidence of Poverty*, 170. Eventually "mothers' pensions" for widows with children spread to many states, but the amounts were small and coverage limited.

24. I divided total spending by five thousand workers, based on Joan Waugh, "'Give This Man work!' Josephine Shaw Lowell, the Charity Organization Society of the City of New York, and the Depression of 1893," *Social Science History* 25 (2001): 217–46, esp. 232–41. White, *Problem of Recovery*, 26–27, on private and government funds for the East Side Committee. Closson, "Unemployed in the Cities," 170, 473, for other examples, such as a Lawrence, Massachusetts, which allotted $50 per person for three months of work.

25. Rezneck, "Unemployment," 331, 344–45; White, *Problem of Recovery*, 28–32. Lowell repudiated the jobs program she had helped to create. Compare Ringenbach, *Tramps and Reformers*, 96 to Waugh, "Give this Man Work!" 239.

26. Faulkner, *Politics, Reform, and Expansion*, 14–19, 164; Rezneck, "Unemployment," 330–31; Robert H. Bremner, *From the Depths: The Discovery of Poverty in the United States*

(New York: New York University Press, 1956), 3–30; Don D. Lescohier, *Working Conditions* (New York: Macmillan, 1935), vol. 3 of John R. Commons, *History of Labour in the United States* (New York: MacMillan, 1918), 120, and 166 for first quotation and Stanley, "Beggars Can't Be Choosers," 1292, for second. Professor Franklin Giddings labeled the unemployed "defective working people," in 1886 (Ross, *Origins of American Social Science,* 128).

27. Rezneck, "Unemployment," 327; Closson, "Unemployed in American Cities," 209–12, 477–78. Denver's experience with seasonal and boom-bust labor markets was important, but as important was that conservatives did not control thought and action; labor did. Farm areas of California had plenty of experience with seasonal work, too, but worker organizations were weak enough to be suppressed.

28. William Allen White is quoted in White, *Problem of Recovery,* 32. Governor Lewelling, in Closson, "Unemployed in Americans Cities," 206; Bremner, *From the Depths,* 21–22, 123–39; see Lescohier, *Working Conditions,* 126–27, for the phrase from the U.S. Industrial Commission. Sautter, *Three Cheers,* 33, points out that no one came out of the 1890s depression working on a thorough analysis of the depression or the problem of widespread vagrancy. Experts often mixed realism and backward ideas, including Lowell and Carlos Closson, an authority on unemployment and relief efforts. See also Fine, *Laissez Faire,* 322–29, and Dorfman, *Economic Mind,* 303–5, on the Tuttle episode.

29. Douglas, *Real Wages,* 460; *HS,* I, 126; Weir "A Century of U.S. Unemployment," 241. The three scholars made a total of forty-eight annual estimates for sixteen years. In only six of the estimates was unemployment under 6.0 percent. Also, see Lescohier, *Working Conditions,* 127–18.

30. For three paragraphs: three quotations: U.S. Bureau of Labor Statistics, *Unemployment in New York City, N.Y.,* Bulletin No. 172 (Washington, D.C.: Government Printing Office, 1915), 5; Ringenbach, *Tramps and Reformers,* 129; David Brody, *Steelworkers in America: The Nonunion Era* (New York: Harper Torchbook, 1969 of 1960 original), 28, and 39. Also Sumner H. Slichter, *The Turnover of Factory Labor* (New York: D. Appleton, 1919), esp. 43–46, 251–54; Hunter, *Poverty,* 28; Kusmer, *Down and Out,* 102; S. J. Kleinberg, *Shadow of the Mills: Working-Class Families in Pittsburgh, 1870–1907* (Pittsburgh: University of Pittsburgh Press, 1989), 2–25; and Walter Licht, *Getting Work, Philadelphia, 1840–1950* (Philadelphia: University of Pennsylvania Press, 1999), 220–55. Melvyn Dubofsky, *Industrialism and the American Worker, 1865–1920,* 3rd ed. (Wheeling, Ill.: Harlan Davidson, 1996), 25–27, believes it was rare for workers to get full-year, full-time work. Keyssar, *Out of Work,* 58, claims that a third of the Massachusetts workforce had substantial unemployment every year. Also, Don Lescohier, *The Labor Market* (New York: Macmillan, 1919), 111–17; Carl Boyd Leon, "The Life of American Workers in 1915," *Monthly Labor Review* (February 2016).

31. Lescohier, *Labor Market,* 272; Whitney Coombs, *The Wages of Unskilled Labor in Manufacturing Industries in the United States, 1890–1914* (Reprinted by AMS Press in 1968 from the Columbia University Studies in the Social Sciences edition,1926, Number

283), 14–20; Andrea Graziosi, "Common Laborers, Unskilled Workers, 1880–1915," *Labor History* 22 (Fall 1981): 511–44, esp. 521 for the quotation, which is from John Commons's *Trade Unionism and Labor Problems* (1905). Also, Higbie, *Indispensable Outcasts*, 25–58.

32. For this and previous items in the list: Higbie, *Indispensable Outcasts*, 8–9, 30–32, 52–57; Graziosi, "Common Laborers," 537, on Ford; Lescohier, *Labor Market*, 117–18; Slichter, *Turnover*, esp. 19, 23, 45–46; John B. Andrews, *A Practical Program for the Prevention of Unemployment in America* (New York: American Association on Unemployment, December 1914, labeled First Tentative Draft), 5–9. Also, Keyssar, *Out of Work*, 54, 125, n7 on 388; Hunter, *Poverty*, 29–32; Kusmer, *Down and Out*, 102–34, 149, 158–59, 249; Hornell Hart, *Fluctuations in Unemployment in Cities of the United States, 1902–1917* (Cincinnati: Studies from the Helen S. Trounstine Foundation, 1918); *CIR*, 106–9. Carleton H. Parker, *The Casual Laborer and Other Essays* (New York: Russell & Russell, 1967 reprint of 1920 original), 50, claimed that a New York department store with slots for three thousand employees had thirteen thousand workers pass through in one year. Also, see Susan Porter Benson, *Counter Cultures: Saleswomen, Managers, and Customers in American Department Stores, 1890–1940* (Urbana: University of Illinois Press, 1988), 184–87. Also, Sautter, *Three Cheers*, 36, and 53; and W. M. Leiserson, "The Problem of Unemployment Today," *Political Science Quarterly* 31 (March 1916): 1–24, esp. 11–12. Of people on the road, a fair number were disabled and there were no laws forcing employers to hire the handicapped. Some tramps rejected "starvation wages in dead-end jobs." I believe that had there been more good jobs, fewer would have been tramps. There is a picture of the horrible sanitation conditions and crushing heat that led to the Wheatland Hop Fields Riot by farm workers in Parker, *Casual Laborer*, 169–99. Also useful is Sanford M. Jacoby and Sunil Sharma, "Employment Duration and Industrial Labor Mobility in the United States, 1880–1980," *Journal of Economic History* 52 (March 1992): 161–79. Regarding small business owners, years ago I read several memoirs and biographies of young socialist intellectuals in this period; many told of the failure of a father's farm or business.

33. Richmond, quoted in John H. Ehrenreich, *The Altruistic Imagination: A History of Social Work and Social Policy in the United States* (Ithaca, N.Y.: Cornell University Press, 1985), 61–65. Case-file quotations from Deborah O'Keefe, "Annals of Social Work," *American Heritage* 36 (February–March 1985), accessed at AmericanHeritage.com. David Wagner sent me this article. See also Ringenbach, *Tramps and Reformers*, 100.

34. In the 1890s, Columbia University professors analyzed records of the New York City Charity Organization Society and concluded that unemployment was a more common cause of poverty and sickness than were laziness and intemperance. Peter Seixas, "Unemployment as a 'Problem of Industry' in Early Twentieth-Century New York," *Social Research* 54 (Summer 1987): 403–30, esp. 406–14; Kusmer, *Down and Out*, 91–96; Trattner, *From Poor Law*, 102–3.

35. Trattner, *From Poor Law*, 163–88, esp. 171, 175; Ehrenreich, *Altruistic Imagination*, 60–65; Carson, *Settlement Folk*, 74–84.

36. Andrews quoted in Yellowitz, *Origins of Unemployment Reform,* 342. Second quotation from Lescohier, *Working Conditions,* 129. Lescohier does mention state officials who were developing more sophisticated views. Also, see Garraty, *Unemployment in History,* 140–45; Kusmer, *Down and Out,* 169–91.

37. Seixas, *Unemployment,* 419; Ringenbach, *Tramps and Reformers,* 109–29, Andrews, *Practical Program,* 37.

38. Seixas, *Unemployment,* 421–27; *CIR,* 108–15; Higbie, 57, *Indispensable Outcasts*; Sautter, *Three Cheers,* 73–94; Rezneck, "Patterns," 298.

39. Sautter, *Three Cheers,* 110. The essence of the AAU program is in Andrews's *Practical Program.*

40. On Taylorism and work slowdowns, Frederick Winslow Taylor, *The Principles of Scientific Management* (New York: Norton Library, 1967 of 1911 original); Stanley B. Mathewson, *Restriction of Output Among Unorganized Workers* (Carbondale: Southern Illinois University Press, 1969, reprint of 1931 original); and, no author, "Lag in Employment: The Causes Are Deeper than the Recession," *Time,* September 29, 1958, 88. See also Yellowitz, "Origins of Unemployment Reform," 345, 356–59. The Socialist Party platform of 1912, letter i. under "Industrial Demands," urged a comprehensive insurance system covering unemployment, old age, and disability. See H. Wayne Morgan, ed. *American Socialism, 1900–1960* (Englewood Cliffs, N.J.: Prentice-Hall, 1964), 58. See also Sautter, *Three Cheers,* 114–15, and the Progressive Party platform online at the American Presidency Project, under Minor/Third Party Platforms.

41. Ringenbach, *Tramps and Reformers,* 51–71, 174–81; Trattner, *From Poor Law,* 181–87; Ehrenreich, *Altruistic Imagination,* 12 and 62; Bruce S. Jansson, *The Reluctant Welfare State: A History of American Social Welfare Policies,* 2nd ed. (Pacific Grove, Calif.: Brooks/Cole Publishing, 1993) 137–40. The quoted phrase is from David Wagner, email to author, May 26, 2010.

42. For the whole section: Lescohier, *Working Conditions,* 129–32, 152, 164; Sautter, *Three Cheers,* 14, 18, 106–20 (first quoted phrase); Dorfman, *Economic Mind,* 455–73, and 474 for the "periodic" phrase, which is from Chicago social worker, Graham Taylor; *CIR,* 22–25, 35–38, 101–12. Leiserson, "The Problem of Unemployment," summarizes the state of learning and prescriptions in 1916. Tannenbaum quoted in Christopher Gray, "Streetscapes: The Municipal Lodging House; A 1909 Home for the Homeless," December 22, 1991, *New York Times,* accessed at nytimes.com, May 2, 2015.

43. For the quoted phrase and other details, "I.W.W. Invaders Seized in Church," *New York Times,* March 5, 1914, accessed from the *New York Times archives*; and Philip S. Foner, *History of the Labor Movement in the United States, Volume IV: The Industrial Workers of the World, 1905–1917* (New York: International Publishers, 1965), 435–50. The Wobblies believed reforms were the way that capitalists co-opted and deflated militancy; in theory they believed strikes were steps to a general strike that would replace capitalism with worker control. But much I.W.W. activity was gritty organizing for immediate ends rather than for the revolution.

44. Ringenbach, *Tramps and Reformers,* 162–70, 178–93; Kusmer, *Down and Out,* 169–91; Graham Taylor's view, 474, in Dorfman, *Economic Mind.*

45. Stricker, "The Wages of Inflation: Workers' Earnings in the World War One Era," *Mid-America: An Historical Review* 63 (April–July 1981): 93–105; Lescohier, 193–208; Sautter, *Three Cheers*, 121–26, 154–80.

46. Melvyn Dubofsky, *We Shall Be All: A History of the Industrial Workers of the World* (Chicago: Quadrangle Books, 1969), 291–318. On farmworker pay, see Douglas, *Real Wages*, 187.

Chapter 2. The Twenties and the Thirties

1. On the economic underside of the twenties, see my "Affluence for Whom? Another Look at Prosperity and the Working Classes in the 1920s," *Labor History* 24 (Winter 1983): 5–33.

2. Russell A. Nixon, "The Historical Development of the Conception and Implementation of Full Employment as Economic Policy," in Alan Gartner, Russell A. Nixon, and Frank Riessman, *Public Service Employment: An Analysis of Its History, Problems, and Prospects* (New York: Praeger Publishers, 1973), 9–27, esp. 15–17; Michael Bleaney, *Underconsumption Theories: A History and Critical Analysis* (New York: International Publishers, 1976), 148.

3. Two paragraphs: quotations from William E. Leuchtenburg, *Franklin Roosevelt and the New Deal, 1932–1940* (New York: Harper Torchbook, 1963), 21; and Ronald Edsforth, *The New Deal: America's Response to the Great Depression* (Malden, Mass.: Blackwell Publishers, 2000), 53. One product of the 1921 conference was *Recent Economic Changes in the United States,* Report of the Committee on Recent Economic Changes of the President's Conference on Unemployment, Herbert Hoover, Chairman (New York: National Bureau of Economic Research and McGraw-Hill, 1929). It included unemployment estimates by Meredith B. Givens, 466–78, in Leo Wolman, "Labor," 425–93.

4. Nixon, "Historical Development," 16–17. Also, see Gertrude Schaffner Goldberg, "Conclusion: Learning from the Successes and Failures of the New Deal," 294–324, esp. 297–300; and Philip Harvey, "The New Deal's Direct Job-Creation Strategy: Providing Employment Assurance for American Workers," 146–79, both in Sheila D. Collins and Gertrude Schaffner Goldberg, *When Government Helped: Learning from the Successes and Failures of the New Deal* (New York: Oxford University Press, 2014).

5. For four paragraphs, Paul H. Douglas, *Real Wages in the United States: 1890–1926* (Boston: Houghton Mifflin, 1930), 204–14, 460; Don D. Lescohier, *Working Conditions* (New York: Macmillan, 1935), Vol. III of John R. Commons, ed., *History of Labour in the United States, 1896–1932* (New York: Macmillan, 1918), 80–91; Richard K. Vedder and Lowell E. Gallaway, *Out of Work: Unemployment and Government in Twentieth-Century America* (New York: New York University Press, 1997), 61–71; Stricker, "Affluence for Whom," esp. 5–8. Douglas, *Real Wages*, 464, found that employees in transportation and manufacturing had 37 percent more in real annual earnings in 1926 than 1914, but much of the advance occurred during the war. Given its reputation for prosperity, it is surprising that real per capita GNP grew less rapidly in the 1920s than in the 1940s, '50s, and '60s. First quotation from Mark Perlman, 122, "Labor in Eclipse," 103–45, in John Braeman, Robert H. Bremner, and David Brody, eds., *Change and Continuity in*

Twentieth-Century America: The 1920s (Columbus: Ohio State University Press, 1968), and second from Lescohier, *Working Conditions* 91. Sumner H. Slichter, "The Current Labor Policies of American Industries," *Quarterly Journal of Economics* 42 (May 1929): 393–435, on welfare capitalism. On productivity and wages, see George Soule, *Prosperity Decade: From War to Depression, 1917–1929* (New York: Harper Torchbook, 1968), 328; Chadbourne, "Debt Is the Only Adventure a Poor Man Can Count On," *American Magazine* 104 (December 1927): 44; and Anonymous, "Says Our Masses Are Not Prosperous," *New York Times,* November 26, 1927, 14, Amusements section.

6. Stricker, "Affluence," 5; *Historical Statistics of the United States: Colonial Times to 1970,* Part I (Washington, D.C.: U.S. Bureau of the Census, 1975), 126. Hereafter *HS.* Slichter, "Current Labor Policies" (425–31), thought there were tight labor markets only in 1923. David Brody, *Workers in Industrial America: Essays on the Twentieth Century Struggle,* 2nd ed. (New York: Oxford University Press, 1993), 59–66; and for quotation, 59. Also Robert S. Lynd and Helen Merrell Lynd, *Middletown: A Study in Modern American Culture* (New York: Harcourt, Brace & World, 1956 paperback edition of 1929 original), 55–59.

7. The unemployment averages comparing 1900–1909 and 1920–1929 are based on numbers from David Weir, as reproduced on 2–82–83, *Historical Statistics of the United States, Millennial Edition,* Vol. 2 (New York: Cambridge University Press, 2006), hereafter as *Millennial HS.* On turnover and quits, see Sanford M. Jacoby, "Industrial Labor Mobility in Historical Perspective," *Industrial Relations* 22 (Spring 1983): 261–82. He adds that fewer immigrants, especially fewer men without families or families back in the old country, may also have contributed to falling quit rates in the 1920s. See, too, Lauren Owen, "History of Labor Turnover in the U.S.," EH.Net Encyclopedia, edited by Robert Whaples, April 29, 2004. Regarding welfare capitalism, U.S. Steel was a leader in breaking unions and expanding benefits.

8. For two paragraphs: Slichter, "Current Labor Policies;" and "The Price of Industrial Progress," *New Republic,* February 8, 1928, 316–18. *HS,* 43, figures rounded. On technological unemployment and other issues, see J. F. Bogardus, "Unemployment Among Organized Labor in Philadelphia," *American Federationist* 35 (August 1928): 935–43, esp. 940; Lescohier, *Working Conditions,*144; and Soule, *Prosperity Decade,* 215–17, 228.

9. In *Real Wages,* Douglas's blue-collar sample represented a fourth of the labor force. The average of Weir's numbers for 1920–1926, in *Millennial HS,* is almost identical to Lebergott's. On counting issues, Royal Meeker, "The Dependability and Meaning of Unemployment and Employment Statistics in the United States," *Harvard Business Review* 8 (July 1930): 385–400, esp. 386, 390; Udo Sautter, *Three Cheers for the Unemployed: Government and Unemployment Before the New Deal* (Cambridge, U.K.: Cambridge University Press, 1991), 149–54.

10. Bogardus, "Unemployment," 939; Lynd and Lynd, *Middletown,* 55–60, and table 3, 512. Also, see Leila Houghteling, *The Income and Standard of Living of Unskilled Laborers in Chicago* (Chicago: University of Chicago Press, 1927), 30–31.

11. Weir's numbers for 1927–1929 are close to Lebergott's except for 1929 at 4.05 percent.

12. Janice Andrews, "Helen Hall and the Settlement House Movement's Response to Unemployment: Reaching Out to the Community," *Journal of Community Practice* 4 (1997): 65–75; Clinch Calkins, *Some Folks Won't Work* (New York: Harcourt, Brace, 1930). *Catholic Charities* magazine carried useful articles on joblessness. Also useful on late twenties unemployment is Christopher C. Wright, *Down But Not Out: The Unemployed in Chicago during the Great Depression* (Ph.D. diss., University of Illinois at Chicago, 2017), 49–50. Sautter, *Three Cheers,* 271–73, on Hoover's familiarity with Foster and Catchings.

13. On unemployment and coping strategies before the Great Depression, see "Unemployment Committee of the National Federation of Settlements," edited by Marion Elderton, *Case Studies of Unemployment* (Philadelphia: University of Pennsylvania Press, 1931); Lynd and Lynd, *Middletown,* 60–63; and no author, "The Problem of the Unskilled Laborer with a Large Family," *Monthly Labor Review* 25 (November 1929): 34–38.

14. A good example of the kind information and perspectives that were available was Bogardus's article on high unemployment in Philadelphia in the non-depression year of 1928. Also see John A. Garraty, *Unemployment in History: Economic Thought and Public Policy* (New York: Harper & Row, 1979), 129–64, especially 156–58, for Keynes in the '20s; Lester V. Chandler, *America's Greatest Depression, 1929–1941* (New York: Harper & Row, 1970), 112–13, 122; William Trufant Foster and Waddill Catchings, *Business Without a Buyer* (Boston: Houghton Mifflin, 1927); Bleaney, *Underconsumption Theories,* 202–4; Alan H. Gleason, "Foster and Catchings: A Reappraisal," *Journal of Political Economy* 67 (April 1959): 156–72; and Joseph Dorfman, *The Economic Mind in American Civilization, 1918–1933,* Vol. 5 (New York: Viking Press, 1959, reprinted by New York: Augustus M. Kelley, 1969), 520–45.

15. Soule, *Prosperity Decade,* 324–32.

16. Broadus Mitchell, *Depression Decade: From New Era through New Deal, 1929–1941* (New York: Harper Torchbooks, 1969), 82–85; Edsforth, *New Deal,* 150; Richard E. Rustin, "Crash of '29 Has Many Lingering Effects, Although '69 Was Rougher on Wall Street," *Wall Street Journal,* October 25, 1979, 46. It took twenty-five years for the stock market to recover Depression-era losses.

17. Annual unemployment numbers are Weir in *Millennial HS,* pp. 2–82 to 2–83, Series Ba476. Also Chandler, *America's Greatest Depression,* 31–41; Edsforth, *New Deal,* 77–79; Nick Taylor, *American-Made: The Enduring Legacy of the WPA: When FDR Put the Nation to Work* (New York: Bantam Books, 2008), 18; Irving Bernstein, *A Caring Society: The New Deal, the Worker, and the Great Depression* (Boston: Houghton Mifflin, 1985), 18; William J. Barber, *From New Era to New Deal: Herbert Hoover, the Economists, and American Economic Policy, 1921–1933* (Cambridge, U.K.: Cambridge University Press, 1985), 53. Women's share of the labor force did not fall in the '30s despite government action and propaganda against women workers. See Susan Ware, *American Women in the 1930s:*

Holding Their Own (Boston: Twayne, 1982), 21–53; and Ruth Milkman, "Women's Work and Economic Crisis: Some Lessons of the Great Depression," *Review of Radical Political Economics* 8 (Spring 1976): 73–97. The Pattersons are in Susan Cohen, *Making a New Deal: Industrial Workers in Chicago, 1919–1939* (Cambridge, U.K.: Cambridge University Press, 1990), 216.

18. Irving Bernstein, *The Lean Years* (Baltimore: Penguin Books, 1966), 324–29; Edsforth, *New Deal,* 83. An exciting feature film about youth transiency in the depression is *Wild Boys of the Road* (1933).

19. For two quotations, Arthur M. Schlesinger Jr., *The Age of Roosevelt: The Coming of the New Deal* (Boston: Houghton Mifflin, 1959), 274; and Taylor, *American-Made,* 36. Business leaders and the press in Muncie, Indiana, claimed that nobody was suffering and that the unemployed could find jobs. Lynd and Lynd, *Middletown in Transition: A Study in Cultural Conflicts* (New York: Harcourt, Brace, 1937), 408–9.

20. Lescohier, *Working Conditions,*173–80; Barber, *From New Era,* 27; William E. Leuchtenburg, *Herbert Hoover* (New York: Henry Holt, 2009), 60–62; and Chandler, *America's Greatest Depression,*110–14, 122–25, for general beliefs about government and depressions. Also, Dorfman, *Economic Mind,* 521; Carolyn Grin, "The Unemployment Conference of 1921: An Experiment in National Cooperative Planning," *Mid-America: An Historical Review* 55 (April 1973): 83–107; Joan Hoff Wilson, *Herbert Hoover, Forgotten Progressive* (Boston: Little, Brown, 1975), 90–102, quotation on 90; Garraty, *Unemployment in History,* 149–50; Robert M. Sobel, *Herbert Hoover and the Onset of the Great Depression* (Philadelphia: J.B. Lippincott, 1975), 16–18, 53.

21. Leuchtenburg, *Hoover,* 52–63; Schlesinger Jr., *Age of Roosevelt,* 177–83; Chandler, *America's Greatest Depression,*111–26.

22. Mitchell, *Depression Decade,* 85–86; Edsforth, *New Deal,* 39–43, 65–66; Sautter, *Three Cheers,* 75–82; Taylor, *American-Made,* 21–25; Steve Babson, *The Unfinished Struggle: Turning Points in American Labor, 1877-Present* (Lanham, Md.: Rowman and Littlefield, 1999), 57. Quotations from Lescohier, *Working Conditions,* 159, and John D. Hicks, *Republican Ascendancy, 1921–1933* (New York: Harper Torchbooks, 1960), 270. Adolf Berle told FDR that most workers could not exercise much individuality when 70 percent of business was controlled by six hundred corporations. See Michael Hiltzik, *The New Deal: A Modern History* (New York: Free Press, 2011), 27–28.

23. The RFC's largest loan, $90,000,000, went to the family bank of former Vice President Charles Dawes, three weeks after he resigned from the RFC board. Mitchell, *Depression Decade,* 88; Lescohier, *Working Conditions,* 160–62.

24. Two paragraphs: Lescohier, *Working Conditions,* 159; Leuchtenburg, *Hoover,* 133–35; Sautter, *Three Cheers,* 82–86. ERCA included loans for public works, but Robert D. Leighninger Jr., *Long-Range Public Investment: The Forgotten Legacy of the New Deal* (Columbia: University of South Carolina Press, 2007), 7–10, writes that only $20 million of $1.6 billion of ERCA money had been distributed by the time FDR took office.

25. Chandler, *America's Greatest Depression,* 114–20, outlines Federal Reserve policy.

26. Hicks, *Republican Ascendancy*, 274–76; Edsforth, *New Deal*, 49–50, and for the quotation, 71; Lescohier, *Working Conditions*, 178; David M. Kennedy, *Freedom from Fear: The American People in Depression and War, 1929–1945* (New York: Oxford University Press, 1999), 79–84. FDR opposed a big bonus bill in 1936.

27. For two paragraphs: Leighninger, *Long-Range Public Investment*, 5–10; Leuchtenburg, *Hoover*, 102–16. There was no help from ethnic benevolent associations and banks; they had invested in the real estate market; when that collapsed, so did ethnic institutions. Chandler, *America's Greatest Depression*, 49; Hicks, *Republican Ascendancy*, 268–75; Mitchell, *Depression Decade*, 99–104; Cohen, *Making a New Deal*, 218–38; Frances Fox Piven and Richard A. Cloward, *Poor People's Movements: Why They Succeed, How They Fail* (New York: Vintage Books, 1979), 60–67. New York City gave needy families $2.39 a week and Los Angeles gave $.50 for a month's staples in early 1933. *The Voice of the Rank and File* (Los Angeles Unemployed Cooperative City Units), No. 4, March 13, 1933, in possession of author. Lescohier, *Working Conditions*, 162; Taylor, *American-Made*, 56. Quotation in Cohen, *Making a New Deal*, 227.

28. Cloward and Piven, *Poor People's Movements*, esp. 41–72; Cohen, *Making a New Deal*, 251–67; Edsforth, *New Deal*, 94–114; Babson, *Unfinished Struggle*, 60–66. Garraty, *Unemployment in History*, exaggerates the apathy of the unemployed, 178–87.

29. Robert S. McElvaine, *The Great Depression: America, 1929–1941* (New York: Times Books, 1993), 95–120; Mitchell, *Depression Decade*, 100–101.

30. Three paragraphs: *HS*, 164, 166, 172. Total consumption spending did not get back to 1929 levels until 1937. Private investment almost stopped and stayed below 1929 levels until 1941 (Chandler, *America's Greatest Depression*, 132). Without more wage growth and consumption, it is hard to see how there could have been a major boom in business investment. There was already excess capacity in many businesses and in agriculture. Larger increases in federal spending would have helped, as they did, in fact, in World War II. The Supreme Court judged the NRA unconstitutional in 1935, but the administration was ready to dump it anyway. See also Raymond Wolters, *Negroes and the Great Depression: The Problem of Economic Recovery* (Westport, Conn.: Greenwood Publishing, 1970), 193–96; McElvaine, *Great Depression*, 156–62. Recovery efforts for farmers included credit and payments not to grow on their acreage. Federal farm policies raised average incomes but also pushed tenants and laborers off the land. Owners used federal subsidies to buy tractors and chemicals. See Edsforth, *New Deal*, 149–80. On various recovery policies, including the influx of gold, see Christina Romer, "Lessons from the Great Depression for Economic Recovery in 2009," paper for presentation at the Brookings Institution, Washington, D.C., March 9, 2009.

31. For two paragraphs: Keynes's *The General Theory* appeared in 1936, but you could read his employment articles in the 1920s, as well as the works of John A. Hobson from before the war (Garraty, *Unemployment in History*, 123–28), and Foster and Catchings. Hoover knew of Foster and Catchings (Sautter, *Three Cheers*, 271–73, 291–95).

32. Iwan W. Morgan, *Deficit Government: Taxing and Spending in Modern America* (Chicago: Ivan R. Dee, 1995). Job numbers in *HS*, 126. Three million unemployed were

in government work relief programs. They were not considered regular, permanent employees, but Michael R. Darby thinks they should have been in "Three-and-a-Half Million U.S. Employees Have Been Mislaid: Or an Explanation of Unemployment,1934–1941," *Journal of Political Economy* 84 (February 1976): 1–16.

33. Two paragraphs: Morgan, *Deficit Government*, 24–40. Annual federal deficits in the thirties reached $3 billion, but were offset by state and local surpluses (helped by federal grants). In 1943 the deficit exceeded $55 billion.

34. Bernstein, *Caring Society*, 155–60, 291; John A. Salmond, *The Civilian Conservation Corps, 1933–1942: A New Deal Case Study* (Durham, N.C.: Duke University Press, 1967); and Neal M. Maher, *Nature's New Deal: The Civilian Conservation Corps and the Roots of the American Environmental Movement* (New York: Oxford University Press, 2008), 17–41. After Eleanor Roosevelt protested, sixty-four hundred women worked in eighty-six special camps. These, according to Leighninger, *Long-Range Public Investment*, 17, were part of the WPA, not the CCC. The best short analysis of New Deal job programs is Harvey, "The New Deal's Direct Job-Creation Strategy," copy from the author.

35. For two paragraphs: Bernstein, *Caring Society*, 155–60; Olen Cole Jr., *The African-American Experience in the Civilian Conservation Corps* (Gainesville: University Press of Florida, 1999); Edsforth, *New Deal*, 138; Maher, *Nature's New Deal*, 87–91; Leighninger, *Long-Range Public Investment*, 16–17; Salmond, *Civilian Conservation Corps*, 47–54, 102–20.

36. For two paragraphs: Bernstein, *Caring*, 156–58; Leighninger, *Long-Range Public Investment*, 23–27; Salmond, *Civilian Conservation Corps*, 4, 121; Maher, *Nature's New Deal*, 43–65, 71, 146–80.

37. The typical PWA work week was thirty hours. On poverty lines for the '30s and other periods, see Gordon M. Fisher, "From Hunter to Orshansky: An Overview of (Unofficial) Poverty Lines in the United States from 1904 to 1965," 30–31, 1997 revised version, at www.census.gov/hhes/ poverty/povmeas/papers/hstorsp4. html. Ickes tested his staff by circulating a proposal with a section of *Alice in Wonderland*. When three divisions missed it and approved the proposal, Ickes hit the roof (Leighninger, *Long-Range Public Investment*, 41). Also, McElvaine, *Great Depression*, 152–53; Leighninger, *Long-Range Public Investment*, 80–101, 129; and on PWA housing, see Wolters, *Negroes and the Great Depression*, 196–209 and Richard Rothstein, *The Color of Law: A Forgotten History of How Our Government Segregated America* (New York: Liveright Publishing, 2017), 20–24.

38. For $250 million of the program, states had to contribute three dollars for every federal dollar; the other $250 million was for areas that could not afford the match. Anthony J. Badger, *The New Deal: The Depression Years, 1933–1940* (New York: Noonday Press, 1989), 192–96; Chandler, *America's Greatest Depression*, 194–202; Paul A. Kurzman, *Harry Hopkins and the New Deal* (Fair Lawn, N.J.: R.E. Burdick, 1974), 79–99; Bonnie Fox Schwartz, *The Civil Works Administration, 1933–1934: The Business of Emergency Employment in the New Deal* (Princeton, N.J.: Princeton University Press, 1984), esp. 30.

39. Chandler, *America's Greatest Depression*, 198–99, esp. table 11–5; Taylor, *American-Made*, 110–15; Kurzman, *Harry Hopkins*, 80; Schwartz, *Civil Works Administration*, 25–35.

40. A fourth of those on FERA work projects were so poorly paid that they also received direct relief. See Schwartz, *Civil Works Administration*, 35, 47–48, 117–34, 183–87, esp. 186; Leighninger, *Long-Range Public Investment*, 50–54.

41. Schlesinger Jr., *Age of Roosevelt*, 270–71, 277; Taylor, *American-Made*, 124–25; "Senate Group Asks Relief Accounting," *New York Times*, April 12, 1935; Forrest A. Walker, *The Civil Works Administration: An Experiment in Federal Work Relief, 1933–1934* (New York: Garland Publishing, 1979), 125–29. Many social welfare professionals did not stick up for the CWA because it had no role for them in awarding relief benefits and managing individual programs of rehabilitation. On protests against CWA shutdowns, see Schwartz, *Civil Works Administration*, 208–12, 233.

42. Nancy E. Rose, *Put to Work: Relief Programs in the Great Depression* (New York: Monthly Review Press, 1994), 33–34, 47–53. There is nothing on Latinos and little on blacks in Schwartz, *Civil Works Administration*, but plenty on women (166–80).

43. Schwartz, *Civil Works Administration*, 213–19; Rose, *Put to Work*, 66–70, 78–80; Taylor, *American-Made*, 166–68.

44. Leuchtenburg, *New Deal*, 122–23; Taylor, *American-Made*, 133–41; Schlesinger Jr., *Age of Roosevelt*, 275; Jacob Baker, "Work Relief: The Program Broadens," *New York Times*, November 11, 1934, 6, 17; Schwartz, *Civil Works Administration*, 180–96, 213–14, 221–52; William W. Bremer, "Along the 'American Way:' The New Deal's Work Relief Programs for the Unemployed," *Journal of American History* 62 (December 1975): 636–52, esp. 642; Leighninger, *Long-Range Public Investment*, 48.

45. Three paragraphs: *HS*, 126, McElvaine, *Great Depression*, 224–54; Searle F. Charles, *Minister of Relief: Harry Hopkins and the Depression* (Syracuse, N.Y.: Syracuse University Press, 1963), 94–113; Edsforth, *New Deal*, 222–26; Chandler, *America's Greatest Depression*, 204–5; Taylor, *American-Made*, 429, 321–31, 359, 523. Also, WPA workers helped develop the unemployment survey. More on that in my chapter 6. NYA textbox based on Edsforth, *New Deal*, 229–30; Badger, *New Deal*, 207–8; and Bernstein, *Caring Society*, 160–64.

46. For four paragraphs: McElvaine, *Great Depression*, 269–74; Taylor, *American-Made*, 282–302, 311–14, 409–14, 453, 492. Not enough was spent on tools and materials because the aim was to spend as much as possible on wages. Prior to wartime, the WPA had only small training programs for foremen and household workers. See Alden T. Briscoe, "Public Service Employment in the 1930s: The WPA," 95–115, in Harold L. Sheppard et al., eds., *The Political Economy of Public Service Employment* (Lexington, Mass.: D.C. Heath, 1972). On skills, see Donald S. Howard, *The WPA and Federal Relief Policy* (New York: Da Capo Press, 1973 reprint of 1943 original), 229–43; and Bremer, "Along the 'American Way.'" In 1939 Congress limited WPA workers to eighteen months; a laid-off employee could be recertified as needy but had to go to the end of the line. This congressional action caused strikes and demonstrations.

47. Two paragraphs based on Taylor, *American-Made*, 171, 218, 477, 495–97; Badger, *New Deal*, 208–11; Lyle W. Dorsett, *Franklin Roosevelt and the City Bosses* (Port Washington, N.Y.: Kennikat Press, 1977), throughout, for example, 88–89.

48. For three paragraphs: attacks on the WPA are in Howard, *The WPA*; Badger, *New Deal*, 211–27; McElvaine, *Great Depression*, 265–67; E. Wight Bakke, *The Unemployed Worker: A Study of the Task of Making a Living Without a Job* (New Haven, Conn.: Yale University Press, 1940), esp. the last chapter and 368–70, 410; Schwartz, *Civil Works Administration*, 254–55. Bremer, "Along the 'American Way,'" notes (649–50) that we don't know much about WPA worker morale. Howard, *The WPA*, 812, for "cringing." Other quotations from Kurzman, *Harry Hopkins*, 109, and Don D. Lescohier, "The Hybrid WPA," *Survey Midmonthly* 85 (June 1939): 169. On relief issues for large families and discrimination against women and older workers, see Gertrude Springer, "Border Lines and Gaps," *Survey* 71 (November 1935): 332–33; Springer, "You Can't Eat Morale," Survey 72 (March 1936): 76–77; and Howard, *The WPA*, 192–97. Private employers did not seem to feel that WPA participation ruined the skills and work discipline of job-seekers.

49. Taylor, *American-Made*, 148, 153; Kennedy, *Freedom from Fear*, 254; Edsforth, *New Deal*, 228–29; McElvaine, *Great Depression*, 193. Illegal immigrants were excluded from the WPA, and in 1938 only American citizens were accepted. Painter Willem de Kooning had to resign and filmmaker John Houseman was fired. See Taylor, *American-Made*, 403; Eric Rauchway, *The Great Depression and the New Deal: A Very Short Introduction* (New York: Oxford University Press, 2008), 68.

50. McElvaine, *Great Depression*, 182; Rose, *Put to Work*, 100–103.

51. Such "unemployables" as the aged and female-heads of families were supposed to get assistance under welfare provisions of the Social Security Act. Springer, "Border Lines and Gaps," 332–33; Cloward and Piven, *Poor People's Movements*, 82–85, McElvaine, *Great Depression*, 268. Adding WPA, CCC, and NYA jobs, Phil Harvey, "U.S. Job Creation Programs in the 1930s" (manuscript compliments of the author), finds that at a high point in 1937, the three agencies employed 52.4 percent of the unemployed, but on average only 37 percent. See also Bakke, *Unemployed Worker*, 391. James T. Patterson, *America's Struggle Against Poverty in the Twentieth Century* (Cambridge, Mass.: Harvard University Press, 2000), claims (60), that WPA officials simply miscalculated the need.

52. Theda Skocpol and Kenneth Finegold, "State Capacity and Economic Intervention in the Early New Deal," *Political Science Quarterly* 97 (Summer 1982): 255–78; Kennedy, *Freedom from Fear*, 171–75; Bakke, *Unemployed Worker*, 404; Tony Badger, "FDR: A Model for Obama?" *Nation*, January 26, 2009, 20–22.

53. Taylor, *American-Made*, 95–101, 106. New Dealers often improvised, using old agencies for new functions. See Schwartz, *Civil Works Administration*, 41. The story of CWA checks is in Schwartz, 48–49, 66, and Taylor, *American-Made*, 116–20.

54. Four paragraphs: Bakke, *Unemployed Worker*, 320, 368–410; "The Fortune Survey: XXVII: The People of the U.S.A.—a self-portrait," *Fortune*, February, 1940, 14, 20, 28, 133, 134, 136; Rauchway, *Great Depression*, 69; Sidney Verba and Kay Lehman Schlozman, "Unemployment, Class Consciousness, and Radical Politics: What Didn't Happen in the Thirties," *Journal of Politics* 39 (May 1977): 291–323, esp. 302, 307, 318;

also Howard, *The WPA,* 257–58, 153–55; Charles, *Minister of Relief,* 235; Patterson, *America's Struggle,* 65; "Relief Top Issue, Survey Indicates," *New York Times,* June 4, 1939, L27; Cloward and Piven, *Poor People's Movements,* 83–85; and *Public Opinion, 1935–1946,* under the editorial direction of Hadley Cantril. Prepared by Mildred Strunk (Princeton, N.J.: Princeton University Press, 1951), 893–97; Michael Rogin, "How the Working Class Saved Capitalism: The New Labor History and *The Devil and Miss Jones," Journal of American History* 89 (June 2002): 87–114.

55. Surprisingly, conservative Ronald Reagan recalled in 1981 that others remembered boondoggles, "But I can take you to our town and show you things, like a river front that I used to hike through once that was swamp and is now a beautiful park place built by WPA" (Badger, *New Deal,* 215). That memory did not keep President Reagan from cutting work programs. John L. Palmer, ed., *Creating Jobs: Public Employment Programs and Wage Subsidies* (Washington, D.C.: Brookings Institution, 1978), including Robert Haveman's point (230) about the "moratorium on research on the economics of special pubic employment" over 1940–1970. Also see Briscoe, "Public Service Employment, in Sheppard, and Alan S. Blindner, "What's the Matter With Economics," *New York Review of Books,* December 18, 2014, 55.

56. Elizabeth Fones-Wolf, *Selling Free Enterprise: The Business Assault on Labor and Liberalism: 1945–1960* (Urbana and Chicago, University of Illinois Press, 1994). On recent attitudes, Anon., "Some Unemployed Find Fault in Extension of Jobless Benefits," *New York Times,* October 7, 2011, via CNBC; and Saul J. Blaustein, Christopher J. O'Leary, and Stephen A. Wandner, "Policy Issues: An Overview," 1–49, in O'Leary and Wandner, eds. *Unemployment Insurance* (Kalamazoo, Mich.: W.E. Upjohn, 1997), esp. 6, 15; Seymour Martin Lipset and Gary Marks, *It Didn't Happen Here: Why Socialism Failed in the United States* (New York: W.W. Norton, 2000), 289. In five countries, a majority of low-income respondents agreed that government should provide a job for everyone. Among high-income respondents, only 32 percent in the United States, but 77 percent in West Germany thought so.

57. Peter Fearon, *War, Prosperity and Depression: The U.S. Economy, 1917–45* (Lawrence: University Press of Kansas, 1987), 248, 250; Badger, *New Deal,* 211–17. The WPA spent $11.4 billion, more than a billion a year. Total federal revenues in 1935 were just $3.609 billion and total expenditures $6.412. Executive Office of the President of the United States, *Historical Tables: Budget of the United States Government, Fiscal Year, 1997* (Washington, D.C.: GPO, 1996), 19. Goldberg discusses Roosevelt's bill of rights in "Conclusion: Learning from the Successes and Failures of the New Deal," 292, 297–98.

Chapter 3. Full Employment

1. Easy credit also played a role. See Iwan W. Morgan, *Deficit Government: Taxing and Spending in Modern America* (Chicago: Ivan R. Dee, 1995), 51; and Harold G. Vatter, *The U.S. Economy in World War II* (New York: Columbia University Press, 1985), esp. 21. Also, Executive Office of the President of the United States, Office of Manage-

ment and Budget, *Historical Tables: Budget of the United States Government, Fiscal Year, 1997* (Washington, D.C.: Government Printing Office, 1996), 21.

2. Margaret Weir, *Politics and Jobs: The Boundaries of Employment Policy in the United States* (Princeton, N.J.: Princeton University Press, 1992), 27–129; Morgan, *Deficit Government,* 3–147; Herbert Stein, *Presidential Economics: The Making of Economic Policy from Roosevelt to Clinton,* 3rd revised ed. (Washington, D.C.: American Enterprise Institute, 1994), 65–233. The Committee on Economic Development, a business group, supported recession deficits and tax-cut deficits.

3. Gene Smiley, *Rethinking the Great Depression* (Chicago: Ivan R. Dee, 2002), 133–48; Richard K. Vedder and Lowell E. Gallaway, *Out of Work: Unemployment and Government in Twentieth-Century America* (New York: New York University Press, 1997), 150–75. *Historical Statistics of the United States: Colonial Times to 1970,* Part I (Washington, D.C.: U.S. Bureau of the Census, 1975), 126. Hereafter as *HS.* Morgan, *Deficit Government,* 47; Vatter, *World War II,* 42–44, 104–6. According to *Historical Tables,* 19, from 1941 to 1945, federal spending totaled $311 billion, of which $175 billion was borrowed. *The Life and Times of Rosie the Riveter* (Clarity Films, 1980), uses government recruiting films that showed how easily domestic skills could be adapted to war work.

4. Vatter, *World War II,* 121. Officials allowed that at the start of a collective bargaining agreement, union members had fifteen days to opt out of the union.

5. Two paragraphs based on Foster Rhea Dulles and Melvyn Dubofsky, *Labor in America: A History,* 5th ed. (Arlington Heights, Ill.: Harlan Davidson, 1993), 319–24; Samuel Rosenberg, *American Economic Development Since 1945: Growth, Decline, and Rejuvenation* (New York: Palgrave Macmillan, 2003), 19–39; Vatter, *World War II,* 78–79, 90–97, 121–35. There were sixty-three government seizures. The War Labor Disputes Act [Smith-Connally] of 1943 made it a crime to encourage strikes in war plants. The National War Labor Board allowed wage increases to correct gross pay inequities and substandard living levels and did not subject fringe benefits and bonuses to the Little Steel restriction (Rosenberg, *American Economic Development,* 31). Fifths data in Vatter, *World War II,* 143–44, is before taxes and inflation. *HS,* 164, 225. People faced many shortages. The last car for civilians was produced on February 10, 1942. Housing was in short supply, and tires, gasoline, and hundreds of other items were rationed. The percentage of disposable income not spent jumped from 5.5 percent to 25.2 percent (1940–1944). Workers bought bonds, adding to their savings, and that helped fuel economic growth after the war.

6. Helen Ginsburg, *Full Employment and Public Policy: The United States and Sweden* (Lexington, Mass.: Lexington Books, 1983), 13. Gary Mucciaroni, *The Political Failure of Employment Policy, 1945–1982* (Pittsburgh: University of Pittsburgh Press, 1990), 23, for the public opinion survey.

7. G. J. Santoni, "The Employment Act of 1946," Federal Reserve Bank of St. Louis, November, 1986, 5–16, esp. 10; Vedder and Gallaway, *Out of Work,* 162; Weir, *Politics and Jobs,* 190, n64; Stein, *Presidential Economics,* 76–77.

8. Santoni "Employment Act of 1946"; Rosenberg, *American Economic Development,* 44–47; Ginsburg, *Full Employment,* 3–17. The law required an annual economic report

from the president, a Joint Economic Committee in Congress, and a Council of Economic Advisors to advise the president. It did not include the right to a decent job.

9. Vedder and Gallaway, *Out of Work*, 154–72. In the fall of 1945, President Truman won tax cuts, but the decline in government spending was much larger than the tax cuts. See Barton J. Bernstein and Allen J. Matusow, eds., *The Truman Administration: A Documentary History* (New York: Harper Colophon, 1968), 49–52. Dollar figures in text compare mid-1945 to early 1946.

10. Vedder and Gallaway, *Out of Work*, 167–68; Vatter, *World War II*, 136–38, for the Hutchins statement; U.S. Department of Labor Children's Bureau Publication 289, *Wartime Employment of Boys and Girls Under 18* (Washington, D.C.: Government Printing Office, 1943).

11. Quoting Vatter, *World War II*, 15; Alvin H. Hansen, *The Postwar American Economy: Performance and Problems* (New York: W.W. Norton, 1964), esp. vii, 23–24; Morgan, *Deficit Government*, 53–85. Federal budgets in the 1920s were about $3 billion and usually in surplus. $3 billion was the equivalent of $4.6 billion in 1955. Actual spending in 1955 was $68 billion.

12. *HS*, 225, 293, and column 725 on 164; Harold Vatter, *The U.S. Economy in the 1950s: An Economic History* (New York: W.W. Norton, 1963). For background, see Frank Stricker, *Why America Lost the War on Poverty—And How to Win It* (Chapel Hill: University of North Carolina Press, 2007), 9–31, esp. 21.

13. Defense expenditures jumped from $13.2 billion (1949) to $52.8 billion (1953). Then they began to fall, but they were still 52.2 percent of all on-budget outlays in 1960. See *Historical Tables*, 43–44. Also, Hansen, *Postwar American Economy*, 24; Rosenberg, *American Economic Development*, 58; Stricker, *Why America Lost*, 11–12.

14. Nonfarm job numbers at BLS.gov, Series CES0000000001. Eva E. Jacobs, ed., *Handbook of U.S. Labor Statistics, 1999* (Lanham, Md.: Bernan Press, 1999), hereafter cited as *HLS99*, 154–55, 158, 177–78, for other numbers including the Household/CPS job numbers. *HS*, 15, series 125 and 126, for the population of twenty-five- to thirty-four-year-olds.

15. For two paragraphs: Thomas J. Sugrue, *The Origins of the Urban Crisis: Race and Inequality in Postwar Detroit* (Princeton, N.J.: Princeton University Press Paperback, 1998), 119–54, esp. 119–20 and 135; *HLS99*, 164; Harold L. Sheppard, Louis A. Ferman, and Seymour Faber, *Too Old to Work, Too Young to Retire: A Case Study of a Permanent Plant Shutdown*, U.S. Senate, 86th Cong., 1st sess., Special Committee on Unemployment Problems (Washington, D.C.: Government Printing Office, 1960); and for general background, Stricker, *Why America Lost*, 11, figure 1.2 on 16, and 25–26. As to sluggish growth, of sixteen quarters in 1957–1960, GDP growth rates declined in six quarters and increased little in three others.

16. Stanley Lebergott, "Unemployment: A Perspective," 1–53 in Lebergott, ed., *Men Without Work: The Economics of Unemployment* (Englewood Cliffs, N.J.: Prentice-Hall, 1964).

17. Irving Bernstein, *Promises Kept: John F. Kennedy's New Frontier* (New York: Oxford University Press, 1993), 160. Dominic A. Pacyga, *Chicago: A Biography* (Chicago: Uni-

versity of Chicago Press, 2009), 308–21; Rosenberg, *American Economic Development,* 127. United Auto Workers President Walter Reuther accepted automation as inevitable, as did John Lewis and Harry Bridges. See Nelson Lichtenstein, *Walter Reuther: The Most Dangerous Man in Detroit* (Urbana: University of Illinois Press, 1997), 281–98.

18. First quotation, Sheppard, *Too Old to Work,* 10; second, A. H. Raskin, "Hard-Core Unemployment a Rising National Problem," *New York Times,* April 6, 1961, reprinted in Harold L. Sheppard, ed., *Poverty and Wealth in America* (Chicago: Quadrangle Books, 1970), 200–9. Also, Lichtenstein, *Walter Reuther,* 283. Anxieties about age discrimination against white-collar workers are reflected in two movies: *The High Cost of Living* (1958) and hostility to older career women in the Nina Foch character in *Cash McCall* (1959).

19. U.S. Senate, *Unemployment Problems, Hearings Before the Special Committee on Unemployment Problems,* 86th Cong., 1st sess., pt. 7 (December 1, 1959), 2732–39; Bernstein, *Promises Kept,* 165–66; Charles Denby, *Workers Battle Automation* (Detroit: News & Letters, 1971 reprint of 1960 original). Rosy views win out in *Desk Set (*1957); "Painless Automation," *Time,* January 4, 1960, 66; and "Business in 1961: Automation Speeds Recovery, Boosts Productivity, Pares Jobs," *Time,* December 29, 1961, 50–54. See also, U.S. Congress, Joint Economic Committee, *Staff Report on Employment, Growth, and Price Levels* (Washington, D.C.: Government Printing Office, 1960), 168; phrase quoted from Sheppard, *Too Old to Work,* 4.

20. Hansen, *Postwar American Economy,* 17–19, 24; *HS,* 225; Lebergott, "Unemployment," 22–23. Robert Aaron Gordon, *Economic Instability and Growth: The American Record* (New York: Harper & Row, 1974), 122–29; *HLS99,* 17. Regarding the recession, in the second half of 1959 and all of 1960, there was just one quarter of strong growth.

21. For four paragraphs: James L. Sundquist, *Politics and Policy: The Eisenhower, Kennedy, and Johnson Years* (Washington, D.C.: Brookings Institution, 1968), 13, 25–35, and n57; also, Allen J. Matusow, *The Unraveling of America: A History of Liberalism in the 1960s* (New York: Harper Torchbooks, 1984); 30–59. For this whole section: *HLS99,* 163; Morgan, *Deficit Government,* 83–90. Heller thought that training programs could push unemployment below 4 percent without much inflation by adding trained workers to the labor supply and easing wage pressures. Inflation numbers in the text measure the CPI from December to December. Business got another tax break in mid-1962 when the Treasury Department issued guidelines for accelerated depreciation. That put more cash in corporate accounts.

22. Initially, White House economists expected the 1964 tax cut to produce a large deficit; that would have raised economic demand, which was the point of Keynesian deficits. But when President Johnson was massaging Congress to pass the tax cut, he promised to cut spending at least for the first year. On-budget spending in 1965 (FY) was a billion dollars lower than in 1964 (FY), and the budget was virtually balanced. That doesn't fit the Keynesian script for deficits, but White House economists were concerned, above all, to avoid a budget surplus and the "fiscal drag" on growth that came as businesses expanded, people moved into higher tax brackets, and govern-

ment revenues rose. Also, President Johnson told supporters of deficit spending to accept one year of balanced budgets. Once the cuts were law, deficits could be brought back. Deficits did, indeed, follow, especially as Vietnam spending surged. On business fears of full employment and liberal critiques of the tax cut, see Rosenberg, *American Economic Development*, 105–10, and for Harrington's phrase, 53, Matusow, *Unraveling of America*.

23. Herbert Stein, *The Fiscal Revolution in America: Policy in Pursuit of Reality*, 2nd rev. ed. (Washington, D.C.: American Enterprise Institute, 1996), 372–453; Gordon, *Economic Instability*, 152–53. GDP data is after inflation and comes from the U.S. Bureau of Economic Analysis at bea.gov. Here jobs are nonfarm CES/payroll numbers, measured from December to December, at BLS.gov.

24. Two paragraphs: *HLS99*, 163–64; Stein, *Presidential Economics*, 71–75; 97; Paul A. Samuelson and Robert M. Solow, "The Problem of Achieving and Maintaining a Stable Price Level: Analytical Aspects of Anti-Inflation Policy," *American Economic Review* 50 (May 1960): 177–94, esp. 192–93; Gordon, *Economic Instability*, 143–46; Rosenberg, *American Economic Development*, 112–18. The 4.7 percent rate is measured from December 1967 to December 1968.

25. The consumer price index increased a total of 6 percent between December 1961 and December 1965 but 18.6 percent between December 1965 and December 1969. See also Gordon, *Economic Instability*, 137–70; *Historical Tables*, 20, 45; Morgan, *Deficit Government*, 109–14.

26. Weir, *Politics and Jobs*, 62–86; Matusow, *Unraveling of America*, 104; Garth L. Mangum and John Walsh, *A Decade of Manpower Development Training* (Salt Lake City: Olympus Publishing, 1973).

27. Mangum and Walsh, *Manpower Development Training*, 47 and 32–48. Harry Levin, "A Decade of Policy Developments in Improving Education and Training for Low-Income Populations," 168–79, in Robert H. Haveman, ed., *A Decade of Federal Anti-poverty Programs* (New York: Academic Press, 1977). Daniel Friedlander, David H. Greenberg, and Philip K. Robins, "Evaluating Government Training Programs for the Economically Disadvantaged," *Journal of Economic Literature* 35 (December 1997): 1809–55, conclude that the programs did not make "substantial inroads in reducing poverty, income inequality, or welfare use."

28. There were two other motives for opposing a jobs program: LBJ did not want to raise taxes when he had just fought to cut them, and he seemed to think a new WPA would look like welfare. See Mucciaroni, *Political Failure*, 50–59. Most programs in the War on Poverty were not designed to directly create jobs, but various new agencies employed thousands of poor people at low-wage jobs and thousands of middle-class Americans in bureaucratic and professional capacities. See Bennett Harrison, "Ghetto Employment and the Model Cities Program," *Journal of Political Economy* 82 (March–April 1974): 353–71; Ralph M. Kramer, *Participation of the Poor: Comparative Community Case Studies in the War on Poverty* (Englewood Cliffs, N.J.: Prentice-Hall, 1969), 210–11, 231; Frances Fox Piven and Richard Cloward, *Regulating the Poor: The Functions of Pub-*

lic Welfare (New York: Vintage Books, 1971), n37 on 274–75; and Nancy A. Naples, *Grassroots Warriors: Activist Mothering, Community Work, and the War on Poverty* (New York and London: Routledge, 1998). There was a federal initiative under the rubric of New Careers for the Poor, which recognized that people needed jobs as much as they needed training. It subsidized new, low-level jobs in social and human services areas, especially in the nonprofit sector. Minority women got many of the jobs. The program's founders assumed that such jobs could be the first rung on a ladder that led to professional positions, but that part did not work out. See Claire Dunning, "New Careers for the Poor: Human Services and the Post-Industrial City," *Journal of Urban History* 44:4 (2017): 669–90.

29. Matusow, *Unraveling of America,* 237–40; "The Administration: 'My Neighbor Needs Me,'" *Time,* March 5, 1965, 21; Irwin Unger, *The Best of Intentions: The Triumphs and Failures of the Great Society under Kennedy, Johnson, and Nixon* (New York: Doubleday, 1996), 175, 179; John Bainbridge, "The Job Corps," *New Yorker,* May 21, 1966, in Gerald Leinwand, ed., *Poverty and the Poor* (New York: Washington Square Press, 1968), 129–39. Also, Robert Weisbrot, *Freedom Bound: A History of America's Civil Rights Movement* (New York: Plume, 1991), 165; Levin, "Decade of Political Developments, 171–72; Robert A. Levine, *The Poor Ye Need Not Have with You: Lessons from the War on Poverty* (Cambridge, Mass.: M.I.T. Press, 1970), 121–28; Sar Levitan, *The Great Society's Poor Law: A New Approach to Poverty* (Baltimore: Johns Hopkins University Press, 1969), 285.

30. Levitan, *Great Society's Poor Law,* 306; Sar A. Levitan and Benjamin H. Johnston, *The Job Corps: A Social Experiment that Works* (Baltimore: Johns Hopkins University Press, 1975), 42–43, 71; David Sullivan, "Labor's Role in the War on Poverty," *AFL-CIO American Federationist,* April 1966, 10–11; David Wellman, "Putting-On the Poverty Program," from *Steps,* reprinted in David M. Gordon, ed., *Problems in Political Economy: An Urban Perspective,* 2nd ed. (Lexington, Mass.: D.C. Heath, 1977), 120–28; Charles E. Silberman, and the Editors of *Fortune, The Myths of Automation* (New York: Harper and Row, 1966), 124–25. The Marine Cooks and Stewards Union ran a successful Job Corps program in the early 1970s. It offered real jobs at the end of the program.

31. Mucciaroni, *Political Failure,* 73–75. The Kerner Commission on the riots recommended the creation of a million jobs. See Gareth Davies, *From Opportunity to Entitlement: The Transformation and Decline of Great Society Liberalism* (Lawrence: University of Kansas Press, 1996), 203–8. Instead of making a fundamental change in policy, President Johnson tried to get proof that the Soviet Union was financing the riots.

32. DOL, "A Sharper Look at Unemployment in U.S. Cities and Slums," 1967, available at eric.ed.gov/ERIC; William J. Spring, "Underemployment: The Measure We Refuse To Take," 189, in Harold L. Sheppard, Bennett Harrison, and William J. Spring, eds., *The Political Economy of Public Service Employment* (Lexington, Mass.: D.C. Heath, 1972). Sheldon H. Danziger, Robert H. Haveman, and Robert D. Plotnik, "Antipoverty Policy: Effects on the Poor and the Nonpoor," 50–77 in Sheldon H. Danziger and Daniel H. Weinberg, eds., *Fighting Poverty: What Works and What Doesn't* (Cambridge, Mass.: Harvard University Press, 1986), 70; Elliot Liebow, *Tally's Corner: A Study of Negro*

Streetcorner Men (Boston: Little, Brown, 1967). Barry Bluestone, et al., *Low Wages and the Working Poor* (Ann Arbor, Mich.: Institute of Labor and Industrial Relations, 1973), argued that bad jobs caused people to quit their jobs more often, thus generating more unemployment.

33. The quoted phrase is from "A Sharper Look at Unemployment." The 1970 DOL supplement to the census surveyed fifty-one poor urban areas and nine rural counties. The official national unemployment rate was 4.9 percent and the official rate in the fifty-one areas was 9.6 percent. The special survey added discouraged workers, part-timers who wanted full-time work, and the working poor, yielding a 31 percent subemployment rate. Most of the subemployed were looking for work or working. See William Spring, Bennett Harrison, and Thomas Vietorisz, "In much of the inner city 60% don't earn enough for a decent standard of living," *New York Times Magazine,* November 5, 1972, 42; and T. Vietorisz, R. Mier, and J. Giblin, "Subemployment: Exclusion and Inadequacy Indexes," *Monthly Labor Review* 98 (May 1975): 3–12.

34. Spring, Harrison, Vietorisz, "In much of the inner city," 52–53; and excerpts from U.S. Department of Labor, *Manpower Report of the President, 1968,* 109–117, in Robert E. Will and Harold G. Vatter, eds., *Poverty in Affluence,* 2nd ed. (New York: Harcourt Brace & World, 1970).

35. Rosenberg, *American Economic Development,* 114–23. Policy in 1968–1970 seemed to aim at cooling the economy without a full-blown recession. Efforts to cut federal spending and tighten credit seesawed with efforts to do the opposite. But the main effect, starting with a 1968 tax increase and a budget surplus that carried into Richard Nixon's first year as president, was a recession. Stein, *Presidential Economics,* 119–24, 150–52; Morgan, *Deficit Government,* 112–19. Increases in consumer prices from January to January: 1969–1970: 6.2 percent, 1970–1971: 5.3 percent, 1971–1972: 3.3 percent, 1972–1973: 3.6 percent, 1973–1974: 9.4 percent. The deficit rose to $23 billion in fiscal years 1971 and 1972.

36. For three paragraphs, Stein, *Presidential Economics,* 139, 150–51; Rosenberg, *American Economic Development,* 118–23, 183–207; and BLS.gov, for unemployment rate and consumer price index.

37. Clair Brown, "Unemployment Theory and Policy, 1946–1980," *Industrial Relations* 22 (Spring 1983): 164–85, esp. 178–79; Rosenberg, *American Economic Development,* 189; and a 1975 presentation to Congress, Barry Bluestone and Bennett Harrison, "Taking Public Employment Seriously," 130, in Gordon, *Problems.* Connally quoted in Ginsburg, *Full Employment,* 33. Also, *Annual Report of the Council of Economic Advisers, in Economic Report of the President, 1972* (Washington, D.C.: Government Printing Office, 1972), 113–16.

38. Morgan, *Deficit Government,* 123–27; *Historical Tables,* 23. There was almost no deficit in fiscal year '74, a large one in FY '75, and an even larger one in FY '76.

39. Quotation, 72, in Peter B. Doeringer and Michael J. Piore, "Unemployment and the 'Dual Labor Market'," *Public Interest* 38 (Winter 1975): 67–79. Background in Stricker, *Why America Lost,* 91–98.

40. Quoting Spring, "Underemployment." Also, Spring, "Manpower Programs: The Lessons of the 1960s," 157–64, in Alan Gartner, Russell A. Nixon, and Frank Riessman, eds., *Public Service Employment: An Analysis of its History, Problems and Perspectives* (New York: Praeger Publishers, 1973); 53–133, in Gordon, *Problems,* esp. Bennett Harrison, "Institutions on the Periphery," 102–7. Doeringer and Piore, "Unemployment and the 'Dual Labor Market,'" 72–73, noted that much training occurs on the job; thus, racism and other isms keep people from getting jobs where they can get relevant training.

41. Robert F. Cook, Charles F. Adams Jr., V. Lane Rawlins, and Associates, *Public Service Employment: The Experience of a Decade* (Kalamazoo, Mich.: W.E. Upjohn Institute for Employment Research, 1985), 5–7. "Puny" from Robert Lekachman, "Public Jobs and the New Economy," 94–95, in Gartner, *Public Service Employment.*

42. Cook, *Public Service Employment,* 7–10; Weir, *Politics and Jobs,* 117–23; Mucciaroni, *Political Failure,* 86–89.

43. Two paragraphs: Robert Lekachman, "Managing Inflation in a Full Employment Society," *Annals of the American Academy of Political and Social Science* 418 (March 1975): 85–93; Bennett Harrison, "Inflation and Unemployment: Jobs Above All," *Social Policy* 5 (March–April 1975): 36–42. Harrison (40) noted that GM raised prices ten times from the fall of 1973 to the fall of 1974, even as sales fell 21 percent. Doubts about the natural theory are mentioned in Roger E. A. Farmer, *How the Economy Works: Confidence, Crashes, and Self-Fulfilling Prophecies* (New York: Oxford University Press, 2010), 61–62. As noted in the next chapter, Friedman was quoted on the need for higher unemployment in *Business Week.*

44. Economists Tom Larson and Jim Devine helped me here. Also, Brown, "Unemployment Theory." Lloyd Ulman, "The Uses and Limits of Manpower Policy," originally 1974, reprinted in Gordon, *Problems,* 117, noted that in two surveys, most people found new jobs while working at their old jobs. People did not normally quit a job to devote all their time to finding a new one, as some theorists assume. So, there are quite a few job-searchers who are working while searching and many who are in the sidelines who are looking for work but not officially listed as searching.

45. These issues are also discussed in my introduction and in chapter 6. BLS tables on labor force flows, especially LNU07100000 and LNU07200000, show churning among labor force categories. For example, from August 2016 to September 2016, 4.7 million people went from "Not in the Labor Force" and not counted as searching for a job and unemployed to being employed. Provocative and very helpful is Kim B. Clark and Lawrence H. Summers, "Labor Force Transitions and Unemployment," Working Paper No. 277 (Cambridge, Mass.: National Bureau of Economic Research, April 1978); and Monica D. Castillo, "Persons Outside the Labor Force Who Want a Job," *Monthly Labor Review,* July 1998, 34–42.

Chapter 4. Low Unemployment + Low Inflation

1. The opening section title is from Michael Mandel, "Plenty of Workers Waiting in the Wings," *Business Week,* March 13, 1989, 90–91. Pay levels in table 4.1 are for

nonfarm, private-sector production and nonsupervisory workers and come from *Economic Report of the President, 1984* (Washington, D.C.: Government Printing Office, 1984), table B-38, p. 264; and *Economic Report of the President, 2016* (Washington, D.C.: Government Printing Office, 2016), table B-15, p. 418, hereafter as *ERP.*

2. Many articles and online sites offer the basics on the immigration laws. For example, see Ballotpedia for the Immigration and Naturalization Act of 1965, and Tom Gjelten, "The Immigration Act that Inadvertently Changed America," *Atlantic,* October 2, 2015, accessed January 8, 2019, at theatlantic.com. A useful general article from the period is Eli Ginzberg, "The Job Problem," *Scientific American* 237 (November 1977): 43–51.

3. Sarah Shannon, Christopher Uggen, Melissa Thompson, Jason Schnittker, and Michael Massoglia, "Growth in the U.S. Ex-Felon and Ex-Prisoner Population, 1948–2010," presented at the Population Association of America Annual Meeting, March 31–April 2, 2011, Washington, D.C.

4. Samuel Rosenberg, *American Economic Development Since 1945: Growth, Decline and Rejuvenation* (New York: Palgrave Macmillan, 2003), 183–89. *Statistical Abstract of the United States, 1981* (Washington, D.C.: Bureau of the Census, 1981), tables 779, 780, and 1094. Food prices climbed 46 percent in 1972–1976.

5. Quoting Herbert Stein, *Presidential Economics: The Making of Economic Policy from Roosevelt to Clinton,* 3rd revised ed. (Washington, D.C.: American Enterprise Institute, 1994), 189.

6. For five paragraphs: Rosenberg, *American Economic Development,* 189; James G. Devine, "The 'Natural' Rate of Unemployment," 126–32, in Edward Fullbrook, ed., *A Guide to What's Wrong With Economics* (London: Anthem Press, 2004); Anonymous, "How to Fight Inflation and Recession," *Business Week,* December 7, 1974, 84–88; Jefferson Cowie, *Stayin' Alive: The 1970s and the Last Days of the Working Class* (New York: New Press, 2010), 221–24. For the quoted phrase, which is italicized in the original, 101 of Sanford Rose, "We've Learned How to Lick Inflation," *Fortune,* September, 1976, 100–105, 180, 182, 184. Rose asserted that wage hikes caused inflation and unemployment had to be high to cut wages. More factual were Anonymous, "1976: Labor's Year of Compromise," *Business Week,* December 1, 1975, 44–50; and Irwin Ross, "How to Tell When the Unions Will Be Tough," *Fortune,* July, 1975, 100–103, 151–52, 156.

7. For two paragraphs: Executive Office of the President of the United States, Office of Management and Budget, *Historical Tables: Budget of the United States Government, Fiscal Year, 1997* (Washington, D.C.: Government Printing Office, 1996); Iwan W. Morgan, *Deficit Government: Taxing and Spending in Modern America* (Chicago: Ivan R. Dee, 1995), 122–23; and Stein, *Presidential Economics,* 189, on recession as the "old-time religion" approach to fighting inflation. Carter tried voluntary controls, without success. Untried was a Tax-Based Incomes Policy, discussed in note 14. There was little support for mixed policies, for example, that government would restrain total spending and access to credit, dampening overall economic growth and inflation, but directly create public-service jobs for the unemployed. See Gary Mucciaroni, *The Political Fail-*

ure of Employment Policy, 1945–1982 (Pittsburgh: University of Pittsburgh Press, 1990), 85–91; Lawrence A. Mayer, "First Aid for Recession's Victims," *Fortune,* February, 1975, 74–77, 158, 160. Jeff Madrick, *Seven Bad Ideas: How Mainstream Economists Have Damaged America and the World* (New York: Knopf, 2014), 136–37, on the fact that high wages can stimulate higher productivity, which lowers costs. In Ford's administration extreme right-wingers like Treasury Secretary William Simon wanted to "Balance the Budget, Period," even at the risk of a bigger recession. Quoted in Stein, *Presidential Economics,* 211.

8. For the list and the preceding paragraph: Andrew Levison, *The Full Employment Alternative* (New York: Coward, McCann & Geoghegan, 1980), 13–33; "Jobs, Skilled and Unskilled, Go Begging in Many Cities," *New York Times,* July 1, 1975, 1, 60; Clair Brown, "Unemployment Theory and Policy, 1946–1980," *Industrial Relations* 22 (Spring 1983): 164–85. Helen Ginsburg, *Unemployment, Subemployment, and Public Policy* (New York: New York University, School of Social Work, Center for Studies in Income Maintenance Policy, 1975), 25–28; Ginsburg, *Full Employment and Public Policy: The United States and Sweden* (Lexington, Mass.: D.C. Heath, 1985), 25–48, esp. 33; Walter Guzzardi Jr., "How to Deal with the 'New Unemployment,'" *Fortune,* October 1976, 132–35, 208, 210, 212, 214, 216. Evaluations of aspects of the new unemployment theory include a model that showed that if the United States had eliminated unemployment insurance in 1976, the average duration of unemployment would have fallen from 4.3 months to 2.8 months. See Lloyd G. Reynolds et al., *Economics of Labor* (Englewood Cliffs, N.J.: Prentice-Hall, 1987), 440; and Robert G. Ehrenberg and Robert S. Smith, *Modern Labor Economics: Theory and Public Policy,* 8th ed. (Boston: Addison Wesley, 2003), 515–16. Also, Kay Lehman Schlozman and Sidney Verba, *Injury to Insult: Unemployment, Class, and Political Response* (Cambridge, Mass.: Harvard University Press, 1979), 31–98, esp. 32, 37, 44–45.

9. For two paragraphs and quoted phrases: Harry Maurer, *Not Working: An Oral History of the Unemployed* (New York: Holt, Rinehart and Winston, 1979), 47–50, 111–14. Also, Schlozman, *Injury to Insult,* 48–54; Daniel Yankelovich, "Work, Values, and the New Breed," 3–26, in Clark Kerr and Jerome K. Rosow, eds., *Work in America: The Decade Ahead* (New York: Van Nostrand Reinhold, 1979).

10. For two paragraphs, Maurer, *Not Working,* 51–56, 192, 230–31, 215–19, 143–44, 139–43, 17–21, 168–69.

11. Maurer, *Not Working,* 76–80, 39–43; Schlozman, *Injury to Insult,* 47–59; Levison, *Full Employment Alternative,* 25–27; Guzzardi, "How to Deal."

12. James K. Galbraith, "Time to Ditch the NAIRU," *Journal of Economic Perspectives* 11 (Winter 1997): 93–108. Galbraith noted that NAIRU-ites never knew what NAIRU levels should be. When unemployment fell below NAIRU without much inflation, they scrambled to find explanations and excuses. Arguments used by Friedman and Robert Lucas seemed to be made-up stories of how workers reacted to inflation. They alleged that as inflation rose, more workers decided not to search for work because it paid less well, but that is not what seemed to happen in the high inflation 1970s when more people went to work to cushion themselves against inflation.

13. Cowie, *Stayin' Alive,* 221–24 and 224 for quoted phrase; Rose, "We've Learned How"; Anonymous, "1976: Labor's Year of Compromise;" Ross, "How to Tell When the Unions Will Be Tough."

14. Two paragraphs: See Alan Blinder's review of Jeff Madrick's *Seven Bad Ideas,* "What's the Matter with Economics," *New York Review of Books,* December 18, 2014, 55–57, and January 8, 2015, 40. Blinder wondered in 1989 if liberals had been too fast to accept NAIRU (comment included in Matthew Yglesias, "The NAIRU Explained: Why Economists Don't Want Unemployment to Drop Too Low," November 14, 2014, VOX, accessed on January 9, 2015). A liberal economist might have supported NAIRU, accepting a little more unemployment—nothing drastic. In parallel fashion, Fed Chair Paul Volcker drove up interest rates to bring on recession in 1981, but he once claimed he was just controlling growth in the money supply, not trying to create more unemployment. See Madrick, *Seven Bad Ideas,* 66, 132. In the '90s, liberal Paul Krugman was a defender of the natural rate and NAIRU, which he said had risen because of costly government benefit programs that made it easy not to work. He claimed that support of natural-rate ideas was "near-universal" among economists. See James Risen, "Fed's Decisions Tied to 'Natural' 6% Jobless Rate," *Los Angeles Times,* August 29, 1994, A1, A4. Also, see Madrick, *Seven Bad Ideas,* 59–65, 131–37; and Madrick, "Why Economists Cling to Discredited Ideas," *American Prospect,* Winter 2015, 75–79. Among stalwart critics of NAIRU were the staff of a magazine called *Dollars and Sense* (for example, Teresa Amott, "The 6% Solution: The Fed Redefines Full Employment," November 1988, 6–8, 21) and many people who worked for a full-employment policy and a strong Humphrey-Hawkins bill.

There is no space to explore the variety of suggestions for controlling inflation that were being discussed. They included wage-and-price controls, which unions opposed. Other possibilities included raising taxes, cutting taxes, deregulating businesses (this was being done in trucking and airlines), and encouraging businesses to invest more to improve productivity (there were supply-side tax-cuts in the late '70s). Despite the latter two, prices surged. The most unusual proposal was a Tax-Based Incomes Policy, which involved tax credits for companies that held wages down and tax surcharges for those that did not. It was quite controversial and it was never tried. See Rosenberg, *American Economic Development,*183–95, and Nancy Ammon Jianakoplos, "A Tax-Based Incomes Policy (TIP): What's It All About?" Federal Reserve Bank of St. Louis, February 1978, 8–12.

15. A very useful short piece on Humphrey-Hawkins with an important section on support groups is Gertrude Schaffner Goldberg, "Trying Again for Full Employment," *Dollars and Sense,* November–December 2018, 7–13. Helen Ginsburg sent me her copy of "A Full Employment Policy for America, A Symposium at UCLA," edited by Paul Bullock (October 12, 1973), which includes the first version of Humphrey-Hawkins, H.R. 15476. She also lent me her copy of the minutes of a conference she participated in: *A Congressional Conference on Full Employment Policy: An Examination of its Implications,* Hearing before the Joint Economic Committee, Congress of the United States, Ninety-

Fourth Congress, First Session, December 10, 1975, U.S. Government Printing Office, Washington, 1976. Helen has been active in full-employment movements for half a century, and she shared many insights in phone conversations.

16. In addition to sources in note 15, this section on Humphrey-Hawkins is based on Public Law 95–523, 95th Congress, October 27, 1978, known as "Full Employment and Balanced Growth Act of 1978." Also, see Cowie, *Stayin' Alive,* 266–93; Mucciaroni, *Political Failure,* esp. 93–105; and for the clearest summary of the Humphrey-Hawkins story, including discussions of the main versions of the bill, Ginsburg, *Full Employment,* 63–81. Also, see Larry Martz et al., "The Inflation Surge: Special Report," *Newsweek,* May 28, 1978, 68–82 (69 for Fellner quotation); Stein, "Full Employment at Last?" *Wall Street Journal,* September 14, 1977. Also Brown, "Unemployment Theory;" and Margaret Weir, *Politics and Jobs: The Boundaries of Employment Policy in the United States* (Princeton, N. J.: Princeton University Press, 1992), 130–62, esp. 137, 157, noting that many economists were monetarists (restrain the money supply and raise unemployment), and free-marketers committed to individual action models (unemployment was caused by individual decisions). Schultze also opposed a Humphrey-Hawkins provision to offer wages of $4 an hour, which he feared would draw low-wage workers from private industry, where they were making $2.50. So much for lifting the working poor. Robert Kuttner, *Everything for Sale: The Virtues and Limits of Markets* (New York: Alfred A. Knopf, 1998), 30–38; Paul Lewis, "Schultze of the C.E.A.," *New York Times,* Business Section, January 9, 1977, 7.

17. Weir, *Politics and Jobs,* 131–38; Mucciaroni, *Political Failure,* 95–105. Efforts to argue away unemployment include American Enterprise Institute for Public Policy Research, *Full Employment and Balanced Growth Act: An Update* (Washington, D.C.: American Enterprise Institute, 1978), 17–22. Over time there were fewer devout labor-liberals in Congress, but there were still centers of liberalism such as the Democratic Study Group. The Watergate scandal brought dozens of new Democrats to Congress in 1974, although fewer of them were "emotionally involved with unemployment." Some voted against Humphrey-Hawkins. See Foster Rhea Dulles and Melvyn Dubofsky, *Labor in America: A History,* 5th ed. (Arlington Heights, Ill.: Harlan Davidson, 1993), 385–405; Cowie, *Stayin' Alive,* 235–36; Jacob S. Hacker and Paul Pierson, *Winner-Take-All Politics* (New York: Simon and Schuster, 2010), 108–13, 116. Helen Ginsburg emphasized in a phone conversation the key support of faith-based groups for Humphrey-Hawkins and other full-employment efforts. See also her *Full Employment,* 66–67.

18. Cowie, *Stayin' Alive,* 227–36, 309; Frank Stricker, *Why America Lost the War on Poverty—And How to Win It* (Chapel Hill: University of North Carolina Press, 2007), 1, 165–67, 173–75, 198–99; Hacker and Pierson; Levison, *Full Employment Alternative,* 159, 161; Wikipedia entry on Business Roundtable, December 30, 2011. Bennett Harrison and Barry Bluestone, *The Great U-Turn: Corporate Restructuring and the Polarizing of America* (New York: Basic Books, 1990 pbk.), 7–11, on declining profit rates. Right-wingers seemed more aggressive about pushing their line, and liberal organizations, such as the Brookings Institution, got less liberal. There were new liberal organizations, such

as the Center on Budget Policies and Priorities—founded in 1981—that analyzed federal spending cuts as they affected low-income Americans.

19. For three paragraphs, Donald C. Baumer and Carl E. Van Horn, *The Politics of Unemployment* (Washington, D.C.: Congressional Quarterly Press, 1985), 125–56 and esp. 130 for the quotation from the *Reader's Digest*; Mucciaroni, *Political Failure*, 100–101; Weir, *Politics and Jobs;* Cowie, *Stayin' Alive,* 188–96. Space does not allow discussion of President Carter's effort to reform welfare called The Program for Better Jobs and Income, but see Stricker, *Why America Lost,* 137–38.

20. In the '60s, Democratic policy included supply-side cuts for businesses. Republican supply-siders rarely admitted commonalities with Democrats because supply-side was mostly an excuse for cutting the taxes on rich people and exciting Republicans against liberals, not a coherent economic program. One difference was that existing tax rates were higher in the early 1960s than the 1980s, so the tax cut should have had a bigger impact. An excellent early analysis of Reaganomics is Frank Ackerman, *Hazardous to Our Wealth: Economic Policies in the 1980s* (Boston: South End Press, 1984). Also see Stein, *Presidential Economics,* 237–49.

21. For two paragraphs: Stein, *Presidential Economics,* 256–61, 294; Reagan quotation on 256; and Josh Bivens, "Tax Cuts Didn't Lead to Faster Growth," EPI Economic Snapshot, February 11, 2015. After the tax cuts were enacted, Reagan's budget director, David Stockman, predicted that federal deficits would soar.

22. Information and quotations from Katherine S. Newman, *Declining Fortunes: The Withering of the American Dream* (New York: Basic Books, 1993), 14; and Newman, *Falling from Grace: The Experience of Downward Mobility in the American Middle Class* (New York: Vintage Books, 1989), 69–70.

23. Richard E. Meyer and Barry Bearak, "Poverty: Toll Grows Amid Aid Cutbacks," *Los Angeles Times,* July 28, 1985, 1, 6–7; Stuart Eizenstat, "Comments," in Donald T. Critchlow and Ellis W. Hawley, eds., *Poverty and Public Policy in Modern America* (Chicago: Dorsey Press, 1989), 311–13; Daniel P. McMurrer and Amy B. Chasanov, "Trends in Unemployment Insurance Benefits," *Monthly Labor Review* 118 (September 1995): 30–39.

24. "Plenty of Workers," esp. the judgments of John Hekman; *ERP 2011,* 246, table B-47. The hourly wage is in constant 1982–1984 dollars. Also, see Bob Drogin, "True Victims of Poverty: the Children," *Los Angeles Times,* July 30, 1985, part I, 1, 10–11.

25. Unless otherwise noted, all employment and unemployment numbers are from BLS.gov. The numbers used for table 4.2 and the numbers in the insert comparing total nonfarm jobs and manufacturing jobs are from the BLS's Current Employment Statistics, accessed September 17, 2018. Other information in these paragraphs from Richard Child Hill and Cynthia Negry, "Deindustrialization and Racial Minorities in the Great Lakes Region, USA," in D. Stanley Eitzen and Maxine Baca Zinn, eds., *The Reshaping of America: Social Consequences of the Changing Economy* (Englewood Cliffs, N.J.: Prentice-Hall, 1989), 168–78. Not all deindustrialized workers lost out; Ruth Milkman, *Farewell to the Factory: Auto Workers in the Late Twentieth Century* (Berkeley: University of

California Press, 1997), esp. 93–136, describes a GM buyout in Linden, New Jersey. Some who took the buyout hated the work environment at GM, so they were upbeat about finding other kinds of jobs.

26. Drogin, "True Victims." Anonymous, "Help Wanted Ads Don't Add Up," *Dollars and Sense,* January, 1984, 12–13, 17.

27. UC Berkeley criminologist Elliot Currie quoted in Stanley Meisler and Sam Fullwood III, "Voices of the Poor Echo with Puzzlement, Pain and Survival," *Los Angeles Times,* July 15, 1990, 22–23. Lawrence Mishel, Jared Bernstein, and John Schmitt, *The State of Working America: 2000/2001* (Ithaca, N.Y.: Cornell University Press, 2001), 130–31, show that the percentage of women earning poverty wages stayed around 37 percent over 1979–1989, while the share of men increased from 14 percent to 21 percent. Median household income increased in the 1980s, largely because of more workers per household.

28. The *New York Review of Books* has often published penetrating articles about stop and frisk, poor legal representation for minorities, and similar issues. For example, Adam Hochschild, "Our Awful Prisons: Can They Be Changed?" May 26, 2016, 30, 32; and Michael Greenberg, "'Broken Windows' and the New York Police," November 6, 2014, accessed at nybooks.com on June 13, 2015.

29. On conservative social theorists and liberals who wrote like conservatives, including Pete Hamill, see Stricker, *Why America Lost,* 174–78. Widely debated was Charles Murray, *Losing Ground: American Social Policy, 1950–1980* (New York: Basic Books, 1984). William J. Wilson, sometimes labeled a social democrat, occasionally gave credence to the underclass model in some of his work, but his bigger point was that lack of jobs was the main problem.

30. Barry Bearak, "Poor Share Work Ethic, U.S. Dream," *Los Angeles Times,* July 29, 1985, I, 1, 8–9. While conservatism spread, *the Los Angeles Times* and other good papers continued to carry well-researched pieces on poverty, unemployment, and deindustrialization.

31. Binyamin Appelbaum, "Out of Trouble, but Criminal Records Keep Men Out of Work," *New York Times,* February 28, 2015, accessed December 4, 2016, at nytimes .com; and Alice Goffman, *On the Run: Fugitive Life in an American City* (New York: Picador, 2015).

32. Two paragraphs based on Michele I. Naples and Nahid Aslanbeigui, "Is There a Theory of Involuntary Unemployment in Introductory Textbooks?" 109–21; and Robert Cherry, "Full Employment in Introductory Textbooks," 127–39. Both are in Naples and Aslanbeigui, eds., *Rethinking Economic Principles: Critical Essays on Introductory Textbooks* (Chicago: Irwin-Times Mirror, 1996). Also, Stein, *Presidential Economics,* 426–44; and Rosenberg, *American Economic Development,* 254–57, including 257 for the quoted phrase.

33. For two paragraphs, Hacker and Pierson, *Winner-Take-All-Politics,* 212–13; Rosenberg, *American Economic Development,* 279–312; Iwan Morgan, *Deficit Government,* 189. Pundits talked about a jobless recovery, but job growth was strong in 1992 and 1993;

what was striking was that average pay fell. See Alexander Cockburn, "The '90s Boom Unmasked: It's a Wage Freeze," *Los Angeles Times,* October 30, 1977, B9. Gordon Richards, chief economist of the National Association of Manufacturers, believed that financiers had a "pathological fear of growth," quoted in Robert A. Rosenblatt, "Economic Surge Adds 348,000 Jobs to the U.S. Work Force," *Los Angeles Times,* June 8, 1996, A2, A13. Also, see Rosenblatt, "U.S. Jobless Rate Drops to 24-Year Low of 4.7%," *Los Angeles Times,* January 1, 1997, A1, A14. Job exports are explained in *Wal-Mart: The High Cost of Low Prices* (2005), a film by Robert Greenwald. David Bacon, "How U.S. Policies Fueled Mexico's Great Migration," *Nation,* January 4, 2012, online; Robert E. Scott, Carlos Salas, and Bruce Campbell, "Revisiting NAFTA: Still Not Working for North America's Workers," EPI Briefing Paper #173, September 28, 2006; Joan Grillo, "How Mexicans See NAFTA," *New York Times,* September 25, 2016, Sunday Review, 3.

34. The boast was from Wisconsin's Tommy Thompson. See Stricker, *Why America Lost,* 216–20; and Sharon Hays, *Flat Broke with Children: Women in the Age of Welfare Reform* (New York: Oxford University Press, 2003), 94, 114–17, and 101 for the second phrase. Also, Rosenberg, *American Economic Development,* 287–89.

35. U.S. Census Bureau. *Poverty in the United States: 2000* (Washington, D.C.: Government Printing Office, 2001), 5.

36. For two paragraphs, Mary Williams Walsh, "High January Job Figures Baffle Experts," *Los Angeles Times,* February 5, 2000, A1, A15. Patrice Apodaca, "Job Boom Reaches Fringes of Labor Force," *Los Angeles Times,* April 11, 1998, A1, A19.

37. Wage data on nonsupervisory and production workers in the private, nonfarm sector. For 2000–2008, I calculated the changes from available figures on annual average wages. For 2009–2017, the figures measure real changes from January of one year to another. Thus the 2015 rate measures the change from January 2015 through January 2016.

38. Four paragraphs and quoted phrases: Don Lee, "L.A. County Jobs Surge Since '93 but Not Wages," *Los Angeles Times,* July 26, 1999, A1, A19; Leslie Earnest, "Recruiters Who Fill Low-Skill Jobs Go Begging," *Los Angeles Times,* November 2, 2000, A1, A22; Sylvia Pagan Westphal and Maria Elena Fernandez, "Census Bureau Applicants Plentiful in Most of County," *Los Angeles Times,* March 18, 2000, B1, B5; Don Lee, "Labor Pinch Has Midwest Pitching Woo," *Los Angeles Times,* December 7, 1999, A1, A24; Lee, "Labor Supply Falling Short," *Los Angeles Times,* September 28, 1998, D1, D6; Peter G. Gosselin, "Job Picture Still Rosy as Hiring Gets Creative," *Los Angeles Times,* August 30, 1999, A1, A15. Also Walsh, "High January"; Louis Uchitelle, "Companies Try Digging Deeper into Labor Pool," *New York Times,* March 26, 2000, 1, 26; Julie Hatch and Angeles Clinton, "Job Growth in the 1990s: A Retrospect," *Monthly Labor Review* (December 2000): 3–18; Stricker, *Why America Lost,* 221–22 and n60; Rosenberg, *American Economic Development,* 291–97. Also, see Peter G. Gosselin, "Boom Times Elude Workers with Modest Education, Skills," *Los Angeles Times,* November 27, 1999, A1, A32. Greenspan in Charles M. Kelly, *Class War in America* (Santa Barbara, Calif.: Fithian Press, 2000), 55–56.

39. Davan Maharj, "Layoffs: A Company's Strategy of First Resort," *Los Angeles Times,* November 22, 1998, C1, C7.

40. For two paragraphs: Hatch and Clinton, "Job Growth." In the retail sector, sales increased 70 percent, and there was talk of labor shortages, but real wages increased only 4.5 percent. Lee Romney and Stuart Silverstein, "Economic Boom Boosts Even Blighted Areas," *Los Angeles Times,* August 20, 2000, A1, A24–25. *Poverty in the United States: 2000,* 11, table D; Katherine S. Newman, *No Shame in My Game: The Working Poor in the Inner City* (New York: Russell Sage Foundation and Vintage Books, 2000), 57, 85; data.bls.gov/map/MapToolServlet, for "Local Area Unemployment Statistics Map," for November 1998; Steven Greenhouse, "Low-Paid Jobs Lead Advance in Employment," *New York Times,* October 1, 2000, 1, 56; and *ERP 2011,* table B-47, for real hourly wages.

41. For two paragraphs: Jared Bernstein and Dean Baker, *The Benefits of Full Employment: When Markets Work for People* (Washington, D.C.: Economic Policy Institute, 2003), 46–56; Don Lee, "A Rising Tide Puts the Nation to Work: The Real Winners"; Peter G. Gosselin, "A Rising Tide . . . The Good Times," both in *Los Angeles Times,* April 11, 1999, A1, A30, A31; Stuart Silverstein, "Missing the Boom-Time Bandwagon," *Los Angeles Times,* July 20, 1998, A1, A16.

42. Jared Bernstein and Dean Baker, "The Unemployment Rate at Full Employment: How Low Can It Go?" economix.blogs.nytimes.com2013/11/20.

43. Dean Baker, "The High Priests of the Bubble Economy," accessed November 11, 2008, at tpmcafe. talkingpointsmemo.com/2008/11/11/ the_high_ priests_of_ the_bubble. John Miller, "Economy Sets Records for Longevity and Inequality," *Dollars and Sense,* May–June 2000, 15–19; Robert M. Solow, "Why Were the Nineties So Good? Could It Happen Again?" *Focus* 22 (Summer 2002): 1–7; Newman, *No Shame,* 63. Average annual increases in labor productivity in the business sector were 3 percent in 1996–2001 but only 0.9 percent in another period with low unemployment, 2013–2018. As to real unemployment, the BLS's U-6 rate is too narrow to include all the truly unemployed, but it averaged 8.2 percent over 1995–2001. For one measure of productivity, see the BLS series PRS84006092, and for U-6, series LNU03327709.

Chapter 5. Low Pay, Great Recession

1. Various monthly issues of the BLS's Employment Situation, hereafter as *ES,* for unemployment and employment numbers. See also, BLS. gov, "Civilian Labor Force Participation Rate by Age, Gender, Rate, and Ethnicity," accessed at BLS.gov on February 27, 2017, and also series LNS11300000 for long-term rates. For the Recession's impact on young adults, see Alana Semuels, "Degree Not Needed, College Grads Find," *Los Angeles Times,* September 20, 2013, B1, B5; Heidi Shierholz, Alyssa Davis, and Will Kimball, "The Class of 2014: The Weak Economy is Idling Too Many Young Graduates," Briefing Paper #377, (Washington, D.C.: Economic Policy Institute, May 1, 2014); Philip Oreopoulus, Till von Wachter, and Andrew Heisz, "The Short- and Long-Term Career Effects of Graduating in a Recession," *American Economic Journal,*

Applied Economics 4 (1) (2012): 1–29; Josh Mitchell, "Recent Black College Grads Face Severe Underemployment," *Wall Street Journal,* May 20, 2014, at wsj.com/economics/ 2014/05/20/recent-black-college=grads-face-severe-underemployment; Emily Alpert, "Dim Outlook for Young Adults," *Los Angeles Times,* September 19, 2013, AA1, AA5. Also, see Susan Saulny, "After Recession, More Young Adults Are Living on the Street," *New York Times,* December 18, 2012, accessed 12/19/2012 at nytimes.com. Regarding veterans, in November of 2012, when all 25- to 34-year-olds had unemployment rates of 7.9 percent, for recent veterans, unemployment was 9.5 percent for men and 12.5 percent for women. See also Alana Semuels, "Veterans Face High Unemployment," *Los Angeles Times,* July 11, 2001, A11. Sara Murray, "The Curse of the Class of 2009," *Wall Street Journal,* May 9, 2009, accessed August 17, 2012 at online.wsj.com/article/ SB12418197091500209.html. For long-term trends, Steven Greenhouse, "If You're a Waiter, the Future is Rosy: Training for What?" *New York Times,* March 7, 2004, Wk, 5. Baby boomers (born in the 1940s, '50s, and early '60s) had less unemployment than young workers, but once they lost their jobs, they had more trouble finding work. Many were too young for Medicare and Social Security. Some baby-boomers worked to support elderly parents and their own children. More kids were living at home, but even some older people came back to live with their elderly parents. See Catherine Rampell, "In Hard Economy for All Ages, Older Isn't Better . . . It's Brutal," *New York Times,* February 3, 2013, 1, 17; Walter Hamilton, "A Midlife Moving Crisis," *Los Angeles Times,* April 21, 2014, A1, A9.

2. Heather Long, "U.S. Inequality Keeps Getting Uglier," accessed on February 27, 2017, at money.cnn.com/2016/12/22/news/economy/us-inequality-worse/.

3. Quoting Alan S. Blinder and Janet L.Yellen, *The Fabulous Decade: Macroeconomic Lessons from the 1990s* (New York: Century Foundation Press, 2001), 70. The Fed raised the federal funds rate six times from June 30, 1999 through May 16, 2000, but Greenspan cut rates eleven times in 2001–2003 to fight recession. The National Bureau of Economic Research determined that the 2001 recession began in March 2001 and ended in November 2001. This official dating tells us nothing about when the employment recovery began. There are four concise paragraphs about the 2001 recession in Dean Baker, "Recessions Are Not as Sneaky as Austin Goolsbee Tells You," *Beat the Press,* March 15, 2019, accessed March 18, 2019, at cepr.net/blogs.

4. In 2008 Thomas got a new job and saved enough money to buy a car. But she was laid off in January 2009. Stories and quotations from Peter S. Goodman, *Past Due: The End of Easy Money and the Renewal of the American Economy* (New York: Times Books/ Henry Holt, 2009), 1–5, 71–74, 175–76, 209–11. Quoted phrase on 176.

5. Peter G. Gosselin, "Fed Chief Now Blamed for Inflating Stock Bubble," *Los Angeles Times,* July 21, 2002, A1, A38; *Fabulous Decade;* Board of Governors of the Federal Reserve System, "Intended Federal Funds Rate, Change and Level," accessed July 25, 2012, at *www.federalreserve.gov/monetarypolicy/ openmarket_archive.htm;* Federal Reserve Bank of San Francisco, "Growth in the Post-Bubble Economy," FRBSF Economic Letter, June 20, 2003, accessed July 21, 2012, at *www.frbsf.org/publications/* economics/letter/2003/

el2003–17.html; Thomas S. Mulligan, "Fed's Dilemmas Expose Limits of Its Influence," *Los Angeles Times,* March 15, 2000, A1, A13; Thomas I. Palley, "Chairman Greenspan Wants Your Job," *American Prospect* 22 (October 23, 2000): 26–28; and Warren Vieth, "Congress Seeks Fed Chief's Guidance," *Los Angeles Times,* September 29, 2001, C1, C3. Federal budget deficits jumped from zero to more than $400 billion a year in 2003–2006. See *Historical Tables, Budget of the United States, Fiscal Year, 2009* (Washington, D.C.: U.S. Government Printing Office, 2008), 22; and Michael Mandel, "How Real Was the Prosperity?" *Business Week,* February 4, 2008, 24–27; experts' blind faith in markets in Goodman, *Past Due,* 16, 114. Also, see Dean Baker and David Rosnik, *Will a Bursting Bubble Trouble Bernanke? The Evidence for a Housing Bubble* (Washington, D.C.: Center for Economic and Policy Research, November 2005).

6. David Leonhardt, "For Many, a Boom that Wasn't," *New York Times,* April 9, 2008, accessed online April 13, 2008. Josh Bivens, *Failure By Design: The Story Behind America's Broken Economy* (Ithaca, N.Y.: Economic Policy Institute/Cornell University Press, 2011), links low wages and the crash. Also, Stricker, *Why America Lost the War on Poverty—And How to Win It* (Chapel Hill: University of North Carolina Press, 2007), 232. Bruce Bartlett, "The Fiscal Legacy of George W. Bush," June 12, 2012, Economix, accessed November 7, 2012, at economix.blogs.nytimes.com; and Jacob S. Hacker and Paul Pierson, *Winner-Take-All Politics: How Washington Made the Rich Richer and Turned Its Back on the Middle Class* (New York: Simon and Schuster, 2010). Wage data from annual Economic Reports of the President.

7. Nicholas Riccardi, "Economy's Growing, but Where Are the New Jobs?" *Los Angeles Times,* February 15, 2005, A1, A20; David Leonhardt, "Do Tax Cuts Lead to Economic Growth?" *New York Times,* September 16, 2012, SR, 4; Isaac Shapiro, Richard Kogan, and Aviva Aron Dine, "How Does This Recovery Measure Up?" Center for Budget and Policy Priorities, Washington, D.C., accessed April 10, 2006. Marla Dickerson, "Temping, but Not by Choice," *Los Angeles Times,* November 1, 2002, C1, C6; Louis Uchitelle, "Incentives Lure Many to Quit, Even with a Tight Job Market," *New York Times,* November 11, 2004, 1, 14; and Peter S. Goodman, "Is the Lean Economy Turning Mean? Why It's Even Harder to Find a Job," *New York Times,* March 2, 2008, Business, 1, 8–9; Edmund Andrews, "A Growing Force of Nonworkers," *New York Times,* July 18, 2004, BU 4; Don Lee, "Is Recovery Without Jobs Now the Norm?" *Los Angeles Times,* March 10, 2004, A1, A24–25; Alana Semuels, "Efficient and Exhausted," *Los Angeles Times,* April 7, 2013, A1, A14, and April 8, 2013, A1, A12; Shan Li, "California Jobless Rate Falls to 9.6%," *Los Angeles Times,* March 30, 2013, B1, B3.

8. Luis Alberto Urrea, "Chicago, Upside Down," *New York Times,* February 5, 2006, 13; Joel Havemann, "Job Growth Boosts Fears of Inflation," *Los Angeles Times,* January 6, 2007, C1–C2; Peter G. Gosselin, "U.S. Payroll Growth Slows Sharply in June," *Los Angeles Times,* July 3, 2004, A1, A24. The Fed raised the federal funds rate from 1 percent to 5.25 percent. CES jobs peaked in December 2000 and did not surpass that peak until February 2005.

9. Baker and Rosnik, *Bursting Bubble.* "Harebrained" is in Nicholas D. Kristof, "A Banker Speaks, With Regret," *New York Times,* November 30, 2011, accessed at nytimes

.com, December 4, 2011. Neil Fligstein and Adam Goldstein, "Catalyst of Disaster: Subprime Mortgage Securitization and the Roots of the Great Recession," IRLE Working Paper #113–12, (September, 2011), 31, for second quoted phrase. There isn't space to delve into the debate about Fannie Mae and Freddy Mac, but the reader can start with David Min, "For the Last Time, Fannie and Freddie Didn't Cause the Housing Crisis," *Atlantic,* December 16, 2011, accessed March 6, 2017 at www.theatlantic.com/businesss/archive/2011/12/for-the-last-time-fannie-and-freddie.

10. For the whole section: Goodman, *Past Due,* esp. 122–23; Housing Finance Network, "The Subprime Mortgage and Financial Crisis," accessed July 29, 2012; and Dean Baker, "The Housing Bubble and the Financial Crisis," *Real-World Economic Review* 46 (May 20, 2008): 73–81, accessed July 29, 2012 at www.paecon.net/PAERveview/issue46/Baker46.pdf; and Fligstein and Goldstein, "Catalyst of Disaster." Also, see Joseph E. Stiglitz, *Free Fall: America, Free Markets, and the Sinking of the World Economy* (New York: W.W. Norton, 2010), 87, 362, n2. Eventually, 200,000 African Americans and Hispanics received $335 million in damages because Countrywide pushed them into subprime mortgages even though they qualified for regular mortgages; Pallavi Gogoi and Nedra Pickler, "Bank of America Countrywide Settlement: Bank to Pay $335 Million to Settle Discriminatory Lending Claims," accessed March 1, 2012, at huffingtonpost.com/ 2011/12/21/bank-of-america-countrywide-settlement_n_11. Also, see Kristoff, "A Banker Speaks." By the mid-2000s, 40 percent of new mortgages were subprime or nearly so, and four million additional households were paying half their incomes for housing.

11. John Quiggin, *Zombie Economics: How Dead Ideas Still Walk Among Us* (Princeton, N.J.: Princeton University Press, 2012), 2.

12. Laurence Ball, Brad Delong, and Larry Summers, "Fiscal Policy and Full Employment" (Washington, D.C.: Center on Budget and Policy Priorities, April 2, 2014). Quotation, from 2003, is in Paul Krugman, *End This Depression Now!* (New York: W.W. Norton, 2012), 91.

13. Quoted in Gosselin, "Fed Chief Now Blamed for Inflating Stock Bubble," A38.

14. Krugman, *End this Depression,* 6 and quotation on 103. A partial explanation for falling labor-force participation rates over the long-term was the aging of the population, but another was the plight of prime-age job-seekers.

15. Realty Trac Staff, "More than 1.2 Million Foreclosure Filings Reported in 2006," accessed July 30, 2012 at realtytrac.com/content/press-releases/more-than-12-million-forclosure-filings. AP, "Fed Underestimated Financial Crisis in '07," *Los Angeles Times,* January 19, 2013. Rex Nutting, "Recession Will Be Nasty and Deep, Economist Says," *Market Watch, Wall Street Journal,* August 23, 2006, accessed July 29, 2012; Baker and Rosnik, *Bursting Bubble.*

16. Fligstein and Golstein, "Catalyst of Disaster," 21, 29–31. Quotation from Peter Gosselin, "Why This Downturn May Be No Run-of-the-Mill Recession," *Los Angeles Times,* January 13, 2008, A1, A22. Brian Blackstone and Greg Ip, "Strong Jobs Data Signal Economy Is Gaining Steam," *Wall Street Journal,* July 7–8, 2007, A1-A2; Maura Reynolds and Walter Hamilton, "Job-Growth Numbers Allay Fears of Recession," *Los*

Angeles Times, October 6, 2007, A1, A7; Joel Havemann, "Jobs Grow Steadily in June," *Los Angeles Times,* July 7, 2007, C1,C6; Louis Uchitelle, "Fed Fears Wage Spiral That Is Little in Evidence," *New York Times,* August 1, 2008, accessed at nytimes.com.

17. Krugman, *End this Depression,* 114–16, on Lehman's collapse.

18. Noam Scheiber, *The Escape Artists: How Obama's Team Fumbled the Recovery* (New York: Simon and Schuster, 2011), 65–66. Arguing for breaking up twelve big banks that controlled 69 percent of the industry is Gretchen Morgenson, "How to Cut the Megabanks Down to Size," *New York Times,* January 20, 2013, Sunday Business, 1, 3. Also Maura Reynolds and Tiffany Hsu, "Approval of Bailout Comes Amid Signs that a Steep Recession is Just Beginning," *Los Angeles Times,* Oct. 4, 2008, A1, A12; Stiglitz, *Free Fall,* esp. 123–24; Peter Schweizer, "Why Goldman Sachs, Other Wall Street Titans, Are Not Being Prosecuted," August 14, 2014, accessed July 5, 2017, at thedaily beast. com/articles/2012/08/14/why-goldman-sachs-other-wall-street; Matt Taibbi, "Secrets and Lies of the Bailout," *Rolling Stone,* January 4, 2013, accessed July 18, 2017, at rollingstone.come/politics/ news/secrets-and-lies-of-the-bailout-20130104; and Charles W. Calomiris and Urooj Khan, "An Assessment of TARP Assistance to Financial Institutions," *Journal of Economic Perspectives* 29 (Spring 2015): 53–80.

19. A later study claimed that the Fed gifted the finance sector with $7.8 trillion. See Binyamin Appelbaum, "The Audacious Pragmatist," *New York Times,* August 25, 2013, 1, 4–5; and Kristof, "A Banker Speaks." In constant dollars, personal consumption spending fell in 2008 and 2009. Any fall is rare, and this was the only two-year decline from 1959 through 2017. Data from U.S. Bureau of Economic Analysis.

20. Leonhardt, "Do Tax Cuts"; Mark Zandi, "The Economic Impact of the American Recovery and Reinvestment Act," January 21, 2009, 9, at Zandi's site on Moody's Analytics.

21. A study showing that Republicans have been more partisan than Democrats is Thomas Mann and Norman Ornstein, *It's Even Worse than It Looks: How the American Constitutional System Collided with the New Politics of Extremism* (New York: Basic Books, 2012).

22. Michael Grunwald, *The New New Deal: The Hidden Story of Change in the Obama Era* (New York: Simon and Schuster, 2012), esp. 66–68; and Wikipedia entry on the American Recovery and Reinvestment Act, 2009. ARRA also included $70 billion to soften the Alternative Minimum Tax. This softener was passed every year anyway and should not have been counted as part of a new stimulus.

23. Quoting Michael Hiltzik, "California Would Pay High Price in Tax Plan," *Los Angeles Times,* December 19, 2012, B1, B5; Kenneth Harney, "New Short-Sale Program Offers Relief," *Los Angeles Times,* November, 11, 2012, B9; and Scheiber, *Escape Artists,* 236–42. COBRA stands for the Consolidated Omnibus Budget Reconciliation Act of 1985, but it is commonly used for that part of the act that gave some employees the right to pay to continue health insurance coverage after separating from their employer.

24. Grunwald, *New New Deal,* 194–97, for examples of Republicans who liked infrastructure spending.

25. Simon Johnson, "The Crisis Last Time," *American Prospect* (Spring 2019): 81–82, emphasizes that three central figures, Ben Bernanke, Tim Geithner, and Hank Paulson, did not want reforms that lifted the working class. Also, presidential advisor economist Larry Summer dropped Romer's higher stimulus request without even telling Romer. Scheiber, *Escape Artists,* describes Obama's naive optimism about working with Republicans, 40–41, 95–136, esp. 109. Also, see Grunwald, *New New Deal,* 138, 181–86, 214–16, 234.

26. Ari Berman, "The Austerity Class," *Nation,* November 7, 2011, 11–17. Paul Krugman argued that for some non-conservatives, a hard line on deficits was a form of intellectual machismo—a willingness to take tough positions (even if other people got most of the pain). People in the Hamilton Project at the Brookings Institution may have helped push the anti-deficit line on White House advisors.

27. Two paragraphs: the Tea Party was partly financed by conservative big money, but it had rank-and-file enthusiasm. It may have been catalyzed by Gene Santelli's television rant (280, Grunwald, *New New Deal*) against Obama's plan to help troubled homeowners. At times it seemed a frenetic attempt to hold on to a world that was slipping away—one that Anglo males dominated. See Paul Krugman and Robin Wells, "Getting Away With It," *New York Review of Books,* July 12, 2012, 6, 8, 9; Mark Lilla, "The Great Disconnect," *New York Times Book Review,* September 30, 2012, 1, 12–13; Barbara Ehrenreich, "What Happened to the White Working Class? The Great Die-Off of America's Blue-Collar Whites," *Tom Dispatch,* December 1, 2015, accessed December 11, 2015, at portside.org; and Michael Finnegan, "Another Reason They'll Stand by Trump," *Los Angeles Times,* December 10, 2015, A1, A14-A15. Also, Nancy MacLean, *Democracy in Chains: The Deep History of the Radical Right's Stealth Plan for America* (New York: Penguin Books, 2018), which follows one stream of right-wing libertarianism from its origins in the 1950s.

28. Krugman, *End This Depression,* on conservatives who claimed that deficits caused a shortage of private investment funds. But there was no shortage of funds, only of the will to invest. Big banks increased from zero to $1.6 trillion the amount they left in safe, nearly zero interest accounts with the Federal Reserve. Stephanie Kelton, "Forget the 'Fiscal Cliff'," *Los Angeles Times,* December 21, 2012, A35. Timothy Noah's review of Theda Skocpol and Vanessa Williams, *The Tea Party and the Remaking of Republican Conservatism* in the *New York Times Book Review,* January 8, 2012, 1, 11–12, mentions a poll of South Dakota Tea Partiers showing opposition to cuts in Social Security, Medicare D, and Medicare payments to doctors and hospitals. Also, see Kate Zernike, "With No Jobs, Plenty of Time for Tea Party," *New York Times,* March 27, 2010, accessed October 27, 2012 at nytimes.com/2010/03/28/us/politics/28teaparty.html.

29. Carmen DeNavas-Walt, Bernadette D. Proctor, and Jessica C. Smith/U.S. Census Bureau, *Income, Poverty, and Health Insurance Coverage in the United States, 2011* (Washington, D.C.: Government Printing Office, 2012). The twenty-seven-million figure is from njfac.org for September 2012.

30. Faye Fiore, "Out of Work, and Aid," *Los Angeles Times,* June 26, 2010, A1, A20-A21.

31. AP, various reporters, "Behind the Poverty Numbers," at hosted.ap.org/dynamic/stories/U/US_FACES_OF_POVERTY?SITE=TEXWIC&SEC, accessed on September 26, 2011; Zernike, "With No Jobs." The national food stamp program is now called SNAP—Supplemental Nutrition Assistance Program. Some conservatives claim that needy people could rely more on private giving. Most charitable giving in the United States is not for the poor but for churches and for art and cultural affairs. If we tried to replace food stamps with a church-run program, every individual church in America—including poor ones—would have to raise $50,000 a year. Mark Pattison, "Churches can't afford to do more for poor, says Nun," April 27, 2012, accessed October 31, 2012, at bread.org/media/coverage/news/churches-can't-afford-to-do.html.

32. Robert Pear, "In a Tough Economy, Old Limits on Welfare," *New York Times,* April 11, 2010, 16; and Jason DeParle, "Welfare Limits Left Poor Adrift as Recession Hit," *New York Times*, April 7, 2012, accessed April 13, 2012, at nytimes.com/2012/04/08/us/welfare-limits-left-poor-adrift-as-recession-hit.htm. Motoko Rich, "Forced to Early Social Security, Unemployed Pay a Steep Price," *New York Times,* June 10, 2012, 1, 24.

33. Stephen A. Wandner, *The Response of the U.S. Public Workforce System to High Unemployment during the Great Recession,* Urban Institute, Working Paper 4 (September, 2012), 8, 13. Paul Davidson, "What Do Jobless Do When the Checks Run Out?" *USA Today,* August 3, 2012, 1–2; "Tea Party: People on Unemployment Benefits Are Lazy/Study: People on Unemployment Find Work Faster," accessed May 29, 2012, at democratic underground.com/discuss/duboard.php?az=printer_friendly& forum; Lawrence Rafferty, "Tea Party Congressman Thinks the Unemployed Are Lazy," May 1, 2011, accessed October 27, at jonathanturley.org/2011/05/01/tea-party-congressman-thinks-the-unemployed. Many people who moved to North Dakota found work, but no housing. The fossil fuel boom in Wyoming pushed unemployment below 5 percent and people with low education had good earnings. But working conditions were so dangerous that some people quit good jobs. Overall, migrants to Wyoming had mixed outcomes: They found good jobs, bad ones, or no jobs; and some became homeless. John M. Glionna, "Oil Boom, College Bust," *Los Angeles Times,* September 24, 2013, A6; and Jack Healy, "In Wyoming, Many Jobs, but No Place to Call Home," *New York Times,* January 13, 2013, 17, 20.

34. *ES* for August 2007, table A-9; *ES* for September 2012, table A-12.

35. Stuart Pfeifer, "Former Insurance Agent, Battling Isolation, Finds She Lacks Key Skills," *Los Angeles Times,* September 26, 2010, B1, B9; Mollee Harper, "My Unemployed Life: the Forgotten Woman," accessed November 27, 2010 at jobs.aol.com/articles/2010/11/17/my-unemployed-life-the-forgotten-woman; Judy Kean, "On Craigslist, the Jobless and Desperate Plead for Work," *USA Today,* October 4, 2011, 1A–2A.

36. For some people, getting laid off was not so bad. Lisa Henshall enjoyed more time with her babies. A young man named Ryan Payne, who lost a Wall Street job paying $140,000, was living with his parents in Malibu and earning money trading stocks online. Henshall, "My Unemployed Life: Choosing Happiness Despite Being Laid Off,"

accessed October 30, 2012, at jobs.aol.com/articles/2011/05/17/my-unemployed-life -choosing-happiness. Also Michael Luo, "For Long-Term Unemployed, a Shaky Safety Net," *New York Times*, July 1, 2010, 13, 18. Catherine Rampell, "A Look Back at Extended Unemployment Benefits," *New York Times,* December 16, 2011, accessed November 2, 2012, at economix.blogs.nytimes.com/2011/12/16/a-look-back-at-extended -unemployment; and Robert Pear, "3 Million Could Lose Jobless Pay in Impasse," *New York Times,* December 20, 2013, accessed at nytimes.com on December 21, 2011; "Tea Party: People on Unemployment Benefits Are Lazy," at NELP, November, 2012; "Federal Unemployment Insurance Puts People Back to Work and Back on Their Feet," NELP, accessed November 29, 2012. An earlier study predicted that had the United States eliminated unemployment insurance in 1976, the duration of unemployment would have fallen from 4.3 months to 2.8 months; see Ronald G. Ehrenberg and Robert S. Smith, *Modern Labor Economics: Theory and Public Policy,* 8th ed. (Boston: Addison Wesley, 2003), 515–16. Quotation from Rich McGahey and Teresa Ghilarducci, "Five Myths about the Unemployed," accessed December 8, 2012, at washingtonpost.com/ opinions/five-myths-about-the-unemployed/2012/12/07.

37. Wandner, *The Response,*11; Editorial, "Another Hole in the Safety Net," *New York Times,* April 2, 2012, accessed at nytimes.com on April 3, 2012; Shaila Dewan, "U.S. Winds down Longer Benefits for the Unemployed," *New York Times,* May 28, 2012, accessed May 29, 2012; Stephanie Mencimer, "The Great Florida Experiment," *Mother Jones,* March–April, 2013, 28–33, on the Tea Party in power.

38. J. D. Foster, "Four Basic Facts about the Pending Payroll Tax Hike," June 7, 2012, Issue Brief #3630, The Heritage Foundation, accessed November 8, 2012; Chuck Marr, Chye-Ching Huang, and Chad Stone, "Payroll Tax Cut and Emergency Unemployment Insurance Still Needed to Support the Recovery," October 16, 2012, Center on Budget and Policy Priorities.

39. The Republican Plan for American Job Creators included reducing red tape, reducing unemployment benefits, and adding small business tax breaks. Don Lee, "U.S. Reports Growth Rate of 0.1%," *Los Angeles Times,* March 1, 2013, B2; Binyamin Applebaum, "Fed Ties Rates to Joblessness, with Target of 6.5 percent," *New York Times,* December 12, 2012, accessed December 13, 2012, at nytimes.com.

40. Alana Semuels and Ricardo Lopez, "Minimum Wage a Focus of Protests," *Los Angeles Times,* December 14, 2012, B1, B5. Josh Bivens and Andrew Fieldhouse, "Who Would Promote Job Growth in the Near Term? Macroeconomic Impacts of the Obama and Romney Budget Proposals," Issue Brief, September 26, 2012, Economic Policy Institute.

41. Two paragraphs: Robert Borosage, "Grand Bargain/Betrayal," Campaign for America's Future, November 15, 2012; Paul Krugman, "Hawks and Hypocrites," *New York Times,* November 11, 2012, accessed November 12, 2012, at nytimes.com; Mark Weisbrot, "Economists May Contribute to the 'Lost Decade' for America," accessed January 10, 2012, at Center for Economic and Policy Research. David Cooper, Mary Gable, and Algernon Austin, "The Public Sector Jobs Crisis: Women and Afri-

can Americans Hit Hardest by Job Losses in State and Local Governments," Economic Policy Institute Briefing Paper #339, Washington, D.C., May 2, 2012; Mike Konczal, "Public Sector Layoffs and the Battle Between Obama and Conservative States," June 12, 2012, accessed March 22, 2013 at nextnewdeal.net/rortybomb/public-sector-layoffs-and-battle.

42. The numbers in table 5.1 are CES jobs, covering nonfarm employees and were accessed April 3, 2019.

43. Ronald Brownstein, "The Battle of the Coalitions," *Los Angeles Times,* November 23, 2012, A 31; John Cassidy, "After the Blowup: Laissez-Faire Economists Do Some Soul-Searching and Finger-Pointing," *New Yorker* 85 (January 11, 2010): 28–33.

44. Walter Hamilton, "A Complex View of the Wealthy," *Los Angeles Times,* September 1, 2012, B1, B3.

45. CES numbers at BLS.gov. Changes measured from January 1989 through January 2001, January 2001 through January 2013, and January 2000 through January 2019.

46. The wage numbers here and in table 5.2 derive from *ERP2013* (Washington, D.C.: Government Printing Office, 2013), table B-47; and BLS monthly reports called *Real Earnings,* table A-2. Also see NELP, "The Low-Wage Recovery: Industry Employment and Wages Four Years into the Recovery" (April 2014), which shows that low-wage industries accounted for 22 percent of job losses in the recession, but 44 percent of new jobs in the recovery period.

47. For three paragraphs: Andrew Hacker, "We're More Unequal Than You Think," *New York Review of Books,* February 23, 2012, 34–36; David Cay Johnston, "First Look at US Pay Data, It's Awful," Reuters, October 19, 2011, accessed online. Also Erin Hatton, "The Rise of the Permanent Temp Economy," January 28, 2013, accessed at http://portside.org, November 29, 2013; Kevin G. Hall, "Manufacturing Goes 'Lean' in Recovery Effort," *Los Angeles Times,* January 2, 2014, B5; Dan Dimaggio, "The Jobs Crisis and the Art of Flexible Labor," *Dollars and Sense,* January–February, 2011, 8; Louis Uchitelle, "Factory Jobs Gain, but Wages Retreat," *New York Times,* December 29, 2011, at nytimes.com, accessed April 13, 2012; Charles Fishman, "The Insourcing Boom," *Atlantic,* December, 2012, 45–52; Associated Press, "AP Impact: Middle-Class Jobs Cut in Recession Feared Gone for Good, Lost to Technology," January 25, 2013, accessed February 1, 2013, at washingtonpost.com/business/technology/ap-impact -middle-class-jobs-cut. In-sourcing did not reverse bad pay trends. New workers at G.E, which was bringing back jobs, topped out at $19 an hour. An older generation of G.E. workers was getting $32. Motoko Rich, "Tough Budget Calculus as Technical Schools Face Deep Cuts," *New York Times,* July 10, 2011, 1, 16. The National Association of Manufacturers alleged that its members had 600,000 job openings; but pay levels were not rising to attract workers. Adam Davidson, "Skills Don't Pay the Bills," *New York Times Sunday Magazine,* November 25, 2012, 16, 18. But see Thomas L. Friedman on welders, "If You've Got the Skills, She's Got the Job," *New York Times,* November 18, 2012, Sunday Review, 1, 11.

48. Fast-food workers fought back; Steven Greenhouse, "In the Drive to Unionize, Fast Food Workers Walk Off the Job," November 28, 2012, accessed at nytimes

.com November 30, 2012. Pay rates at www.payscale.com/research/US/Employer=
Macy%27%2c_Inc./Hourly_Rate. Sources for wages and labor force numbers include
ES for December 2012, and for retail sales and food and beverage workers, BLS, *Occupational Outlook Handbook* (2017), accessed January 14, 2019. See also Kari Lydersen,
"Workers on Chicago's Magnificent Mile Start a 'Fight for 15' (Dollars Per Hour)," *In
These Times,* December 5, 2012, accessed through portside.org, December 13, 2012.

49. Caitlin Kelly, *Malled: My Unintentional Career in Retail* (New York: Portfolio Penguin,
2011), on North Face and other retailers, e.g., 134, 158–60. Apple's new C.E.O. took
hundreds of millions of dollars' worth of stock, but Apple's retail workers, many of
whom had college degrees, averaged only $25,000 a year. There were extras for workers; when one store gave a party, every employee got not one but two tacos. Some
employees had hoped for an i-Pad. See David Segal, "Apple's Retail Army, Long on
Loyalty but Short on Pay," *New York Times,* June 24, 2012, 1, 18–19; and Chris Obrien,
"Apple CEO's Pay Tops $4.1 Million for 2012," *Los Angeles Times,* December 28, 2012,
B2. Costco wages from Steven Greenhouse on *The Ed Show,* MSNBC, November 29,
2012. While underpaying staff, Apple stashed $100 billion overseas to avoid taxes and
borrowed at low American interest rates to buy back stock and raise dividends. Chris
O'Brien and Jim Puzzanghera, "Apple Execs Grilled Over Tax Strategy," *Los Angeles
Times,* May 22, 2013, B1, B6. Steven Greenhouse, "A Part-time Life, as Hours Shrink
and Shift," *New York Times,* October 28, 2012, 1, 20. Greenhouse, "No Rest for Retail
Workers: Scheduling Chaos as Retail Competition Grows Fierce," *Los Angeles Times,*
November 24, 2017, A11. An exception to arbitrary scheduling was Macy's flagship
store in Manhattan, where unionized senior workers received their schedules six
months in advance. See also, Natalie Kitroeff, "Rock 'Em and Stock 'Em: The Number
of Warehouses in the State is Rising, Spurred by Online Shopping, but More of the
Work is Going to Robots," *Los Angeles Times,* December 4, 2016, C1, C8.

50. Cashier pay from Occupational Employment Statistics at BLS.gov/oes/current/
oes412011, accessed June 24, 2019. On part-timers in union shops, Matt Hart, a staff
worker for the United Food and Commercial Workers in Orange County, California,
email to the author, January 11, 2013. On minimum wage jobs for union grocery workers, informal conversations of employees with the author. Also, Steven Greenhouse,
"Study of Retail Workers Finds $9.50 Median Pay," *New York Times,* January 16, 2012,
accessed at nytimes.com, January 16, 2012. The BLS defines part-time as less than
thirty-five hours a week. About 18 percent of the workforce has been part-time in
recent years and a third of those are primary wage-earners. Since early 2006, average
weekly hours in retail trade have never been as high as 32 or below 30. In September
2019, the average was 30.7.

51. Mac McClelland, "Shelf Lives: My Brief, Backbreaking, Rage-Inducing, Low-
Paying, Dildo-packing Time Inside the Online-shipping Machine," *Mother Jones,*
March–April, 2012, 46–55; Marc Lifsher, "Wal-Mart is Blamed for Driving Down
Wages," *Los Angeles Times,* June 4, 2012, B2; Jennifer Medina, "As California Warehouses
Grow, Labor Issues Are a Concern," *New York Times,* July 22, 2012, online at nytimes
.com, accessed November 23, 2012; see the statement by Sylvia, in "Doing More with

Less," *Mother Jones,* July–August, 2011, 24; Michael Smith and Lauren Etter, "'Ghost' Staff on Duty, Off Books," *Los Angeles Times,* December 25, 2018, C2; David Cooper and Teresa Kroeger, "Employers Steal Billions from Workers' Paychecks Each Year" (Washington, D.C.: Economic Policy Institute, May 2017). As to job security, years at one's current job for mature (55–64) male workers fell from fifteen to ten between the early 1980s and the 2000s; for women, tenure rose from 4.5 in 1951 to ten years in the 1980s and stayed there. See Craig Copeland, "Employee Tenure Trends, 1983–2012," *Employment Benefit Research Institute* 33 (12) (December 2012), 12–23.

52. BLS.gov/ooh/print/most-new-jobs, accessed April 2, 2014.

53. For two paragraphs, Rebecca Theiss, "The Future of Work: Trends and Challenges for Low-Wage Workers," Briefing Paper #341, Washington, D.C.: Economic Policy Institute, April 27, 2012, table 3. David Streitfeld, "Uncertain Payoff in an Apps Boom," *New York Times,* November 18, 2012, 1, 19; Donald L. Bartlett and James B. Steele, "Programming Jobs Fall, Despite Labor Department's Outlook," accessed December 5, 2012 at americawhatwentwrong.org/story/ programming-jobs-fall; Harry Bradford, "Jobs with the Biggest Talent Shortages: Manpower Group," at huffingtonpost.com/ 2012/05/30/jobs-talent-shortage, accessed November 28, 2012; "Professor Norm Matloff's H-1B Web Page," at heather.cs.ucdavis.edu/h1b.html, accessed November 28, 2012. In the Manpower survey, half the employers said they could not fill openings because of talent shortages, but 56 percent admitted that unfilled jobs had little impact on customers or investors. At Manpower, surveyors claimed that there was a shortage of schoolteachers at a time when teachers were being laid off in many states—thirty-two thousand in California alone. Also, see Patrick May, "'Crowd Labor' Matches Jobs with Online Temps," *Los Angeles Times,* June 9, 2012, B3; Moshe Z. Marvit, "The Wages of Crowdwork," *Nation,* February 24, 2014, 18–22, 24–25.

54. See, for example, Peter S. Goodman, "Trump Has Promised to Bring Jobs Back. His Tariffs Threaten to Send Them Away," *New York Times,* January 6, 2019, accessed January 7, 2019, at nytimes.com.

55. Sources for this section include Anne Case and Angus Deaton, "Mortality and Morbidity in the 21st Century," *Brookings Papers on Economic Activity Conference Drafts,* March 23–24, 2017; and Alex Hollingsworth, Christopher J. Ruhm, and Kosali Simon, "Macroeconomic Conditions and Opioid Abuse," NBER Working Paper No. 23192 (February 2017).

Chapter 6. The U.S. Unemployment Rate

1. Helen Ginsberg, Tom Larson, Edward Kantowicz, Steve Ross, and Deborah Schopp are among those who gave this chapter a critical read. An example of moderate conservative economics is the work of N. Gregory Mankiw, *Macroeconomics,* 9th ed. (New York: Worth Publishers, 2016), especially chapters 7 and 10.

2. Sources for two paragraphs: John A. Garraty, *Unemployment in History: Economic Thought and Policy* (New York: Harper, 1979), 108–09; Margo J. Anderson, *The American Census: A Social History* (New Haven, Conn.: Yale University Press, 1988), 165; Udo Sautter, *Three Cheers for the Unemployed: Government and Unemployment Before the New Deal*

(Cambridge, U.K.: Cambridge University Press, 1991), 42–51, 149–54. Quotation from Herman P. Miller, "Measuring Subemployment in Poverty Areas of Large U.S. Cities," *Monthly Labor Review* (hereafter *MLR*) 96 (October 1973), 10–18. An early government survey of unemployment, mainly of blue-collars workers, was U.S. Department of Labor, Bureau of Labor Statistics, *Unemployment in the United States* 195 (Washington, D.C.: Government Printing Office, 1916). On the "gainful worker" concept, which limited efforts to get a national unemployment rate, see table 1 in David Card, "Origins of the Unemployment Rate: The Lasting Legacy of Measurement without Theory," February 2011, paper prepared for 2011 meetings of the American Economic Association.

3. Anderson, *American Census,* 162–64; Joseph Goldberg and William T. Moye, *The First Hundred Years of the Bureau of Labor Statistics* (Washington, D.C.: Government Printing Office, 1985), 127; Sautter, *Three Cheers,* 42–51, 149–54, 244. More upbeat about the 1921 conference was William A. Berridge, in National Bureau of Economic Research, *The Measurement and Behavior of Unemployment* (Princeton, N.J.: Princeton University Press, 1957), 585–86. Paul H. Douglas, *Real Wages in the United States, 1890–1926* (Boston and New York: Houghton Mifflin, 1930). Also, the estimates by Meredith B. Givens, in Leo Wolman, "Labor," in *Recent Economic Changes in the United States,* Report of the Committee on Recent Economic Changes of the President's Conference on Unemployment, Herbert Hoover, Chairman (New York: National Bureau of Economic Research and McGraw-Hill, 1929), 466–78.

4. For two paragraphs, Goldberg and Moye, *First Hundred Years,* 128–30. In the 1920s, the National Industrial Conference Board and the American Federation of Labor also made unemployment estimates. So did Robert S. Lynd and Helen Merrell Lynd, in *Middletown: A Study in Modern American Culture* (New York: Harcourt, Brace & World, 1956 pbk. of 1929 original). The quotation from Berridge is in Don D. Lescohier, *Working Conditions* (New York: Macmillan 1935), vol. III of John R. Commons, ed. *History of Labor in the United States, 1896–1932,* 138. Lescohier's section on unemployment, 114–15, is very useful. The second quotation is in Kirstin Downey, *The Woman Behind the New Deal: The Life of Frances Perkins, FDR's Secretary of Labor and His Moral Conscience* (New York: Nan Talese/Doubleday, 2009), 110–13; the third quotation is in Anderson, *American Census,* 165. See also Sautter, *Three Cheers,* 150–51. On Walsh, Wagner, Metropolitan Life Insurance, and Persons, see Sautter, *Three Cheers,* 245–51; and Irving Bernstein, *The Lean Years: A History of the American Worker, 1920–1933* (Baltimore: Penguin Books, 1966), 267–69. Wagner also criticized jobless information from the United States Employment Service, calling it "poppycock" and "the most concentrated piffle" ever published at government expense (Sautter, *Three Cheers,* 246). Card, "Origins of the Unemployment Rate," 4, notes that after the 1930 fiasco, Congress authorized a twenty-one-city recount, which came up with an 8.2 percent unemployment rate.

5. For two paragraphs: the first quotation is from Thomas A. Stapleford, *The Cost of Living in America: A Political History of Economic Statistics, 1880–2000* (New York: Cambridge University Press, 2009), 148, but all of 145–159 is useful. The second quotation is from Anderson, *American Census,* 175, whose discussion at 172–77 is important. Also,

see Sautter, *Three Cheers,* 342, and Russell A. Nixon, "The Historical Development of the Conception and Implementation of Full Employment as Economic Policy," in Alan Gartner, Russell A. Nixon, and Frank Riessman, *Public Service Employment: An Analysis of Its History, Problems and Prospects* (New York: Praeger Publishers, 1973), 16–17; and Downey, *Woman Behind the New Deal,* 138–48, about corruption and other problems in the Department of Labor that faced Secretary Perkins.

6. Two paragraphs based on Gertrude Bancroft, "Current Unemployment Statistics of the Census Bureau and Some Alternatives," 63–122, esp. 65 and 102, in *Measurement and Behavior of Unemployment;* and John D. Durand, "Development of the Labor Force Concept, 1930–1940," 80–90, in Louis J. Ducoff and Margaret Jarman Hagood, *Labor Force Definition and Measurement: Recent Experience in the United States* (New York: Social Science Research Council, 1947), 80–90; Card, "Origins of the Unemployment Rate," 6; John D. Biggers, "National Unemployment Census, 1937," *MLR* 46 (February 1938): 355–62; John E. Bregger and Cathryn S. Dippo, "Overhauling the Current Population Survey: Why Is It Necessary to Change?" *MLR* 116 (September 1993), 3–9; Bregger, "The Current Population Survey: a Historical Perspective and the BLS's Role," *MLR* 107 (June 1984): 8–14; Anderson, *American Census,* 159–90; Broadus Mitchell, *Depression Decade: From the New Era through New Deal, 1929–1941* (New York: Harper and Row, 1969 Torchbook of 1947 original), 91–96; and Ewan Clague, *Bureau of Labor Statistics* (New York: Frederick A. Praeger, 1968), 48–50.

7. Bregger, "Current Population Study," 8–9. Anderson, *American Census,* 186–90. Also, see a publication by the Bureau of Labor Statistics and the Census Bureau, *Design and Methodology: Current Population Survey,* Technical Paper 66 (October 2006). One slam-bang attack on the credibility of the numbers came from James Daniel, discussed later. In 2012 there was a splash when the unemployment rate fell by 0.3 percentage points just before the presidential election. Critics of President Obama charged that his administration faked the figures, but experts, including Keith Hall, who had been President Bush's BLS Commissioner, did not think so. See Nelson D. Schwartz, "Political Questions about the Job Report," *New York Times* Economix Blog, November 20, 2013, accessed at economix.blogs.nytimes.com on November 20, 2013. Several conferences and commissions evaluated government methods and published their results in books like these: *Measurement and Behavior of Unemployment* (1957), *Measuring Employment and Unemployment* (1962), and *Counting the Labor Force* (1979). A minor change not discussed in the text was the inclusion of resident military personnel in the labor force in the 1980s. That lowered the national unemployment rate 1/10 of a percent, but it created confusion and the change was reversed.

8. Another issue is the sometimes-startling difference between the results from the household sample, derived from the Current Population Survey (CPS), which is used for the unemployment count, and the survey of establishments for job totals, which generates Current Employment Statistics (CES). Often the two numbers move in the same direction at about the same pace, but occasionally the two are so different that they seem to be measuring two different economies.

9. "How the Government Measures Unemployment," available at BLS.gov. The version I used was last modified October 16, 2009. Do other countries measure unemployment the same way? The U.K.'s methods, for example, seem generally similar to the U.S. approach, and the U.K. method follows definitions employed by the International Labor Organization. The ILO defines the unemployed as those without a job who have actively sought one in the last four weeks and are available for work in the next two weeks. Other nations may utilize different methods, but the Organization of Economic Cooperation and Development publishes harmonized unemployment rates based on the ILO method for forty-two countries. For the fourth quarter of 2018, the United States had the seventh-lowest unemployment rate, at 3.8 percent. The six countries with lower rates were the Czech Republic, Japan, Iceland, Mexico, Germany, and the Netherlands. Those with the highest rates were Italy, Turkey, Spain, Greece, and South Africa. Interestingly, the ILO acknowledges that there are discouraged workers and others who want a job, but aren't currently searching for one, and aren't counted as unemployed. See ILO, "Unemployment Rate," at https://www.ilo.org/ilostat-files/Documents/description_UR_EN.pdf.

10. Those on strike or lockout, ill, on vacation, or on maternity/paternity leave are counted as employed.

11. Data and perspectives from BLS, *Employment Situation—April 2019,* njfac.org; and at BLS.gov., Series LNU05026645. The BLS definition of discouraged workers, which is almost always under a million, is almost useless. You must have searched in the last year, if not in the current month, if you are to be included in the discouraged category. If you are really discouraged about finding a position—because you fear discrimination, or you cannot live on $7.25, or there are few jobs in your region and you can't sell your house and move elsewhere, and therefore don't look for work for a year or more, you are not only not considered unemployed; you are not even considered a discouraged worker. That explains why, even in the pit of the Great Recession, with the most discouraging labor market since the 1930s, the Bureau counted just 1.2 million discouraged workers. Helpful here is Christopher G. Gellner, "Enlarging the Concept of a Labor Reserve," *MLR* 98 (April 1975): 20–28.

12. For background on the late '50s economy, see Stricker, *Why America Lost the War on Poverty—And How to Win It* (Chapel Hill: University of North Carolina Press, 2007), 23–28.

13. James Daniel, "Let's Look at Those 'Alarming' Unemployment Figures," *Reader's Digest* (September 1961), 67–71. Daniel ignored cases where Census Bureau adjustments lowered the unemployment rate. He seems to have read Bancroft, "Current Unemployment Statistics" (compare his 69 and Bancroft's 67–68), but he missed the spirit in which government experts were working. I get no sense from reading the government documents or secondary sources that government statisticians were plotting to inflate unemployment numbers. Some things they did raised the unemployment rate a bit and some lowered it. Judith Eleanor Innes, *Knowledge and Public Policy: The Search for Meaningful Indicators,* 2nd expanded ed. (New Brunswick, N.J.:

Transaction Publishers, 1990), 133–35. Also, Clague, *Bureau of Labor Statistics,* 52–58; and one response to criticisms, President's Committee to Appraise Employment and Unemployment Statistics, *Measuring Employment and Unemployment* (Washington, D.C.: Government Printing Office, 1962), 9–10, 33–35.

14. About the same time as the experimental subemployment survey expanded the count of the unemployed, including discouraged workers, the BLS eliminated from the unemployment count the only group of discouraged workers that had been included as unemployed: those who were not currently searching for a job because it was clear there was no work in their community or line of work. See also, Editors, "Capitalism and Unemployment," *Monthly Review* 27 (June 1975): 1–14; Gross and Moss, "Real Unemployment Is Much Higher than They Say," in Alan Gartner et al., eds., *Public Service Employment: An Analysis of Its History, Problems and Prospects* (New York: Praeger, 1973), 30–36; and Frank Furstenberg and Charles Thrall, "Counting the Jobless: the Impact of Job Rationing on the Measurement of Unemployment," *Annals of the American Academy of Political and Social Science* 418 (March 1975): 45–59.

15. Four paragraphs based on Richard J. Mcdonald, "The 'Underground Economy' and BLS Statistical Data," *MLR* (January 1984): 4–18; Ashlie M. Koehn, "Navigating the Shadow Economy: Only the Shadow Knows," *MLR* (April 2017): 1–4; Niall McCarthy, "The Countries with the Largest Shadow Economies (Infographic)," at www.forbes .com/sites/niallmccarthy/2017/02/09, accessed January 18, 2019.

16. Julius Shiskin, "Employment and Unemployment: The Doughnut or the Hole?" *MLR* 99 (February 1976): 3–10 and the quotation on 4–5. The table of alternative measures was first published in *Employment Situation—January 1977*. It is now table A-15 in the Household Data section.

17. BLS, *The Employment Situation—January 1994,* accessed at BLS.gov, March 5, 2015. Glen Cain said the Levitan commission, of which he was a member, had almost voted to include discouraged workers in the official unemployment count. But conservatives "felt anyone who really wanted a job should be there hustling," and they won. See David Streitfeld, "Jobless Count Skips Millions," *Los Angeles Times,* December 29, 2003, A1, A16–A17, esp. A17; Bregger and Dippo, "Overhauling the Current Population Survey"; Bregger and Steven E. Haugen, "BLS Introduces New Range of Alternative Unemployment Measures," *MLR* 118 (October 1995): 19–26, esp. 23–26. The tighter discouraged category required that people who were not currently looking for work had searched in the past year, be available for work, and have quit looking because of job-related causes. U-6 first appeared in BLS, *Employment Situation—February 1996*. In the 1980s and 1990s, the statistics were tweaked in opposite directions. The report of January 1994 reflected changes that raised the unemployment rate by several tenths of a percentage point. For example, surveyors could no longer assume that a woman at home was a housewife; she may have wanted an outside job. On the other hand, BLS officials revised definitions so that the number of part-timers who wanted full-time work and the number of "discouraged workers" were reduced.

18. There are illuminating BLS tables on labor force flows, especially LNU07100000 and LNU07200000, which show remarkable churning among labor force categories.

For example, from August to September 2016, 4.7 million people went from "Not in the Labor Force" and not counted as searching for a job or unemployed—to being Employed. See also Kim B. Clark and Lawrence H. Summers, "Labor Force Transitions and Unemployment," Working Paper No. 277 (Cambridge, Mass.: National Bureau of Economic Research, April 1978); and Monica D. Castillo, "Persons Outside the Labor Force Who Want a Job," *MLR* (July 1998): 34–42. On people's reasons for not looking for work when they said they wanted a job, data was sent to me for September 2006 and October 2007 by Terrence M. McMenamin, Division of Labor Statistics at the BLS.

19. This is for nonsupervisory and production workers in the nonfarm, private sector. See BLS, *Real Earnings—January 2018*.

20. Natalie Kitroeff, "U.S. Job Market's Strength is Allowing More to Share in Pay Gains," January 5, 2018, at nytimes.com.

21. The BLS series on prime-age male dropouts is LNS11300061. Nicholas Eberstadt, *Men Without Work: America's Invisible Crisis* (West Conshohocken, Pa.: Templeton Press, 2016), has useful facts and a conservative view. Loaded with survey data is Alan B. Krueger, "Where Have all the Workers Gone? An Inquiry into the Decline of the U.S. Labor Force Participation Rate," *Brookings Papers on Economic Activity*, BPEA Conference Drafts, September 7–8, 2017.

22. John Coglianese, "The Rise of In-and-Outs: Declining Labor Force Participation of Prime-Age Men," November 15, 2017, on Coglianese's Harvard website.

23. Phrase quotes Frank Lysy, "The Structural Factors Behind the Steady Fall in Labor Force Participation Rates of Prime Age Workers," posted October 14, 2016, https://aneconomicsense.org/2016/10/14/the- structural-factors. Also, Eberstadt, *Men Without Work*, 110–28; Jim Puzzanghera, "Job Market Mystery: Where Are the Men?" *Los Angeles Times*, November 21, 2016, A8; Binyamin Appelbaum, "Out of Trouble, but Criminal Records Keep Men Out of Work," *New York Times*, February 28, 2015, accessed December 4, 2016, at nytimes.com.; Don Lee and Samantha Masunaga, "Nothing in the Works," *Los Angeles Times*, September 7, 2015, A8; June Zaccone, "The Labor Force Participation Rate and Its Trajectory—Why It Matters," National Jobs for All Coalition, Special Report 5, June 2015; David Leonhardt, "Unemployed and Skewing the Picture," *Los Angeles Times*, March 5, 2008, updated March 7, and accessed online September 29, 2008; David Streitfeld, "Disparate Job Data Add Up To a Mystery," *Los Angeles Times*, August 23, 2004, C1, C5; "Workers or Shirkers," *Economist*, January 29, 2005, 28.

High rates of incarceration interact in several ways with job markets. Lousy job markets for minority males make criminal activity more appealing. Many of the 2.3 million people in American prisons would never have been in prison if there really were full employment and racial equality. On the other side, incarceration makes millions of people less employable when they get out.

24. As mentioned earlier, Furstenberg and Thrall argued that American culture inclines people who think they don't deserve a job not to look for one. Also relevant is that one BLS experiment showed that some people are ashamed of admitting that household members are jobless and report unemployed family members as working

(Bregger and Dippo, "Overhauling the Current Population Survey," 8). See too, Ofer Sharone, "Why Do Unemployed Americans Blame Themselves while Israelis Blame the System?" Reconnecting to Work Conference Presentation, UCLA, April 2, 2011.

Chapter 7. Why So Much Unemployment?

1. Danielle Kurtzleben, "Even Economists Can't Decide the Cause of High Unemployment," May 15, 2012, accessed October 5, 2013, at usnews.com.

2. As wage growth has not matched what is supposed to be a full-employment economy, some mainstream economists and writers are finally deciding that the reason might be that we aren't really in a full-employment economy and that the official unemployment rate does not count all the truly unemployed. See Ben Casselman, "Why Wages Are Finally Rising, 10 Years After the Recession," *New York Times,* May 2, 2019, accessed at nytimes.com on May 3, 2019; and James Pethokoukis, "5 Questions for Adam Ozimek on Unemployment, Wage Growth, and Productivity," October 22, 2018, accessed at aei.org on May 3, 2019. Meanwhile, there are oddities—sometimes unsettling ones—in the monthly employment report. In the report for April 2019, the unemployment rate fell to 3.6 percent. That should mean more jobs. But it did not mean more jobs in the household survey from which we derive unemployment rates. The number of people with jobs fell by 103,000, but because the labor force supposedly declined by a whopping 490,000, the unemployment rate fell. Meanwhile, in the payroll survey, the economy added 263,000 jobs. It seems to be the consensus that we are to rely on the payroll report with its larger sample for job totals. But we must have faith in the household report for unemployment rates—even if we are not supposed to trust the job totals in the household report from which the unemployment rate is calculated.

3. For two paragraphs: Sharon Parrott and LaDonna Pavetti, "Commentary: Cato Gets It Very Wrong: The Safety Net Supports Rather Than Discourages Work," August 21, 2013, Center on Budget and Policy Priorities, accessed August 22, 2013. Anonymous, "Help Wanted Ads Don't Add Up," *Dollars and Sense,* January 1984, 12–13, 17; and Robin Abcarian, "Jobless Dispute Complacency Claim," *Los Angeles Times,* September 12, 2010, A10. A variation on the lazy argument is that black culture and family life are deranged.

4. Quotation in Clare Gordon, "Why Is It So Hard to Get an $8 an Hour Job at Wal-Mart?" September 7, 2012, accessed at jobs.aol.com on May 20, 2013. Also, Marina Villeneuve, "Wal-Mart May Flee D.C. Over Minimum Wage," *Los Angeles Times,* July 20, 2013, B1, B4, on Wal-Mart's resistance to paying $12.50 an hour and some workers' willingness to take less. "Job Openings and Labor Turnover Survey, Highlights, July 2013," September 10, 2013, at BLS.gov, accessed October 1, 2013. Stan Hinden, "Ad for Janitor's Position Draws 350 Applicants," *Washington Post,* August 13, 1991, C1. The Wal-Mart story is in Paul Krugman, "The Summer of Our Discontent," August 26, 2005, accessed at nytimes.com on August 26, 2005; ice cream jobs in Yves Smith, "Why Don't the Unemployed Get Off their Couches," accessed June 4, 2014, at nakedcapitalism.com/ 2014/06/don't-unemployed-get.

5. Somini Sengupta, "Tech Firms Push to Hire More Workers from Abroad," *New York Times,* April 11, 2013, accessed at nytimes.com on April 12, 2013. The fakery about labor shortages is not limited to high-skill occupations. In the summer of 2017, managers at President Trump's Mar-a-Lago tried to hire thirty-five foreign workers without having made a sincere effort to find American applicants. See David A. Farenthold and Lori Rozsa, "'Apply by Fax': Before It Can Hire Foreign Workers, Trump's Mar-a-Lago Club Advertizes at Home—Briefly," *Washington Post,* August 7, 2017, accessed at washingtonpost.com/politics/apply-by-fax on August 8, 2017.

6. Arguing that there is no shortage of educated labor in science, tech, and math fields is Daniel Costa, "STEM Labor Shortages? Microsoft Report Distorts Reality about Computing Occupations," Economic Policy Institute Policy Memorandum #195 (Washington, D.C.: November 19, 2012); and Michael S. Teitelbaum, "Are We Losing the Tech Race?" *New York Times,* April 20, 2014, A19. Unemployment rates by educational level at BLS.gov, series LNS14027660 and LNS 14027662. See also Teresa Kroeger, et al., "The Class of 2016: The Labor Market is Still Far from Ideal for Young Graduates," at epi.org.

7. Peter Cappelli, *Why Good People Can't Get Jobs: The Skills Gap and What Companies Can Do About It* (Philadelphia: Wharton Digital Press, 2012), 26, 45–57; Andrew Hacker, "Where Will We Find the Jobs?" *New York Review of Books,* February 24, 2011, at nybooks .com/articles/archives/2011/feb/24/ where-will- we-find-jobs; John Miller and Jean-nette Wicks-Lim, "Unemployment: A Jobs Deficit or a Skills Deficit?" *Dollars and Sense,* January–February 2011, 9–13. College share of the population in John Schmitt and Janelle Jones, "Where Have All the Good Jobs Gone?" (Washington, D.C.: Center for Economic and Policy Research, July, 2012). Also, Steven Greenhouse, "If You're a Waiter, the Future is Rosy," *New York Times,* March 7, 2004, Wk, 5.

8. In World War II, millions of people, including housewives, trained to become skilled blue-collar workers. Rosie was not born a riveter. View the government film, *Glamour Girls of 1943.* See also Patricia Cohen, "As Demand for Welders Resurges, Community Colleges Offer Classes," *New York Times,* March 10, 2015, accessed at nytimes .com, March 10, 2015.

9. Large employers were shameless about not hiring the long-term unemployed during the Great Recession. Cappelli, *Why Good People,* 37–38, 61–64; Brad Plumer, "Companies Won't Even Look at Resumes of the Long-Term Unemployed," *Washington Post,* April 15, 2013, accessed at washingtonpost.com on May 8, 2013; and Paul Krugman, "The Jobless Trap," *New York Times,* April 21, 2013, accessed at nytimes.com, April 23, 2013.

10. Some employers aren't serious about filling vacancies. They post a position that they may want to fill at some time, but they don't fill it because they haven't found the right applicant at a low enough price, or they fear that a recession or a government shutdown is coming, or that Obamacare costs too much, or whatever. They conduct interviews but never hire. One young man received eighth- and ninth-round call-backs from three different companies, but two of the companies decided not to hire at all. See Thomas L. Friedman, "If You've Got the Skills, She's Got the Job,"

New York Times, Sunday Review, November 18, 2012, 1, 11. Mike McGrorty, "Building Trades: Entry and Success" (unpublished paper provided by the author), says there are usually good jobs for welders but some people cannot get through the training program, which requires math and night school. However, the total number of welding jobs is not large in most locales. On the end of the nursing shortage, CNN Money, "For Nursing Jobs, New Grads Need Not Apply," posted January 15, 2013, accessed May 5, 2013. Also, Alana Semuels and Alejandro Lazo, "Builders Say Good Help Is Hard to Find," *Los Angeles Times,* May 8, 2013, A1, A13. Tiffany Hsu, "Factory Labor Shortage May Rise," *Los Angeles Times,* October 16, 2012, B2; Harold L. Sirkin, "The Coming Shortage of Skilled Manufacturing Workers," January 14, 2013, accessed at businessweek.com on April 24, 2013. Also, see Robert J. Samuelson, "Employers Lack Confidence, Not Skilled Labor," May 5, 2013, accessed at Washingtonpost. com on May 6, 2013; Catherine Rampell, "With Positions to Fill, Employers Wait for Perfection," *New York Times,* March 6, 2013, accessed at nytimes.com, March 7, 2013. Views contrary to mine are Ricardo Lopez, "Jobs for Skilled Workers Are Going Unfilled," *Los Angeles Times,* June 8, 2012, B1, B4; and Claire Cain Miller, "The Numbers of Our Lives," *New York Times Education Life,* April 14, 2013, 18–19, on a shortage of data-scientists.

11. Cappelli, *Why Good People,* 37. Adam Davidson, "Skills Don't Pay the Bills," *New York Times Magazine,* November 25, 2012, 16, 18; Sirkin, "The Coming Shortage;" Natalie Kitroeff, "How This Garlic Farm Went from a Labor Shortage to over 150 People on its Applicant Waitlist," *Los Angeles Times,* February 9, 2017, accessed March 24, 2017 at latimes.com.business.

12. For three paragraphs: table E-16, "Unemployment Rates by Sex, Race, and Hispanic or Latino Ethnicity" (not seasonally adjusted) at BLS.gov. On hiring discrimination, Saru Jayaraman, *Behind the Kitchen Door* (Ithaca, N.Y.: Cornell University Press, 2013), 28–32, 103–29; Joleen Kirschenman and Kathryn M. Neckerman, "'We'd Love to Hire Them, But . . .': The Meaning of Race for Employers," 203–32, in Christopher Jencks and Paul E. Peterson, eds., *The Urban Underclass* (Washington, D.C.: The Brookings Institution, 1991); Binyamin Applebaum, "Out of Trouble, but Criminal Records Keep Men Out of Work," *New York Times,* February 28, 2015, accessed at nytimes.com on December 4, 2016; Will Evans, "Growing Temp Industry Shuts out Black Workers; Exploits Latinos," *Chicago Reporter,* June 8, 2016, accessed at portside.org/2016-6 -13/growing-temp-industry-shuts-out; Alden Loury, "In the Chicago Region. When White People Leave, Jobs Tend to Follow," April 30, 2017, at portside.org, accessed May 1, 2017. On job networks, see Nancy Ditomaso, "How Social Networks Drive Black Unemployment," opinionator.blogs. nytimes.com/ 2013/05/05, accessed May 6, 2013; Deirdre A. Royster, *Race and the Invisible Hand: How White Networks Exclude Black Men from Blue-Collar Jobs* (Berkeley: University of California Press, 2003).

13. For two paragraphs: despite racist attitudes among members, unions have often helped to ease race and gender inequalities. See Meredith Kleykamp and Jake Rosendfeld, "Lost Unions, Lost Ground: The Decline of Organized Labor Has Helped

to Worsen the Racial Wage Gap," *Los Angeles Times,* accessed September 9, 2013, A13. On another issue, Boston job markets improved so much that the black family poverty rate fell from 29.1 percent to 13.4 percent. See Paul Osterman, "Gains from Growth? The Impact of Full Employment on Poverty in Boston," 122–34 in *The Urban Underclass.* For national black unemployment rates, Series LNS 14000006 at BLS.gov.

14. Carmen DeNavas-Walt, Bernadette D. Proctor, and Jessica C. Smith/U.S. Census Bureau, *Income, Poverty, and Health Insurance Coverage in the United States: 2011* (Washington, D.C.: Government Printing Office, 2012), 51, 53.

15. Jared Bernstein and Dean Baker, *The Benefits of Full Employment: When Markets Work for People* (Washington, D.C.: Economic Policy Institute, 2003), 42–50, and Series LNS 14000006 at BLS.gov.

16. Adam Davidson, "Do Illegal Immigrants Actually Hurt the U.S. Economy?" *New York Times,* February 12, 2013, accessed at nytimes.com on October 14, 2013. In recent decades, Hispanic immigrants have powered a rebirth of unionism in California and a push for higher wages. U.S. Bureau of Labor Statistics, *Foreign-Born Workers: Labor Force Characteristics, 2012,* News Release USDL-13–0991, May 22, 2013, at BLS.gov; Nelson Lim, "On the Back of Blacks: Immigrants and the Fortunes of African Americans," 186–227, in Roger Waldinger, ed., *Strangers at the Gates: New Immigrants in Urban America* (Berkeley: University of California Press, 2001); Eduardo Porter, "Cost of Illegal Immigration May Be Less Than Meets the Eye," *New York Times,* April 16, 2006, Business, 3; Aaron Zitner, "Immigrant Tally Doubles in Census," *Los Angeles Times,* March 10, 2001, A1, A12.

17. June Zaccone, "Has Globalization Destroyed the American Middle Class?" presentation to Columbia Seminar on "Full Employment, Social Welfare and Equity," April 2012, revised June 2012; Paul Craig Roberts, "Globalization Creates Unemployment: American Job Loss is Permanent," Global Research, October 28, 2010, accessed June 23, 2013.

18. Job numbers are the CES count at BLS.gov. On mediocre pay at a booming business, see Isaac Shapiro, "$45+ Billion for Apple Shareholders, Nothing Yet for Apple Workers," epi.org, accessed April 23, 2013. Also, Steven Greenhouse, "Going It Alone, Together," *New York Times,* March 24, 2013, 1, 4; Shan Li, "California Jobless Rate Falls to 9.6 percent," *Los Angeles Times,* March 30, 2013, B1, B3.

19. For this section, BLS series for nonfarm and production and nonsupervisory manufacturing jobs, CES0000000001 and CES3000000006. Also, see U.S. Bureau of the Census, Foreign Trade Division, "U.S. Trade in Goods and Services," (1960–2015); Don Lee, "U.S. Manufacturing Faces a Grim Reality," *Los Angeles Times,* August 13, 2016, C1, C5; Robert E. Scott, "Currency Manipulation and Manufacturing Jobs Loss: Why Negotiating 'Great Trade Deals' Is Not the Answer," Economic Policy Institute, July 21, 2016, at epi.org/111038; and Matt Pearce, "For Whites without College Degrees, 'Sea of Despair,'" *Los Angeles Times,* March 25, 2017, A10.

20. For the whole section: Sue Halpern, "How Robots & Algorithms Are Taking Over," *New York Review of Books,* April 2, 2015, 24, 26, 28; Barbara Ehrenreich, "Welcome

to Your Obsolescence," *New York Times Book Review,* May 17, 2015, 1, 26; Dean Baker, "No, Robots Aren't Taking All the Jobs," *Los Angeles Times,* May 7, 2015, A17; Lawrence Mishel and Heidi Shierholz, "Robots, or Automation, Are Not the Problem," Economic Policy Institute Snapshot, February 21, 2017, accessed at epi.org on February 26, 2017; Natalie Kitroeff, "Rock 'Em, Stock 'Em," *Los Angeles Times,* December 4, 2016, C1, C8, on two kinds of modern warehouses—one with plenty of workers and one with almost no workers. Also, see Kevin Drum, "You Will Lose Your Job to a Robot," *Mother Jones,* November–December 2017, 39–47, 68–69.

21. Kate Linthicum, "One Job's Journey: A Tale of Two Cities," *Los Angeles Times,* February 19, 2017, A1, A12-A13.

22. A young researcher, Arnobio Morelix, in "The True Cost of Paying McDonald's Workers a Livable Wage," accessed August 3, 2013, at truthdig.com/earthtotheground, posted July 30, 2013, estimated that McDonald's could double the pay and benefits of every employee by adding 68 cents to the Big Mac and 17 cents to dollar items. And, I'd add, they could raise prices less if executives were excluded from the pay-doubling process. In February 2014, in "The Effects of a Minimum-Wage Increase on Employment and Family Income," the Congressional Budget Office predicted a loss of 500,000 jobs from a $10.10 national minimum wage, but also higher incomes and less poverty for millions of workers. On the local job-creating effects of added spending from a higher minimum wage, see Daniel Flamming and Patrick Burns, *Effects of a Fifteen Dollar an Hour Minimum Wage in the City of Los Angeles* (Los Angeles: Economic Roundtable, 2013), esp. 16–18. Essential is John Schmitt, "Why Does the Minimum Wage Have No Discernible Effect on Employment?" (Washington, D.C.: Center for Economic and Policy Research, February 2013). Some researchers have found a little less employment among teens; employers may think that if they are paying more, they should get more productive, adult workers. Also, Editor's Desk, "Minimum Wage Workers Account for 4.7 Percent of Hourly Paid Workers in 2012," U.S. Bureau of Labor Statistics, accessed September 5, 2013. The Wal-Mart story is in Neil Irwin, "And in This Aisle, Higher Pay," *New York Times,* October 16, 2016, 1, 4.

23. Emmanuel Saez, "Striking It Richer: The Evolution of Top Incomes in the United States (updated with 2012 Preliminary Estimates)," September 3, 2013, accessed online at elsa.berkeley. edu/~saez/ saez-UStopincomes2012.pdf; and "World Top Incomes Database," at topincomes.g-mond.parisschoolof economics.eu/, accessed September 12, 2013. The top 1 percent do pay income taxes, but not enough. And they don't pay a fair share on capital gains, estate transfers, and Social Security. An interesting comparison is that Burger King workers in Copenhagen earn $20 an hour, but in Florida only $9. See Liz Alderman and Steven Greenhouse, "Where Fast Food Pays a Living Wage," *International New York Times,* October 28, 2014, 1, 16. On the trillions held abroad to escape U.S. taxation, see the Americans for Tax Fairness Action Fund, October 10, 2015.

24. This section is based on information in chapters 3, 4 and 5, and the recantation of ex-supply-sider Bruce Bartlett, "I Helped Create the GOP Tax Myth. Trump is Wrong:

Tax Cuts Don't Equal Growth," *Washington Post,* September 28, 2017, accessed the same day online. Statements about wages are based on real hourly rates for nonsupervisory/production workers in the monthly BLS report, *Real Earnings.* Manufacturing totals are under CES 3000000006 on the BLS.gov site.

25. National Bureau of Economic Research, "U.S. Business Cycle Expansions and Contractions," accessed at nber.org on June 2, 2016.

26. Examples of the point: Eileen Shanahan, "Executives Back Job Cut in Split with the President," *New York Times,* October 21, 1968, accessed online from the *New York Times* archive; and Associated Press, "Indexes Fall as Worries About Wages Persist," *New York Times,* B2, April 20, 2017.

27. Arlie Hochschild, "No Country for White Men," *Mother Jones,* September–October, 2016, 21–29. Also, Ronald Brownstein, "Ted Cruz and His Kamikaze Caucus," *Los Angeles Times,* A15, September 27, 2013. Republicans seem more partisan than Democrats. In the spring of 2017, opinion polls showed that Republican approval of specific policies—for example, bombing Syria—was different depending on whether a Democrat or a Republican were president. Democratic views on the issues were more consistent regardless of which party held the White House. Also see, "What the Stimulus Accomplished," *New York Times,* February 23, 2014, SR, 10; and Paul Krugman, "The Damage Done," *New York Times,* October 7, 2013, accessed at nytimes.com, October 18, 2013.

28. Economist James Devine reminds me that during the Great Recession quite a few labor economists supported higher minimum wages. But as far as I know, there has never been a reckoning with the uncritical acceptance of NAIRU by centrist and liberal economists. Alan Blinder wondered in 1989 if liberals had been too fast to accept NAIRU, but he was rare. Blinder comment included in Matthew Yglesias, "The NAIRU Explained: Why Economists Don't Want Unemployment to Drop Too Low," November 14, 2014, VOX, accessed on January 9, 2015. It was well known that recessions and high unemployment are disproportionately hard on lower-income households. That should have given NAIRU supporters pause. See Willem Thorbecke, "Who Pays for Disinflation?" Highlights of Public Policy Brief No. 38A, Levy Economics Institute of Bard College, December 1997. N. Gregory Mankiw, *Macroeconomics,* 9th ed. (New York: Worth Publishers, 2016), especially 184 in chapter 7. In Mankiw's conservative-traditionalist view, much unemployment comes from price and wage rigidities, such as those introduced by unions and minimum wage laws. The author is concerned that high wages may limit employers' ability to hire more workers. I found no evidence that he is worried that very low wages limit workers' willingness to take jobs.

29. Tom Petruno and Josh Friedman, "Wall Street Finds Mixed Blessing in Job Growth," *Los Angeles Times,* April 5, 2004, C1, C5.

30. Quoting Jacob Heilbrun, "Sacrificing Workers in the War on Inflation," *Los Angeles Times,* May 28, 2000, M1, M6. In 2006 a reporter and an economist from Goldman Sachs thought that big companies had enough cash to raise wages without raising prices. It was an unusual admission from Wall Street. I don't think Greenspan weighed in on it. See Joel Havemann, "Big Profits May Hold the Line on Inflation," *Los Angeles*

Times, August 8, 2006, C1, C7. Also, Charles M. Kelly, *Class War in America: How Economic and Political Conservatives Are Exploiting Low- and Middle-Income Americans* (Santa Barbara, Calif.: Fithian Press, 2000), 35–59; Dean Baker, "Why the Fed Should Not Raise Interest Rates," *Los Angeles Times,* August 19, 2016, A11, on Greenspan's 1996 decision not to raise interest rates, although Janet Yellen and others were urging him to do so. Also, Robert Kuttner, "Trump: The Wrong Version of the Right Policy, Take Two," *American Prospect,* June 21, 2019, accessed online June 22, 2019; and on the complexities of policy at the Fed, see Don Lee, "The Fed Holds Line on Rates," *Los Angeles Times,* June 20, 2019, C1, C6.

31. David Wolpe, "The Compassion Deficit," *Los Angeles Times,* September 8, 2013, A28; Daniel Goleman, "Rich People Just Care Less," *New York Times* Opinionator, October 5, 2013, accessed October 7, 2013; Karen Kaplan, "How Money Affects Happiness," *Los Angeles Times,* December 26, 2017, B2; Elise Gould, Lawrence Mishel, and Heidi Shierholz, "Already More than a Lost Decade: Income and Poverty Trends Continue to Paint a Bleak Picture," September 18, 2013, accessed at epi.org, on September 20, 2013; and Andrew Tangel, "Wall Street Perks Take a Drubbing," *Los Angeles Times,* September 21, 2013, B1, B4. Average Wall Street trader bonuses fell from $191,360 to $121,890—not so bad considering what the recession cost working-class families.

32. Thomas C. Cochran and William Miller, *The Age of Enterprise: A Social History of Industrial America,* revised ed. (New York: Harper and Row, 1961), 139, 182.

33. Business leaders liked railroad subsidies and having soldiers, courts, and police suppress strikes.

34. Irving G. Wyllie, *The Self-Made Man in America: The Myth of Rags to Riches* (New York: The Free Press, 1954), 157–59; and see the discussion of Beecher in my chapter 1; Alexander Keyssar, *Out of Work: The First Century of Unemployment in Massachusetts* (New York: Cambridge University Press, 1986), 251, 257. Nineteenth-century economics was often merely propaganda for capitalism and against socialism. John Bates Clark supposedly "proved" that every worker was paid what he or she actually contributed. He hadn't proved it. Moshe Adler, *Economics for the Rest of Us: Debunking the Science that Makes Life Dismal* (New York: New Press, 2010), 133–50.

35. Keyssar, *Our of Work,* notes, 279–80, that when unemployment insurance was discussed in the 1920s, it was sometimes denounced as a Soviet-style attempt to reward sluggards.

36. For the whole section, Thomas E. Weisskopf, Samuel Bowles, and David M. Gordon, "Two Views of Capitalist Stagnation: Underconsumption and Challenges to Capitalist Control," *Science and Society* 49 (Fall 1985): 259–86, esp. 264, 276; and Raford Boddy and James Crotty, "Class Conflict and Macro Policy: The Political Business Cycle," *Review of Radical Political Economics* 7 (Spring 1975): 1–19.

37. Jonathan Martin, Jim Rutenberg, and Jeremy W. Peters, "Fiscal Crisis Sounds the Charge in the G.O.P.'s 'Civil War,'" *New York Times,* October 20, 2013, 1, 20–21.

Chapter 8. Real Full Employment

1. On wage issues, see Economic Policy Institute, "Raising America's Pay," June 4, 2014, at epi.org.

2. On the tariff issue, see Peter S. Goodman, "Trump Has Promised to Bring Jobs Back. His Tariffs Threaten to Send Them Away," *New York Times,* January 6, 2019, accessed January 7, 2019, at nytimes.com. See the Hamilton Project, "The Closing of the Jobs Gap: A Decade of Recession and Recovery," August 4, 2017, accessed August 5, 2017 at the Brookings Institution site. For the sixteen million number, "April 2019 Unemployment Data—the Full Count," at njfac.org.

3. See LaDonna Pavetti, "Improving Opportunity: Building on Past Successes," January 11, 2016, Center on Budget and Policy Priorities, accessed February 7, 2016. On the problem of rural unemployment and poverty, discussed in point 5, see Eduardo Porter, "Abandoned America," *New York Times,* December 16, 2018, SR, 1, 6–7; Nathan Arnosti and Amy Liu, "Why Rural America Needs Cities," Brookings Report, November 30, 2018; and Arlie Hochschild, "Silicon Holler: A Bipartisan Effort to Revitalize the Heartland, One Tech Job at a Time," September 23, 2018, SR, 4–5.

4. The text of the modern Humphrey-Hawkins bill can be found as H.R. 1000, at njfac. org. My section on 2029 benefited from suggestions made by many people, including James Devine, Helen Ginsburg, William Darity Jr., Darrick Hamilton, Philip Harvey, Trudy Goldberg, June Zaccone, and Scott Myers-Lipton. See also, Harvey's *Securing the Right to Employment: Social Welfare Policy and the Unemployed in the United States* (Princeton, N.J.: Princeton University Press, 1989); Mark Paul, William Darity Jr., and Darrick Hamilton, *The Federal Job Guarantee—A Policy to Achieve Full Employment,* March 9, 2018, the Center on Budget and Policy Priorities; and Russell A. Nixon, "The Historical Development of the Conception and Implementation of Full Employment as Economic Policy," in Alan Gartner, Russell A. Nixon, and Frank Riessman, eds., *Public Service Employment: An Analysis of Its History, Problems and Prospects* (New York: Praeger Publishers, 1973), 9–27.

5. Tyler Cowen, "All in All, a More Egalitarian World," *New York Times,* July 20, 2014, BU, 6.

6. On the related issue of currency manipulation, see Dean Baker and Jared Bernstein, *Getting Back to Full Employment: A Better Bargain for Working People* (Washington, D.C.: Center for Economic and Policy Research, 2014), 63–71; and Robert E. Scott, "Currency Manipulation and Manufacturing Job Loss: Why Negotiating 'great trade deals' is Not the Answer," Economic Policy Institute, July 21, 2016, at epi.org/111038. A case study of the complexities of tariff policy in the wood floor industry is Guy Lawson, "Floored," *New York Times Magazine,* December 2, 2018, 46–52. Here, the Chinese factory owner was moving his plant, which provided an important stage in the American manufacturing process, to Cambodia to escape new tariffs.

7. Republican speaker of the House John Boehner was attacking lazy people in the fall of 2014. See Paul Krugman, "Those Lazy Jobless," *New York Times,* September 21, 2014, accessed September 21, 2014, at nytimes.com.

8. Learning-by-earning is in Jared Bernstein, "The CBPP Full Employment Project: Overview," Center on Budget and Policy Priorities, April 2, 2014, 3.

9. The fraction of workers earning poverty wages has long been about one-fourth. Some conservatives urge even lower wages than the pathetically low federal minimum of $7.25 as a way to create jobs. See Michael R. Strain, "A Job Agenda for the Right," *National Affairs* 18 (Winter 2014): 3–20. Also, Economic Policy Institute, "Raising America's Pay."

10. Timothy J. Bartik, in *Jobs for the Poor: Can Labor Demand Policies Help?* (New York: Russell Sage Foundation, 2001), thinks tax credits for employers can add a million jobs a year (289–98). He wants short-term jobs with below-market wages to force people into the private sector as soon as possible. On the Work Opportunity Tax Credit, in existence since 1996, a large share of credits in some states were going to a few big employers of high-turnover, low-wage workers. Sample the following: LaDonna Pavetti, "Subsidized Jobs: Providing Paid Employment Opportunities When the Labor Market Fails," April 2, 2014, at cbpp.org.; Elizabeth Lower-Basch, "Rethinking Work Opportunity: From Tax Credits to Subsidized Job Placements," November 2011, at clasp.org; Anne Roder and Mark Elliot, "Stimulating Opportunity: An Evaluation of ARRA-Funded Subsidized Employment Programs," Economic Mobility Corporation, September 2013; Michael Ettlinger, "Would a New Jobs Tax Credit Help?" Center for American Progress, December 3, 2009, accessed December 18, 2009, at American Progress.org.; H. Luke Shaefer and Kathryn Edin, "It's Time to Complete the Work-Based Safety Net," *Pathways* (Spring 2017), 27–31. The TANF-EF part of Obama's stimulus program employed welfare recipients and had some success. A third of the participants kept their jobs after the subsidy ended. A broad critique of Enterprise Zones and tax-break programs is David Neumark, "Rebuilding Communities Job Subsidies," in Jay Shambaugh and Ryan Nunn, eds., *Place-Based Policies for Shared Economic Growth* (Washington, D.C.: Brookings Institution: The Hamilton Project, September 2018), 81–90.

11. William D. Cohan, "How Quantitative Easing Contributed to the Nation's Inequality Problem," *New York Times,* October 22, 2014, accessed at nytimes.com on October 31, 2014; and Timothy A. Canova, "Who Runs the Fed?" *Dissent,* Summer 2015, accessed December 9, 2015, at www.dissentmagazine.org/article/who-runs -federal-reserve-2008-crash.

12. To evidence in earlier chapters, add Phil Harvey, *Back to Work: A Public Jobs Proposal for Economic Recovery,* March 10, 2011, at demos.org, 6; and Lawrence Mishel, "Even Better Than a Tax Cut," *International New York Times,* February 23, 2015, accessed February 24, 2015, at nytimes.com. Also, see Colin Gordon, "Union Membership and the Income Share of the Top Ten Percent," posted October 7, 2013, on epi.org/blog, accessed August 2, 2014.

13. Tax cuts for the rich and corporations do not generate so much additional business activity and tax revenue that they pay for themselves. See David Sirota, "Should We Devote 40 percent of the Stimulus to Tax Cuts?" January 5, 2009, accessed on Janu-

ary 5, 2009 at ourfuture.org.blogentry/2009010205/should-we-devote. David Leonhardt, "Do Tax Cuts Lead to Economic Growth?" *New York Times,* September 16, 2012, SR, 4; Nigel Duara, "Why Liberals, Conservatives are Watching Kansas Closely," *Los Angeles Times,* March 5, 2017, A2; N. Gregory Mankiw, "Cut Taxes, Sure. But Remember the Budget Deficit," *New York Times,* June 4, 2017, BU, 3.

14. Baker and Bernstein, *Getting Back,* 61–62; Tiffany Hsu, "Factory Output in State Surges Despite Job Losses," *Los Angeles Times,* July 16, 2014, B1, B6. Hsu shows that over fifteen years, output in California's factories increased by 73 percent while employment declined 34 percent. Another reason that tax cuts for the rich aren't as effective today is that the highest tax rates aren't so high anymore. In 1963 the top income tax rate was 91 percent; lowering the top rate to 70 percent tripled the amount of income that rich people could keep after taxes. In recent times, the rate has seesawed up and down from 28 percent to 39.6 percent. Cuts of a few points haven't increased domestic investment much. On tax avoidance, see David Sirota, "Microsoft Admits Stashing $92B Offshore to Avoid $29B in U.S. Taxes," *International Business Times,* August 22, 2014, accessed at portside.org, August 30, 2014. Apple was holding $138 billion abroad, mainly in Ireland.

15. We used to see wild assertions from the right that government never creates jobs, but obviously it does, massively so in periods of war and military build-ups, but in many other ways all the time.

16. For a review of job programs in the twentieth century, see Clifford M. Johnson and Ana Carricchi Lopez, "Shattering the Myth of Failure: Promising Findings from Ten Public Job Creation Initiatives," December 22, 1997, cbpp.org, accessed June 30, 2014. Also, Sylvester J. Schieber and John B. Shoven, *The Real Deal: The History and Future of Social Security* (New Haven, Conn.: Yale University Press, 1999), 44–47, on the successful low-tech rollout of Social Security in the 1930s and 1940s.

17. Thirty-six of thirty-seven leading economists agreed that the stimulus package lowered unemployment. Justin Wolfers, "What Debate? Economists Agree the Stimulus Lifted the Economy," at nytimes.com/2014/07/30/upshot/what-debate-economists-agree-the-stimulus, accessed July 31, 2014; Doyle McManus, "Washington's Competence Deficit," *Los Angeles Times,* October 5, 2014, A22. Also, Jeff Madrick, "Innovation: The Government Was Crucial After All," *New York Review of Books,* April 24, 2014, accessed at nybooks.com on June 20, 2014. An example of private responsibility for a government flub is that Deloitte, the largest U.S. accounting firm, messed up the modernization of California's unemployment benefits system. One can also study Medicare fraud. See Reed Abelson and Erich Lichtblau, "Pervasive Medicare Fraud Proves Hard to Stop," *New York Times,* August 15, 2014, accessed at nytimes.com on August 16, 2014. Medicare relies on private entities to deliver health care, to manage payments, and to investigate fraud. Medicare fraud usually involves crime by private businesses—doctors, clinics, and so on. Rick Scott, once governor and now senator from Florida and an opponent of government social programs, headed a company that stole from federal health-care programs. Another interesting case about alleged

government failures: the Social Security Administration is not perfect. Nor are people in the system. Some people are listed as deceased who are not. But erroneous payouts are less than 1 percent, the cost of keeping perfect records would require more spending, and congressional conservatives won't support that. See Michael Hiltzik, "60 Minutes Bungles Another Hit Piece on Social Security," March 16, 2015, *Los Angeles Times,* at latimes.com/business/hiltzik/la-fi-mh-60-minutes-bungles-20150316.

18. HH21, aka the "Jobs for All Act," was introduced into the 115th Congress, 1st Session, as H.R. 1000, on February 9, 2017, and again in the 116th Congress on February 6, 2019.

19. Helen Lachs Ginsburg and Gertrude Schaffner Goldberg, "Decent Work and Public Investment: A Proposal," *New Labor Forum* 17 (Spring 2008): 123–33; Robert Pollin, *Back to Full Employment* (Cambridge, Mass.: Boston Review/MIT Press, 2012), 103–6; Robert Pollin and Dean Baker, "Reindustrializing America: A Proposal for Reviving U.S. Manufacturing and Creating Millions of Good Jobs," *New Labor Forum* 19 (Spring 2012): 17–34. Low-pay temp jobs are proposed by Bartik and Dimitri B. Papadimitriou, Jerome Levy Economics Institute Public Policy Brief, No. 53A, July 1999, "Full Employment Has Not Been Achieved." See also Harvey, *Back to Work.*

20. Pollin and Baker, "Reindustrializing America," 27–30.

21. American Society of Civil Engineers, "2017 Infrastructure Report Card," infrastructurereportcard.org/, accessed May 7, 2017.

22. Philip Elliott, "School Maintenance Report Shows Need for $542 Billion to Update, Modernize Buildings," Huff Post, Politics, March 12, 2013, accessed July 7, 2014; Jim Puzzanghera, "Who Pays for Rotten Roads?" *Los Angeles Times,* December 2, 2018, 1, 7.

23. Clare McCann, "Head Start Exceeds Requirement that Half of Teachers Earn BA in Early Childhood," May 9, 2013, Early Ed Watch Blog, New America Foundation; Danielle Paquette, "Child-care Workers Are Likely to Live in Poverty," *Los Angeles Times,* July 12, 2016, C2.

24. Michael Grunwald, *The New New Deal: The Hidden Story of Change in the Obama Era* (New York: Simon and Schuster, 2012), 271–75, 352–79.

25. Julie Grant, "One of Offshore Wind Power's Best Hopes Is Fading on Lake Erie," July 16, 2014, accessed August 29, 2014, at pri.org/stories/2014-07-16/one-offshore-wind-powers-best-hopes-fading-lake; Bobby Magill, "Wind Could Power 35% of U.S. Electricity By 2050," March 12, 2015, accessed on March 14, 2015 at portside.org; Maddie Oatman, "The Gust Belt," *Mother Jones,* May–June, 2017, 70–71; Tom Kiernan, "Wind Energy Works to Create American Jobs," *The Hill,* March 3, 2017, accessed July 31, 2017 at thehill.com/blogs/pundits-blog/energy-environment/325630-wind-energy.

26. Wage data by county is available from the Wages and Hours Division of the Department of Labor. It is somewhat shocking to find that prevailing wages for craft workers in some counties of Mississippi were close to poverty: for plumbers $11.42 an hour and for electricians $9.38.

27. The cut-off level for homeowners was raised in ARRA from the poverty line to 200 percent of the poverty line. My weatherization section is based on an email

from labor expert Mike McGrorty, July 7, 2014; a GAO evaluation, "Progress and Challenges in Spending Weatherization Funds," at gao.gov/assets/590/ 587064; Becca Aaronson, "Despite Rocky Start, Texas' Weatherization Program Thrives," *Texas Tribune,* October 30, 2011, accessed July 9, 2014. Also, see three reports on the Climate Progress site: Jorge Madrid and Adam James, "Home Weatherization Grows 1,000% under Stimulus, Creating Jobs, Saving Low-Income Families $400 a Year," September 19, 2011; Richard W. Caperton, Adam James, and Matt Kasper, "One Millionth Home Weatherized: Federal Efficiency Program a Winner on All Counts," September 28, 2012; and Patrick Maloney, "Time to Reauthorize Weather Assistance Programs, Which Returns $2.50 in Savings for Every Dollar Invested," accessed at thinkprogress.org/climate on July 7, 2014, July 9, 2014; and November 19, 2014. Also U.S. House of Representatives, Committee on Oversight and Government Reform, Staff Report, *The Department of Energy's Weatherization Program: Taxpayer Money Spent, Taxpayer Money Lost* (March 20, 2012), accessed August 27, 2014; Grunwald, *The New, New Deal,* 306–11.

28. In July 2014, House Republicans proposed to allow companies to write off costs for buildings and equipment more quickly, a gift of $29 billion a year, but one whose contribution to job creation and deficit reduction was dubious. On affordable housing, see Rick Cohen, "The National Housing Trust Fund on the Congressional Cutting Block Unless Advocates Act?" at nonprofitquarterly.org/ 2015/06/10-the-national-housing-trust-fund-on-the-congressional.

29. State efforts to entice foreign companies to locate in the United States are expensive. Tennessee paid $288,500 *per job* to get VW to move a plant from Germany. Hsu, "Factory Output;" Steven Rattner, "The Myth of Industrial Rebound," *New York Times,* Sunday Review, January 26, 2014, 1, 8; Don Lee, "U.S. Manufacturing Faces a Grim Reality," *Los Angeles Times,* August 13, 2016, C1, C5; Frank Stricker. "Can We Bring Back Many Factory Jobs? Let's Do the Math," *Counterpunch,* September 8, 2016.

30. Nelson D. Schwartz and Reed Abelson, "Health Act Repeal Could Threaten Job Engine," *New York Times,* May 7, 2017, 1, 14; Dan Mangan, "500,000 Jobs Added to Health-Care Sector under Obamacare, Goldman Sachs Estimates," March 23, 2017, accessed August 5, 2017, at cnbc/2017/03/23/500000-jobs-added-to-health-sector -under-obamacare-goldman; Vann R. Newskirk II, "Repealing Obamacare Could Kill Jobs," *Atlantic,* January 10, 2017, accessed August 5, 2017, at theatlantic.com/politics/ archive/ 2017/01/obamacare-economic-effects-repeal.

31. See the productivity and pay table in *Mother Jones,* "All Work and No Pay," July– August 2011, 21. Catherine Reutschlin and Amy Traub, "A Higher Wage Is Possible: How Wal-mart Can Invest in Its Workforce Without Costing Customers a Dime," demos.org, November, 2013. U-6 is BLS series LNU03327709.

32. On dealing with inflation at real full employment, see https://njfac.org/ wp-conten/uploads/208/05/Anti-Inflationary-Features-of-HR-1000-pdf.

33. For three paragraphs: in the fall elections of 2014, there was a disconnect between widespread support for minimum-wage increases and the election of Republican opponents of a higher minimum wage. To some commentators that meant that

Democrats were too conservative; a more left or populist message would have won more votes. See *The Nation*, December 1–8, 2014, esp. 6–7, 13–18. In the Washington Post/Kaiser Family/Harvard University *Role of Government Survey* (October 2010), see items 5, 12, and 16 to 20; Gallup poll, "Americans Widely Back Government Job Creation Proposals," March 20, 2013, at gallup.com/poll/161438/americans-widely -back-government-job creation, accessed August 9, 2014; David Callahan and J. Mijin Cha, *Stacked Deck: How the Dominance of Politics by the Affluent and Business Undermines Economic Mobility in America*, accessed at demos.org/stacked-deck on August 13, 2014; Michael Ollove, "Despite Governors' Opposition, Strong Southern Support for Medicaid Expansion," Stateline, Pew Charitable Trusts, May 21, 2013, accessed August 8, 2014. In a November 2014, NBC News/Wall Street Journal Survey, 75 percent supported increased spending on roads and highways; 9 percent opposed it. Also, see Gertrude Schaffner Goldberg, "Strategic and Political Challenges to Large-Scale Federal Job Creation," *Review of Black Political Economy*, published online, December 2, 2011. Quotation from Binyamin Appelbaum and Robert Gebeloff, "Even Critics of the Safety Net Increasingly Depend on It," *New York Times*, February 11, 2012, at nytimes.com, accessed May 19, 2016. Also, see Gary Younge, "Working Class Voters: Why America's Poor Are Willing to Vote Republican," accessed August 6, 2014, at theguardian.com/ world/2012/oct/29/working-class-voters-america-republican. In the Post/Kaiser/ Harvard survey, respondents gave a C+ to the federal government. It is fascinating that in some Appalachian counties that lead the country in dependence on federal income programs, those who vote now vote Republican and cheer proposals to add work requirements to benefit programs. They may believe that liberal Democrats are the reason mining jobs are shrinking. See Eduardo Porter, "Where Government is a Dirty Word, but Its Checks Pay the Bills," accessed December 23, 2018, at nytimes .com/2018/12/21.

34. See item 12 in the Post/Kaiser survey. Other surveys show that people understand that it is harder to get ahead than it was for past generations; Elizabeth Warren, quoted in John Cassidy's review of her *A Fighting Chance* in the *New York Review of Books*, May 22, 2014, 6, column 3. Also, see Russell Shorto, "Water Works," *New York Times Magazine*, April 23, 2014, 20–23. On attitudes toward social welfare in other countries, see Ofer Sharone, "Why Do Unemployed Americans Blame Themselves While Israelis Blame the System?" Conference on Reconnecting to Work, Institute for Research on Labor and Employment, UCLA, April 2, 2011. Also, Jackie Calmes, "In Poorest States, Political Stigma is Depressing Participation in the Health Law," *New York Times*, April 27, 2014, 1, 22; final quoted phrase is from Michael Tomasky, "Now We Face 2016!" *New York Review of Books*, December 18, 2014, accessed on March 7, 2015, at nybooks .com.

35. Whether Democrats should have been more aggressive in telling the truth about Obamacare in conservative states came up in West Virginia. There, the right-wing fright-machine told people that everyone who signed up for Obamacare would have a chip embedded in their bodies and that medical decisions would be in the hands of

"death panels." Democrats and the medical establishment did not offer much push-back against that narrative, and the Democratic governor did not accept federal funds to market Obamacare. But he did support the expansion of Medicaid, which was part of Obamacare. State workers deemphasized the program's connection to Obama. There was a jump in the number of West Virginians on Medicaid, but many people were in denial that their new benefit came from a black president. David Lauter, "A Healthcare Gap in Red and Blue," *Los Angeles Times,* August 6, 2014, A9. In West Virginia uninsured rates were cut in half. Kentucky added 500,000 people under Obamacare but its Senator, Mitch McConnell, led the fight to abolish the program. The lies from the opponents of Obamacare have been extreme, even for American politicians. See also Tomasky, "Now We Face 2016."

36. A concise history of Republicans and race is Elizabeth Drew, "The Republicans: Divided & Scary," *New York Review of Books,* February 19, 2015, 32, 34–35. Libertarian defenders of segregation and even of slavery are described in Sam Tanenhaus and Jim Rutenberg, "Rand Paul's Mixed Inheritance," *New York Times,* January 26, 2014, 1, 20–21. One southerner who, starting in the 1950s, helped to bind a conservative movement for resegregation and racial oppression with a movement to protect the rich from liberal government was economist James McGill Buchanan. He is a key figure in Nancy MacLean's *Democracy in Chains: The Deep History of the Radical Right's Stealth Plan for America* (New York: Penguin Books, 2018). Eventually, the Koch brothers, with tons of fossil fuel money, linked up with Buchanan and his associates. The leaders of the extremist-libertarian empire that includes the Federalist Society, the Cato Institute, the Heritage Foundation, and the Mercatus Center at George Mason University oppose most liberal federal programs. They are nineteenth-century social Darwinians; William Graham Sumner would like them. They hate Social Security, public schools, the progressive income tax, government efforts to promote equality, and democracy. One of Buchanan's primary assertions was that democracy—voting by the masses—leads to the welfare state, which steals from the rich and gives to the undeserving. If the libertarians have their way, most of the United States will look like Texas and more of its cities will look like the favelas, the slums, of Rio de Janiero. And that will be good. So wrote Tyler Cohen of the Mercatus Center (MacLean, *Democracy in Chains,* 212–13).

37. National Employment Law Project (NELP), "City Minimum Wage Laws: Recent Trends and Economic Evidence," April, 2016. On Obama's failure to make the most of his opportunities, see Robert L. Borosage, "From the Rearview Mirror," *The Nation,* May 8/15, 2017, 35–37.

38. The Obama administration allotted significant money to retraining efforts in Appalachian coal counties, but many of the programs were and are hugely under-subscribed, sometimes because there are no jobs at the end of the program, but also because miners are waiting for mining jobs to return. President Trump encourages them in that vain hope. See Valerie Volcovici, "Awaiting Trump's Coal Comeback, Miners Reject Training," November 1, 2017, accessed at reuters.com, on December 28,

2018; Jenny Jarvie, "Black Lung, Grim Future for Younger Miners," *Los Angeles Times,* December 26, 2018, 1, 10.

39. For five paragraphs, Associated Press, "American Airlines Announces Pay Raises, and Investors Balk," latimes.com/business/la-fi-american-airlines-raises -20170427-story, accessed May 7, 2017. Sasha Abramsky, "A New Campaign to Turn the Blue Ridge Mountains Blue," *The Nation,* October 8/15, 2018, 22–25; Jim Tankers- ley, "Democrats' Next Big Thing," nytimes.com, May 22, 2018, accessed December 16, 2018; David Leonhardt, "The Secret to Winning in 2020," December 16, 2018, nytimes .com, accessed December 19, 2018.

Index

FRANK STRICKER is a professor emeritus of history, interdisciplinary studies, and labor studies at California State University, Dominguez Hills. He is the author of *Why America Lost the War on Poverty—and How to Win It*. He is a member of the National Jobs for All Coalition/Network and a regular contributor on the organization's web site.

The University of Illinois Press
is a founding member of the
Association of University Presses.

—————————————

University of Illinois Press
1325 South Oak Street
Champaign, IL 61820-6903
www.press.uillinois.edu